UP NHM

Staff Nurse Exam

Latest Edition

Practice Kit

10 Tests

02 Previous Year Paper

08 Mock Test

Based On Real Exam Pattern

✓ Thoroughly Revised and Updated

✓ Detailed Analysis of all MCQs

Title : UP NHM Staff Nurse Exam
Author Name : Mr. Rohit Manglik
Published By : EduGorilla Community Pvt. Ltd.
Publishers Address : 12/651, First Floor Opp. Arvindo Park, Near Jama Masjid, Indira Nagar, Lucknow, Uttar Pradesh-226016, India

Copyright EduGorilla

ISBN : 978-93-55565-34-1
First Edition

Disclaimer EduGorilla

Compiled and created by EduGorilla Community Pvt. Ltd

ROHIT MANGLIK
CEO, EduGorilla

Dear Applicants,

People say *"Success comes to those who work hard."* But I've seen people working hard for their exams day in and day out for marginal success. While others succeed in their examinations by putting in just half the work. So are they God Gifted? No! I believe that it's because they work *smart* and not just *hard*. Similarly, for your exams, you should strategize your preparation so as to increase the likelihood of success. Well with EduGorilla get ready to increase your *chances of selection* in your exam by *16x*.

EduGorilla helps you in not only working *hard* but also working in a *smart and strategic* manner. With EduGorilla's preparation package, you get a chance to make your exam preparation easy, and a fun learning path towards selection. Finding the right path to your preparations can be difficult if you don't know in which direction to head. Don't worry, we have you covered! EduGorilla will be your guide to success in your journey. With our Preparation Package, you can prepare strategically and beat the exam in just one attempt.

EduGorilla's Preparation Package includes-

- **Test Series**
- **Books**

Our preparation package is handcrafted as per the latest changes, expert opinions, and students' discretion. Thus, enabling you to get through each stage of the selection process for your exam.

Our Books are designed by the teachers and experts of the respective exam with a combined 150+ years of experience; to provide you with easy, efficient, and effective learning. Our books are smart, in the sense that not only do they give you the answers to the questions but also provide similar questions for practice.

EduGorilla's competent Test Series gives you real-time experience and confidence through which you can clear your offline or online exam in just one attempt. We currently host 83,000+ mock tests for 1,440+ competitive and academic exams.

Thus, EduGorilla misses no chance to assist you in your preparation and covers all stages of the exam, so that you don't have to look anywhere else.

We provide complete preparation packages for defense, banking, teaching, and other National & State-Level exams. Hence, it doesn't matter which exam you aspire to because you will reach your success.

ALL THE BEST !

Let EduGorilla be your Guide to Success.

Rohit Manglik,
Founder and CEO, EduGorilla

Editor's Note

INTRODUCTION

EduGorilla focuses on guiding students to succeed in their examinations. With that in mind, our book, titled "UP NHM : Staff Nurse Exam", has been drafted through the collective efforts of our distinguished experts with 150+ years of combined experience. This book consists of questions that are created following the latest changes in the syllabus and exam pattern. We compiled the book on the basis of questions that are most likely to appear in the UP NHM Staff Nurse Book. Through EduGorilla's "UP NHM : Staff Nurse Exam" your chances of success will increase 16x.

EduGorilla does this through our Complete Preparation Package. This package consists of well-conceptualized and structured content in the form of questions that are tailor-made according to your needs and will help you practice for exams in a smart way by pinpointing all the necessary information. It also provides hints and solutions, along with a smart answer sheet for your self-evaluation. You can assess your shortcomings and work accordingly on areas that may require more of your attention.

EduGorilla promises to help you succeed in your examination and accomplish your dream goals. We believe in our aspirants and see them at the top of the merit list. And the first step towards the top is to start preparing with us. EduGorilla's "UP NHM : Staff Nurse Exam" includes the following attributes.

- Well-Researched Content
- Top-Notch Quality
- Detailed Answers and Analysis
- Smart Answer Sheet
- Exam Relevant Questions

Therefore, EduGorilla fortifies your preparation and makes it durable enough to help you stand tall and beat the examination.

UP NHM Staff Nurse Book
Scan QR code for Eligibility, Exam Pattern, Syllabus and more.

Book ID: 1199

TABLE OF CONTENTS

Mock Test 1-150

Mock Test - 1 1-18

Mock Test - 2 19-37

Mock Test - 3 38-55

Mock Test - 4 56-73

Mock Test - 5 74-92

Mock Test - 6 93-111

Mock Test - 7 112-130

Mock Test - 8 131-150

Previous Year Paper 151-185

24 January 2021 (1st Shift) 151-168

24 January 2021 (2nd Shift) 169-185

Mock Test 01

Discipline

Q.1 Fundal height of a pregnant woman is measured from _________.

A. The middle of the pubic bone to the top of the uterus
B. The top of the pubic bone to the middle of the uterus
C. The bottom of the pubic bone to the top of the uterus
D. The top of the pubic bone to the top of the uterus

Q.2 Sarah is a seventeen-year-old female who has not gotten her first period and is visiting her doctor for an exam. She has displayed the normal growth and development of several secondary sex characteristics. The nurse would describe to the doctor that Sarah is showing signs of _________.

A. Oligomenorrhe
B. Secondary amenorrhea
C. Primary amenorrhea
D. Secondary dysmenorrhea

Q.3 Hanna is a 21-year-old woman who is presenting at the emergency room for severe vaginal bleeding. She is 32 weeks pregnant. Upon further examination, she is found to be suffering from abruptio placentae. Which of the following assessment findings would be of least concern to the nurse?

A. Shortness of breath
B. Bleeding from oral mucosa
C. Small red dots on the skin
D. A tender uterus

Q.4 Which of the following is not a risk factor for gestational diabetes?

A. High blood pressure
B. Asian ethnicity
C. Advanced maternal age
D. Prior birth of a child with a congenital disorder

Q.5 Andrea comes to the office for a prenatal visit. She mentions that lately, she has been excessively hungry, thirsty, and very tired. Which of the following would the nurse suspect?

A. Anemia
B. Parvovirus B19
C. Pre-eclampsia
D. Gestational diabetes

Q.6 Your patient is under 24-hour fetal monitoring and observation. The fetal monitoring strip begins to show decelerations, starting after the peak of contractions and recovering late. Which of the following interventions does the nurse anticipate doing?

A. Increasing rate of oxytocin
B. Administering medication
C. Removing oxygen supplementation
D. Reposition mother

Q.7 The nurse is observing the fetal monitoring strip of a 37-week-old fetus. He observes a visually apparent and abrupt increase in fetal heart rate (FHR) from a baseline of 140 to a peak of 159. The FHR returns to baseline after 20 seconds. What type of fetal heart rate characteristic has occurred?

A. Recurrent acceleration
B. Deceleration
C. Acceleration
D. Prolonged acceleration

Q.8 The nurse observes an electronic fetal monitoring strip. Upon review, the fetal heart rate (FHR) undulates from 140bpm to 160bpm and back down to 140bpm in a consistent cycle over a period of 35 minutes. What type of fetal heart rate characteristic is occurring on this electronic fetal monitoring strip?

A. Variable
B. Bradycardia
C. Recurrent
D. Sinusoidal

Q.9 At what point does preeclampsia develop into eclampsia?

A. At the initiation of kidney failure
B. When there is evidence of vascular dysregulation
C. When blood pressure exceeds 160/95 mmHg
D. At the progression into seizures

Q.10 The chief complication of pertussis is:

A. Bronchitis
B. Bronchopneumonia
C. Bronchiectasis
D. All of the above

Q.11 A 23-year-old patient in the 27th week of pregnancy has been hospitalized on complete bed rest for 6 days. She experiences sudden shortness of breath, accompanied by chest pain. Which of the following conditions is the most likely cause of her symptoms?

A. Myocardial infarction due to a history of atherosclerosis.
B. Pulmonary embolism due to deep vein thrombosis (DVT).
C. Anxiety attacks due to worries about her baby's health.
D. Congestive heart failure due to fluid overload.

Q.12 Thrombolytic therapy is frequently used in the treatment of suspected stroke. Which of the following is a significant risk associated with thrombolytic therapy?

A. Air embolus
B. Cerebral hemorrhage
C. Expansion of the clot
D. None of these

Q.13 A priority goal of involuntary hospitalization of the severely mentally ill patient is:

A. Re-orientation to reality
B. Elimination of symptoms
C. Protection from harm to self or others
D. Return to independent functioning

Q.14 The nurse is assessing an infant with developmental dysplasia of the hip. Which finding would the nurse anticipate?

A. Unequal leg length

B. Limited adduction
C. Diminished femoral pulses
D. Symmetrical gluteal folds

Q.15 On admission to the psychiatric unit, the Patient is trembling and appears fearful. The nurse's initial response should be to:

A. Give the Patient orientation materials and review the unit rules and regulations.
B. Introduce him/her and accompany the Patient to the Patient's room.
C. Take the Patient to the day room and introduce her to the other Patients.
D. Ask the nursing assistant to get the Patient's vital signs and complete the admission search.

Q.16 The nurse is caring for a person with a long leg cast. During discharge teaching about appropriate exercises for the affected extremity, the nurse should recommend:

A. Isometric **B.** Range of motion
C. Aerobic **D.** Isotonic

Q.17 While explaining an illness to a 10-year-old, what should the nurse keep in mind about the cognitive development at this age?

A. They are able to make simple associations of ideas.
B. They are able to think logically in organizing facts.
C. Interpretation of events originates from their own perspective.
D. Conclusions are based on previous experiences.

Q.18 What should a nurse focus on to diagnose nursing in a person with severe depression?

A. Nutrition **B.** Elimination
C. Activity **D.** Safety

Q.19 Ablative surgery refers to:

A. Surgery aimed to relieve pain or reduce symptoms caused by a disease
B. Surgery that replaces malfunctioning structures
C. Surgery used to restore structure or function
D. Surgery carried out in order to remove disease body parts

Q.20 An anxiolytic is:

A. A drug used to dry up secretions
B. A type of anaesthetic
C. A medication or any other intervention that relieves anxiety
D. A controlled drug

Q.21 The overarching aim of performing preoperative checks is to:

A. Comply with trust policy
B. Comply with Royal College of Nursing's Code of Conduct
C. Reduce the risk of errors occurring
D. None of the above

Q.22 In wedge resection:

A. The whole lung is removed
B. An aspect of lung tissue is removed
C. A biopsy is taken
D. None of these

Q.23 The mediastinum contains the:

A. Heart and liver
B. Heart, lungs, trachea, great vessels, oesophagus
C. Kidneys, lungs, great vessels
D. Heart, stomach, oesophagus

Q.24 Haemothorax is:

A. A collection of air in the pleural space
B. A collection of pus in the pleural space
C. A collection of blood in the pleural space
D. A collection of synovial fluid in the pleural space

Q.25 In stem cell transplantation antibiotics, immunosuppressant medication and steroids can be given to treat:

A. Shock
B. Haemorrhage
C. Graft-versus-host disease
D. Infection

Q.26 In postoperative coronary artery bypass graft, the person should be encouraged to:

A. Reduce mobility
B. Drink 3 L of fluid as soon as possible
C. Splint the incision when coughing and moving
D. Close the eyes when coughing

Q.27 The valve most likely to be repaired is:

A. The pulmonary valve
B. The mitral valve
C. The aortic valve
D. The hydrocephalic valve

Q.28 In _________ method of health education people learn by exchanging their views and experiences.

A. Syposium **B.** Work shop
C. Role play **D.** Group discussion

Q.29 Story telling is a_________method of health education.

A. Modern **B.** Traditional
C. One way **D.** None of these

Q.30 Safeguards to help limit liability in patient communication by phone and e-mail include:

A. Allow any staff member within the facility to officially change the protocols by a group e-mail
B. Require patients to sign off on all protocols
C. Review protocols annually and maintain discontinued ones
D. Use a checklist format for protocols

Q.31 Which communication technique is being used in this nurse-patient interaction?

Patient: "When I get angry, I get into a fistfight with my wife, or I take it out of the kids."

Nurse: "I notice that you are smiling as you talk about this physical violence."

A. Encouraging comparison

B. Exploring
C. Formulating a plan of action
D. Making observations

Q.32 Which therapeutic communication technique is being used in this nurse-client interaction?

Client: "My father spanked me often."

Nurse: "Your father was a harsh disciplinarian."

A. Restatement
B. Offering general leads
C. Focusing
D. Accepting

Q.33 A nurse is assessing a client diagnosed with schizophrenia for the presence of hallucinations. Which communication technique used by the nurse is an example of making observations?

A. "You appear to be talking to someone I do not see."
B. "Please describe what you are seeing."
C. "Why do you continually look in the corner of this room?"
D. "If you hum a tune, the voices may not be so distracting."

Q.34 An instructor is correcting a nursing student's clinical worksheet. Which instructor statement is the best example of effective feedback?

A. "Why did you use the client's name on your clinical worksheet?"
B. "You were very careless to refer to your client by name on your clinical worksheet."
C. "Surely you didn't do this deliberately, but you breached confidentiality by using the client's name."
D. "It is disappointing that after being told, you're still using client names on your worksheet."

Q.35 After assertiveness training, a formerly passive client appropriately confronts a peer in group therapy. The group head nurse states, "I'm so proud of you for being assertive. You are so good!" Which communication technique has the head nurse employed?

A. The non-therapeutic technique of giving approval
B. The non-therapeutic technique of interpreting
C. The therapeutic technique of presenting reality
D. The therapeutic technique of making observations

Q.36 Which nutrient deficiency is the main reason for microcytic anemia?

A. Folic acid **B.** Amino acids
C. Iron **D.** Vitamin C

Q.37 Which disease is caused by the deficiency of protein?

A. Pellagra **B.** Marasmus
C. Beri-Beri **D.** Rickets

Q.38 Which of the following is used for grading protein-energy malnutrition?

A. Ballard's scale **B.** Gomez scale
C. Bishop scoring **D.** Krammer's rule

Q.39 Which of the following is caused due to extreme lack of proteins?

A. Malaria **B.** Typhoid
C. Kwashiorkor **D.** None of these

Q.40 Which of the following are mostly first class of proteins?

A. Animal proteins **B.** Plant proteins
C. Both (A) and (B) **D.** Neither (A) nor (B)

Q.41 The enzyme which forms the peptide bond is known as:

A. Carbonic unhydrase **B.** Peptidase
C. Carbohydrate **D.** Peptidyl transferase

Q.42 You are alone first aider and have an unconscious non-breathing adult, what should you do first?

A. Start CPR with 30 chest compressions.
B. Give five initial rescue breaths.
C. Call 911/112 requesting AED (defibrillator) and ambulance.
D. Give two initial rescue breaths.

Q.43 Which of the following is the correct sequence for the chain of survival?

A. 911/112, CPR, Defibrillation, Advanced care
B. CPR, Defibrillation, 911/112, Advanced care
C. Defibrillation, CPR, 911/112, Advanced care
D. Defibrillation, 911/112, CPR, Advanced care

Q.44 Which of the following are the techniques used in First Aid?

A. Dressing **B.** Bandage
C. Transport technique **D.** All of the above

Q.45 Which medical condition will develop from severe blood loss?

A. Hypovolemic shock **B.** Hypoglycaemia
C. Anaphylaxis **D.** Hypothermia

Q.46 What steps would you take to control bleeding from a nose?

A. Sit casualty down, lean forward, and pinch soft part of nose.
B. Sit casualty down, lean backward, and pinch part of the nose.
C. Lie casualty down and pinch the soft part of the nose.
D. Lie casualty down and pinch the top of the nose.

Q.47 What causes Anaphylactic shock?

A. Choking
B. Insect sting or spider bites
C. 3rd degree burns
D. Heart attack

Q.48 What is the first thing you should do for severe bleeding?

A. Put the victim in the recovery position
B. Direct pressure with a clean cloth or hand to the bleeding wound
C. Cover with a clean cloth
D. Give oxygen

Q.49 Which hormone is secreted by the testis?

A. Testosterone **B.** Progesterone
C. T.S.H. **D.** Insulin

Q.50 As per the text 'Charaka Samhita' how many bones are there in a human body?

A. 206 **B.** 360 **C.** 370 **D.** 208

Q.51 How many bones are there in human spinal column?

A. 33 **B.** 32 **C.** 31 **D.** 30

Q.52 The femur bones of the human body are also known as _____.

A. Wrist bones **B.** Thigh bones
C. Shoulder bones **D.** Collar bones

Q.53 The ends of limbs are covered with what to reduce the friction in joints?

A. Ligament **B.** Cartilage
C. Muscle **D.** Tendon

Q.54 The element found in teeth and bones is:

A. Potassium and Calcium
B. Calcium and Magnesium
C. Calcium and Phosphorus
D. Phosphorus and Sulfur

Q.55 In which part of the body are the Tarsal bones found?

A. Ear **B.** Leg **C.** Head **D.** Hand

Q.56 According to Gordon's classification of prevention of disease includes all except one:

A. Primary prevention
B. Universal prevention
C. Selective prevention
D. Indicated prevention

Q.57 A nurse manager has identified a problem on the nursing unit and holds unit meetings for all shifts. The nurse manager presents an analysis of the problem and proposals for actions to team members and invites the team members to comment and provide input. Which style of leadership is the nurse manager specifically employing?

A. Situational **B.** Laissez-faire
C. Participative **D.** Authoritarian

Q.58 What are the factors affecting ward management?

A. Size of room **B.** Treatment room
C. Dirty utility room **D.** All of the above

Q.59 Cross sectional study is included in which type of epidemiology study?

A. Analytical **B.** Descriptive
C. Randomised control **D.** Ecological study

Q.60 Advantages of cohort study are all except:

A. Incidence cannot be calculated
B. Bias minimised
C. Relative risk can be estimated
D. Dose response ratio can be calculated

Q.61 A nurse manager is planning to implement a change in the method of the documentation system for the nursing unit. Many problems have occurred as a result of the present documentation system, and the nurse manager determines that a change is required. The initial step in the process of change for the nurse manager is which of the following?

A. Plan strategies to implement the change
B. Set goals and priorities regarding the change process
C. Identify the inefficiency that needs improvement or correction
D. Identify potential solutions and strategies for the change process

Q.62 1st step of investigation of an epidemic is:

A. Confirmation of existence
B. Varification of diagnosis
C. Analysis of data
D. Search the cases

Q.63 A sense of belongingness and spirit of working together to achieve objectives effectively refers to as:

A. Unity of direction **B.** Esprit de corps
C. Unity of command **D.** Centralization

Q.64 Which is not a type of screening:

A. Mass Screening **B.** Multiple Screening
C. Low risk Screening **D.** High risk Screening

Q.65 What is the most important nursing intervention to correct skin dryness is?

A. Consult the dietitian about increasing the patient's fat intake, and take necessary measures to prevent infection.
B. Ask the physician to refer the patient to a dermatologist, and suggest that the patient wear home-laundered sleepwear.
C. Encourage the patient to increase his fluid intake, use non-irritating soap when bathing the patient, and apply lotion to the involved areas.
D. Avoid bathing the patient until the condition is remedied, and notify the physician.

Q.66 When bathing a patient's extremities, the nurse should use long, firm strokes from the distal to the proximal areas. This technique _____________.

A. provides an opportunity for skin assessment
B. avoids undue strain on the nurse
C. increases venous blood return
D. causes vasoconstriction and increases circulation

Q.67 What should the nurse do when planning nursing care for a client with a different cultural background?

A. Allow the family to provide care during the hospital stay so no rituals or customs are broken.
B. Identify how these cultural variables affect the health problem
C. Speak slowly and show pictures to make sure the client always understands.
D. Explain how the client must adapt to hospital routines to be effectively cared for while in the hospital.

Q.68 The nurse is interviewing a newly admitted psychiatric patient. Which nursing statement is an example of offering a general lead?

A. "Do you know why you are here?"
B. "Are you feeling depressed or anxious?"

C. "Can you chronologically order the events that led to your admission?"
D. "Yes, I see. Go on."

Q.69 Nursing interventions that can help the patient to relax and sleep restfully include all of the following except:
A. Have the patient take a 30- to 60-minute nap in the afternoon.
B. Turn on the television in the patient's room.
C. Provide quiet music and interesting reading material.
D. Massage the patient's back with long strokes.

Q.70 Restraints can be used for all of the following purposes except ____.
A. Prevent a confused patient from removing tubes, such as feeding tubes, I.V. lines, and urinary catheters.
B. Prevent a patient from falling out of bed or a chair.
C. Discourage a patient from attempting to ambulate alone when he requires assistance for his safety.
D. Prevent a patient from becoming confused or disoriented.

Q.71 Which of the following is the nurse's legal responsibility when applying restraints?
A. Document the patient's behavior
B. Document the type of restraint used
C. Obtain a written order from the physician except in an emergency, when the patient must be protected from injury to himself or others
D. All of the above

Q.72 Which nursing statement is a good example of the therapeutic communication technique of offering self?
A. "I think it would be great if you talked about that problem during our next group session."
B. "Would you like me to accompany you to your electroconvulsive therapy treatment?"
C. "I notice that you are offering help to other peers in the milieu."
D. "After discharge, would you like to meet me for lunch to review your outpatient progress?"

Q.73 A terminally ill patient usually experiences all of the following feelings during the anger stage except ___________.
A. rage
B. envy
C. numbness
D. resentment

Q.74 A female child, age 2 , is brought to the emergency department after ingesting an unknown number of aspirin tablets about 30 minutes earlier. On entering the examination room, the child is crying and clinging to the mother. Which data should the nurse obtain first?
A. Heart rate, respiratory rate, and blood pressure
B. Recent exposure to communicable diseases
C. Number of immunizations received
D. Height and weight

Q.75 When assessing a child's cultural background, the nurse in charge should keep in mind that:
A. Cultural background usually has little bearing on a family's health practices
B. Physical characteristics mark the child as part of a particular culture
C. Heritage dictates a group's shared values
D. Behavioral patterns are passed from one generation to the next

Q.76 Nurse Gloria questions the parents of a child with oppositional defiant disorder about the roles of each parent in setting rules of behavior. The purpose of this type of questioning is to assess which element of the family system?
A. Anxiety levels
B. Generational boundaries
C. Knowledge of growth and development
D. Quality of communication

Q.77 Which behavioral assessment in a child is most consistent with a diagnosis of conduct disorder?
A. Arguing with adults
B. Gross impairment in communication
C. Physical aggression toward others
D. Refusal to separate from caretaker

Q.78 Martin Sanchez is a nine (9)-year-old child admitted to a psychiatric treatment unit accompanied by Mr. and Mrs. Sanchez. To establish trust and position of neutrality, which action would the nurse take?
A. Encourage Mr. and Mrs. Sanchez to leave while Martin is being interviewed.
B. Interview Martin with his parents together, observing their interaction.
C. Provide diversion for Martin, and interview Mr. and Mrs. Sanchez alone.
D. Review the clinical record prior to interviewing Mr. and Mrs. Sanchez.

Q.79 12-year-old Caroline has recurring nephrotic syndrome. Which of the following areas of potential disturbances should be a prime consideration when planning ongoing nursing care?
A. Body image
B. Sexual maturation
C. Muscle coordination
D. Intellectual development

Q.80 Mrs. Johnson tells the nurse that she is very worried because her 2-year-old child does not finish his meals. What should the nurse advise the mother?
A. Make the child seat with the family in the dining room until he finishes his meal
B. Provide quiet environment for the child before meals
C. Do not give snacks to the child before meals
D. Put the child on a chair and feed him

General Aptitude / Reasoning / General Awareness / Basic Computer knowledge

Q.81 A train leaves from a station and moves at 40 km/hr. After 2 hours, another train leaves from the same station and moves in the same direction at a certain speed. If the second train catches up with the first train in 4 hours, what is the speed of the second train?

A. 55 km/hr **B.** 50 km/hr **C.** 60 km/hr **D.** 65 km/hr

Q.82 Three unbiased coins are tossed. What is the probability of getting at least 2 heads?

A. $\frac{1}{4}$ **B.** $\frac{1}{2}$ **C.** $\frac{1}{3}$ **D.** $\frac{1}{8}$

Q.83 The average of five consecutive odd numbers is 51. What is the difference between the highest and lowest number?

A. 3 **B.** 7 **C.** 8 **D.** 11

Q.84 The base of a triangular field is three times its height. If the cost of cultivating the field at Rs. 36.72 per hectare is Rs. 495.72, find the height and base of the triangular field: (1 hectare = 10000 m^2)

A. 480 m, 1120 m **B.** 400 m, 1200 m
C. 300 m, 900 m **D.** 250 m, 650 m

Q.85 The selling price of glass is Rs 1965 and the loss percentage is 25%. If the selling price is Rs 3013, then what will be the profit percentage?

A. 13% **B.** 10% **C.** 15% **D.** 20%

Q.86 Prasanna went 15 m to the west from my house, then turned left and walked 20 m. He then turned East and walked 25 m and finally turning left covered 20 m. How far was he from his house?

A. 10 m **B.** 20 m **C.** 30 m **D.** 40 m

Q.87 The nearest coming year, which will be a perfect square is:
[Uttarakhand Public Service Commission (UKPSC), 2016]

A. 2027 **B.** 2030 **C.** 2025 **D.** 2032

Q.88 A functional clock shows $10am$. How many degrees will its hour hand rotate to show $6pm$ the same day?

A. 120° **B.** 240° **C.** 360° **D.** 550°

Q.89 Direction: Study the following information carefully to answer the given question.

M 1 E & D 2 G 9 $ F @ 4 N Z W © 8 C Y A * 6

If all the numbers in the above arrangement are dropped, then which of the following will be the tenth from the right end?

A. $ **B.** D **C.** F **D.** Z

Q.90 Deepak introduced Raju saying, "He is the husband of the granddaughter of the father of my father. "How is Raju related to Deepak?
[RRB (NTPC), 2017]

A. Son-in-law **B.** Brother-in-law
C. Son **D.** Brother

Q.91 The Uttar Pradesh government has introduced a system of issuing a unique ____ digit Unicode to mark all kinds of landholdings in the state.

A. 12 **B.** 14 **C.** 16 **D.** 18

Q.92 The Supreme Court of India tenders advice to the President of India on matters of law or fact:

A. On its own initiative (on any matter of larger public interest)
B. If he seeks such advice
C. Only if the matters of the citizens
D. None of the above

Q.93 Khizr Khan belonged to which of the following dynasties?
[UPSSSC Forest Guard, 2018]

A. Slave Dynasty **B.** Khilji Dynasty
C. Sayyid Dynasty **D.** Shah Dynasty

Q.94 The landform which is raised and is flat-surfaced is classified as

A. hill **B.** plateau **C.** plain **D.** valley

Q.95 Who has been appointed as head of the panel that is set up to strengthen the assessment and accreditation of higher educational institutions?

A. K. Radhakrishnan **B.** Kasturi Rangan
C. Amitabh Kant **D.** V. K. Paul

Q.96 Verification of a login name and password is known as:

A. Configuration **B.** Accessibility
C. Authentication **D.** Logging in

Q.97 The _______ key is used to make the internet browser window full-screen.
[Rajasthan Police Constable, 2020]

A. F8 **B.** F9 **C.** F10 **D.** F11

Q.98 An example of application software is:

A. Data processing **B.** Processing Unit
C. Control Unit **D.** MS Word

Q.99 Which of the following is not a valid function in MS Excel?

A. SUM() **B.** COUNT()
C. SUBTRACT() **D.** COUNTA()

Q.100 Which of the following is the shortcut to create a new presentation in MS PowerPoint?
[Allahabad High Court ARO, 2020]

A. Alt + W **B.** Ctrl + Q **C.** Alt + H **D.** Ctrl + N

// Smart Answer Sheet //

Correct Indicates percentage of students who answered questions correctly.

Skipped Indicates percentage of students who skipped questions.

Q.	Ans.	Correct	Skipped
1	D	57.38 %	1.82 %
2	C	25.22 %	3.48 %
3	D	62.63 %	1.62 %
4	B	61.14 %	1.78 %
5	D	55.32 %	1.27 %
6	D	10.09 %	4.39 %
7	C	20.92 %	4.42 %
8	D	22.76 %	3.14 %
9	D	67.57 %	1.01 %
10	D	45.23 %	1.78 %
11	B	32.33 %	3.48 %
12	B	41.49 %	1.29 %
13	C	89.01 %	0.0 %
14	A	18.46 %	4.97 %
15	B	46.28 %	1.06 %
16	A	40.33 %	1.01 %
17	B	49.62 %	1.75 %
18	D	54.51 %	1.4 %
19	D	78.4 %	0.0 %
20	C	78.58 %	0.0 %
21	C	57.1 %	1.4 %
22	B	82.67 %	0.0 %
23	B	53.55 %	1.65 %
24	C	82.33 %	0.0 %
25	C	24.57 %	3.2 %
26	C	58.22 %	1.68 %
27	B	51.74 %	1.01 %
28	D	85.34 %	0.0 %
29	B	63.68 %	1.07 %
30	D	68.97 %	1.68 %
31	D	86.17 %	0.0 %
32	A	42.01 %	1.44 %
33	A	48.0 %	1.66 %
34	C	82.18 %	0.0 %
35	A	20.61 %	3.51 %
36	C	54.12 %	1.38 %
37	B	66.74 %	1.78 %
38	B	47.44 %	1.21 %
39	C	48.03 %	1.84 %
40	A	60.77 %	1.4 %
41	D	66.17 %	1.4 %
42	C	49.37 %	1.58 %
43	A	51.69 %	1.61 %
44	D	84.91 %	0.0 %
45	A	80.54 %	0.0 %
46	A	48.06 %	1.7 %
47	B	49.23 %	1.34 %
48	B	61.45 %	1.34 %
49	A	68.08 %	1.97 %
50	B	52.35 %	1.23 %
51	A	63.89 %	1.48 %
52	B	42.13 %	1.35 %
53	B	21.68 %	3.03 %
54	C	66.81 %	1.06 %
55	B	43.31 %	1.73 %
56	A	15.69 %	4.9 %
57	C	85.91 %	0.0 %
58	D	70.0 %	1.53 %
59	A	66.01 %	1.37 %
60	A	45.64 %	1.53 %
61	C	60.67 %	1.15 %
62	B	84.63 %	0.0 %
63	B	53.17 %	1.48 %
64	C	88.68 %	0.0 %
65	C	56.95 %	1.1 %
66	C	49.65 %	1.06 %
67	B	27.16 %	4.58 %
68	D	53.19 %	1.69 %
69	A	82.26 %	0.0 %
70	D	62.77 %	1.35 %
71	D	31.15 %	4.14 %
72	B	29.38 %	4.25 %
73	C	63.1 %	1.27 %
74	A	28.31 %	3.92 %
75	D	62.32 %	1.01 %
76	B	50.51 %	1.64 %
77	C	56.42 %	1.73 %
78	B	22.98 %	3.35 %
79	A	68.7 %	1.69 %
80	C	52.25 %	1.19 %

Q.	Ans.	Correct	Skipped
81	C	83.09 %	0.0 %
82	B	87.03 %	0.0 %
83	C	84.59 %	0.0 %
84	C	76.21 %	0.0 %

Q.	Ans.	Correct	Skipped
85	C	77.04 %	0.0 %
86	A	79.47 %	0.0 %
87	C	81.86 %	0.0 %
88	B	78.72 %	0.0 %

Q.	Ans.	Correct	Skipped
89	C	83.18 %	0.0 %
90	B	77.98 %	0.0 %
91	C	63.55 %	1.47 %
92	B	13.95 %	3.94 %

Q.	Ans.	Correct	Skipped
93	C	41.25 %	1.29 %
94	B	56.54 %	1.8 %
95	A	67.25 %	1.65 %
96	C	18.22 %	4.75 %

Q.	Ans.	Correct	Skipped
97	D	87.35 %	0.0 %
98	D	55.07 %	1.63 %
99	C	67.43 %	1.05 %
100	D	47.77 %	1.64 %

Performance Analysis	
Avg. Score (%)	34.0%
Toppers Score (%)	63.0%
Your Score	

//Hints and Solutions//

1. The fundal height of a pregnant woman is measured from the top of the pubic bone to the top of the uterus.

Fundal height (sometimes referred to as McDonald's rule) is measured in centimeters from the top of the pubic bone to the top of the uterus. The top of the uterus may also be called the fundus of the uterus. It is used to assess the growth and development of the fetus inside the womb.

Hence, the correct option is (D).

2. The nurse would describe to the doctor that Sarah is showing signs of primary amenorrhea.

Primary amenorrhea occurs when a female is fourteen years old and has not gotten her first period and has not developed secondary sex characteristics. Primary amenorrhea also occurs when a female sixteen or older has not gotten her first period but has developed secondary sex characteristics. Primary dysmenorrhea refers to painful menstruation not linked to a physiological disorder. Secondary dysmenorrhea refers to painful menstruation due to an underlying cause such as endometriosis. Oligomenorrhea refers to the absence of a period, typically for at least 35 days.

Hence, the correct option is (C).

3. A tender uterus assessment findings would be of least concern to the nurse.

Abruptio placentae is a serious condition where the placenta inappropriately and prematurely detaches from the uterus. Women with obstetric complications such as abruptio placentae can quickly develop disseminated intravascular coagulation (DIC). DIC is a clotting disorder in which the blood inappropriately clots. Severe bleeding can also occur as clotting proteins become scarce. Symptoms of DIC include blood clots, and bleeding into the tissues such as the skin and oral mucosa. Decreasing blood pressure is concerning due to the severe bleeding caused by the combination of DIC and abruptio placentae. Shortness of breath could indicate the presence of a blood clot. Although uterine tenderness is of concern, it is common with abruptio placentae and does not indicate an immediately life-threatening condition.

Hence, the correct option is (D).

4. Asian ethnicity is not a risk factor for gestational diabetes.

Asian ethnicity is not considered a risk factor. Hispanic, Native American, and African American ethnicities are considered risk factors for gestational diabetes. Others include maternal obesity, previous pregnancies with gestational diabetes, delivery of a very large baby, and a family history of diabetes.

Hence, the correct option is (B).

5. Gestational diabetes would the nurse suspect.

Gestational diabetes is a type of diabetes that is first seen in a pregnant woman who did not have diabetes before she was pregnant. Some women have more than one pregnancy affected by gestational diabetes. Gestational diabetes usually shows up in the middle of pregnancy.

Hence, the correct option is (D).

6. Reposition mother of the following interventions does the nurse anticipate doing.

Late decelerations are caused by uteroplacental insufficiency. The nurse should anticipate many interventions to promote uteroplacental blood flow. Initially, the nurse should implement oxygen supplementation, stop the oxytocin infusion, reposition the mother to the left side, and introduce a fluid bolus of lactated Ringer's solution (LR).

Hence, the correct option is (D).

7. Acceleration type of fetal heart rate characteristic has occurred.

An acceleration in fetal heart rate is defined as a visually apparent and abrupt increase in FHR, where the FHR increases from the onset of the acceleration to the peak in less than 30 seconds. At less than 32 weeks, the acceleration must peak at least 10 bpm above baseline and last at least 10 seconds. At more than 32 weeks, the acceleration must peak at least 15 bpm above baseline and last at least 15 seconds. A prolonged acceleration follows the same guidelines as acceleration, but lasts more than 2 minutes and is no longer than 10 minutes in duration; after 10 minutes, it is a change in baseline FHR. Deceleration is a visually apparent decrease in FHR from the baseline, gradual or abrupt, that returns to the original baseline. Recurrent accelerations occur with more than 50% of contracts in any 20-minute window. Tachycardia is a baseline FHR of more than 160 bpm.

Hence, the correct option is (C).

8. A Sinusoidal type of fetal heart rate characteristic is occurring on this electronic fetal monitoring strip.

A sinusoidal pattern is a visually apparent, smooth, sine wave-like undulating pattern in fetal heart rate baseline with a cycle frequency of at least 3–5/min that persists for more than 20 minutes. Variable describes an abrupt deceleration of visually apparent decrease and return in fetal heart rate (FHR) from baseline lasting less than 30 seconds. Bradycardia occurs when the baseline FHR is less than 110 bpm. Intermittent describes an acceleration or deceleration occurring with less than 50% of contractions in any 20-minute window. Recurrent describes an acceleration or deceleration occurring with more than 50% of contractions in any 20-minute window.

Hence, the correct option is (D).

9. Preeclampsia develops into eclampsia at the onset of seizures. Seizures are tonic-clonic and may appear during pregnancy, during labor, or postpartum. It is relatively rare, affecting only approximately 1.2-1.8% of pregnancies.

Hence, the correct option is (D).

10. The chief complication of pertussis are Bronchitis, Bronchopneumonia and Bronchiectasis.

Pertussis, also known as whooping cough, is a highly contagious respiratory disease. It is caused by the bacterium Bordetella pertussis. Pertussis is known for uncontrollable, violent coughing which often makes it hard to breathe.

Hence, the correct option is (D).

11. In a hospitalized patient on prolonged bed rest, the most likely cause of sudden onset shortness of breath and chest pain is pulmonary embolism. Pregnancy and prolonged inactivity both increase the risk of clot formation in the deep veins of the legs. These clots can then break loose and travel to the lungs.

Hence, the correct option is (B).

12. When treating a stroke victim with thrombolytic therapy intended to dissolve a suspected clot, cerebral hemorrhage is a significant risk. The success of the treatment demands that it be instituted as soon as possible, often before the cause of stroke has been determined.

Hence, the correct option is (B).

13. A priority goal of involuntary hospitalization of the severely mentally ill patient is protection from self-harm and harm to others. Involuntary hospitalization may be required for persons considered dangerous to self or others or for individuals who are considered gravely disabled.

Hence, the correct option is (C).

14. Unequal leg length is a sign of developmental dysplasia of the hip. The hip is a "ball-and-socket" joint. In a normal hip, the ball at the upper end of the thigh bone (femur) fits firmly into the socket, which is part of the large pelvis bone. In babies and children with developmental dysplasia (dislocation) of the hip (DDH), the hip joint has not formed normally. The ball is loose in the socket and may be easy to dislocate.

Hence, the correct option is (A).

15. On admission to the psychiatric unit, the Patient is trembling and appears fearful. The nurse's initial response should be to introduce him/herself and accompany the Patient to the Patient's room.

Anxiety is triggered by change that threatens the individual's sense of security. In response to anxiety in Patient, the nurse should remain calm, minimize stimuli, and move the Patient to a calmer, more secure/safe setting.

Hence, the correct option is (B).

16. The nurse should instruct the person on isometric exercises for the muscles of the affected extremity instruct the person to alternately contract and relax muscles without moving the affected part.

Isometric exercises are contractions of a particular muscle or group of muscles. During isometric exercises, the muscle doesn't noticeably change length and the affected joint doesn't move. Isometric exercises help maintain strength.

Hence, the correct option is (A).

17. While explaining an illness to a 10-year-old, the nurse should keep in mind about the cognitive development at this age that they are able to think logically in organizing facts. Cognitive development means the growth of a child's ability to think and reason. This growth happens differently from ages 6 to 12, and from ages 12 to 18. Children ages 6 to 12 years old develop the ability to think in concrete ways. These things are called concrete because they're done around objects and events.

Hence, the correct option is (B).

18. The safety of a person with depression is a priority for care. Depression can be effectively treated in primary care settings using an evidence-based collaborative approach in which primary care providers are systematically supported by mental health providers in the care of patients with the condition.

Hence, the correct option is (D).

19. Ablative surgery refers to surgery carried out in order to remove disease body parts. An ablative surgery is a type of procedure to remove or reprogram tissue in the body that is damaged or causing interference. For example, a doctor might use an ablation procedure to destroy (ablate) a small amount of heart tissue that's causing abnormal heart rhythms or to treat tumors in the lung, breast, thyroid, liver or other areas of the body.

Hence, the correct option is (D).

20. An anxiolytic is a medication or any other intervention that relieves anxiety. Anxiolytics, or anti-anxiety drugs, are a category of drugs used to prevent anxiety and treat anxiety related to several anxiety disorders.

These include:

- Alprazolam (Xanax)
- Chlordiazepoxide (Librium)
- Clonazepam (Klonopin)
- Diazepam (Valium)
- Lorazepam (Ativan)

Hence, the correct option is (C).

21. The overarching aim of performing preoperative checks is to reduce the risk of errors occurring. The ultimate goals of preoperative medical assessment are to reduce the patient's surgical and anesthetic perioperative morbidity or mortality, and to return him to desirable functioning as quickly as possible.

Hence, the correct option is (C).

22. In wedge resection, an aspect of lung tissue is removed. A wedge resection is the surgical removal of a wedge-shaped portion of tissue from one, or both, lungs. A wedge resection is typically performed for the diagnosis or treatment of small lung nodules. A lung biopsy is a procedure in which a small sample of lung tissue is removed through a small incision between the ribs.

Hence, the correct option is (B).

23. The mediastinum contains the heart, lungs, trachea, great vessels, oesophagus. The mediastinum is a space in the thorax that contains a group of organs, vessels, nerves, lymphatics and their surrounding connective tissue. It lies in the midline of the chest between the pleura of each lung and extends from the sternum to the vertebral column.

Hence, the correct option is (B).

24. Haemothorax is a collection of blood in the pleural space. By far the most common cause of hemothorax is trauma. Penetrating injuries of the lungs, heart, great vessels, or chest wall are obvious causes of hemothorax; they may be accidental, deliberate, or iatrogenic in origin.

Hence, the correct option is (C).

25. In stem cell transplantation antibiotics, immunosuppressant medication, and steroids can be given to treat Graft-versus-host disease (GvHD). GvHD happens when particular types of white blood cell (T cells) in the donated stem cells or bone marrow attack your own body cells. This is because the donated cells (the graft) see your body cells (the host) as foreign and attack them.

Hence, the correct option is (C).

26. In postoperative coronary artery bypass graft (CABG), the person should be encouraged to splint the incision when coughing and moving. The following aspects of postoperative care apply to all patients who've had CABG surgery:

- Maintain airway patency.
- Monitor vital signs and record intake and output hourly.
- Assess the patient's hemodynamic and cardiac status.
- Perform peripheral and neurovascular assessments hourly for the first 8 hours.

Hence, the correct option is (C).

27. The valve most likely to be repaired is the mitral valve. The mitral valve is one of four valves in the heart. It regulates blood flow from the upper left chamber (left atrium) into the lower left chamber (left ventricle). The left ventricle is the heart's main pumping chamber. A normal mitral valve has two flaps, or leaflets.

Hence, the correct option is (B).

28. In the Group discussion method of health education, people learn by exchanging their views and experiences.

Group discussion involves the free flow of communication between a facilitator and two or more participants. In most group discussions the subject of the discussion can be taken up and shared equally by all the members of the group.

Hence, the correct option is (D).

29. Story telling is a Traditional method of health education.

Story telling, the art of narrating a tale from memory rather than reading it is one of the oldest of all art forms, reaching back to prehistoric times. Story telling is the original form of teaching and has the potential of fostering emotional intelligence and help the child gain insight into human behaviour.

Hence, the correct option is (B).

30. Safeguards to help limit liability in patient communication by phone and e-mail include Use a checklist format for protocols.

Checklist is intended as an aid in suggesting a format for writing protocols and in identifyingissues that scientists should consider as they design a study or surveillance system. When usingthe checklist, investigators should select the items that apply to their specific project. It is notexpected that every item on the checklist is applicable to each protocol for a study or surveillance system.

Hence, the correct option is (D).

31. Making observations communication technique is being used in this nurse-patient interaction.

The nurse is using the communication technique of making observations when noting that the patient smiles when talking about physical violence. The technique of making observations encourages the patient to compare personal perceptions with those of the nurse.

Hence, the correct option is (D).

32. Restatement communication technique is being used in this nurse-client interaction.

The nurse is using the therapeutic communication technique of restatement. Restatement involves repeating the main idea of what the client has said. The nurse uses this technique to communicate that the client's statement has been heard and understood.

Hence, the correct option is (A).

33. "You appear to be talking to someone I do not see." communication technique used by the nurse is an example of making observations.

Making observations involves verbalizing what is observed or perceived. This encourages the client to recognize specific behaviors and make comparisons with the nurse's perceptions.

Hence, the correct option is (A).

34. The instructor's statement, "Surely you didn't do this deliberately, but you breached confidentiality by using the client's name." is an example of effective feedback.

Feedback is a method of communication to help others consider a modification of behavior. Feedback should be descriptive, specific, and directed toward behavior that the person has the capacity to modify and should impart information rather than offer advice or criticize the individual.

Hence, the correct option is (C).

35. The non-therapeutic technique of giving approval communication technique has the head nurse employed.

Giving approval implies that the head nurse has the right to pass judgment on whether the client's ideas or behaviors are "good" or "bad." This creates a conditional acceptance of the client.

Hence, the correct option is (A).

36. Microcytic anemias are caused by conditions that prevent your body from producing enough hemoglobin. Hemoglobin is a component of your blood. It helps transport oxygen to your tissues and gives your red blood cells their red color. Iron deficiency causes most microcytic anemias.

Hence, the correct option is (C).

37. Marasmus is caused by the deficiency of protein. Nutrient deficiency is the main cause of marasmus. It occurs in children that don't ingest enough protein, calories, carbohydrates, and other important nutrients. This is usually due to poverty and a scarcity of food. There are several types of malnutrition.

Hence, the correct option is (B).

38. Gomez scale is used for grading protein-energy malnutrition. Gomez scale is one of the earliest systems for classifying protein-energy malnutrition in children, based on the percentage of expected weight for age:

- Over 90% is normal.
- 76–90% is mild (first degree) malnutrition.
- 61–75% is moderate (second degree) malnutrition.
- Less than 60% is severe (third degree).

Hence, the correct option is (B).

39. Kwashiorkor is caused due to extreme lack of proteins. Kwashiorkor is a severe form of malnutrition. It's most common in some developing regions where babies and children do not get enough protein or other essential nutrients in their diet. The main sign of kwashiorkor is too much fluid in the body's tissues, which causes swelling under the skin (oedema).

Hence, the correct option is (C).

40. Proteins which contains most of the essential amino acids are termed as first-class proteins, while those which do not are called second class proteins. Animal proteins are the first class proteins and Plant proteins are second class proteins.

Hence, the correct option is (A).

41. The enzyme which forms the peptide bond is known as Peptidyl transferase. Peptidyl transferase is an enzyme that catalyzes the addition of an amino acid residue in order to grow the polypeptide chain in protein synthesis. It is located in the large ribosomal subunit, where it catalyzes the peptide bond formation.

Hence, the correct option is (D).

42. If you are alone first aider and have an unconscious non-breathing adult, you should Call 911/112 requesting AED (defibrillator) and ambulance.

An AED, or automated external defibrillator, is used to help those experiencing sudden cardiac arrest. It's a sophisticated, yet easy-to-use, medical device that can analyze the heart's rhythm and, if necessary, deliver an electrical shock, or defibrillation, to help the heart re-establish an effective rhythm.

Hence, the correct option is (C).

43. The correct sequence for the chain of survival is 911/112, CPR, Defibrillation, Advanced care.

The International Telecommunication Union has officially set 911/112 two standard emergency phone numbers for countries to use in the future. 911 is currently used in North America, while 112 is standard across the EU and in many other countries worldwide.

Cardiopulmonary resuscitation (CPR) is a lifesaving technique that's useful in many emergencies, such as a heart attack or near drowning, in which someone's breathing or heartbeat has stopped.

Defibrillators are devices that restore a normal heartbeat by sending an electric pulse or shock to the heart.

Hence, the correct option is (A).

44. The following are the techniques used in First Aid:

- Dressings
- Bandages
- Fast evacuation techniques (single-rescuer)
- Transport techniques

Dressing:

A dressing is a protective covering applied to a wound to:

- prevent infection,
- absorb discharge,
- control bleeding,
- avoid further injury, and
- reduce pain.

Bandage:

- A bandage is a fairly long strip of material such as gauze used to protect, immobilize, compress, or support a wound or injured body part.

Fast evacuation techniques:

- In case the casualty is in a dangerous situation following are possible one-rescuer evacuation techniques to move an unconscious casualty over a very short distance to get him into safety.

Transport technique:

- After appropriate first aid has been given, the patient may need to be transported.

Hence, the correct option is (D).

45. The hypovolemic shock will develop from severe blood loss.

Hypovolemic shock is an emergency condition in which severe blood or other fluid loss makes the heart unable to pump enough blood to the body. This type of shock can cause many organs to stop working.

Hence, the correct option is (A).

46. Sit casualty down, lean forward, and pinch soft part of nose to control bleeding from a nose.

Sit down and firmly pinch the soft part of your nose, just above your nostrils, for at least 10-15 minutes.

Lean forward and breathe through your mouth – this will drain blood into your nose instead of down the back of your throat.

Hence, the correct option is (A).

47. An insect sting or spider bite causes Anaphylactic shock.

Insect stings and bites can cause severe allergic reactions. Doctors call this "anaphylaxis." A spider bite can cause allergic reactions doctors call "anaphylactic shock." It can be fatal. Call 911 if you have any of these symptoms: Rapid swelling of the lips, tongue, throat, or around the eyes.

Hence, the correct option is (B).

48. The first thing you should do for severe bleeding is Direct pressure with a clean cloth or hand to the bleeding wound.

Apply direct pressure on the cut or wound with a clean cloth, tissue, or piece of gauze until bleeding stops. If blood soaks through the material, don't remove it. Put more cloth or gauze on top of it and continue to apply pressure. If the wound is on the arm or leg, raise the limb above the heart, if possible, to help slow bleeding. Wash your hands again after giving first aid and before cleaning and dressing the wound. Do not apply a tourniquet unless the bleeding is severe and not stopped to prevent irritation. Apply antibiotic cream to reduce the risk of infection and cover with a sterile bandage.

Hence, the correct option is (B).

49. The testis is the primary reproductive organ in males. The testes are situated outside the abdominal cavity within a pouch called the scrotum. The scrotum helps in maintaining the low temperature of the testes (2–2.5°C lower than the normal internal body temperature) necessary for spermatogenesis.

Testis performs dual functions as a primary sex organ as well as an endocrine gland. The testis is composed of seminiferous tubules and stromal or interstitial tissue. The Leydig cells or interstitial cells, which are present in the intertubular spaces produce a group of hormones called androgens mainly testosterone.

Testosterone plays a key role in the development of male reproductive tissues such as the testes and prostate, as well as promoting secondary sexual characteristics such as increased muscle and bone mass, and the growth of body hair.

Hence, the correct option is (A).

50. As per the text 'Charaka Samhita' 360 bones are there in a human body.

- It was authored by Maharshi Charaka.
- The Charaka Samhita mentioned that the content of the book was first taught by Atreya Punarvasu.
- It is one of the foundational Hindu texts of medicines that have survived from ancient India.
- As per the text 'Charaka Samhita' there are 360 bones in a human body.
- Charaka studied the anatomy of the human body and concluded that there are 360 bones including teeth, present in the human body.
- As per the text Charaka Samhita, there are four important parts of medical practice:

1. The patient.
2. The physician.
3. The nurse.
4. The medicines.

- Human body composed of around 270 bones by birth.
- The number of bones will be reduced to around 206 bones by adulthood after some bones get fused together.

Hence, the correct option is (B).

51. The human spinal column is made up of 33 bones. Vertebrae separated by intervertebral discs.

Each vertebra is given a name according to its location.

Region	No of vertebrae
cervical region	7
thoracic region	12
lumbar region	5
sacral region	5
coccygeal region	4

Formula - C7 T12 L5 S5 C4
The first vertebral column is Atlas which is connected with the skull.

Hence, the correct option is (A).

52. The femur bones of the human body are also called thigh bones.

- The femur is the only bone located within the human thigh.
- It is the longest and the strongest bone in the human body.
- The head of the femur articulates with the acetabulum in the pelvic bone forming the hip joint.
- While the distal part of the femur articulates with the tibia and kneecap, forming the knee joint.

Hence, the correct option is (B).

53. The ends of limbs are covered with Cartilage to reduce the friction in joints.

- Hyaline Cartilage: It is the most well-endowed form of cartilage. cartilage is found lining bones in joints (articular cartilage). it's additionally gifted within bones, serving as a centre of ossification or bone growth. additionally, cartilage forms the embryonic skeleton.
- Elastic Cartilage: Elastic animal tissue is found within the pinna of the ear and several other tubes, like the walls of the modality and eustachian canals and vocal organs. Elastic animal tissue is comparable to cartilage however contains elastic bundles (elastin) scattered throughout the matrix. This provides a tissue that's stiff nonetheless elastic.
- Fibrocartilage: cartilage could be a specialized form of animal tissue found in areas requiring robust support or nice durability, like between bone disks, at the bone and different symphyses, and at sites connecting tendons or ligaments to bones.

Hence, the correct option is (B).

54. The element found in teeth and bones is Calcium and Phosphorus.

Bone:

- It is a type of connective tissue.
- It provides protection and movement to the body.
- It works to make RBC and WBC.

- It stores a lot of minerals inside itself.
- It contains the highest amount of calcium and phosphorus.
- The cells present in it are called osteocyte which is also called Mature bone.

Teeth: They are not living tissue.

They're comprised of four different types of tissue:

- Dentin
- Enamel
- Cementum
- Pulp

Dentin is that part of the tooth that is beneath enamel and cementum.

Enamel is the hardest substance in the body. It has no nerves. Though some remineralization of enamel is possible, it can't regenerate or repair itself if there's significant damage. This is why it's important to treat tooth decay and cavities sooner rather than later.

The cementum covers the root, under the gum line, and helps the tooth stay in place. Teeth also contain other minerals, but do not have any collagen. Because teeth are not living tissue, it's important to maintain good oral hygiene, since early damage to teeth cannot be naturally repaired.

The pulp is the innermost part of a tooth. It contains blood vessels, nerves, and connective tissue. The pulp is surrounded by dentin, which is covered by the enamel.

Hence, the correct option is (C).

55. Tarsal bones are found in the Leg.

The tarsal bones consist of seven small bones located in the proximal region of the Leg in the ankle area. They are arranged in proximal and distal rows. The metatarsals connect the phalanges to the tarsals. The bones of the Leg provide mechanical support for the soft tissues.

Hence, the correct option is (B).

56. According to Gordon's classification of prevention of disease includes all except one Primary prevention.

Primary Prevention is trying to prevent yourself from getting a disease. Examples include: legislation and enforcement to ban or control the use of hazardous products (e.g. asbestos) or to mandate safe and healthy practices (e.g. use of seatbelts and bike helmets) education about healthy and safe habits (e.g. eating well, exercising regularly, not smoking)

Hence, the correct option is (A).

57. The participative style of leadership is the nurse manager specifically employing.

Participative leadership is a managerial style that invites input from employees on all organizational decisions. Two other leadership styles often used in nursing practice are situational leadership and autocratic leadership.

Hence, the correct option is (C).

58. All of the above are the factors affecting ward management.

FGI guidelines suggest the following space for a patient/family centered patient room: 250-square foot minimum and an additional 30 square feet per family member.

A treatment room is a place in the hospital where your child receives medical care. Healthcare providers can test your child's blood, insert an IV (small tube that goes into a vein), place a feeding tube, or change a bandage in a treatment room.

The Dirty utility room provides a space for the decontamination and storage of bedpans, urinals and bowls, testing and disposal of patient specimens, disposal of clinical and other wastes.

Hence, the correct option is (D).

59. A cross-sectional study is included in the analytical type of epidemiology study.

The purpose of an analytic study in epidemiology is to identify and quantify the relationship between an exposure and a health outcome. The hallmark of such a study is the presence of at least two groups, one of which serves as a comparison group.

Hence, the correct option is (A).

60. Advantages of cohort study are all except incidence cannot be calculated.

Cohort studies are a type of longitudinal study is an approach that follows research participants over a period of time (often many years).

Hence, the correct option is (A).

61. The initial step in the process of change for the nurse manager is to identify the inefficiency that needs improvement or correction. Idetifying the problem first will ease the process of correction.

A basic purpose of the nursing documentation is the creation of a data base in which the patients' files are included. The information, that is contained in a file can form a valuable source of elements for research. The care plan can bring up useful information on the care of many patients.

Hence, the correct option is (C).

62. 1st step of investigation of an epidemic is varification of diagnosis.

Verifying the diagnosis is important: (a) to ensure that the disease has been properly identified, since control measures are often disease-specific; and (b) to rule out laboratory error as the basis for the increase in reported cases. First, review the clinical findings and laboratory results.

Hence, the correct option is (B).

63. A sense of belongingness and spirit of working together to achieve objectives effectively refers to as Esprit de corps.

- The Esprit de corps is the feeling of unity, trust, and belonging to the organization among the employees.

- It is the practice of pulling each other together to achieve organizational goals.
- It is an art to make the employees believe that they are the organization.

Hence, the correct option is (B).

64. Low risk Screening is not a type of screening.

There appear to be four main aims of screening, although seven terms are used to describe them: case-finding, mass screening, multiple screening, opportunistic screening, High risk Screening, periodical health examination, prescriptive screening, and targeted screening.

Hence, the correct option is (C).

65. The most important nursing intervention to correct skin dryness is to encourage the patient to increase his fluid intake, use non-irritating soap when bathing the patient, and apply lotion to the involved areas.

Dry skin will eventually crack, ranking the patient more prone to infection. To prevent this, the nurse should provide adequate hydration through fluid intake, use non-irritating soaps or no soap when bathing the patient, and lubricate the patient's skin with lotion. In most cases, dry skin responds well to lifestyle measures, such as using moisturizers and avoiding long, hot showers and baths. Moisturizers provide a seal over the skin to keep water from escaping. Apply moisturizer several times a day and after bathing.

Hence, the correct option is (C).

66. When bathing a patient's extremities, the nurse should use long, firm strokes from the distal to the proximal areas. This technique increases venous blood return.

Washing from distal to proximal areas stimulates venous blood flow, thereby preventing venous stasis. Good personal hygiene is essential for skin health but it also has an important role in maintaining self-esteem and quality of life. Supporting patients to maintain personal hygiene is a fundamental aspect of nursing care.

Hence, the correct option is (C).

67. The nurse should identify how these cultural variables affect the health problem.

Without assessment and identification of the cultural needs, the nurse cannot begin to understand how these might influence the health problem or health care management. Culture is influential at many levels in health, ranging from the formation of new diagnostic groups to the diagnosis of disease to the determination of what is called a disease or no symptoms and disease cues.

Hence, the correct option is (B).

68. The nurse's statement, "Yes, I see. Go on." is an example of the therapeutic communication technique of a general lead. Offering a general lead encourages the patient to continue sharing information. It indicates that the nurse is listening and following what the patient is saying without taking away the initiative for the interaction.

Hence, the correct option is (D).

69. Nursing interventions that can help the patient to relax and sleep restfully include all of the following except having the patient take a 30- to 60-minute nap in the afternoon.

Napping in the afternoon is not conducive to nighttime sleeping. There are a few considerations about naps. For example, a short daytime nap of 15-30 minutes can be restorative for elders and will not interfere with nighttime sleep. On the other hand, insomniacs are cautioned to avoid naps. Quiet music, watching television, reading, and massage usually will relax the patient, helping him to fall asleep.

Hence, the correct option is (A).

70. Restraints can be used for all of the given purposes except prevent a patient from becoming confused or disoriented.

By restricting a patient's movements, restraints may increase stress and lead to confusion, rather than prevent it. Restraints in a medical setting are devices that limit a patient's movement. Restraints can help keep a person from getting hurt or doing harm to others, including their caregivers. They are used as a last resort. The other choices are valid reasons for using restraints.

Hence, the correct option is (D).

71. All of the above are the nurse's legal responsibility when applying restraints.

When applying restraints, the nurse must document the type of behavior that prompted her to use them, document the type of restraints used, and obtain a physician's written order for the restraints. Nurses are accountable for providing, facilitating, advocating, and promoting the best possible patient care and to take action when patient safety and well-being are compromised, including when deciding to apply restraints.

Restraint use should be continually assessed by the health care team and reduced or discontinued as soon as possible. After the discontinuing restraints, inter professional teams should debrief with the patient, patient's family, or substitute decision maker to discuss intervention, previous interventions and alternatives to restraints.

There are three types of restraints: physical, chemical and environmental. Physical restraints limit a patient's movement. Chemical restraints are any form of psychoactive medication used not to treat illness, but to intentionally inhibit a particular behaviour or movement. Environmental restraints control a patient's mobility.

With any intervention, such as restraint use, nurses need to ensure they actively involve the patient, patient's family, substitute decision-makers and the broader health care team. Nurses are also accountable for documenting nursing care provided, including assessment, planning, intervention and evaluation. In emergency situations, nurses may apply restraints without consent when a serious threat of harm to the patient or others exists and only after all alternative interventions were unsuccessful.

Hence, the correct option is (D).

72. "Would you like me to accompany you to your electroconvulsive therapy treatment?" is a good example of the therapeutic communication technique of offering self.

This is an example of the therapeutic communication technique of offering self. Offering self-makes the nurse available on an unconditional basis, increasing the patient's feelings of self-worth. Professional boundaries must be maintained when using the technique of offering self.

Hence, the correct option is (B).

73. A terminally ill patient usually experiences all of the following feelings during the anger stage except numbness.

Numbness is typical of the depression stage when the patient feels a great sense of loss. Depression is perhaps the most immediately understandable of Kubler-Ross's stages and patients experience it with unsurprising symptoms such as sadness, fatigue, and anhedonia. Spending time in the first three stages is potentially an unconscious effort to protect oneself from this emotional pain, and, while the patient's actions may potentially be easier to understand, they may be more jarring in juxtaposition to behaviors arising from the first three stages.

Hence, the correct option is (C).

74. The nurse obtain first heart rate, respiratory rate, and blood pressure.

The most important data to obtain on a child's arrival in the emergency department are vital sign measurements. Salicylate toxicity is a medical emergency. Intentional ingestion or accidental overdose can cause severe metabolic derangements, making treatment difficult. In an acute salicylate overdose, the onset of symptoms will occur within 3 to 8 hours. The severity of symptoms is dependent on the amount ingested.

Hence, the correct option is (A).

75. When assessing a child's cultural background, the nurse in charge should keep in mind that behavioral patterns are passed from one generation to the next.

A family's behavioral patterns and values are passed from one generation to the next. Pediatric health care providers must be aware of the demographic trends and be culturally competent to deliver the safest, highest quality care possible to children of widely differing groups.

Hence, the correct option is (D).

76. The purpose of this type of questioning is to assess generational boundaries of the family system.

An important element in assessing the family system is determining if the parents establish and maintain appropriate generational boundaries, establishing clear rules and expectations as part of the parental role. Provide clear behavioral guidelines, including consequences for disruptive and manipulative behavior.

Hence, the correct option is (B).

77. Physical aggression toward others is a significant criterion consistent with the diagnoses of conduct disorder. Conduct disorder (CD) lies on a spectrum of disruptive behavioral disorders, which also include oppositional defiant disorder (ODD). In some cases, ODD is a precursor to CD. CD is characterized by a pattern of behaviors that demonstrate aggression and violation of the rights of others and evolves over time.

Hence, the correct option is (C).

78. It is important for the nurse to be seen as a neutral person who is interested in the family as an adaptive functioning unit. By conducting the admission interview with the parents and child together, the nurse establishes this neutral role from the beginning. Relationships with child and adolescent patients differ from those with adult patients and nurses build relationships in a different way with adults.

Hence, the correct option is (B).

79. Because of edema associated with nephrotic syndrome, potential self-concept, and body image disturbances related to changes in appearance and social isolation should be considered. Nephrotic syndrome is a condition that causes the kidneys to leak large amounts of protein into the urine. This can lead to a range of problems, including swelling of body tissues and a greater chance of catching infections.

Hence, the correct option is (A).

80. If the child is hungry he/she is more likely to finish his meals. Therefore, the mother should be advised not to give snacks to the child. Set times for meals and snacks and try to stick to them.

Hence, the correct option is (C).

81. Distance covered by the first train in 2 hrs = 40 × 2 = 80 km

Let the speed of the second train be x km/hr

According to the question

Speed = $\frac{Distance}{Time}$

⇒ $(x - 40) = \frac{80}{4}$

⇒ $x - 40 = 20$

⇒ $x = 20 + 40$

∴ $x = 60$ km/hr.

Hence, the correct option is (C).

82. Here,

$S = \{TTT, TTH, THT, HTT, THH, HTH, HHT, HHH\}$

Let $E =$ event of getting at least two heads

$= \{THH, HTH, HHT, HHH\}$

$\therefore P(E) = \frac{n(E)}{n(S)} = \frac{4}{8} = \frac{1}{2}$

Hence, the correct option is (B).

83. Let the numbers be $x, x+2, x+4, x+6$ and $x+8$.

According to question,

$\frac{[x+(x+2)+(x+4)+(x+6)+(x+8)]}{5} = 51$

$\Rightarrow 5x + 20 = 255$

$\Rightarrow x = 47$

So, required difference $= (47 + 8) - 47 = 8$

Hence, the correct option is (C).

84. Area of field $= \frac{495.72}{36.72} = 13.5$ hectare

$= 135000\ m^2$

$h = x, b = 3x$

$\frac{1}{2} \times b \times h = 135000$

$\frac{1}{2} \times x \times 3x = 135000$

$x = 300\ m$

& base $= 3x = 900\ m$

Hence, the correct option is (C).

85. According to the question,

Selling price of glass = Rs. 1965

And loss = 25%

$\therefore CP = \frac{1965}{75} \times 100 =$ Rs. 2620

If selling price = Rs. 3013

$\therefore$ Profit $\% = \frac{(3013-2620)}{2620} \times 100$

$= \frac{3930}{262} = 15\%$

Hence, the correct option is (C).

86.

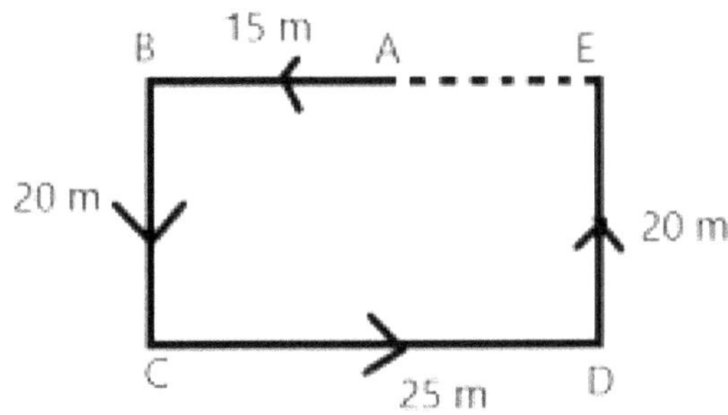

The movements of Prasanna are as shown in the figure.

Therefore, Prasanna's distance from his house at A

$= AE = (BE - BA)$

$= (CD - BA)$ ($\because$ BE = CD)

$= (25 - 15)$ m

$= 10$ m

Hence, the correct option is (A).

87. Perfect square - A given number that can be expressed as the square of a number from the same number system.

So, the nearest coming year which will be perfect square $=$ 2025

whose square number is 45

$\therefore$ The next coming year is 2025.

Hence, the correct option is (C).

88. The hour hand rotates $360°$ in 12 hours.

There are 8 hours from 10 to $6pm$.

So it covers degrees: $\frac{360}{12} \times 8 = 240°$

Hence, the correct option is (B).

89. Given series:

Left Side M 1 E & D 2 G 9 $ F @ 4 N Z W © 8 C Y A * 6 Right Side

If all the numbers are dropped:

M E & D G $ F @ N Z W © C Y A *

Then, the letter/symbol that is tenth from the right end is 'F'.

Hence, the correct option is (C).

90. Preparing the family tree using the following symbols:

Symbol in Diagram	Meaning
○	Female
□	Male
═	Married couple
—	Siblings
|	Difference of a generation

Deepak is talking about his father's daughter which would be his sister. Since Raju is his sister's husband, Deepak is Raju's Brother-in-law.

So, the possible tree diagram is:

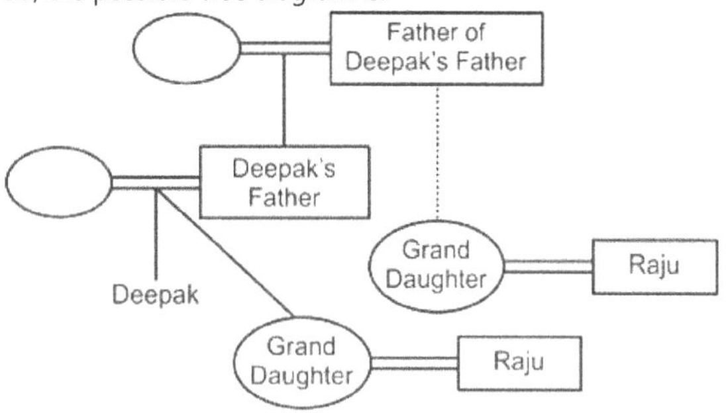

So, Deepak is Raju's Brother-in-law.

Hence, the correct option is (B).

91. The Uttar Pradesh government has introduced a system of issuing a unique 16 digit Unicode to mark all kinds of landholdings in the state.

The Unicode will be provided by the Revenue Department for marking all forms of residential, agriculture, and commercial land. The first six digits will be based on the population of the land while the next four digits will determine the unique identity of the land. The digits from 11 to 14 in the Unicode will be the number of the division of the land in the state.

The last two digits of the Unicode will have the details of the category, through which, the residential, agricultural and commercial land will be identified.

Hence, the correct option is (C).

92. The supreme court of India tenders advice to the President of India on matters of law or fact if he seeks such advice.

Article 143 of the Indian Constitution confers upon the Supreme Court advisory jurisdiction. According to Article 143 of the Indian Constitution, the President may seek the opinion of the Supreme Court on any question of law or fact of public importance on which he thinks it expedient to obtain such an opinion.

Hence, the correct option is (B).

93. Khizr Khan belonged to Sayyid Dynasty.

The Sayyid dynasty was the fourth dynasty of the Delhi Sultanate, with four rulers who ruled from 1414 to 1451. It was the ruling dynasty of the Delhi sultanate, in northern India after the invasion of Timur and the fall of the Tughlaq dynasty. He was the Governor of Multan under the Tughlaq ruler, Firuz Shah Tughlaq.

Hence, the correct option is (C).

94. A plateau is a flat, elevated landform that rises sharply above the surrounding area on at least one side. Plateaus occur on every continent and take up one-third of the Earth's land. They are one of the four major landforms, along with mountains, plains, and hills.

Hence, the correct option is (B).

95. The Central Government has set up a high-level panel to strengthen the assessment and accreditation of higher educational institutions. The committee has been formed under the chairmanship of K. Radhakrishnan, chairperson, Board of Governors, IIT Kanpur. He is also the chairperson of IIT Council Standing Committee.

Hence, the correct option is (A).

96. Verification of a login name and password is known as authentication. User authentication is a process that allows a device to verify the identify of someone who connects to a network resource.

Hence, the correct option is (C).

97. The F11 key is used to make the internet browser window full-screen. F11 key can be used by combined with Shift, Ctrl, Alt keys.

Some of the uses of the F11 key in MS Word.

- SHIFT + F11 = Go to the previous field.
- CTRL + F11 = Lock a field.
- CTRL + SHIFT + F11 = Unlock a field.
- ALT + F11 = Display Microsoft Visual Basic Code.
- ALT + SHIFT + F11 = Display Microsoft Visual Studio Code.

Hence, the correct option is (D).

98. An example of application software is MS Word.

Application software is a type of software or program that is designed to complete a specific task. The first user deal with system software after that he/she deals with application software. It is also known as an end-user program or a productivity program.

Examples of Application Software - Word processing software, Spreadsheets Software, Presentation, Graphics, CAD/CAM, Sending email, etc.

Hence, the correct option is (D).

99. SUBTRACT() is not a valid function in MS Excel.

Subtract two or more numbers in a cell:

1. Click any blank cell, and then type an equal sign (=) to start the formula.
2. After the equal sign, type a few numbers that are separated by a minus sign (-). for example, 100-50-30.
3. Press RETURN, then the result is 20.

Hence, the correct option is (C).

100. Ctrl + N is the shortcut to create a new presentation in MS PowerPoint.

Microsoft PowerPoint is a software application that is particularly used to present data and information by using text, diagrams with animation, images, and transitional effects, etc in the form of slides. It is used to make presentations for personal and professional purposes.

Hence, the correct option is (D).

Mock Test 02

Discipline

Q.1 Which of the following drugs is commonly used as a wound disinfectant?

A. Neosporin **B.** Prednisolone
C. Povidone iodine **D.** Bacitracin powder

Q.2 The difference between systolic and diastolic blood pressure is called:

[UPPSC Staff Nurse, 2017]

A. Blood Pressure **B.** Pulse Pressure
C. Apical Pressure **D.** Lateral Pressure

Q.3 Epidemic Dropsy is caused by:

[UPPSC Staff Nurse, 2017]

A. Sanguinarine **B.** B.O.A.A.
C. Drug borne **D.** Ergot

Q.4 At what angle is the intradermal injection given?

[UPPSC Staff Nurse, 2017]

A. 15° angle **B.** 30° angle
C. 45° angle **D.** 90° angle

Q.5 When CPR on a person If done, how deep will the pressure be on the chest?

[UPPSC Staff Nurse, 2017]

A. $1\frac{1}{2}$ inch **B.** 2 inch **C.** $2\frac{1}{2}$ inch **D.** 3 inch

Q.6 For a patient with Crohn's disease, the medical surgical nurse recommends a diet:

[UPPSC Staff Nurse, 2017]

A. High in fiber and low in protein and calories
B. High in potassium
C. Low in Fiber and High in Protein and Calories
D. Low in potassium

Q.7 TNM classification system is used in clinical staging of:

[UPPSC Staff Nurse, 2017]

A. Pain **B.** Depression
C. Cancer **D.** Obesity

Q.8 Match List-I with List-II and select the correct answer from the codes given below:

List-I	List-I
A. obstruction in the urinary tract	1. laser lithotripsy
B. treatment of renal stone	2. ileal conduit
C. stress incontinance	3. hydronephrosis
D. one type of urinary diversion	4. kegel exercises

[UPPSC Staff Nurse, 2017]

A. A - 1, B - 3, C - 4, D - 2
B. A - 2, B - 4, C - 1, D - 3
C. A - 4, B - 1, C - 3, D - 2
D. A - 3, B - 1, C - 4, D - 2

Q.9 The risk for vertical transmission of HIV is higher in:

[UPPSC Staff Nurse, 2017]

A. Anterior period **B.** Intranatal period
C. Postural period **D.** Breast feeding

Q.10 _______ approach to health education is based on the assumption that humans are rational decision-makers, this approach relies heavily upon the provision of information about the risks and benefits of certain behaviours.

A. Behaviour change
B. Community development
C. Biomedical
D. None of these

Q.11 Which of the following is a characteristic of the community development approach to health education?

A. Improving individual attitudes and beliefs is key to successful health education.
B. There is a close relationship between individual health and its social and material contexts, thus are relevant when developing initiatives for change.
C. Individuals need to change personal behaviour rather than to change the environment to promote health.
D. All of these

Q.12 A patient with a diagnosis of major depression who has attempted suicide says to the nurse, "I should have died! I've always been a failure. Nothing ever goes right for me." Which response demonstrates therapeutic communication?

A. "You have everything to live for."
B. "Why do you see yourself as a failure?"
C. "Feeling like this is all part of being depressed."
D. "You've been feeling like a failure for a while?"

Q.13 When the community health nurse visits a patient at home, the patient states, "I haven't slept the last couple of nights." Which response by the nurse illustrates a therapeutic communication response to this patient?

A. "I see."
B. "Really?"
C. "You're having difficulty in sleeping?"
D. "Sometimes, I have trouble sleeping too."

Q.14 Which of the following is not true of communication from a nursing perspective?

A. It includes the exchange of information, ideas, or opinions
B. Does not affect patient safety and quality of care provided
C. It is interactive
D. All of the above

Q.15 Nonverbal Behavior when engaging in healthcare communication includes:

A. Posture **B.** Tone of voice
C. Facial expression **D.** All of the above

Q.16 Working to increase effective communication can lead to:
A. Improved quality of care
B. A decrease in patient safety
C. Lack of team cohesiveness
D. Decreased nurse satisfaction

Q.17 What is the purpose of a nurse providing appropriate feedback?
A. To give the client good advice.
B. To advise the client on appropriate behaviors.
C. To evaluate the client's behavior.
D. To give the client critical information.

Q.18 A patient who is homeless has been admitted to the hospital with multiple health care problems. The nursing case manager, physician, social worker, and clinical dietician work together to care for the patient. This interprofessional interaction is referred to as:
A. Collaboration **B.** Consultation
C. Continuity **D.** Coordination

Q.19 To treat an infected foot, a patient with Medicare Part A is prescribed a two-week course of IV antibiotics, wound care, and physical therapy for mobility training. The nursing case manager recommends discharge to:
A. A skilled nursing facility.
B. An acute care hospital.
C. An acute rehabilitation facility.
D. Home health services.

Q.20 The nursing case manager reviews information about the number of patients with asthma who have received care by a specialist, those who have not, and the number of emergency department visits and inpatient hospitalizations for both groups. When comparing the data to develop interventions, the nurse engages in:
A. Aggregate data analysis
B. Benchmarking
C. Collaboration
D. Integrated data solutions

Q.21 To cover the cost of durable medical equipment, a patient who is enrolled in Medicare is required to:
A. Appeal for coverage
B. Request coverage
C. Seek supplemental insurance
D. Share in the cost

Q.22 A doctor wants to order a brand-name fibromyalgia medication that is not covered by a patient's insurance provider. As the patient has failed multiple agents prior to this prescription, the nursing case manager:
A. Advises the doctor that the medication is not covered and suggests revisiting some medications that were ordered before.
B. Directs the patient to the website of the drug company's patient assistance program for alternative medications.
C. Negotiates the self-pay cost for the brand-name medication with the pharmacy.
D. Submits the request for prior authorization to the insurance company with accompanying medical justification.

Q.23 In synthesizing data for a disease management program, the nursing case manager uses which source of data triangulation to validate a conclusion?
A. Cost, containment, and length of stay.
B. Method, cause, and reaction.
C. Reason, rationale, and resolution.
D. Time, space, and person.

Q.24 What is true of a patient classification system (PCS)?
A. It is a method of grouping patientsaccording to length or duration ofnursing care
B. It is a measuring tool used todescribe the progress of a patient'sstatus
C. It depends on the complexity ofnursing care requirements of thepatient
D. All of the above

Q.25 In the hospital, your department is using the functional method of patient care modality.What is it all about?
A. One nurse is responsible forgiving bedside care, another onefor administering medicationsand another one for treatments,and so on
B. It is a one on one constant patientcare for a period of time.
C. The nurse has the responsibility forgiving nursing care to the clientfrom admission until discharge.
D. A team leader has the task ofcoordinating the total care of agroup of patients.

Q.26 The nursing professional development specialist facilitates selection by using thedecision-making technique of:
A. Brainstorming
B. Convergent thinking
C. Consensus
D. Group think

Q.27 Nurses and other healthcare providers often have difficulty helping a terminally ill patient through the necessary stages leading to acceptance of death. Which of the following strategies is most helpful to the nurse in achieving this goal?
A. Taking psychology courses related to gerontology.
B. Reading books and other literature on the subject of thanatology.
C. Reflecting on the significance of death.
D. Reviewing varying cultural beliefs and practices related to death.

Q.28 A nurse is preparing to change the parenteral nutrition (PN) solution bag and tubing. The patient's central venous line is located in the right subclavian vein. The nurse asks the client to take which essential action during the tube change?
A. Turn the head to the right.
B. Inhale deeply, hold it, and bear down.
C. Breathe normally.
D. Exhale slowly and evenly.

Q.29 A nurse caring for a patient with an infectious disease who requires isolation should refers to guidelines published by the ________________.

A. National League for Nursing (NLN)
B. Centers for Disease Control (CDC)
C. American Medical Association (AMA)
D. American Nurses Association (ANA)

Q.30 To institute appropriate isolation precautions, the nurse must first know the ______________.

A. organism's mode of transmission
B. organism's Gram-staining characteristics
C. organism's susceptibility to antibiotics
D. patient's susceptibility to the organism

Q.31 Which is the correct procedure for collecting a sputum specimen for culture and sensitivity testing?

A. Have the patient place the specimen in a container and enclose the container in a plastic bag.
B. Have the patient expectorate the sputum while the nurse holds the container.
C. Have the patient expectorate the sputum into a sterile container.
D. Offer the patient an antiseptic mouthwash just before he expectorates the sputum.

Q.32 An autoclave is used to sterilize hospital supplies because:

A. more articles can be sterilized at a time.
B. steam causes less damage to the materials.
C. a lower temperature can be obtained.
D. pressurized steam penetrates the supplies better.

Q.33 The best way to decrease the risk of transferring pathogens to a patient when removing contaminated gloves is to:

A. wash the gloves before removing them.
B. gently pull on the fingers of the gloves when removing them.
C. gently pull just below the cuff and invert the gloves when removing them.
D. remove the gloves and then turn them inside out.

Q.34 After having an I.V. line in place for 72 hours, a patient complains of tenderness, burning, and swelling. Assessment of the I.V. site reveals that it is warm and erythematous. This usually indicates ______________.

A. infection **B.** infiltration
C. phlebitis **D.** bleeding

Q.35 What should a nurse do to ensure homogenization when diluting a powder medicine in a vial?

A. Shake the vial vigorously.
B. Roll the vial gently between the palms.
C. Invert the vial and let it stand for 1 minute.
D. Do nothing after adding the solution to the vial.

Q.36 Proteins are made up of:

A. Lipids **B.** Amino acids
C. Fatty acids **D.** Glycogen

Q.37 Amino acids are joined by:

A. Hydrogen bond **B.** Peptide bond
C. Ionic bond **D.** Glycosidic bond

Q.38 The building blocks of proteins are polymers of:

A. Glucose **B.** Vitamins
C. Amino Acids **D.** Starch

Q.39 Proteins are soluble in:

A. Benzene **B.** Anhydrous acetone
C. Aqueous alcohol **D.** Anhydrous alcohol

Q.40 Osteomalacia in adults and rickets in children are due to the deficiency of which vitamin?

A. Vitamin C **B.** Vitamin D
C. Vitamin A **D.** Vitamin E

Q.41 Which of the following is not included in kwashiorkor?

A. Edema **B.** Weight loss
C. Fatty liver **D.** Skin changes

Q.42 A bio-fertilizer used as supplemental food for cattle, especially for harnessing bovines is _______.

A. Azotobacter **B.** Azospirillum
C. Rhizobium **D.** Azolla

Q.43 The gas involved in the photosynthesis process is __________.

A. Ozone **B.** Oxygen
C. Hydrogen **D.** Carbon dioxide

Q.44 What are the signs and symptoms of fluoride deficiency?

A. Weak bones
B. Yellow-brown staining of teeth
C. Dermatitis
D. Stiffness in joints

Q.45 What symptoms are associated with heat exhaustion?

A. Cool, moist, pale, or flushed skin
B. Rapid weak pulse
C. Rapid, shallow breathing
D. All of the above

Q.46 A man is having a heart attack, he has medication with him, what should You do?

A. Give the medicine to him placing it under the tongue, Call 108
B. Assist him with the medicine, Call 108, reassure him until help arrives
C. Call 108, place medicine in mouth and begin CPR
D. Have the victim lay down, Call 108

Q.47 A victim has lost a lot of blood through a deep cut in his leg. He is breathing fast and seems pail and restless. He is probably:

A. Having a stroke
B. Having a heart attack
C. In shock
D. Choking

Q.48 What do you do for a victim who has a bleeding injury to the mouth and you are sure that there is no head, neck, or spine injury?

A. Keep victim seated with head tilted slightly forward
B. Keep victim seated with head tilted slightly backward
C. Have the victim lie down on their side
D. Either (A) or (C)

Q.49 In general, a splint should be________.

A. Loose, so that the victim can still move the injured limb
B. Comfortable, but not so tight that it slows circulation
C. Tied with cravats over the injured area
D. None of the above

Q.50 A boy has cut his finger, what action would be the best?

A. Put the severed end of the finger back in place, wrap the entire finger in sterile gauze and transport it to the hospital immediately.
B. Wrap the severed finger in sterile gauze, place it in a plastic bag, put the bag on ice transport, both finger and the victim to the hospital
C. Place the severed finger in a plastic bag, have the boy place the bag under his armpit, transport immediately to the hospital
D. Place a tourniquet at the stub where the finger was severed to control bleeding transport to the hospital immediately

Q.51 Dressing and bandages are used to:

A. Reduce the victim's pain
B. Reduce internal bleeding
C. Help control bleeding and prevent infection
D. Make it easier to take the victim to the hospital

Q.52 Which would you do when caring for a seizure victim?

A. Remove nearby objects that might cause injury
B. Place a small object, such as a rolled-up piece of cloth, between the victim's teeth
C. Try to hold the person still
D. All of the above

Q.53 A boy enters your bus, you smell alcohol, he passes out before you get to his bus stop, what should you do?

A. Take the boy back to school
B. Stop the bus, check for breathing and pulse, Call 911
C. Allow the boy to sleep it off and take him home
D. Drive the boy to the nearest fire station or hospital

Q.54 What is the normal Gestation period of human beings?

A. 400 days **B.** 120 days **C.** 200 days **D.** 270 days

Q.55 The fertilized cell is called-

A. Embryo **B.** Uterus
C. Zygote **D.** None of the above

Q.56 T cells mature in ____.

A. Thyroid gland **B.** Thymus gland
C. Spleen **D.** Bone marrow

Q.57 Match List - I with List-II and select the correct answer from the codes given below the lists:

List - I (Hormone)	List – II (Function)
A. Aldosterone	1. Maintains female secondary sex characteristics
B. Oestrogen	2. Controls circadian rhythm
C. Melatonin	3. Salt-retaining hormone
D. Progesterone	4. Sustains the pregnancy

A. A-4, B-2, C-1, D-3 **B.** A-4, B-1, C-2, D-3
C. A-3, B-2, C-1, D-4 **D.** A-3, B-1, C-2, D-4

Q.58 Which gland controls the functioning of other endocrine glands?

A. Thyroid Gland **B.** Pineal Gland
C. Adrenal glands **D.** Pituitary gland

Q.59 Which of the following is an exocrine secretion?

A. Oxytocin **B.** Saliva
C. Thyroxine **D.** Vasopressin

Q.60 The juxtra glomerular apparatus is a part of which of the following cells in mammals?

A. Oocyte **B.** Myocyte **C.** Neurons **D.** Nephron

Q.61 Name the filtration units of the excretory system in humans.

A. Ureter **B.** Nephron **C.** Neuron **D.** Ueuron

Q.62 What is the main excretory product in birds and reptiles?

A. Urea **B.** Uric acid
C. Ammonia **D.** Guanine

Q.63 A nurse is assessing an 18-year-old woman who has come into the emergency department for bilateral abdominal pain. Which of the following should the nurse not consider a risk factor for ectopic pregnancy?

A. Endometriosis
B. Chlamydia trachomatis
C. Uterine fibroids
D. Yeast infection

Q.64 A woman arrives at the birthing center for evaluation. She thinks she may be in labor. She is multiparous and experiencing contractions every 3 minutes. Upon examination, the nurse notes that she is 5cm dilated and 50% effaced. Which stage and phase of labor is the woman experiencing?

A. Stage 2, phase 1 **B.** Stage 2, phase 2
C. Stage 1, phase 3 **D.** Stage 1, phase 2

Q.65 The nurse is called to a room by a laboring patient. The patient complains of backache and appears restless. Her fingers are trembling and beads of sweat fall from her forehead. The nurse suspects she might be experiencing which stage of labor?

A. Stage 3, phase 1 **B.** Stage 1, phase 3
C. Stage 2, phase 2 **D.** Stage 1, phase 2

Q.66 Which of the following describes a category II fetal heart rate (FHR) tracing?

A. Baseline FHR 90bpm; marked variability; zero accelerations; late decelerations

B. Baseline FHR145 bpm; moderate variability; two accelerations; zero decelerations

C. Baseline FHR170 bpm; moderate variability; two accelerations; zero decelerations

D. Baseline FHR 100bpm; minimal variability; zero accelerations; variable decelerations

Q.67 In a fetus positioned at the left occiput anterior (LOA), where should the nurse assess the fetal heart rate (FHR)?

A. Below umbilicus on mother's left side
B. Above umbilicus on mother's left side
C. Above umbilicus on mother's right side
D. Below umbilicus on mother's right side

Q.68 What is the triad of presenting symptoms with endometriosis?

A. Hirsutism, infertility, and oligomenorrhea
B. Dysmenorrhea, infertility, and dyspareunia
C. Dysmenorrhea, metrorrhagia, and dysuria
D. Menorrhagia, infertility, and dyspraeunia

Q.69 Which is the best method of health communication to motivate an eligible couple for adopting contraceptive practice?

A. Group discussion
B. Use of internet
C. Face to face communication
D. None of these

Q.70 A nurse was assessing the neighborhood near the health agency. The nurse drove around observing the condition of the buildings, sidewalks, and the people in the community. Which of the following best describes the actions of the nurse?

A. A drive-through
B. A neighborhood observation
C. A quick overview
D. A windshield survey

Q.71 Which of the following information is important to be conveyed by a nurse giving nutritional counseling to a patient with cholecystitis?

A. The patient must maintain a low-calorie diet.
B. The patient must maintain a high protein/low carbohydrate diet.
C. The patient should limit sweets and sugary drinks.
D. The patient should limit fatty foods.

Q.72 A patient hospitalized with myocardial infarction develops severe pulmonary edema. Which of the following symptoms would the nurse expect in the patient?

A. Slow and deep breaths
B. Strider(a noisy or high-pitched sound during breath)
C. Bradycardia
D. Breathlessness

Q.73 A nurse is caring a patient diagnosed with pulmonary embolism. Which of the following symptoms the nurse will observed in the patient?

A. The patient's decreased response to the family
B. The patient suddenly complain of chest pain and shortness of breath
C. The patient has developed a wet cough and the nurse hears crackles on auscultation of the lungs
D. The patient has fever, chills, and feels loss of appetite

Q.74 A nurse in the emergency department is observing a 4-year-old child for signs of increased intracranial pressure after a fall from a bicycle, resulting in head trauma. Which of the following signs or symptoms would be cause for concern?

A. Bulging anterior fontanel
B. Frequent vomiting
C. Symptoms of falling asleep early
D. Inability to read smaller words

Q.75 After six months of age:

A. Breast feeding should be stopped and complimentary feeding should be started
B. Continue breast feeding and no complimentary feeding
C. Continue breast feeding and start complimentary feeding
D. Stop breast feeding

Q.76 Below what weight Hepatitis B vaccine is not recommended to be given?

A. 1 kg **B.** 2 kg **C.** 2.5 kg **D.** 3 kg

Q.77 Anterior fontanelle is ossified at ______________in infants.

A. one month after birth
B. 6 months after birth
C. 18 month after birth
D. 25 month after birth

Q.78 Neonatal Mortality rate is calculated by estimating the number newborn death within _________.

A. 24 hours **B.** 28 days
C. one week **D.** one year

Q.79 After birth Umbilical vein converted into:

A. Foramen ovale
B. Ligamentum venosusm
C. Ligamentum arteriosus
D. Ligamentum teres

Q.80 In Marasmus infants which is the principal lacking factor?

A. Protein **B.** Energy **C.** Vitamins **D.** Calcium

General Aptitude / Reasoning / General Awareness / Basic Computer knowledge

Q.81 A tank can be filled by pipe A in 2 hours and pipe B in 6 hours. At 10 A.M. pipe A was opened. At what time will the tank be filled if pipe B is opened at 11 A.M.?

A. 12.45 A.M. **B.** 5 P.M.
C. 11.45 A.M. **D.** 12 P.M.

Q.82 A certain sum of money at simple interest amounts to Rs. 690 in 3 years and to Rs. 750 in 5 years. What is the principal?

A. Rs. 500 **B.** Rs. 550 **C.** Rs. 600 **D.** Rs. 650

Q.83 The speed of a boat in still water is 20 km/h, and the speed of the stream is 2 km/h. In how many hours would the boat cover a distance of 198 km downstream?

A. 11 hours **B.** 6 hours **C.** 9 hours **D.** 15 hours

Q.84 What will come in the place of the question mark ' $?$' in the following question?

$\sqrt{400} \times 2 - 30 = \sqrt{256} - 12 + ?$

A. 4 **B.** 6 **C.** 8 **D.** 3

Q.85 The HCF of two numbers is 7. Which of the following can be LCM of these two numbers.

A. 161 **B.** 872 **C.** 587 **D.** 697

Q.86 If TOUR is written as 1234, CLEAR is written as 56784 and SPARE is written as 90847, find the code for CARE.

[Intelligence Bureau Security Assistant, 2017]

A. 1247 **B.** 4847 **C.** 5247 **D.** 5847

Q.87 Direction: Read the given statement(s) and conclusions carefully and select which of the conclusions logically follow(s) from the statement(s).

Statements:

I. All bottle is plastic

II. Some bags are plastic

Conclusions:

I. Some bags are not bottle

II. Some plastic are not bags

A. Only conclusion I follows

B. Only conclusion II follows

C. None follows

D. All Follows

Q.88 Direction: In the following question, identify the pair of words which has a relationship similar to the pair in the question.

Fan : Heat

A. Water : Drink **B.** Light : Day

C. Teach : Student **D.** Food : Hunger

Q.89 Direction: In the question below a statement is given followed by two conclusions, I and II. You have to consider the statement to be true, even if it seems to be at variance from commonly known facts. You have to decide which of the given conclusions definitely is drawn from the given statement.

Statement: Last year, the total accident count in India was 464,674 which caused 148,707 traffic-related deaths.

Conclusions:

I. Some of the traffic accidents were fatal.

II. The bad condition of the road was also responsible for such a high number.

A. If only conclusion I follows

B. If only conclusion II follows

C. If neither I nor II follows

D. If both I and II follow

Q.90 Direction: Three of the four following number pairs are alike in a certain way, and one is different. Pick up the odd one from the given alternatives.

A. $9:90$ **B.** $7:56$ **C.** $5:30$ **D.** $8:66$

Q.91 The state tree of Uttar Pradesh is ______.

A. Banayan tree **B.** Ashoka Tree

C. Mango Tree **D.** None of the above

Q.92 Who won 'Outstanding Performance by a Female Actor in a Leading Role' award at the Screen Actor Guild Awards, held in California, on 2022?

A. Jessica Chastain

B. Bryce Dallas Howard

C. Diane Kruger

D. Mackenzie Foy

Q.93 Which state has won "Ranji Trophy 2022" Title ?

A. Bihar **B.** Madya Pradesh

C. Maharashtra **D.** Odisha

Q.94 Which country is the host of the International Solar Alliance's Fifth Assembly in 2022?

A. Bangladesh **B.** India

C. Nepal **D.** Thailand

Q.95 Teej is a Hindu festival dedicated to which goddess?

A. Laxmi **B.** Saraswati

C. Parvati **D.** Durga

Q.96 WORM stands for:

[Allahabad High Court Review Officer (RO), 2019]

A. Write Once, Read Many

B. Write Read Memory

C. Wipe Only, Read Memory

D. Read Write Memory

Q.97 Which of the following is not a part operation of instruction cycle?

[Allahabad High Court Review Officer (RO), 2019]

A. Fetch **B.** Indirect **C.** Execute **D.** Memory

Q.98 Which of the following is not a web browser?

A. Google Chrome **B.** Mozilla Firefox

C. Internet Explorer **D.** File Explorer

Q.99 Which of the following words/expressions is not related to the keyboard of a computer?

[Rajasthan Police Constable, 2020]

A. QWERTY **B.** function keys

C. Numeric keypad **D.** Master key

Q.100 Which of the following attack-based checks WebInspect cannot do?

A. cross-site scripting **B.** directory traversal

C. parameter injection **D.** injecting shell code

// Smart Answer Sheet //

Correct Indicates percentage of students who answered questions correctly.

Skipped Indicates percentage of students who skipped questions.

Q.	Ans.	Correct	Skipped
1	C	78.95 %	0.0 %
2	B	68.67 %	1.73 %
3	A	58.1 %	1.97 %
4	A	55.17 %	1.63 %
5	B	46.89 %	1.75 %
6	C	12.44 %	3.26 %
7	C	65.64 %	1.85 %
8	D	18.58 %	3.31 %
9	B	29.8 %	4.6 %
10	A	66.93 %	1.87 %
11	B	57.48 %	1.4 %
12	D	67.59 %	1.68 %
13	C	86.19 %	0.0 %
14	D	53.3 %	1.73 %
15	D	61.79 %	1.52 %
16	A	57.37 %	1.97 %
17	D	51.7 %	1.67 %
18	A	50.18 %	1.13 %
19	A	54.62 %	1.74 %
20	A	46.85 %	1.68 %
21	D	54.44 %	1.5 %
22	D	42.94 %	1.27 %
23	D	42.73 %	1.8 %
24	C	66.12 %	1.32 %
25	A	17.4 %	3.15 %
26	C	66.98 %	1.48 %
27	C	45.68 %	1.76 %
28	B	89.6 %	0.0 %
29	B	56.46 %	1.01 %
30	A	48.27 %	1.68 %
31	C	88.16 %	0.0 %
32	D	29.34 %	4.0 %
33	C	89.07 %	0.0 %
34	C	32.69 %	3.72 %
35	B	52.16 %	1.26 %
36	B	68.62 %	1.91 %
37	B	89.95 %	0.0 %
38	C	58.52 %	1.25 %
39	C	54.34 %	1.25 %
40	B	42.46 %	1.76 %
41	B	40.06 %	1.68 %
42	D	68.27 %	1.22 %
43	D	46.06 %	1.06 %
44	A	48.07 %	1.49 %
45	A	65.4 %	1.09 %
46	B	54.7 %	1.09 %
47	D	43.42 %	1.69 %
48	D	23.64 %	3.97 %
49	B	59.53 %	1.35 %
50	B	46.56 %	1.36 %
51	C	81.52 %	0.0 %
52	A	55.72 %	1.77 %
53	B	43.21 %	1.62 %
54	D	65.04 %	1.1 %
55	C	57.36 %	1.11 %
56	B	54.44 %	1.63 %
57	D	50.58 %	1.67 %
58	D	57.0 %	1.65 %
59	B	41.08 %	1.82 %
60	D	65.55 %	1.55 %
61	B	45.12 %	1.91 %
62	B	54.06 %	1.66 %
63	D	17.06 %	3.03 %
64	D	63.82 %	1.56 %
65	B	41.04 %	1.17 %
66	D	25.62 %	3.64 %
67	D	12.65 %	4.73 %
68	B	59.83 %	1.55 %
69	C	50.25 %	1.91 %
70	D	59.17 %	1.4 %
71	D	65.82 %	1.27 %
72	D	19.65 %	4.27 %
73	B	64.64 %	1.73 %
74	B	64.78 %	1.32 %
75	C	41.77 %	1.75 %
76	B	83.67 %	0.0 %
77	C	56.82 %	1.3 %
78	B	60.03 %	1.17 %
79	D	69.7 %	1.96 %
80	B	89.62 %	0.0 %

Q.	Ans.	Correct / Skipped
81	C	85.19 % / 0.0 %
82	C	81.49 % / 0.0 %
83	C	76.4 % / 0.0 %
84	B	80.64 % / 0.0 %

Q.	Ans.	Correct / Skipped
85	A	79.57 % / 0.0 %
86	D	89.63 % / 0.0 %
87	C	86.85 % / 0.0 %
88	D	80.5 % / 0.0 %

Q.	Ans.	Correct / Skipped
89	A	87.49 % / 0.0 %
90	D	25.72 % / 4.7 %
91	B	64.11 % / 1.58 %
92	A	48.07 % / 1.29 %

Q.	Ans.	Correct / Skipped
93	B	88.27 % / 0.0 %
94	B	55.4 % / 1.8 %
95	C	11.51 % / 4.65 %
96	A	67.0 % / 1.64 %

Q.	Ans.	Correct / Skipped
97	D	56.17 % / 1.21 %
98	D	56.65 % / 1.94 %
99	D	40.98 % / 1.35 %
100	D	81.77 % / 0.0 %

Performance Analysis	
Avg. Score (%)	61.0%
Toppers Score (%)	75.0%
Your Score	

//Hints and Solutions//

1. Povidone iodine:

- It is available as a topical solution, surgical scrub, mouth wash, ointment and vaginal pessary.
- This disinfectant is highly effective against viruses, bacteria, protozoa, yeasts and fungi.
- Its repeated use is prohibitive because of its insolubility, volatility, and its staining and stimulating properties.
- Povidone Iodine aids in the treatment of a range of acute and chronic wounds.
- Povidone iodine is bactericidal against gram-positive and gram-negative organisms.
- Povidone iodine has several properties that place it exceptionally well in the group of wound healing drugs, including its broad antimicrobial spectrum, lack of resistance, efficacy against biofilms, good tolerability, and its effect on excessive inflammation .

Therefore, the drug povidone iodine is commonly used as a wound disinfectant.

Hence, the correct option is (C).

2. The difference between systolic and diastolic blood pressure is called Pulse Pressure.

- Pulse pressure is the difference between systolic BP and diastolic BP.
- Normal blood pressure is 120/80 mmHg.
- So the normal pulse pressure is 40 mmHg.

Hence, the correct option is (B).

3. Epidemic Dropsy is caused by Sanguinarine.

- Sanguinarine is a major alkaloid of Argemone oil.
- Epidemic dropsy occurs when edible oils are adultered by Argemone oil.
- Sanguinarine acts on capillaries. There is capillary dilatation, proliferation, and increased capillary permeability. It leads to edema and hypovolemia.
- Epidemic dropsy is characterized by gastroenteric symptoms followed by cutaneous erythema and pigmentation.
- Respiratory and cardiac symptoms may also be present.

Hence, the correct option is (A).

4. At 15° angle is the intradermal injection given.

- Intradermal injections are delivered into the dermis, or the skin layer underneath the epidermis (which is the upper skin layer).
- ID injection is given at an angle of administration of 5 to 15 degrees angle.

Hence, the correct option is (A).

5. When CPR on a person If done, 2 inch deep will the pressure be on the chest.

- CPR is emergency care requires to restore the vital function of the body in life-threatening conditions.
- Press (compress) the chest straight down at least 2 inches (5 cm) but no more than 2.4 inches (6 cm)

Steps:

- A-Airway
- B-Breathing
- C-C circulation
- D-Defibrillation

Hence, the correct option is (B).

6. For a patient with Crohn's disease, the medical surgical nurse recommends a diet Low in Fiber and High in Protein and Calories.

- Crohn's disease is a type of inflammatory bowel disease (IBD).
- It causes inflammation of your digestive tract, which can lead to abdominal pain, severe diarrhoea, fatigue, weight loss, and malnutrition.
- People with Crohn's disease are at increased risk for malnutrition and nutrient deficiencies. Poor nutrition makes it more difficult for your body to heal and fight infection.
- So, people with Crohn's disease should follow a balanced diet and be sure to get enough calories, protein, vitamins, minerals, and fluid.
- A low-fibre with a low-residue diet can help lessen abdominal pain, cramping, and diarrhoea.

Hence, the correct option is (C).

7. TNM classification system is used in clinical staging of Cancer.

- The TNM staging system (officially known as the TNM classification system of malignant tumors) is a cancer staging system overseen and published by the Union for International Cancer Control (UICC).
- The TNM staging is mainly used to describe cancers that form solid tumors, such as breast, colon, and lung cancers.

The extent and spread of cancer in the patient's body are detected using the TNM system.

- T refers to the size of the tumor and any spread of cancer to nearby tissue.
- N refers to the spread of cancer to nearby lymph nodes.
- M refers to metastasis (spread of cancer to other parts of the body).

Hence, the correct option is (C).

8.

List-I	List-I
A. obstruction in the urinary tract	hydronephrosis

B. treatment of renal stone	laser lithotripsy
C. stress incontinance	kegel exercises
D. one type of urinary diversion	ileal conduit

- Hydronephrosis is a condition of excess urine accumulation in the kidney(s) that causes swelling of the kidneys. This causes pain during urination, nausea, and vomiting.
- Laser lithotripsy is a procedure to break apart kidney stones in the urinary tract. It is done with a scope that can be passed into the tubes of the urinary tract.
- Kegel exercise, also known as pelvic-floor exercise, involves repeatedly contracting and relaxing the muscles that form part of the pelvic floor, sometimes referred to as the "Kegel muscles.
- An ileal conduit urinary diversion is one of various surgical techniques for urinary diversion.

Hence, the correct option is (D).

9. The risk for vertical transmission of HIV is higher in intranatal period.

- HIV (human immunodeficiency virus) is a virus that attacks the body's immune system. If HIV is not treated, it can lead to AIDS (acquired immunodeficiency syndrome)
- Acquired immunodeficiency syndrome (AIDS) is a chronic, potentially life-threatening condition caused by the human immunodeficiency virus (HIV). By damaging your immune system, HIV interferes with your body's ability to fight infection and disease.
- Vertical transmission refers to the generational transmission of viruses from parents to their offspring.
- HIV can be transmitted via the exchange of a variety of body fluids from infected people, such as blood, breast milk, semen and vaginal secretions.
- HIV can also be transmitted from a mother to her child during pregnancy and delivery.

Therefore, the Intranatal period has a higher risk of vertical transmission because transmission might occurs with placenta.

Hence, the correct option is (B).

10. The behaviour change approach to health education is based on the assumption that humans are rational decision-makers, this approach relies heavily upon the provision of information about the risks and benefits of certain behaviours.

The behaviour change approach promotes health through individual changes in lifestyle that are appropriate to people's settings. The simple logic is that some behaviour leads to ill-health, and so persuading people directly to change their behaviour must be the most efficient and effective way to reduce illness.

Hence, the correct option is (A).

11. There is a close relationship between individual health and its social and material contexts, thus is relevant when developing initiatives for change of the following is a characteristic of the community development approach to health education.

Adults who are socially active tend to live longer and be healthier than their more isolated peers. Social relationships are important for maintaining good health. Conversely, social isolation poses health risks. Studies have shown that for patients with coronary artery disease, social isolation poses an additional risk of death. Working through roles, social networks, and status, social structure can influence health, values, occupational attainment, and a sense of belonging in society. Several studies show that people who are part of social networks are less likely to be negatively affected by stressful life events and less likely to become ill.

Hence, the correct option is (B).

12. "You've been feeling like a failure for a while?" response demonstrates therapeutic communication. Responding to the feelings expressed by a patient is an effective therapeutic communication technique. The correct option is an example of the use of restating. It's frequently useful for nurses to summarize what patients have said after the fact. This demonstrates to patients that the nurse was listening and allows the nurse to document conversations. Ending a summary with a phrase like "Does that sound correct?" gives patients explicit permission to make corrections if they're necessary.

Hence, the correct option is (D).

13. "You're having difficulty in sleeping?" response by the nurse illustrates a therapeutic communication response to this patient.

The correct option uses the therapeutic communication technique of restatement. Although restatement is a technique that has a prompting component to it, it repeats the patient's major theme, which assists the nurse in obtaining a more specific perception of the problem from the patient.

Hence, the correct option is (C).

14. All of the above are not true of communication from a nursing perspective.

Nurses act as the hub of communication, relaying and interpreting information between physicians, caregivers, family members and patients. The ability to establish effective communication in nursing is imperative to providing the best care and patient outcomes possible.

Hence, the correct option is (D).

15. Nonverbal Behavior when engaging in healthcare communication includes Posture, Tone of voice, and Facial expression.

In humans, one of the means of communication is the posture of the body, in addition to facial expressions, personal distances, gestures and body movements. Posture conveys information about: Interpersonal relations. Personality traits such as confidence, submissiveness, and openness.

The tone of voice in communication is defined as 'the way a person speaks to someone'. It is how you use your voice to get your point across.

The human face is extremely expressive, able to convey countless emotions without saying a word. And unlike some forms of nonverbal communication, facial expressions are universal. The facial expressions for happiness, sadness, anger, surprise, fear, and disgust are the same across cultures.

Hence, the correct option is (D).

16. Working to increase effective communication can lead to Improved quality of care.

The effective communication to Improve Quality strategy identifies effective communication behaviors for patients, families, and clinicians that are the foundation for partnerships throughout the hospital stay. The strategy supports behavior change through individual tools.

Hence, the correct option is (A).

17. The purpose of providing appropriate feedback is to give the client critical information. Delivered well, feedback can motivate the recipient to improve performance and achieve desired outcomes. Delivered harshly, it can produce the opposite effect and inspire anger, hurt feelings, and resentment.

Hence, the correct option is (D).

18. This interprofessional interaction is referred to as collaboration.

Collaboration means 'to work with another person or group in order to achieve or do something'. Workplace collaboration requires interpersonal skills, communication skills, knowledge sharing and strategy, and can occur in a traditional office or between members of a virtual team.

Hence, the correct option is (A).

19. To treat an infected foot, a patient with Medicare Part A is prescribed a two-week course of IV antibiotics, wound care, and physical therapy for mobility training. The nursing case manager recommends discharge to a skilled nursing facility.

A skilled nursing facility (SNF) is an institution (or a distinct part of an institution) licensed under applicable state laws and primarily engaged in providing skilled nursing care and related services for residents who require medical or nursing care; or rehabilitation services for the rehabilitation of injured.

Hence, the correct option is (A).

20. When comparing the data to develop interventions, the nurse engages in aggregate data analysis.

Aggregate data refers to analysis or non-numerical information that is aggregated from multiple sources and/or multiple measures, variables, or individuals and compiled into a data summary or summary report, usually for public reporting or statistical analysis. For purposes- ie. Examine trends.

Hence, the correct option is (A).

21. To cover the cost of durable medical equipment, a patient who is enrolled in Medicare is required to share in the cost.

If you are in a skilled nursing facility (SNF) or are a hospital inpatient, DME is covered by Part A. Whether you have Original Medicare or a Medicare Advantage Plan, the types of Medicare-covered equipment should be the same. Examples of DME include: Wheelchairs.

Hence, the correct option is (D).

22. As the patient has failed multiple agents prior to this prescription, the nursing case manager submits the request for prior authorization to the insurance company with accompanying medical justification.

Accepted medical practices define medical necessity as any reasonable service, procedure, or treatment that will help to prevent the onset of a condition, reduce the effects of an illness or condition, or help a person reach and maintain maximum functional capacity.

Hence, the correct option is (D).

23. In synthesizing data for a disease management program, the nursing case manager uses time, space, and person source of data triangulation to validate a conclusion. Disease management programs are designed to improve the health of persons with chronic of baseline data on the natural course of the targeted disease.

Hence, the correct option is (D).

24. "It depends on the complexity ofnursing care requirements of thepatient" is true for a patient classification system (PCS).

The Patient classification system (PCS), also known as patient acuity system, is a tool used for managing and planning the allocation of nursing staff in accordance with the nursing care needs. Thus, PCS is used to assist nurse leaders determine workload requirements and staffing needs.

Hence, the correct option is (C).

25. In the hospital, your department is using the functional method of patient care modality. It is all about One nurse is responsible forgiving bedside care, another onefor administering medicationsand another one for treatments.

Functional nursing is a nursing model that focuses on efficiency and getting as many tasks as possible done in the shortest time. It is task-oriented as it involves giving a particular nursing function to each worker.

Hence, the correct option is (A).

26. The nursing professional development specialist facilitates selection by using thedecision-making technique of Consensus. Medical consensus is a public statement on a particular aspect of medical knowledge at the time the statement is made that a representative group of experts agree to be evidence-based and state-of-the-art (state-of-the-science) knowledge.

Hence, the correct option is (C).

27. Reflecting on the significance of death this strategy is most helpful to the nurse in achieving this goal.

According to thanatologists, reflecting on the significance of death helps to reduce the fear of death and enables the health care provider to better understand the terminally ill patient's feelings. It also helps to overcome the belief that medical and nursing measures have failed, when a patient cannot be cured. Thanatology is the science and study of death and dying from multiple perspectives medical, physical, psychological, spiritual, ethical, and more.

Hence, the correct option is (C).

28. The patient should be asked to perform the Valsalva maneuver during tubing changes. This helps avoid air embolism during tube changes. The nurse asks the patient to take a deep breath, hold it, and bear down. Make sure all connections are clamped and closed. Clamp catheter, position patient in left Trendelenburg position, call health care provider, and administer oxygen as needed.

Hence, the correct option is (B).

29. A nurse caring for a patient with an infectious disease who requires isolation should refer to guidelines published by the Centers for Disease Control (CDC).

The Center of Disease Control (CDC) publishes and frequently updates guidelines on caring for patients who require isolation. CDC is responsible for controlling the introduction and spread of infectious diseases, and provides consultation and assistance to other nations and international agencies to assist in improving their disease prevention and control, environmental health, and health promotion activities.

Hence, the correct option is (B).

30. To institute appropriate isolation precautions, the nurse must first know the organism's mode of transmission.

Before instituting isolation precaution, the nurse must first determine the organism's mode of transmission. For example, an organism transmitted through nasal secretions requires that the patient be kept in respiratory isolation, which involves keeping the patient in a private room with the door closed and wearing a mask, a gown, and gloves when coming in direct contact with the patient.

Hence, the correct option is (A).

31. Having the patient expectorate the sputum into a sterile container is the correct procedure for collecting a sputum specimen for culture and sensitivity testing.

Placing the specimen in a sterile container ensures that it will not become contaminated. A sputum specimen is obtained for culture to identify the microorganism responsible for lung infections; identify cancer cells shed by lung tumors; or aid in the diagnosis and management of occupational lung diseases. The other answers are incorrect because they do not mention sterility and because antiseptic mouthwash could destroy the organism to be cultured (before sputum collection, the patient may use only tap water for nursing the mouth).

Hence, the correct option is (C).

32. An autoclave is used to sterilize hospital supplies because pressurized steam penetrates the supplies better.

An autoclave, an apparatus that sterilizes equipment by means of high-temperature pressurized steam, is used because it can destroy all forms of microorganisms, including spores. Autoclaves operate at high temperatures and pressure in order to kill microorganisms and spores. They are used to decontaminate certain biological waste and sterilize media, instruments, and labware.

Hence, the correct option is (D).

33. The best way to decrease the risk of transferring pathogens to a patient when removing contaminated gloves is to gently pull just below the cuff and invert the gloves when removing them.

Turning the gloves inside out while removing them keeps all contaminants inside the gloves. They should then be placed in a plastic bag with soiled dressings and discarded in a soiled utility room garbage pail (double bagged). The other choices can spread pathogens within the environment.

Hence, the correct option is (C).

34. After having an I.V. line in place for 72 hours, a patient complains of tenderness, burning, and swelling. Assessment of the I.V. site reveals that it is warm and erythematous. This usually indicates phlebitis.

Tenderness, warmth, swelling, and, in some instances, a burning sensation are signs and symptoms of phlebitis. Superficial phlebitis affects veins on the skin surface. The condition is rarely serious and, with proper care, usually resolves rapidly. Sometimes people with superficial phlebitis also get deep vein thrombophlebitis, so a medical evaluation is necessary.

Hence, the correct option is (C).

35. To ensure homogenization when diluting powdered medication in a vial, the nurse should roll the vial gently between the palms.

Gently rolling a sealed vial between the palms produces sufficient heat to enhance the dissolution of powdered medication.

Hence, the correct option is (B).

36. Proteins are made up of hundreds or thousands of smaller units called amino acids, which are attached to one another in long chains. There are 20 different types of amino acids that can be combined to make a protein. Bonding within protein molecules helps stabilize their structure, and the final folded forms of proteins are well-adapted for their functions.

Hence, the correct option is (B).

37. Amino acids are joined by Peptide bond. Within a protein, multiple amino acids are linked together by peptide bonds, thereby forming a long chain. Peptide bonds are formed by a biochemical reaction that extracts a water molecule as it joins the amino group of one amino acid to the carboxyl group of a neighboring amino acid.

Hence, the correct option is (B).

38. The building blocks of proteins are polymers of amino Acids. Each amino acid has a central carbon that is linked to an amino group, a carboxyl group, a hydrogen atom, and an R group or side chain. Each amino acid is linked to its neighbors by a peptide bond. A long chain of amino acids is known as a polypeptide.

Hence, the correct option is (C).

39. Proteins are soluble in aqueous alcohol. Of all the seeds of cereals thus far examined, rice is the only one from which an alcohol-soluble protein or prolamine has not been isolated in considerable quantity. Most of the prolamines are readily soluble in 60 to 70 per cent alcohol at room tem- perature.

Hence, the correct option is (C).

40. Osteomalacia in adults and rickets in children are due to deficiency of vitamin D.

Osteomalacia is a condition in which the bones are soft due to insufficient calcium, phosphate, and vitamin D, defective bone mineralization, or reabsorption of calcium. In children, this is known as rickets. Signs and symptoms may include diffuse joint pain and bone pain, positive Chvostek sign (hypocalcemia), pelvic flattening, etc. It can be managed with vitamin D and calcium supplementation and exposure to sunlight.

Hence, the correct option is (B).

41. Kwashiorkor is a disease caused by a deficiency of protein intake. Kwashiorkor does not cause weight loss. Due to accumulation of water in the body, swelling occurs. Hair color becomes lighter. And the hair starts breaking easily. Protein is needed for muscle growth and other mechanisms of homeostasis. Proteins are essential for the healthy growth and development of a child.

Hence, the correct option is (B).

42. Azolla is a biofertilizer used as supplemental food for cattle, especially for bovine harnessing. Azolla is also known as mosquito fern aquatic fern. Azolla is typically small in size, not looking at all like the typical fern, but resembling dubweed or some moss. It can be used as animal feed, human food, medicine, and water purifier.

Hence, the correct option is (D).

43. The gas involved in the photosynthesis process is carbon dioxide. Photosynthesis is the process used by plants to make their food items. The process of making this food usually involves water, sunlight, and carbon dioxide. By absorbing sunlight, water from the roots, and carbon dioxide from the air, plants perform the photosynthesis process to make glucose and oxygen.

Hence, the correct option is (D).

44. The maximum amount of fluoride is deposited in the bones and teeth. High levels of fluoride cause tooth discoloration and poor mineralization. Low levels of fluoride can lead to cavities and weakened bones. Natural water is the main source of fluoride, besides spinach, potatoes, grapes, raisins, black tea and wine also contain fluoride.

Hence, the correct option is (A).

45. Cool, moist, pale, or flushed skin are the symptoms are associated with heat exhaustion. Heat exhaustion is a less serious condition than heat stroke. Symptoms can include: Normal or only slightly elevated body temperature, Cool, moist (clammy), pale skin.

Hence, the correct option is (A).

46. A man is having a heart attack, he has medication with him, you should assist him with the medicine, Call 108, reassure him until help arrives. Have the person sit down, rest, and try to keep calm. Loosen any tight clothing. Ask if the person takes any chest pain medicine, such as nitroglycerin for a known heart condition, and help them take it.

108 emergency is when someone needs help right away because of an injury or an immediate danger.

Hence, the correct option is (B).

47. A victim has lost a lot of blood through a deep cut in his leg. He is breathing fast and seems pail and restless. He is probably choking. If you notice a person having difficulty breathing, they may be choking. Other signs include gagging, wheezing, and coughing. If the object is completely blocking their airway, they may not be able to talk or breath at all.

Hence, the correct option is (D).

48. For a victim who has a bleeding injury to the mouth and you are sure that there is no head, neck, or spine injury you should either Keep the victim seated with the head tilted slightly forward or Have the victim lie down on their side.

Provide as much first aid as possible without moving the person's head or neck. If the person shows no signs of circulation (breathing, coughing or movement), begin CPR, but do not tilt the head back to open the airway. Use your fingers to gently grasp the jaw and lift it forward.

Hence, the correct option is (D).

49. In general, a splint should be comfortable, but not so tight that it slows circulation.

Splint should be tied firmly to immobilize the fractured limb, then check for blood circulation to ensure the splinting is not too tight. Correct splinting provides pain relief. If the fractured limb is bent with a sharp bone end protruding through the skin, keep it motionless.

Hence, the correct option is (B).

50. A boy has his finger severed cut off, you should wrap the severed finger in sterile gauze, place it in a plastic bag, put the bag on ice to transport both finger and the victim to the hospital.

Wrap the amputated part in a damp paper towel and place it in a sealed, watertight bag or container. Put the sealed bag into another sealed container on ice. Do not allow the severed part of the finger to touch the ice directly, as this could further damage it.

Hence, the correct option is (B).

51. Dressing and bandages are used to help control bleeding and prevent infection. Dressings are pads of gauze or cloth that can be placed directly against the wound to absorb blood and other fluids. Cloth bandages cover dressings and hold them in place.

Hence, the correct option is (C).

52. When you caring for a seizure victim you should remove nearby objects that might cause injury. Clear hard or sharp objects away from the person. Don't try to hold them down or stop the movements. Place them on their side, to help keep their airway clear. Look at your watch at the start of the seizure, to time its length.

Hence, the correct option is (A).

53. A boy enters your bus, you smell alcohol, he passes out before you get to his bus stop, you should stop the bus, check for breathing and pulse, Call 911. Take care of the boy until the helps come.

Hence, the correct option is (B).

54. The gestation period of Humans has a mean of 266 days and a standard deviation of 16 days. This can be roughly considered as 270 days.

Gestation (pregnancy) can be defined as the time duration between conception and birth (delivery) of the foetus. It includes the development of the embryo in the uterus. The duration of the gestation period is variable in different species.

Hence, the correct option is (D).

55. The fertilized cell is called the zygote. A zygote is a product of fertilization. The zygote divides repeatedly and travels down the oviduct soon after fertilization.

Sexual reproduction consists of the formation of male and female gametes. A zygote is formed by the fusion of gametes. A zygote is formed inside the body of the organism.

Hence, the correct option is (C).

56. T cells mature in the thymus gland.

1. T cells migrate from the bone marrow and mature in the thymus gland.
2. T cells are also called T lymphocytes are one of the major components of the adaptive immune system.
3. T cells originate from hematopoietic stem cells which are produced in the bone marrow.
4. The thymus gland is located behind the sternum and between lungs and is only active until puberty.
5. Thymosin is the hormone produced by the thymus and it stimulates the development of disease-fighting T cells.

Hence, the correct option is (B).

57. Aldosterone:

- Aldosterone (salt retention hormone), the main mineralocorticoid hormone, is a steroid hormone produced in the adrenal gland by the zona glomerulosa of the adrenal cortex.
- It is essential for sodium conservation in the kidneys, salivary glands, sweat glands and colon.

Estrogen:

- Estrogen is one of the main female sex hormones.
- While both women and men produce estrogen, it plays a large role in women's bodies.
- Estrogen is produced by your hormonal (endocrine) system and passes through the entire bloodstream.

Melatonin:

- The pituitary gland secretes a hormone called melatonin.
- Melatonin plays a very important role in the regulation of our body's 24-hour (diurnal) rhythm.
- For example, it helps to maintain the normal rhythm of the sleep-wake cycle, body temperature.
- A circadian rhythm is a natural, internal process that regulates the sleep-wake cycle and recurs every 24 hours on each rotation of the Earth.

Progesterone:

- Females have a pair of ovaries located in their abdomen. The ovary is the primary female sex organ that produces an ovum during each menstrual cycle. In addition, the ovaries also make two groups of steroid hormones called estrogen and progesterone.

Hence, the correct option is (D).

58. The pituitary gland controls the functioning of other endocrine glands. The pituitary is often called the master gland because its hormones control another part of the endocrine system like thyroid glands, ovaries, and testes.

The pituitary gland has two parts which are the anterior lobe and posterior lobe. Both parts have separate functions. This gland is located at the base of the brain and it is one-third of an inch diameter.

Hence, the correct option is (D).

59. Saliva is secreted by the salivary glands. Mammals have 4 pairs of salivary glands:

- Infra-orbital glands: located under the orbit of the eye. The ducts of these glands open near the 2 molar teeth of the upper molars.
- Parotid-Glands: These are the largest salivary glands. Located below the auditory-capsule (ear). Their ducts are called parotid duct / Stenson's duct which opens into the buccal-vestibule.
- Submaxillary glands: located at the junction of the upper and lower jaws. Their duct is called Wharton's duct which opens in the lower dentine just behind the jaw teeth.
- Sublingual Gland: These are the smallest salivary glands located in the lower jaw. Their ducts called ducts of the rectinus open into the bucopharyngeal cavity on the ventral side of the tongue.

Hence, the correct option is (B).

60. The functional units of the mammalian kidney are called nephrons.

These nephrons perform the function of filtration of blood and deposition of urine in the collecting duct.

This urine is later expelled from the body through the orifice of the urethra.

A nephron has three main parts:

1. Proximal nephron
2. Loop of Henle
3. Distal nephron

Hence, the correct option is (D).

61. The nephron is the part called the filtration unit of the excretory unit.

Human Excretory System: The system of that organ which is used to remove waste products from the body is called human excretory system. The major waste product produced in the human body is urea, along with some other toxins. Urea is eliminated by the kidneys through the process of urination and solid waste is removed from the body by the intestines.

- In the kidney, the nephron is a functional unit, with each kidney containing 1 million nephrons in each human kidney.
- The basic function of the nephron is to carry out the secretion as well as the process of excretion and is also called the filtration unit of the human excretory system.
- Each nephron is composed of a renal corpuscle.
- There are two types of nephrons which are cortical nephron and juxtamedullary nephron.

Hence, the correct option is (B).

62. Birds and reptiles secrete uric acid as their main excretory product because uric acid is a very low toxic waste and does not require much water for its extraction. Uric acid is excreted as semisolid feces.

Hence, the correct option is (B).

63. The nurse should not consider Yeast infection a risk factor for ectopic pregnancy.

Uterine conditions such as endometriosis and uterine fibroids increase the risk of ectopic pregnancy. Endometriosis is the inappropriate growth of uterine tissue outside the uterus. Uterine fibroids are benign tumors within the uterus. Sexually transmitted infections can cause a condition called pelvic inflammatory disease which can result in scarring. Scarring of the reproductive system greatly increases the risk of ectopic pregnancy and infertility. Yeast infections are common after antibiotic therapy and are treated with over-the-counter medication. They generally do not cause permanent damage to the body.

Hence, the correct option is (D).

64. The woman is experiencing the 1 stage of labor and the 2 phase. The 1 stage of labor exists when the woman's cervix is dilating from 0-10cm. The 2 phase of the 1 stage occurs during dilation from 4-7cm and when the cervix is 40-80% effaced. The 2 stage of labor is when the cervix is dilated 10cm until the delivery of the baby. The 3 stage of labor is the delivery of the placenta. The 1 phase of labor is the onset of labor until the cervix is dilated 3cm. The 3 phase of labor is when the cervix fully dilates from 7cm to 10cm.

Hence, the correct option is (D).

65. The nurse suspects she might be experiencing Stage 1, phase 3 of labor.

During the third phase of the first stage of labor, the cervix dilates from 8-10 cm and effacement reaches 80-100%. The woman will be less able to focus on other things and may require more support from support persons. Labor may progress quickly and the nurse should be preparing for the second stage of labor, in which the cervix is fully dilated at 10cm.

Hence, the correct option is (B).

66. Baseline FHR 100bpm; minimal variability; zero accelerations; variable decelerations describe a category II fetal heart rate (FHR) tracing.

A category II fetal heart rate tracing includes all FHR tracings that are not a category I or category III. Category I FHR tracings are as follows: baseline 110-160bpm, moderate variability, absent late or variable decelerations, present or absent early decelerations, and present or absent accelerations. Category III FHR tracings are as follows: absent baseline FHR variability, recurrent late decelerations, recurrent variable decelerations, bradycardia, and sinusoidal patterns.

Hence, the correct option is (D).

67. In a fetus positioned at the left occiput anterior (LOA), the nurse should assess the fetal heart rate (FHR) Below the umbilicus on the mother's right side.

When considering where to hear fetal heart rate best, the nurse must consider the location of the fetal back. Weeks gestation or size may also affect the location of the best place to assess fetal heart rate. LOA, or left occiput anterior, is the most common fetal lie. A fetus in LOA is in vertex presentation with the fetal occiput on the mother's left side toward the front of her pelvis. In LOA, the FHR is best heard below the umbilicus on the mother's left side.

In LOP (left occiput posterior), the FHR is best heard on the mother's left side at the level of the umbilicus. In ROA (right occiput anterior): the mother's right side below the umbilicus. In ROP (right occiput posterior): the mother's right side at the level of the umbilicus. In LSA (left sacrum anterior): the mother's left side above the umbilicus. In RSA (right sacrum anterior): the mother's right side above the umbilicus.

Hence, the correct option is (D).

68. Dysmenorrhea, infertility, and dyspareunia is the triad of presenting symptoms with endometriosis.

The triad of presenting symptoms for endometriosis is dysmenorrhea (painful menses), infertility, and dyspareunia (pain on sexual intercourse). The most common presenting symptom is extreme, intense uterine cramps which may radiate to the back or down the thighs. Endometriosis is also a common cause of infertility due to a local paracrine effect. Pain on intercourse may be due to the implantation of endometrial cells in the vagina or the area around the cervix. Endometriosis will not necessarily result in menorrhagia or excessively heavy bleeding. Hirsutism, infertility, and oligomenorrhea are symptoms commonly seen in polycystic ovarian syndrome (PCOS), rather than endometriosis.

Hence, the correct option is (B).

69. Face to face communication is the best method of health communication to motivate an eligible couple for adopting contraceptive practice. Face to face communication is also known as personal communication because people through this type of communication process can send and receive key information one-on-one.

Hence, the correct option is (C).

70. A windshield survey is an informal survey where the health professional drives around the community/area they are researching, and records his/her observations.This data provides background and context for working in the community or for conducting a community assessment. This is one way that the nurse can get a feel for the community that cannot be obtained from just reading about it.

Hence, the correct option is (D).

71. The nurse giving nutritional counseling for a patient with cholecystitis will advise the patient to consume fatty foods in limited quantities.

Cholecystitis, an inflammation of the gallbladder, is usually caused by the presence of gallstones, which can block bile (essential for the absorption of fat) from entering the intestines. Patients should reduce dietary fat by limiting foods such as fatty meats, fried foods and creamy desserts to avoid gallbladder irritation.

Hence, the correct option is (D).

72. Patients with pulmonary edema experience shortness of breath, anxiety and tearfulness. Symptoms may also include coughing up blood or bloody froth. They have difficulty breathing while lying down. They also feel "drowning" (this feeling is called "paroxysmal nocturnal dyspnea" if it wakes you up 1 to 2 hours after sleeping).

Hence, the correct option is (D).

73. The nurse will see the patient have sudden chest painand shortness of breath.

The suddenly complains of chest pain and shortness of breath in the patient is the symptom of pulmonary embolism. Typical symptoms of pulmonary embolism include chest pain, shortness of breath, and anxiety.

Hence, the correct option is (B).

74. A cause for concern will be frequent vomiting. Increased pressure due to bleeding or swelling within the skull can damage delicate brain tissue and become life-threatening. Frequent vomiting may be an early sign of pressure because the vomiting center within the marrow is stimulated.

Hence, the correct option is (B).

75. The World Health Organization recommends that babies should be exclusively breastfed for the first six months of life, followed by introduction of nutritionally adequate and safe complementary foods, and with continued breastfeeding up to two years old or beyond. Babies who are breastfed are 60 percent less likely to die from SIDS compared to those not breastfeed. The effect is even greater for infants exclusively breastfed. Thus after six months of age continue breast feeding and start complimentary feeding.

Hence, the correct option is (C).

76. Hepatitis B vaccine is not recommended to be given below 2 kg weight. The baby will get the first dose of Hepatitis B vaccine at 1 month of age or when the baby is discharged from the hospital. The vaccine is not recommended if your child is currently sick, although simple colds or other minor illnesses should not prevent immunization.

Hence, the correct option is (B).

77. Anterior fontanelle is ossified at 18 month after birth in infants.

A newborn baby has six fontanelles: the anterior and posterior, two posterolateral, and two anterolateral. The anterior fontanelle is the most prominent, the most variable in size, and clinically important. It is diamond (rhomboid) shaped and located at the junction of the two parietal and two frontal bones.

Hence, the correct option is (C).

78. Neonatal Mortality rate is calculated by estimating the number newborn death within 28 days.

The neonatal period is defined as the period from birth up to but not including 28 days. The numerator of the neonatal mortality rate therefore is the number of deaths among children under 28 days of age during a given time period. The denominator of the seonatal mortality rate, like that of the infant mortality rate, is the No. of live births reported during the same time period.

The NMR is usually expressed per 1,000 live births.

$$\text{NMR} = \frac{\text{No. of deaths under 28 days of age}}{\text{No. of live births during the same period}} \times 1000$$

Hence, the correct option is (B).

79. After birth Umbilical vein converted into ligamentum teres. The umbilical vein is a vein present during fetal development that carries oxygenated blood from the placenta into the growing fetus. The umbilical vein provides convenient access to the central circulation of a neonate for restoration of blood volume and for administration of glucose and drugs.

Hence, the correct option is (D).

80. In Marasmus infants energy is the principal lacking factor. Marasmus is a condition primarily caused by a deficiency in calories and energy, whereas kwashiorkor indicates an associated protein deficiency, resulting in an oedematous appearance.

Hence, the correct option is (B).

81. Part filled by A in 1 hour (i.e. till 11 A.M.) $= \frac{1}{2}$

Part filled by A and B in 1 hour $(60$ minutes$)$ $= \frac{1}{2} + \frac{1}{6} = \frac{3+1}{6} = \frac{2}{3}$

Time taken by A and B to fill $\frac{1}{2}$ part

$= \frac{60\times3}{2} \times \frac{1}{2}$

$= 45$ minutes

∴ Tank will be filled at 11.45 A.M.
Hence, the correct option is (C).

82. Given,

Amount after 3 years = Rs. 690

Amount after 5 years = Rs. 750

If the amount of 3 years is subtracted from the amount of 5 years, the simple interest of 2 years will be obtained.

Simple interest of 2 years $= 750 - 690 =$ Rs. 60

Simple interest of 1 year $= \frac{60}{2} =$ Rs. 30

Simple interest of 3 years $= 30 \times 3 =$ Rs. 90

Principal $=$ Amount of 3 years $-$ Simple interest for 3 years

Principal $= 690 - 90 = 600$

Hence, the correct option is (C).

83. Given:

Speed of boat $= 20$ km/h

Speed of stream $= 2$ km/h

We know that:

Distance $=$ Speed $\times$ Time

Downstream speed $=$ Speed of boat $+$ Speed of stream

Downstream speed $= 20 + 2 = 22$ km/h

∴ Required time $= \frac{198}{22} = 9$ hours

Hence, the correct option is (C).

84. We know that:

Follow the BODMAS rule according to the table given below:

B	Brackets in order ( ), { } , [ ]	ब्रैकेट ( ), { } , [ ] क्रम में
O	of	का
D	Division $(\div)$	विभाजन $(\div)$
M	Multiplication (x)	गुणा (x)
A	Addition (+)	जोड़ (+)
S	Subtraction (-)	घटाव (–)

Given:

$\sqrt{400} \times 2 - 30 = \sqrt{256} - 12+?$

$\Rightarrow 20 \times 2 - 30 = 16 - 12+?$

$\Rightarrow 40 - 30 = 4+?$

$\Rightarrow 10 - 4 =?$

$\Rightarrow ? = 6$

∴ 6 will come in place of the question mark (?).

Hence, the correct option is (B).

85. Given,

HCF of two numbers $= 7$

As we know,

LCM = HCF $\times$ Co - Prime number

LCM should always will be divisible by HCF.

Option (A):

$161 \div 7$

Quotient $= 23$

Remainder $= 0$

Option (B):

$872 \div 7$

Quotient $= 124$

Remainder $= 4$

Option (C):

$587 \div 7$

Quotient $= 83$

Remainder $= 6$

Option (D):

$697 \div 7$

Quotient $= 99$

Remainder $= 6$

∴ LCM of these 2 number is 161.

Hence, the correct option is (A).

86. The code for TOUR is:

T	O	U	R
1	2	3	4

The code for CLEAR is:

C	L	E	A	R
5	6	7	8	4

The code for SPARE is:

S	P	A	R	E
9	0	8	4	7

Similarly,

The code for CARE is:

C	A	R	E
5	8	4	7

So, '5847' is the correct answer.

Hence, the correct option is (D).

87. The least possible Venn Diagram for the given statements will be as follows:

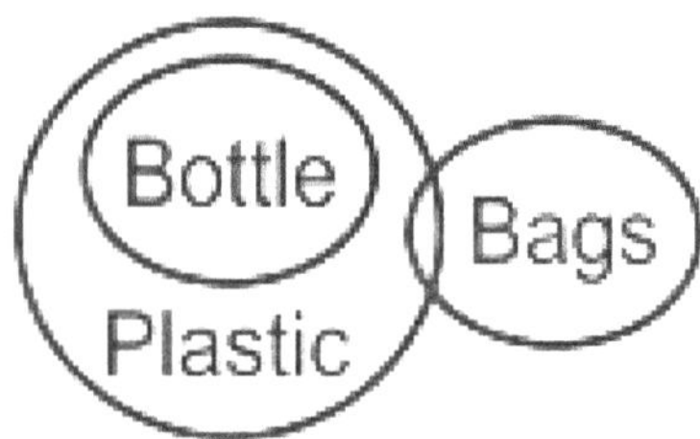

I. Some bags are not bottle → False (There is no direct relation given between bottle and bags so it can be possible but not definite, hence, false)

II. Some plastic are not bags → False (As "Some bags are plastic" given so some plastic can be bags it can be possible but some plastic are not bags it is not definite, hence, false)

So,None follows.

Hence, the correct option is (C).

88. When it is hot, fan circulates air to keep us cool. Similarly, we eat food to satiate our hunger.

Hence, the correct option is (D).

89. In the statement, it is clearly mentioned that there were traffic-related deaths and no information is given regarding the bad condition of the road, therefore only conclusion I follows.

Hence, the correct option is (A).

90. The logic is here is:

1st number × (1st number + 1) = 2nd number

Option (A): $9:90$

Now, follow the logic:

$9 \times (9+1) = 9 \times 10 = 90 = 2$nd number

This option follows the pattern.

Option (B): $7:56$

$7 \times (7+1) = 7 \times 8 = 56 = 2$nd number

This option follows the pattern.

Option (C): $5:30$

$5 \times (5+1) = 5 \times 6 = 30 = 2$nd number

This option follows the pattern.

Option (D): $8:66$

Now, follow the logic:

$8 \times (8+1) = 8 \times 9 = 72 \neq 2$nd number

This option do not follow the pattern.

So, pair " $8:66$" is an odd one.

Hence, the correct option is (D).

91. The state tree of Uttar Pradesh is Ashoka Tree. Uttar Pradesh day is celebrated on 24 January. On 24 January 1950, the United Provinces was renamed as Uttar Pradesh. It was formed on 1 April 1937 as the United Province. Uttar Pradesh has an area of 2,40,928 square km. Uttar Pradesh has a population of 19,9,812,341.

Hence, the correct option is (B).

92. Jessica Chastain won 'Outstanding Performance by a Female Actor in a Leading Role' award at the Screen Actor Guild Awards, held in California, on 2022.

Screen Actor Guild Awards were held in California. Outstanding Performance by a Female Actor in a Leading Role was won by Jessica Chastain (The Eyes of Tammy Faye). Outstanding Performance by a Male Actor in a Leading Role Will Smith (King Richard). Outstanding Performance by a Cast in a Motion Picture was won by CODA, which included Eugenio Derbez, Daniel Durant, Emilia Jones, and more.

Hence, the correct option is (A).

93. Madya Pradesh has won "Ranji Trophy 2022" Title by defeating Mumbai by six wickets in the final at the M. Chinnaswamy Stadium in Bengaluru. Mumbai and Uttar Pradesh played the second semi-final which was a draw and it led to the advancing of Mumbai in the final due to their first-innings lead.

Hence, the correct option is (B).

94. International Solar Alliance's Fifth Assembly is to be hosted by India in New Delhi on October 17-20, 2022.

Union Minister for Power and New and Renewable Energy RK Singh unveiled the curtain raiser to the Fifth Assembly of ISA. India holds the office of the President of the ISA Assembly. The Fifth Assembly will deliberate on key initiatives of ISA on three critical issues: energy access, energy security, and energy transition.

Hence, the correct option is (B).

95. Teej festival is an important festival for married women and much awaited monsoon festival. It is dedicated to celebrate the sacred union of Lord Shiva and Goddess Parvati and the flourishing of nature during monsoon. "Teej" refers to the third day after the new moon and the third day after the full moon. Teej festival is widely celebrated in northern and western India.

Hence, the correct option is (C).

96. WORM stands for Write Once, Read Many.

It is an optical disk technology that allows users to write data onto a disk just once.

- After writing the data, it becomes permanent and can be read any number of times.

- The data is stored on WORM devices.
- The data stored in these devices are in a non-rewritable format to prevent users from accidentally erasing or altering sensitive information.

Hence, the correct option is (A).

97. Memory is not a part operation of instruction cycle.

A program residing in the memory unit of a computer consists of a sequence of instructions. In a basic computer, each instruction cycle consists of the following phases:

- Fetch the instruction from memory.
- Decode the instruction.
- Read the effective address from memory.
- Execute the instruction.

Hence, the correct option is (D).

98. File Explorer is not a web browser. File Explorer is comprised form of folders. Web browser is an application. We use it to link different pages on the Internet for information. It can be used to upload or download data on an FTP server. Mozilla Firefox, Google Chrome, Microsoft Internet Explorer, Apple Safari and Opera are some of the commonly used web browsers.

Hence, the correct option is (D).

99. The master key is not related to the keyboard of a computer.

- The keyboard is an input device used in computers.
- It consists of various keys like function keys, numeric keypad and QWERTY keypad.
- There is no such key as a master key in a computer keyboard.

Hence, the correct option is (D).

100. WebInspect can check whether a web server is properly configured or not by attempting for common attacks such as Cross-site scripting, directory traversal, and parameter injection. But it cannot inject malicious shell code in the server.

Hence, the correct option is (D).

Mock Test 03

Discipline

Q.1 The nurse needs to carefully assess the complaints of pain of the elderly because old people-

A. Have a decreased pain threshold
B. Have altered mental function
C. Are expected to experience chronic pain
D. Experience reduced sensory perception

Q.2 Valsalva maneuver can result in bradycardia. Which of the following activities will not stimulate Valsalva's maneuver?

A. Use of stool softners
B. Enema administration
C. Gagging while toothbrushing
D. Lifting heavy objects

Q.3 After Billroth II surgery, the client developed dumping syndrome. Which of the following should be nurse excluded in the plan of care?

A. Sit upright for at least 30 minutes after meals
B. Take only sips of H_2O between bits of the solid food
C. Eat small meals every 2-3 hours
D. Reduce the amount of simple carbohydrates in the diet

Q.4 The pleural space is:

A. A potential space
B. A space infected
C. A cavity around the heart
D. Also known as the diaphragm

Q.5 When examining a patient who is paralyzed below the T4 level, the medical-surgical nurse expects to find:

A. Flaccidity of the upper extremities
B. Hyperreflexia and spasticity of the upper extremities
C. An impaired diaphragmatic function requiring ventilator support
D. Independent use of upper extremities and efficient cough

Q.6 Removal of the spleen will:

A. Result in death
B. Render a man infertile
C. Cause urinary tract infections
D. None of the above

Q.7 The key objective in coronary artery bypass graft is to:

A. Extend life
B. Improve blood flow and oxygen supply to the heart
C. Improve blood flow and oxygen supply to the lungs
D. Relieve pain

Q.8 Cardiac valves allow for:

A. One-way, low-resistance blood flow
B. Two-way, low-resistance blood flow
C. One-way, high-resistance blood flow
D. Two-way, high-resistance blood flow

Q.9 Varicose veins are often:

A. Long and thick
B. Short and thin
C. Dilated and tortuous
D. Constricted and tortuous

Q.10 ______ approach to health education aims to improve and promote health by addressing socioeconomic and environmental determinants of health within the community.

A. Behaviour change approach
B. Community development approach
C. Biomedical approach
D. None of these

Q.11 Conference can be used as a method in_________approach of health education.

A. Individual
B. Group
C. Mass
D. None of these

Q.12 _________________is the first step in planning a health education programme.

A. Assessing the needs
B. Identifying community resources
C. Selecting content
D. Lesson plan

Q.13 Nurse Patrick is interviewing a newly admitted psychiatric client. Which nursing statement is an example of offering a general lead?

A. "Do you know why you are here?"
B. "Are you feeling depressed or anxious?"
C. "Yes, I see. Go on."
D. "Can you chronologically order the events that led to your admission?"

Q.14 A nurse states to a client, "Things will look better tomorrow after a good night's sleep." This is an example of which communication skills?

A. Giving advice
B. Defending
C. Presenting reality
D. Giving false reassurance

Q.15 In__________method of group teaching, there is no active participation from learners.

A. Lecture
B. Group discussion
C. Symposium
D. Role play

Q.16 What are the aims of health education?

A. Increase the efficacy of health services
B. Curative as well as preventive
C. To improve productivity by reducing occupational diseases
D. All of the above

Q.17 When interviewing a client, which nonverbal behavior should a nurse employ?

A. Maintaining indirect eye contact with the client.

B. Providing space by leaning back away from the client.

C. Sitting squarely, facing the client.

D. Maintaining open posture with arms and legs crossed.

Q.18 Ms. Caputo is newly promoted to a patient care manager position. She updates her knowledge on the theories in management and leadership in order to become effective in her new role. She learns that some managers have low concern for services and high concern for staff. Which style of management refers to this?

A. Organization Management

B. Impoverished Management

C. Country Club Management

D. Team Management

Q.19 Epidemiological triad does not include:

A. Host **B.** Agent

C. Risk factors **D.** Environment

Q.20 Which among the following leadership style is most effective in medical field?

A. Laissez-Faire Leadership

B. Autocratic Leadership

C. Democratic Leadership

D. Bureaucratic Leadership

Q.21 Pecularity of a hospital as an organization is all except:

A. Production can be quantified

B. Dual Authority

C. Personlised Services

D. No unity in line of command

Q.22 Organisation effectiveness comprises all except:

A. Productivity power

B. Adaptabilty to change

C. Flexibility in structure & strategy

D. Rigidity in structure

Q.23 Which is not the basis of classification of a hospital?

A. Specialty **B.** Functional

C. Size **D.** Shape

Q.24 Which of the following is a functional division of hospital?

A. Outpatient Department

B. Surgical Department

C. Nursing Department

D. All of the above

Q.25 The concept behind changing the role of the hospital from indoor care to outpatient care includes all except:

A. Rising cost of hospital care

B. Shortage of hospital bed

C. Economic importance

D. Increase of hospital beds

Q.26 Which of the service is not a part of preventive care?

A. Sentinel surveillance

B. Nutritional counseling

C. Non communicable disease prevention

D. OPD services

Q.27 The nurse is teaching a patient to prepare a syringe with 40 units of U-100 NPH insulin for self-injection. The patient's first priority concerning self-injection in this situation is to:

A. assess the injection site.

B. select the appropriate injection site.

C. check the syringe to verify that the nurse has removed the prescribed insulin dose.

D. clean the injection site in a circular manner with an alcohol sponge.

Q.28 A patient must receive 50 units of Humulin regular insulin. The label reads 100 units = 1 ml. How many milliliters should the nurse administer?

A. 0.5 ml **B.** 0.75 ml **C.** 1 ml **D.** 2 ml

Q.29 How should the nurse prepare an injection for a patient who takes both regular and NPH insulin?

A. Draw up the NPH insulin, then the regular insulin, in the same syringe.

B. Draw up the regular insulin, then the NPH insulin, in the same syringe.

C. Use two separate syringes.

D. Check with the physician.

Q.30 A patient has just received 30 mg of codeine by mouth for pain. Five minutes later he vomits. What should the nurse do first?

A. Call the physician

B. Remedicate the patient

C. Observe the emesis

D. Explain to the patient that she can do nothing to help him

Q.31 A patient is catheterized with a #16 indwelling urinary (Foley) catheter to determine if:

A. trauma has occurred.

B. his 24-hour output is adequate.

C. he has a urinary tract infection.

D. residual urine remains in the bladder after voiding.

Q.32 A staff nurse who is promoted to assistant nurse manager may feel uncomfortable initially when supervising her former peers. How she can best decrease this discomfort?

A. Writing down all assignments.

B. Making changes after evaluating the situation and having discussions with the staff.

C. Telling the staff nurses that she is making changes to benefit their performance.

D. Evaluating the clinical performance of each staff nurse in a private conference.

Q.33 What could cause a geriatric patient to have difficulty retaining knowledge about prescribed medications?

A. Decreased plasma drug levels

B. Sensory deficits

C. Lack of family support

D. History of Tourette syndrome

Q.34 When examining a patient with abdominal pain the nurse in charge should assess ___________.

A. any quadrant first
B. the symptomatic quadrant first
C. the symptomatic quadrant last
D. the symptomatic quadrant either second or third

Q.35 The nurse is assessing a postoperative adult patient. Which of the following should the nurse document as subjective data?

A. Vital signs
B. Laboratory test result
C. Patient's description of pain
D. Electrocardiographic (ECG) waveforms

Q.36 How many amino acids are produceed by our bodies?

A. 20 **B.** 30 **C.** 40 **D.** 10

Q.37 Which one of the following groups of chemical is not a food nutrient?

A. Carbohydrates **B.** Vitamins
C. Proteins **D.** Enzymes

Q.38 The eutrophication of a water body is by ______.

A. Lack of oxygen
B. Increase in algae formation
C. High amounts of nitrogen nutrients and orthophosphates
D. Immersing fetish in the water body

Q.39 Which of the following plant hormones inhibit growth?

A. Cytokinin **B.** Abscisic acid
C. Gibberellin **D.** Auxin

Q.40 The milk of which of the following mammal has highest content of fat?

A. Buffalo **B.** Human **C.** Goat **D.** Cow

Q.41 Infected milk can cause disease:

A. Anthrax **B.** Gastritis
C. Aeolian **D.** Tonsillitis

Q.42 The addition of dilute iodine to foods is a confirmatory test for:

A. Starch **B.** Protein
C. Carbohydrate **D.** Fat

Q.43 Glycogen is an example of which type of carbohydrate?

A. Monosaccharide **B.** Disaccharide
C. Polysaccharide **D.** Both (B) and (C)

Q.44 Due to the deficiency of which of the following, milk is no longer called a balanced diet?

A. Iron and Vitamin C
B. Calcium and Vitamin C
C. Magnesium and Vitamin D
D. Iron and Vitamin A

Q.45 How long would you check to see if an unconscious casualty is breathing normally?

A. No more than 10 seconds.
B. Approximately 10 seconds.
C. Exactly 10 seconds.
D. At least 10 seconds.

Q.46 Which test should you use if you suspect that a person has had a stroke?

A. Face, Arm, Speech tests
B. Alert, Voice, Pain, Unresponsive
C. Response, Airway, Breathing, Circulation
D. Pulse, Respiratory Rate, Temperature

Q.47 What are the symptoms of third degree burn?

A. Charred skin, no pain
B. Charred skin, pain
C. Blisters and pain
D. Red and pain

Q.48 What is the main purpose of the "Route" emergency transportation technique when providing treatment to a passenger?

A. To relocate the passenger
B. To administer rescue breathing
C. To remove a blockage in the victim's airway
D. To remove a blockage in the victim's airway

Q.49 How can you recognize arterial bleeding?

A. Blood flows equally out of the wound.
B. Blood flows slowly out of the wound.
C. Blood flow out of the wound with high pulses.
D. None of these

Q.50 A person is allergic to peanut butter and is going into anaphylactic shock. What do you do next?

A. Have them sit with their head between her knees and have them breathe deeply
B. Arrange medical attention
C. Give them some aspirin immediately
D. Both B and C

Q.51 What is a scald?

A. A burn by liquid or gas
B. A burn by fire
C. A break in your leg
D. Being beaten with a stick

Q.52 What do you do when someone has broken his arm?

A. Scream and run
B. Put a plaster on it
C. Use an antisceptic wipe
D. Put the arm in a sling

Q.53 When caring for a student who is suffering from heat cramps:

A. Apply cold packs
B. Give cool water or sports drink
C. Have the student keep walking slowly to work the cramp out
D. Massage the muscle vigorously to increase circulation

Q.54 The system affected by AIDS disease is:

A. Digestive system
B. Respiratory system
C. Central nervous system
D. Immune system

Q.55 Which of the following hormones is called the fight-or-flight hormone?

A. Adrenaline **B.** Thyroxine
C. Glucagon **D.** Dopamine

Q.56 Which one of the following is a female sex hormone?

A. Androgens **B.** Progesterone
C. Estradiol **D.** All of these

Q.57 Bowman's capsule is associated with which of the following organ system?

A. Circulatory System
B. Digestive System
C. Excretory System
D. Reproductive System

Q.58 A boy remains dwarf because of less secretion of hormone from _________ gland.

A. Pituitary **B.** Thyroid Gland
C. Pancreas **D.** Adrenal Gland

Q.59 Which one of the following make up Central Nervous System together with the brain?

A. Neuron **B.** Brain
C. Spinal Cord **D.** None of these

Q.60 The circular muscle found at the junction of the stomach and duodenum is:

A. Anal sphincter **B.** Cardiac sphincter
C. Meissner's plexus **D.** Pyloric sphincter

Q.61 Which one of the following organs will not feel any pain on being pricked by a needle?

A. Skin **B.** Brain **C.** Heart **D.** Eye

Q.62 Glial cells are the most abundant cells in:

A. Lungs **B.** Kidney
C. Gallbladder **D.** Nervous system

Q.63 Which of the following increases risk of ectopic pregnancy?

A. History of pelvic inflammatory disease
B. Endometriosis
C. Post-tubal ligation
D. All of these

Q.64 Which of the following conditions can be triggered by Rh incompatibility between mother and fetus?

A. Hyperemesis gravidaru
B. Preeclampsia
C. Postpartum hemorrhage
D. Hemolytic disease of the newborn

Q.65 A woman is admitted with suspected placenta previa. What test does the nurse expect will be done to confirm the diagnosis?

A. Internal exam
B. Nonstress test
C. Oxytocin challenge test
D. Ultrasound

Q.66 While caring for a laboring patient, the nurse is called into the room because her patient felt a "gush" of fluid. Which of the following should be the nurse's next action?

A. Turn the mother to her right side
B. Assess fetal heart rate
C. Alert the physician
D. Change the sheets

Q.67 What are the signs and symptoms of ectopic pregnancy?

A. Nausea and diplopia
B. Abdominal pain and vaginal bleeding
C. Fundal tenderness and vertigo
D. Cramping and abdominal mass

Q.68 The nurse advises a woman with mild pre-eclampsia to do all of the following except ________.

A. weigh herself daily
B. keep track of fetal movement
C. measure the protein in her urine
D. limit water intake

Q.69 A nurse know that the most positive evidence of active tuberculosis is:

A. A positive skin test result
B. A raised total leucocyte count
C. Positive chest X-ray findings
D. Sputum culture findings

Q.70 The usefulness of a 'screening test' in a community depends on its:

A. Reliability **B.** Sensitivity
C. Specificity **D.** Credibility

Q.71 A nurse is administering a shot of Vitamin K to a 30 day-old infant. Which of the following target areas is the most appropriate?

A. Gluteus maximus **B.** Gluteus minimus
C. Vastus lateralis **D.** Vastus medialis

Q.72 A nurse taking care of a gastritis patient, will recommend which of the following medications contraindicated for this patient?

A. Naproxen sodium **B.** Calcium carbonate
C. Clarithromycin **D.** Furosemide

Q.73 A nurse is caring for a patient with peripheral vascular disease (PVD). The patient complains of burning and tingling of the hands and feet and cannot tolerate touch of any kind. Which of the following is the most likely explanation for these symptoms?

A. Inadequate tissue perfusion leading to nerve damage.
B. Fluid overload leading to compression of nerve tissue.
C. Sensation distortion due to psychiatric disturbance.
D. Inflammation of the skin on the hands and feet.

Q.74 A patient in the cardiac unit is concerned about the risk factors associated with atherosclerosis. Which of the following are hereditary risk factors for developing atherosclerosis?

A. Family history of heart disease
B. Overweight
C. Smoking
D. Age

Q.75 What is the most common cause of death in children suffering from diarrhoea?

A. Dehydration **B.** Abdominal pain
C. Vomiting **D.** Lethargy

Q.76 Growth chart is also known as:

A. New Ballard scale **B.** Road to health chart
C. Apgar Score **D.** GCS score

Q.77 A child grasps fingers when palm touch occurs at the age of:

A. 4 months **B.** 9 months
C. 6 months **D.** 3 months

Q.78 Which is the predisposing condition for the occurrence of rheumatic fever in children?

A. Pharyngitis **B.** Otitis media
C. Rhinitis **D.** Chondritis

Q.79 On second post operative day after repair of cleft palate which is the suitable method of feeding?

A. Cup
B. Straw
C. Rubber tipped syringe
D. Large holed nipple

Q.80 Total lung capacity in a newborn is:

A. 100 ml **B.** 350 ml **C.** 500 ml **D.** 150 ml

General Aptitude / Reasoning / General Awareness / Basic Computer knowledge

Q.81 Three pipes A, B, and C can fill a tank in 6 hours. After working at it together for 2 hours, C is closed and A and B can fill the remaining part in 7 hours. The number of hours taken by C alone to fill the tank is

A. 10 **B.** 12 **C.** 14 **D.** 16

Q.82 In what time will ₹ 1000 amount to ₹ 1331 at 20% per annum, compounded half-yearly?

A. $\frac{3}{2}$ years **B.** 2 years
C. 1 year **D.** $2\frac{1}{2}$ years

Q.83 A boat can travel with a speed of 13 Km/hr in still water. If the speed of the stream is 4 Km/hr, find the time taken by the boat to go 68 km downstream.

A. 2 hours **B.** 3 hours **C.** 4 hours **D.** 5 hours

Q.84 What will come in the place of the question mark $'?'$ in the following question?

$240 \div 6 + \sqrt{529} \times 17 = ? + 150\%$ of 80

A. 311 **B.** 310 **C.** 309 **D.** 312

Q.85 Find the HCF of $36, 54$, and 72.

A. 18 **B.** 3 **C.** 6 **D.** 12

Q.86 In certain code, "LIFE" is written as "3965", then how must "FUN" be written?

A. 635 **B.** 634 **C.** 633 **D.** 629

Q.87 Direction: Read the given statement(s) and conclusions carefully and select which of the conclusions logically follow(s) from the statement(s).

Statement:

All dark is night.

Some dark are black.

Conclusion:

I. All black is night.

II. Some black is not night.

A. Only I follows
B. Only II follows
C. Either I or II follows
D. Neither I nor II follows

Q.88 Direction: In the following question, select the pair of words which is related in the same way as the pair in question.

Arc : Circle

A. Number : Count
B. Fraction : Percentage
C. Pie : Slice
D. Segment : Line

Q.89 Direction: In the question below a statement is given followed by two conclusions, I and II. You have to consider the statement to be true, even if it seems to be at variance from commonly known facts. You have to decide which of the given conclusions definitely is drawn from the given statement.

Statement: Adversity makes a man wise.

Conclusions:

I. The poor are wise.

II. Men learn from bitter experiences

A. Only Conclusion I follows
B. Either Conclusion I or II follows
C. Only Conclusion II follows
D. Neither Conclusion I nor II follow

Q.90 Direction: Select the odd figure out of the given series of figures.

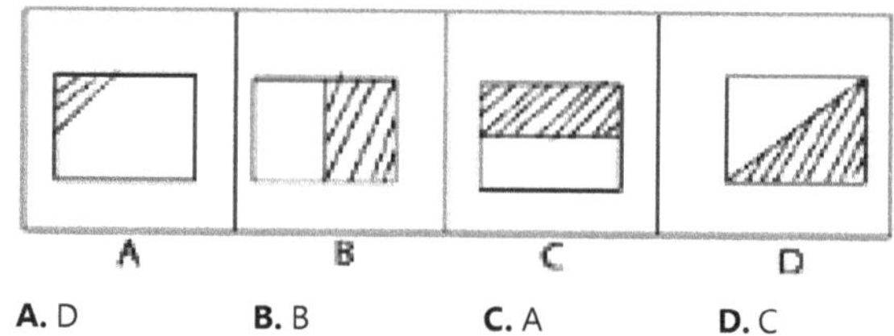

A. D **B.** B **C.** A **D.** C

Q.91 Who appoints the governor of Uttar Pradesh?

A. Chief Minister
B. Parliament
C. President
D. None of the above

Q.92 Who was awarded the 2017 Sahitya Academy award for his English novel 'The Black Hill'?

[RRB/RRC Group D, 2018]

A. Vikram Seth
B. Chetan Bhagat
C. Amitav Ghosh
D. Mamang Dai

Q.93 Which of the following are the all-time record holders for the most number of Olympic medals in tennis?

A. Kathleen McKane Godfree and Venus Williams
B. Kathleen McKane Godfree and Serena Williams
C. Venus Williams and Serena Williams
D. Gigi Fernandez and Mary Joe Fernandes

Q.94 Which is the most powerful rocket launched from the Earth, as of November 2022?

A. Minuteman Heavy
B. Falcon Heavy
C. Long March 5b
D. PSLV 52

Q.95 Ujali or Aneri Holi is associated with:

A. Jaunsari Tribe
B. Bhotia Tribe
C. Tharu Tribe
D. Raaji Tribe

Q.96 URL Stands for _____.

[Army Public School (PRT), 2019]

A. Universal Resource Locator
B. Uniform Resource Locator
C. Uniform Resource Label
D. Universal Research Locator

Q.97 Choose the correct answer from the given options for the process of Debugging.

A. Rolling out a software program
B. Modifying a software program
C. Checking errors in a software program
D. Changing the design structure of a program

Q.98 What is the first webpage of the website called?

A. First page
B. Main page
C. Home page
D. None of these

Q.99 Computer joystick _____.

[Rajasthan Police Constable, 2020]

A. is an input device
B. is a processing device
C. is an output device
D. is a memory device

Q.100 Which of the following commandinterface is normally used forwindows operating system ?

[HTET PGT - Computer Science, 2020]

A. Menu driven interface
B. Command line interface
C. Graphical user interface
D. Icon interface

// Smart Answer Sheet //

Correct Indicates percentage of students who answered questions correctly.

Skipped Indicates percentage of students who skipped questions.

Q.	Ans.	Correct	Skipped
1	D	48.04 %	1.21 %
2	A	18.77 %	4.96 %
3	A	27.07 %	3.86 %
4	A	88.71 %	0.0 %
5	D	50.54 %	1.41 %
6	D	86.54 %	0.0 %
7	B	40.4 %	1.18 %
8	A	84.99 %	0.0 %
9	C	50.55 %	1.59 %
10	B	47.36 %	1.1 %
11	B	52.9 %	1.17 %
12	A	65.97 %	1.95 %
13	C	85.55 %	0.0 %
14	D	48.18 %	1.51 %
15	D	50.9 %	1.48 %
16	C	56.25 %	1.19 %
17	C	65.35 %	1.19 %
18	C	62.58 %	1.17 %
19	C	55.37 %	1.98 %
20	C	81.95 %	0.0 %
21	C	68.82 %	1.19 %
22	C	52.67 %	1.68 %
23	D	85.33 %	0.0 %
24	D	65.77 %	1.91 %
25	C	42.58 %	1.51 %
26	D	77.41 %	0.0 %
27	C	76.89 %	0.0 %
28	A	25.14 %	3.6 %
29	B	58.5 %	1.95 %
30	C	78.98 %	0.0 %
31	B	23.87 %	4.36 %
32	B	80.72 %	0.0 %
33	B	51.67 %	2.0 %
34	C	41.04 %	1.9 %
35	C	85.02 %	0.0 %
36	D	40.94 %	1.9 %
37	D	68.46 %	1.3 %
38	C	78.09 %	0.0 %
39	B	54.82 %	1.48 %
40	A	42.32 %	1.27 %
41	A	54.58 %	1.74 %
42	A	64.15 %	1.51 %
43	C	53.13 %	1.66 %
44	A	44.87 %	1.33 %
45	A	80.96 %	0.0 %
46	A	67.68 %	1.05 %
47	A	64.75 %	1.64 %
48	A	43.17 %	1.4 %
49	C	60.36 %	1.5 %
50	D	44.53 %	1.51 %
51	A	11.1 %	3.39 %
52	D	43.08 %	1.85 %
53	B	66.25 %	1.21 %
54	D	45.89 %	1.88 %
55	A	58.33 %	1.21 %
56	B	69.68 %	1.88 %
57	C	42.86 %	1.76 %
58	A	42.15 %	1.51 %
59	C	65.85 %	1.2 %
60	D	69.89 %	1.23 %
61	B	42.48 %	1.44 %
62	D	54.97 %	1.15 %
63	D	53.07 %	1.29 %
64	D	32.35 %	3.95 %
65	D	59.49 %	1.95 %
66	B	69.18 %	1.75 %
67	B	58.38 %	1.24 %
68	D	16.3 %	4.21 %
69	C	83.47 %	0.0 %
70	B	58.25 %	1.45 %
71	C	85.41 %	0.0 %
72	A	40.19 %	1.28 %
73	A	89.51 %	0.0 %
74	A	86.24 %	0.0 %
75	A	51.2 %	1.1 %
76	B	78.94 %	0.0 %
77	D	49.31 %	1.77 %
78	A	60.96 %	1.01 %
79	A	77.03 %	0.0 %
80	D	40.45 %	1.29 %

Q.	Ans.	Correct / Skipped
81	C	79.67 % / 0.0 %
82	A	83.98 % / 0.0 %
83	C	81.08 % / 0.0 %
84	A	86.67 % / 0.0 %

Q.	Ans.	Correct / Skipped
85	A	78.14 % / 0.0 %
86	A	85.87 % / 0.0 %
87	C	87.46 % / 0.0 %
88	D	83.66 % / 0.0 %

Q.	Ans.	Correct / Skipped
89	C	81.41 % / 0.0 %
90	C	79.92 % / 0.0 %
91	C	68.8 % / 1.18 %
92	D	67.78 % / 1.41 %

Q.	Ans.	Correct / Skipped
93	A	12.98 % / 4.16 %
94	B	40.41 % / 1.35 %
95	C	86.81 % / 0.0 %
96	B	52.49 % / 1.06 %

Q.	Ans.	Correct / Skipped
97	C	47.83 % / 1.28 %
98	C	79.34 % / 0.0 %
99	A	84.75 % / 0.0 %
100	C	65.12 % / 1.38 %

Performance Analysis	
Avg. Score (%)	53.0%
Toppers Score (%)	65.0%
Your Score	

//Hints and Solutions//

1. The nurse needs to carefully assess the complaints of pain of the elderly because old people experience reduced sensory perception.

During old age, degenerative changes occur. The response of pain in the olderly may be lessened because of reduced acuity of touch, alternations of the neural pathways, and diminished process of sensory data.

Hence, the correct option is (D).

2. Valsalva maneuver can result in bradycardia. The use of stool softeners will not stimulate Valsalva's maneuver.

Straining and bearing down activities can cause vagal stimulation that leads to bradycardia. The use of stool softeners promotes easy bowel evacuation that prevents straining or the Valsalva maneuver.

Hence, the correct option is (A).

3. After Billroth II surgery, the client developed dumping syndrome. Sitting upright for at least 30 minutes after meals should be nurse excluded in the plan of care.

One of the causes of peptic ulcer is H pylori infection. It releases a toxin that destroys the gastric and duodenal mucosa which decreases the gastric epithelium's resistance to acid digestion. Giving antibiotics will control the infection and Ranitidine which is a histamine-2 blocker, will reduce the acid secretion that leads to ulcers.

Hence, the correct option is (A).

4. The pleural space is a potential space. It is the space enclosed by the pleura, which is a thin layer of tissue that covers the lungs and lines the interior wall of the chest cavity. The pleural cavity, with its associated pleurae, aids optimal functioning of the lungs during breathing. The pleural cavity also contains pleural fluid, which acts as a lubricant and allows the pleurae to slide effortlessly against each other during respiratory movements.

Hence, the correct option is (A).

5. When examining a patient who is paralyzed below the T4 level, the medical-surgical nurse expects to find independent use of upper extremities and efficient cough. So for example, complete injury to spinal nerves at the T4 bone is known as T4 paraplegia. The same applies below this in the lumbar region, where the first vertebra is called the L1 running downwards to L5, and then below this again in the sacral region.

Hence, the correct option is (D).

6. Removal of the spleen will cause none of the above. Splenectomy is a surgical procedure to remove your spleen. The spleen is an organ that sits under your rib cage on the upper left side of your abdomen. It helps fight infection and filters unneeded material, such as old or damaged blood cells, from your blood.

Hence, the correct option is (D).

7. The key objective in coronary artery bypass graft is to improve blood flow and oxygen supply to the heart. A coronary artery bypass graft involves taking a blood vessel from another part of the body (usually the chest, leg or arm) and attaching it to the coronary artery above and below the narrowed area or blockage. This new blood vessel is known as a graft.

Hence, the correct option is (B).

8. Cardiac valves allow for one-way, low-resistance blood flow. These valves prevent the backward flow of blood. These valves are actual flaps that are located on each end of the two ventricles (lower chambers of the heart). They act as one-way inlets of blood on one side of a ventricle and one-way outlets of blood on the other side of a ventricle.

Hence, the correct option is (A).

9. Varicose veins are often Dilated and tortuous. Causes of varicose veins:

Getting older, as the valves in veins start to weaken over time.

Genetic history of family members with varicose veins.

Pregnancy, as the growing uterus places extra pressure on a person's veins.

Being overweight.

Sitting down for long time periods.

Hence, the correct option is (C).

10. The community development approach to health education aims to improve and promote health by addressing socioeconomic and environmental determinants of health within the community.

The community development approach is a way of working with communities and people to set agendas and organise. Community development is a long–term value based process which aims to address imbalances in power and bring about change founded on social justice, equality and inclusion. Social justice and human rights.

Hence, the correct option is (B).

11. The conference can be used as a method in the Group approach of health education.

The groups are many – mothers, school children, patients, industrial workers – to whom we can direct health teaching. The choice of subject in group health teaching is very important; it must relate directly to the interest of the group. For instance, mothers may be taught about baby care; school children about oral hygiene; a group of TB patients about tuberculosis, and industrial workers about accidents.

Hence, the correct option is (B).

12. Assessing the needs is the first step in planning a health education programme.

A needs assessment is a systematic process that examines what criteria must be met in order to reach a desired outcome. For example, a marketing needs assessment might be used to build a business case for replacing software the company uses to conduct direct email campaigns.

Hence, the correct option is (A).

13. The nurse's statement, "Yes, I see. Go on." is an example of the communication skill of a general lead. Offering a general lead encourages the client to continue sharing information.

General leads indicate that the nurse is listening and following what the client is saying without taking away the initiative for the interaction.

Hence, the correct option is (C).

14. This is an example of giving false reassurance communication skill.

The nurse's statement, "Things will look better tomorrow after a good night's sleep." is an example of the nontherapeutic technique of giving false reassurance. Giving false reassurance indicates to the client that there is no cause for anxiety, thereby devaluing the client's feelings.

Hence, the correct option is (D).

15. In the Lecture method of group teaching, there is no active participation from learners.

Lectures are the most popular method of health teaching. In this, communication is mostly one-way, i.e. the people are only passive listeners' there is no active participation on their part in learning.

Lecture method is the oldest method of teaching. It is based on the philosophy of idealism. This method refers to the explanation of the topic to the students. The emphasis is on the presentation of the content.

Hence, the correct option is (A).

16. All of the above are the aims of health education.

Health education is one of the factors of development because it contributes to: increase the efficacy of health services, curative as well as preventive; to improve productivity by reducing occupational diseases and accidents; to change the social climate of communities by getting the people to participate. The ultimate goal of health education is: Improve the health of the individual and community level. Reduce the incidence of disease. Reduction of disabilities and deaths.

Hence, the correct option is (D).

17. When interviewing a client, the nurse should employ the nonverbal behavior of sitting squarely, facing the client.

Facilitative skills for active listening can be identified by the acronym SOLER. SOLER includes sitting squarely facing the client (S), open posture when interacting with a client (O), leaning forward toward the client (L), establishing eye contact (E), and relaxing (R).

Hence, the correct option is (C).

18. Country Club Management style refers to this.

Country club management style puts concern for the staff as the number one priority at the expense of the delivery of services. He/she runs the department just like a country club where everyone is happy including the manager. This leadership style assumes that if people are happy in their job, they will naturally work harder.

Hence, the correct option is (C).

19. The epidemiological triad does not include risk factors.

Health risk factors are attributes, characteristics or exposures that increase the likelihood of a person developing a disease or health disorder.

Hence, the correct option is (C).

20. Democratic Leadership style is most effective in medical field.

Democratic leadership is one of the most effective leadership styles because it allows lower-level employees to exercise authority they'll need to use wisely in future positions they might hold.

Hence, the correct option is (C).

21. Pecularity of a hospital as an organization is all except personlised services.

Personalized health services (PHS) is an overarching framework for care that unifies predictive technologies with an engaged patient to coordinate care with the primary aim of promoting health and preventing disease.

Hence, the correct option is (C).

22. Organisation effectiveness comprises all except flexibility in structure & strategy.

Strategic flexibility is composed of the capability of organizational goals and the capability of management to external and internal environment.

Organizational effectiveness is a term often used to describe an organization's capacity to achieve outcomes efficiently and effectively.

Hence, the correct option is (C).

23. Shape is not the basis of the classification of hospitals.

Hospitals are institutions that provide medical assistance to the injured and sick people. This is the general concept behind all hospitals.

The criteria-based classification of the hospitals include:

- Functionality
- Size
- Location
- Ownership
- Specialization

Hence, the correct option is (D).

24. All of the above are functional division of hospital.

Hospital, an institution that is built, staffed, and equipped for the diagnosis of disease; for the treatment, both medical and surgical, of the sick and the injured; and for their housing during this process.

Outpatient department (OPD), Surgical Department, Inpatient Service (IP), Nursing Department, Physical Medicine, Paramedical Department, and Rehabilitation Department, Dietary Department, Pharmacy Department, Operation Theatre Complex (OT), Radiology Department (X-ray), and Non-professional Services are some of the functional divisions of hospital.

Hence, the correct option is (D).

25. The concept behind changing the role of hospitals from indoor care to outpatient care includes all except economic importance.

Inpatient care starts with admission to the hospital for medical treatment. Most patients enter inpatient care from a hospital's Emergency Room (ER) or through a pre-booked surgery or treatment. In most cases, the treatment must be serious and require in-depth observation and monitoring. Once discharged from the hospital by the doctor, the patient becomes an outpatient.

Outpatient care involves any sort of care provided without admission into the hospital. Procedures within an outpatient clinic include consultations, rehabilitation, tests, etc. These are all performed outside the hospital setting—traditionally in clinics or other facilities.

Hence, the correct option is (C).

26. OPD services are not a part of preventive care.

OPD Services : It is known as outpatient department in which we provide the facility of diagnosis and take care of the patients who can not stay overnight. It also includes in-patient services and physicians and surgeons who take care of inpatients in the ward and are the consultant in the OPD.

Hence, the correct option is (D).

27. The patient's first priority concerning self-injection in this situation is to check the syringe to verify that the nurse has removed the prescribed insulin dose.

When the nurse teaches the patient to prepare an insulin injection, the patient's first priority is to validate the dose accuracy. The next steps are to select the site, assess the site, and clean the site with alcohol before injecting the insulin.

Hence, the correct option is (C).

28. A patient must receive 50 units of Humulin regular insulin. The label reads 100 units = 1 ml. The nurse should administer 0.5 ml.

There are 3 primary methods for calculation of medication dosages; Dimensional Analysis, Ratio Proportion, and Formula or Desired Over Have Method. Desired Over Have or Formula Method uses a formula or equation to solve for an unknown quantity (x) much like ratio proportion. Drug calculations require the use of conversion factors, for example, when converting from pounds to kilograms or liters to milliliters. Simplistic in design, this method allows clinicians to work with various units of measurement, converting factors to find the answer.

Hence, the correct option is (A).

29. The nurse should draw up the regular insulin, then the NPH insulin, in the same syringe.

Drugs that are compatible may be mixed together in one syringe. In the case of insulin, the shorter-acting, clear insulin (regular) should be drawn up before the longer-acting, cloudy insulin (NPH) to ensure accurate measurements.

Hence, the correct option is (B).

30. A patient has just received 30 mg of codeine by mouth for pain. Five minutes later he vomits. The nurse should observe the emesis first.

After a patient has vomited, the nurse must inspect the emesis to document color, consistency, and amount. Nausea or vomiting is another commonly seen adverse effect that is expected to diminish the following days to weeks of continued codeine exposure. Antiemetic therapies, in oral and rectal formulations, are available for the treatment of nausea or vomiting.

Hence, the correct option is (C).

31. A patient is catheterized with a #16 indwelling urinary (Foley) catheter to determine if his 24-hour output is adequate.

A 24-hour urine output of less than 500 ml in an adult is considered inadequate and may indicate kidney failure. This must be corrected while the patient is in the acute state so that appropriate fluids, electrolytes, and medications can be administered and excreted. Indwelling catheterization is not needed to diagnose trauma, urinary tract infection, or residual urine.

Hence, the correct option is (B).

32. A staff nurse who is promoted to assistant nurse manager may feel uncomfortable initially when supervising her former peers. She can best decrease this discomfort by making changes after evaluating the situation and having discussions with the staff.

A new assistant nurse manager should not make changes until she has had a chance to evaluate staff members, patients, and physicians. Changes must be planned thoroughly and should be based on a need to improve conditions, not just for the sake of change.

Hence, the correct option is (B).

33. Sensory deficits could cause a geriatric patient to have difficulty retaining knowledge about prescribed medications.

Age-related decline of the five classical senses (vision, smell, hearing, touch, and taste) poses significant burdens on older adults. The co-occurrence of multiple sensory deficits in older adults is not well characterized and may reflect a common mechanism resulting in global sensory impairment.

Hence, the correct option is (B).

34. When examining a patient with abdominal pain the nurse in charge should assess the symptomatic quadrant last.

The nurse should systematically assess all areas of the abdomen, if time and the patient's condition permit, concluding with the symptomatic area. Otherwise, the nurse may elicit pain in the symptomatic area, causing the muscles in other areas to tighten. This would interfere with further assessment.

Hence, the correct option is (C).

35. The nurse is assessing a postoperative adult patient. The nurse should document the patient's description of pain as subjective data.

Subjective data come directly from the patient and usually are recorded as direct quotations that reflect the patient's opinions or feelings about a situation. Subjective data provide clues to possible physiologic, psychological, and sociologic problems. They also provide the nurse with information that may reveal a client's risk for a problem as well as areas of strengths for the client. The information is obtained through interviewing. Vital signs, laboratory test results, and ECG waveforms are examples of objective data.

Hence, the correct option is (C).

36. Humans can produce 10 of the 20 amino acids. The others must be supplied in the food. Failure to obtain enough of even 1 of the 10 essential amino acids, those that we cannot make, results in degradation of the body's proteins-muscle and so forth-to obtain the one amino acid that is needed.

Hence, the correct option is (D).

37. Enzymes groups of chemicals are not a food nutrient. Nutrients are compounds in foods essential to life and health, providing us with energy, the building blocks for repair and growth and substances necessary to regulate chemical processes. There are six major nutrients: Carbohydrates (CHO), Lipids (fats), Proteins, Vitamins, Minerals, Water.

Hence, the correct option is (D).

38. The water body is eutrophicated with high amounts of nitrogen nutrients and orthophosphate. The enrichment of water by inorganic plant nutrients is called eutrophication. This phenomenon can be caused by various sources, both artificial and natural. Eutrophication has relevant effects on water bodies: the main ones being algae bloom, excessive aquatic macrophyte growth, and oxygen deprivation. When algae are dense, they form a visible green or yellowish-brown covers that appear to float on the surface of the water. It blocks sunlight that is needed by organisms in the water and further reduces oxygen.

Hence, the correct option is (C).

39. Abscisic acid inhibits hormone growth. Auxins, gibberellins, and cytokinins promote plant growth. Abscisic acid is involved in stopping the dormancy of stomata, seeds and inhibiting other hormonal functions. It plays an important role in seed maturation. It also has an important role in the synthesis of proteins and corresponding osmolytes, which enable plants to tolerate stresses caused by environmental or biological factors.

Hence, the correct option is (B).

40. Buffalo milk has the highest amount of fat in comparison to the milk from cow, sheep and goat. Buffalo milk is the second highest consumed milk after the cow's milk. Apart from fat, buffalo milk is also rich in SNF, calcium, magnesium, and phosphorus content.

Buffalo milk	
Calories	237
Water	83 % 83 % 83%
Carbs	12 grams
Protein	9 grams
Fat	17 grams
Lactose	13 grams
Calcium	32 % 32 % 32%of the Daily Value (DV)

Hence, the correct option is (A).

41. Anthrax disease is a serious disease caused by bacteria called Bacillus anthracis. Anthrax disease can cause pneumonia, blood infection and even death. Infected milk can cause anthrax disease. The greater danger from the milk of an animal infected with anthrax is coming in contact with its surroundings and its feces, urine, milk and other food items.

Hence, the correct option is (A).

42. The addition of dilute iodine to foods is a confirmatory test for starch.

Testing for Starch:

1. Take a small amount of any food or raw material. Put 2-3 drops of dilute iodine solution on it.
2. Observe if there is any change in the color of the food items.
3. A blue-black color indicates that it contains starch.

Hence, the correct option is (A).

43. Glycogen is an example of a polysaccharide carbohydrate. Carbohydrates are usually polyhydroxy aldehydes or ketones composed of C, H, and O in a 1:2:1 ratio, with a few exceptions. The general formula for carbohydrates is $C_n(H_2O)n$. 1 gram of carbohydrate makes 17 KJ of energy. These makeup about 1% of our body weight and can be oxidized to act as a source of energy in the body. The main sources of carbohydrates are potatoes, fruits, cereals, sugar, honey, bread, milk, etc.

Hence, the correct option is (C).

44. Due to the lack of iron and vitamin C, milk is no longer called a balanced diet. Iron and vitamin C is not found in good amounts in milk. The top food source for calcium is milk. Milk is a top source of calcium, potassium, and vitamin D. Full-fat milk contains a maximum of 0.35 mg/dl of vitamin C. Phosphorus, Vitamin A, B12, Riboflavin is found in milk. A naturally good source of milk is cow's milk. Cow's milk does not contain enough vitamin C.

Hence, the correct option is (A).

45. To check to see if an unconscious casualty is breathing normally you should not take more than 10 seconds.

To check if a person is still breathing: look to see if their chest is rising and falling. Listen over their mouth and nose for breathing sounds. Feel their breath against your cheek for 10 seconds.

Hence, the correct option is (A).

46. You should use Face, Arm, Speech tests if you suspect that a person had a stroke.

There's a quick test anyone can do if you think someone is having a stroke. It's called the fast test.

- F = Face (Ask the person to smile. Is the smile uneven?)
- A = Arms (Ask the person to raise both their arms. Is one arm weaker than the other?)
- S = Speech (Ask the person to say something. Does it sound slow or funny?)
- T = Time (If the person can't do any one of these things, then call 911 for help.)

Hence, the correct option is (A).

47. Charred skin, no pain are the symptoms of third degree burns.

Third degree burns have the following symptoms:

- Dry and leathery skin.
- Black, white, brown, or yellow skin.
- Swelling.
- Lack of pain because nerve endings have been destroyed.

Hence, the correct option is (A).

48. To relocate the passenger is the main purpose of the "Route" emergency transportation technique when providing treatment to a passenger.

Regional ETRs have been defined as priority routes targeted during an emergency for rapid damage assessment and debris-clearance and used to facilitate life-saving and life-sustaining response activities, including the transport of first responders (e.g., police, fire and emergency medical services), fuel.

Hence, the correct option is (A).

49. Blood flow out of the wound with high pulses in arterial bleeding.

Arterial bleeding is characterized by rapid pulsing spurts, sometimes several meters high, and has been recorded as reaching as much as 18-feet away from the body. Because it's heavily oxygenated, arterial blood is said to be bright red.

Hence, the correct option is (C).

50. A person is allergic to peanut butter and is going into anaphylactic shock. Give them some aspirin immediately and Arrange medical attention is what you should do next.

Antihistamines block histamine, a symptom-causing chemical released by your immune system during an allergic reaction.

Hence, the correct option is (D).

51. A burn by liquid or gas is called a scald.

Burns and scalds are damage to the skin usually caused by heat. Both are treated in the same way. A burn is caused by dry heat – by an iron or fire, for example. A scald is caused by something wet, such as hot water or steam.

Hence, the correct option is (A).

52. When someone has broken his arm then put the arm in a sling.

A shoulder fracture, elbow fracture, or wrist fracture may require that you wear a sling. 1 It is important after a fracture to immobilize your arm to ensure that the bones heal properly. The sling keeps your arm still and in place to be sure this occurs.

Hence, the correct option is (D).

53. The student who is suffering from heat cramps give him cool water or sports drink. Heat cramps usually go away on their own, but you can try one of these home remedies: Rest in a cool place and drink a sports drink, which has electrolytes and salt, or drink cool water.

Hence, the correct option is (B).

54.

<table>
<tr><td colspan="2">Acquired immunodeficiency syndrome (AIDS) is a fatal viral infection that destroys the immune system.</td></tr>
<tr><td>Causative Agent</td><td>Human immunodeficiency virus (HIV)</td></tr>
<tr><td>Mode of Acquiring</td><td>Through sexual contact</td></tr>
<tr><td>Affects</td><td>Immune system</td></tr>
<tr><td>Symptoms</td><td>Early-stage
• Fever, chills
• Muscle pain, joint pain, weakness, and Weight loss
• Red rashes
• Enlarged glands
Late-stage
• Blurred vision
• Night sweats
• Diarrhea
• White spots on the tongue
• Makes person vulnerable to other infections and diseases like tuberculosis, pneumonia, cancer, etc.</td></tr>
</table>

Hence, the correct option is (D).

55. Adrenaline hormone is called the fight-or-flight hormone. Adrenaline is secreted by Adrenal Gland. Adrenal Gland has two tissues, they are called the Adrenal Medulla and Adrenal Cortex. Adrenal Medulla secretes two hormones called Adrenaline and noradrenaline in response to any kind of stress or emergency situation. So, they are called Emergency Hormones or Stress Hormones.

Hormones	Gland
Thyroxine	Thyroid Gland
Glucagon	Pancreas
Dopamine	Neurons

Hence, the correct option is (A).

56. Progesterone:

- The adrenal glands, ovaries, and placenta produce the hormone progesterone.

- Progesterone level increases during ovulation and spur during pregnancy.
- It helps in stabilizing the menstrual cycle.
- Prepares the body for pregnancy.
- Its lower level leads to irregular periods and increases complications during pregnancy.

Therefore progesterone is the female sex hormone.

Hence, the correct option is (B).

57. Bowman's capsule is associated with the Excretory System. It is a cup-like structure in the functional unit of the mammalian kidney i.e. the nephron.

The first step of blood filtration starts here to form the urine. The Circulatory system consists of the heart and the blood vessels.

The Digestive system starts from the mouth and continues up to the anus. It comprises of the esophagus, stomach pancreas, gall bladder, and intestines. The Reproductive system consists of gonads, ducts, etc. It differs in males and females.

Hence, the correct option is (C).

58. The Growth of the person is dependent upon the growth hormone secreted by the pituitary gland.

The pituitary gland controls the functioning of other endocrine glands.

Glands	Location	Hormones	Functions
Pituitary gland	At the base of the brain	Growth Hormone Adrenocorticotropic hormone	-Stimulates the growth of bones -Stimulates adrenal gland
Adrenal Gland	The anterior end of each kidney	Adrenaline and Nor-adrenaline	Controls behavior during crisis and emotional situations
Thymus	In the thoracic cage, near the heart	Thymosin	Controls the cells which give rise to immunity

Hence, the correct option is (A).

59. Central Nervous System (CNS) is also known as the central processing unit of the body. The CNS includes the Brain and the Spinal cord and is the site of information processing and control. The brain is an organ that's made up of large mass of nerve tissue that's protected within the skull.

Some of its main functions include - processing sensory information, regulating blood pressure and breathing, releasing hormones, etc.

Hence, the correct option is (C).

60. The circular muscle found at the junction of the stomach and duodenum is pyloric sphincter. The pyloric sphincter is a band of smooth muscle at the junction between the pylorus of the stomach and the duodenum of the small intestine. It plays an important role in digestion, where it acts as a valve to controls the flow of partially digested food from the stomach to the small intestine.

Hence, the correct option is (D).

61. Brain organs will not feel any pain on being pricked by a needle.

The brain is a painless organ.

- So pricking or even removing a part of the brain, while a person is conscious, does not cause any pain.

Operating brain in a conscious state is a common procedure which is known as "awake craniotomy".

- A cover around the brain is a painful structure. Pricking it can cause severe pain.

There are no pain nor tactile (touch) receptors of any type in the brain itself.

- So, a needle or even more invasive brain surgery is not associated with any "sensation" of the brain being touched in the patient.

Hence, the correct option is (B).

62. The nervous system is primarily made up of two types of cells, Neurons & Glial cells.

1. **Neurons:** These are the structural and functional units of the nervous system. Neurons are microscopic structures that perform the function of conduction of electrical impulses carrying information.
2. **Glial cells:** These are also called neuroglia cells. They are majorly found in the brain and the spinal cord. They do not conduct electrical impulses.

- Their primary function is to provide support to the neurons.
- About 50% of the total brain cells are neuroglial cells.
- There are different types of neuroglial cells present in the CNS & PNS respectively.

Neuroglial cells of CNS:

Astrocytes/Macroglia	• These are moderately large cells with numerous processes. These are of two types namely fibrous astrocytes of white matter and the protoplasmic astrocytes of grey matter. • They provide a repair mechanism and replace lost tissues.
Oligodendrocytes	• Smaller than astrocytes, they play a metabolic role in the formation and preservation of myelin sheath in the nerve fibres of the CNS
Microglial cells	• These are found in the diffused states through both grey and white matter. • These are specialized

		macrophages and the scavengers of the nervous system.
Ependymal cells	•	These form the Epithelium that lines the ventricles and central canal of the spinal cord.

Neuroglial cells of PNS:

Schwann cells	•	These cells encircle PNS axons. They form the myelin sheath around axons
Satellite cells	•	These are flat cells that surround the cell bodies of neurons of PNS ganglia.

Hence, the correct option is (D).

63. All of these increase the risk of ectopic pregnancy.

Ectopic pregnancy is a serious condition in which an embryo implants in tissue outside the uterus. Risk factors include pelvic inflammatory disease, tubal ligation, endometriosis, tobacco smoking, history of infertility, and the use of assisted reproductive technology.

Endometriosis is an often painful disorder in which tissue similar to the tissue that normally lines the inside of your uterus.

If you do conceive after having a tubal ligation, there's a risk of having an ectopic pregnancy. This means the fertilized egg implants outside the uterus, usually in a fallopian tube.

Pelvic inflammatory disease (PID) is an infection of the female reproductive organs. It most often occurs when sexually transmitted bacteria spread from your vagina to your uterus, fallopian tubes or ovaries.

Hence, the correct option is (D).

64. Hemolytic disease of the newborn can be triggered by Rh incompatibility between mother and fetus.

Of the conditions listed, the only one that is associated with Rh incompatibility between mother and fetus is hemolytic disease of the newborn (otherwise known as hemolytic disease of the fetus and newborn). In this condition, antibodies from the mother's blood attack the blood of the fetus. This is a major cause of fetal and newborn mortality and morbidity.

Hence, the correct option is (D).

65. Ultrasound test does the nurse expect will be done to confirm the diagnosis.

Placenta previa is a condition in which the placenta lies very low in the uterus and covers all or part of the cervix.

An ultrasound scan uses high-frequency sound waves to make an image of a person's internal body structures. Doctors commonly use ultrasound to study a developing fetus (unborn baby), a person's abdominal and pelvic organs, muscles and tendons, or their heart and blood vessels.

Hence, the correct option is (D).

66. Assess fetal heart rate should be the nurse's next action.

The nurse must suspect rupture of the membranes (amniotic sac). Assess fetal heart rate if a rupture of the membranes may have occurred. With rupture comes the potential for cord prolapse. Assess fetal heart rate for baseline variability. Marked variability may be cause for concern and the nurse should monitor the patient for signs of infection.

Hence, the correct option is (B).

67. The most common symptoms of ectopic pregnancy are moderate to severe abdominal pain and vaginal bleeding.

Abdominal pain is pain that occurs between the chest and pelvic regions. Abdominal pain can be crampy, achy, dull, intermittent or sharp.

Vaginal bleeding can have causes that aren't due to underlying disease. Examples include menstruation, objects in the body (such as an IUD), medication side effects or childbirth.

Hence, the correct option is (B).

68. The nurse advises a woman with mild pre-eclampsia to do all of the following except limit water intake.

It is not necessary to limit water intake in women with pre-eclampsia. It is important that women with pre-eclampsia drink at least 8 glasses of water per day. The ingestion of water may even help reduce swelling. Checking blood pressure and body weight frequently are important in tracking fluid levels. It is also important to keep track of fetal movement and notify a provider immediately if a decrease in movement is noted. Women who are preeclamptic may spill protein into their urine as a result of malfunctioning kidneys.

Hence, the correct option is (D).

69. A nurse know that the most positive evidence of active tuberculosis is positive chest X-ray findings. Tuberculosis (TB) is caused by a bacterium called Mycobacterium tuberculosis. Tuberculosis (TB) is a potentially serious infectious disease that mainly affects the lungs.

The bacteria that cause TB are spread when an infected person coughs or sneezes. Most people infected with the bacteria that cause tuberculosis don't have symptoms. When symptoms do occur, they usually include a cough, weight loss, night sweats and fever.

Hence, the correct option is (C).

70. The usefulness of a 'screening test' in a community depends on its sensitivity. A screening test is done to detect potential health disorders or diseases in people who have any symptoms of disease. Examples of Screening Tests are Pap smear, mammogram, clinical breast exam, blood pressure determination, cholesterol level, eye examination/vision test, and urin analysis.

Hence, the correct option is (B).

71. A nurse giving a shot of vitamin K to a 30-day-old baby. The target area vastus lateralis would be best suited. The drugs are injected into the widest part of the vastus lateral thigh muscle, the muscle located on the lateral part of the thigh.

Vitamin K helps the blood to clot and prevents serious bleeding. In newborns, vitamin K injections can prevent a now rare, but potentially fatal, bleeding disorder called 'vitamin K deficiency bleeding' (VKDB), also known as 'haemorrhagic disease of the newborn' (HDN).

Hence, the correct option is (C).

72. A nurse taking care of a gastritis patient, will recommend Naproxen sodium medications contraindicated for this patient.

Naproxen sodium is a nonsteroidal anti-inflammatory drug that can cause inflammation of the upper GI tract. For this reason, it is contraindicated in a patient with gastritis. Naproxen is used to relieve pain from various conditions such as headache, muscle aches, tendonitis, dental pain, and menstrual cramps.

Hence, the correct option is (A).

73. Patients with peripheral vascular disease often have nerve damage as a result of inadequate tissue fusion. Ischemic pain is more worrying. This refers to extreme pain that is caused by a combination of PVD and inadequate fusion. Ischemic pain is often intensified due to poor cardiac output.

Hence, the correct option is (A).

74. A family history of heart disease is an inherited risk factor that is not subject to a lifestyle change. Having a first-degree relative with heart disease has been shown to significantly increase risk.

Atherosclerosis is thickening or hardening of the arteries caused by a buildup of plaque in the inner lining of an artery. Risk factors may include high cholesterol and triglyceride levels, high blood pressure, smoking, diabetes, obesity, physical activity, and eating saturated fats.

Hence, the correct option is (A).

75. Dehydration is the most common cause of death in children suffering from diarrhoea.

Diarrhoea is a condition in which faeces are discharged from the bowels frequently and in a liquid form. Diarrhoea is having 3 or more loose or liquid stools (poos) in one day, or more frequently than normal.

Hence, the correct option is (A).

76. Growth chart is also known as road to health chart.

Road to health chart: also known as a Growth chart. Designed by: David Morley Modified by: World Health Organization (WHO). Road to health chart used by pediatrician and other health care professionals to follow a child's growth.

Hence, the correct option is (B).

77. A child grasps fingers when palm touch occurs at the age of 3 months.

Motor Development in Infants: It disappears around 3 months of age. It means Touch of palm of hand of infant and flexion occurs. Prehension: It occurs around 5-6 months of age. It means Grasps objects between fingers and opposing thumb. Eg: Can hold drinking cup parachute Reflex: It appears around 7 to 9 months as a protective arm mechanism. It means when infant is suddenly thrust downward when prone. Pincer Grasp: It is well established by 1 year of age. It means coordination of index finger and thumb.

Hence, the correct option is (D).

78. Rheumatic fever is an inflammatory disease that can develop when strep throat or scarlet fever. Bacteria called group A Streptococcus (group A strep) cause these infections.

Pharyngitis is inflammation of the pharynx also called a sore throat. Pharyngitis can also cause scratchiness in the throat and difficulty swallowing. It is most commonly caused by viral infections such as the common cold, influenza, or mononucleosis. In some cases Bacterial infection also. The incubation period is typically 2 to 5 days. Common signs and symptoms include sneezing, runny nose, headache, cough, fatigue, body aches, chills, fever, etc.

Hence, the correct option is (A).

79. A cleft palate is a split or opening in the top of the child's mouth. It can involve the bony front portion of the soft back portion of their mouth. Clefts are congenital disorders that may cause problems with eating, drinking and speech. Cleft lip or palate most commonly occur as isolated birth defects but are also associated with many inherited genetic conditions or syndromes. Cleft palate surgery generally occurs when a child is around 12 months old (before the child learns to talk). On the second postoperative day after the repair of the cleft palate feeding suitable is with a cup.

Hence, the correct option is (A).

80. Total lung capacity in a newborn is 150 ml.

Total lung capacity is the volume of air present in the chest after full inspiration. In new born babies Oxygen and carbon dioxide flow through the blood in the placenta. Most of it goes to the heart and flows through the baby's body. At birth, the baby's lungs are filled with fluid so they are not fully inflated so the lung capacity is around 120-150 ml in new burns.

Hence, the correct option is (D).

81. Given,

Part filled in 2 hours $= \frac{2}{6} = \frac{1}{3}$

Remaining part $= \left(1 - \frac{1}{3}\right) = \frac{2}{3}$

∴ (A+B)'s 7 hours work $= \frac{2}{3}$

(A+B)'s 1 hours work $= \frac{2}{21}$

∴ C's 1 hours work $=$ {(A+B+C)'s 1 hours work} $-$ {(A+B)'s 1 hours work}

$= \left(\frac{1}{6} - \frac{2}{21}\right) = \frac{1}{14}$

∴ C alone can fill the tank in 14 hours.

Hence, the correct option is (C).

82. Let the required time $= t$ years

Interest is compounded half-yearly

$t = 2t$ half years and rate $= \frac{20}{2} = 10\%$

We know that:

$\because A = P\left(1 + \frac{r}{100}\right)^t$

$\therefore 1000\left(1 + \frac{10}{100}\right)^{2t} = 1331$

$\Rightarrow \left(\frac{11}{10}\right)^{2t} = \frac{1331}{1000}$

$\Rightarrow \left(\frac{11}{10}\right)^{2t} = \left(\frac{11}{10}\right)^3$

$\Rightarrow 2t = 3$

$\therefore t = \frac{3}{2}$ years

Hence, the correct option is (A).

83. We know that:

Speed of the boat in still water $= 13$ km/hr

Speed of stream $= 4$ km/hr

We are given that the boat travels downstream i.e. with the current, so the new speed of the boat is,

$13 + 4 = 17$ km/hr.

Therefore, time taken to complete distance of 68 km is,

As we know:

Speed \(= frac{ Distance}{Time)\)

$T = \frac{68}{17}$

$= 4$ hours

Hence, the correct option is (C).

84. Given:

$240 \div 6 + \sqrt{529} \times 17 = ? + 150\%$ of 80

$\Rightarrow 40 + 23 \times 17 = ? + 120$

$\Rightarrow 40 + 391 = ? + 120$

$\Rightarrow 431 - 120 = ?$

$\Rightarrow ? = 311$

$\therefore$ The value of $?$ is 311.

Hence, the correct option is (A).

85. Given:

The numbers are $36, 54$, and 72.

Concept used:

HCF (highest common factor): this is the largest positive integer that divides each integer. This is sometimes called the greatest common divisor (G.C.D).

Factor of $36 = 1 \times 2 \times 2 \times 3 \times 3$

Factor of $54 = 1 \times 2 \times 3 \times 3 \times 3$

Factor of $72 = 1 \times 2 \times 2 \times 2 \times 3 \times 3$

So from the above, we can say that the highest common integer $= 3 \times 3 \times 2 = 18$

$\therefore$ The HCF of $36, 54$, and 72 is 18.

Hence, the correct option is (A).

86. According to the given coding language,

A	B	C	D	E	F	G	H	I	J	K	L	M
1	2	3	4	5	6	7	8	9	10	11	12	13
Z	Y	X	W	V	U	T	S	R	Q	P	O	N
26	25	24	23	22	21	20	19	18	17	16	15	14

L = 12 (1 + 2) = 3
I = 9
F = 6
E = 5
Similarly,
F = 6
U = 21 (2 + 1) = 3
N = 14 (1 + 4) = 5
So, FUN corresponds to 635.

Hence, the correct option is (A).

87. The least possible Venn Diagram for the given statements will be as follows:

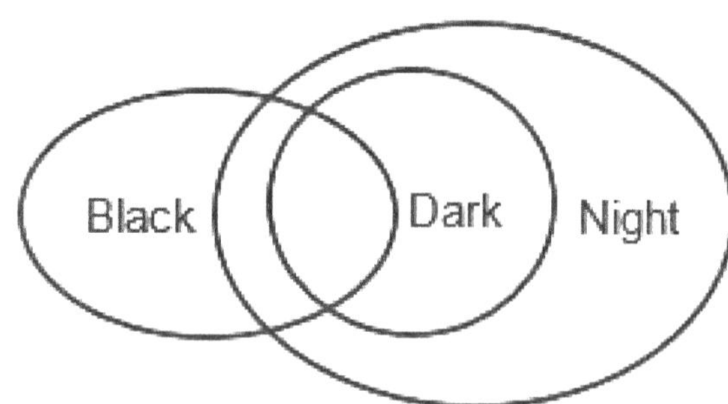

I. All black is night. → False (It is possible but not definite)

II. Some black is not night. → False (It is possible but not definite)

So, Either I or II follows.

Hence, the correct option is (C).

88. As Arc is a part of Circle similarly segment is a part of line.

Hence, the correct option is (D).

89. As per the given statement Adversity makes a man wise.

Conclusion:

I. The poor are wise is false as there is no relation with the given statement.

II. Men learn from bitter experiences is true as Adversity means difficult/unpleasant situation which makes a person wise.

Thus, Only conclusion II follows.

Hence, the correct option is (C).

90.

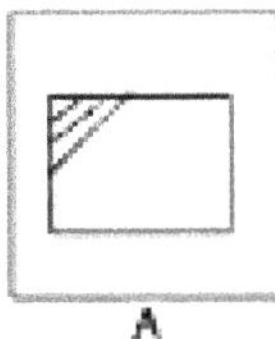

A

In all figures except figure A, half a portion of each figure is shaded.

Hence, the correct option is (C).

91. President appoints the governor of Uttar Pradesh. The appointment of the Governor by the president is given under Article 155. Article 153 explains that there shall be a Governor for each State. A person can be appointed as governor for two or more States. Article 156 explains the term of office of the Governor. The Governor shall hold office during the pleasure of the President. The person has to complete the age of thirty-five years for the governor's post. Smt. Anandiben Patel is the current Governor of Uttar Pradesh.

Hence, the correct option is (C).

92. Mamang Dai was the winner of the Sahitya Akademi Award 2017 from the above.

- She won the award for her English novel The Black Hill.
- Ramesh Kuntal Megh also won 2017 Sahitya Akademi award for the work Vishw Mithak Sarit Sagar, a literary criticism in Hindi.
- Sahitya Akademi announces its annual Sahitya Akademi Awards in 24 languages. The award is in the form of a casket containing an engraved copper-plaque, a shawl and a cheque of Rs. 1 lakh.
- Anees Salim won the 2018 Sahitya Akademi award in the English language for his novel 'The Blind Lady's Descendants'.

Hence, the correct option is (D).

93. Venus Williams (four gold, one silver) and Kathleen McKane Godfree (one gold, two silvers, and two bronzes) are the all-time record holders for the most Olympic tennis medals, with five each. Serena Williams and Venus Williams won a record four gold medals.

Hence, the correct option is (A).

94. Falcon Heavy is the most powerful rocket launched from Earth till November 2022.

SpaceX launched its Falcon Heavy rocket, sending several U.S. military satellites into orbit. This is the most powerful launched ever from the Earth.

This was SpaceX's 50th launch of 2022 as SpaceX's workhorse Falcon 9 rocket has launched 49 missions so far this year. The present pace of the space company is a launch every 6.10 days.

Hence, the correct option is (B).

95. Ujali or Aneri Holi festivals are associated with Tharu Tribe. The community belongs to the Terai lowlands, amid the Shivaliks of the lower Himalayas. Most of them are forest dwellers and some practiced agriculture. The word Tharu is believed to be derived from Sthavir, meaning followers of Theravada Buddhism. The Tharus live in both India and Nepal.

Hence, the correct option is (C).

96. URL stands for Uniform Resource Locator and is used to specify addresses on the World Wide Web. A Uniform Resource Locator (URL), colloquially termed a web address, is a reference to a web resource that specifies its location on a computer network and a mechanism for retrieving it.

Hence, the correct option is (B).

97. Debugging is the process of detecting and removing existing and potential errors (also called 'bugs') in a software program that can cause it to behave unexpectedly or crash.

To prevent incorrect operation of a software or system, debugging is used to find and resolve bugs or defects.

Hence, the correct option is (C).

98. When a web browser is launched, it will automatically open at least one web page. This is the browser's home page, which is also called its start page.

Hence, the correct option is (C).

99. The computer joystick is an input device.

- A joystick is an input device that consists of a stick that pivots on a base and reports its angle or direction to the device it is controlling.
- It is often used in gaming.

Hence, the correct option is (A).

100. Graphical user interface is command interface normally used for windows operating system.

graphical user interface (GUI): CLIs accept as input commands that are entered by keyboard; the commands invoked at the command prompt are then run by the computer. Today, most vendors offer the graphical user interface (GUI) as the default for operating systems (OSes) such as Windows, Linux and macOS.

Hence, the correct option is (C).

Mock Test 04

Discipline

Q.1 A pregnant woman at 43 weeks gestation is having labor augmented with oxytocin infusion. Which of the following best categorizes this particular drug?

A. Erythropoietin
B. Growth hormone
C. Antidiuretic hormone
D. Prolactin

Q.2 Basal body temperature is determined by ________.

A. Taking the temperature before bed
B. Taking the temperature in the afternoon
C. Taking the temperature mid-morning
D. Taking the temperature before rising

Q.3 Which of the following symptoms is not a dangerous sign of pregnancy?

A. Fever or chills
B. Swelling in face or fingers
C. Vaginal bleeding
D. Increased urination

Q.4 A 25-year-old female primigravida presents to the clinic for a prenatal visit and is concerned with new-onset skin changes she has noticed lately. The nurse caring for this client is aware that there are several skin changes associated with pregnancy. All of the following are skin changes associated with pregnancy except ________.

A. Linea nigra
B. Chloasma gravidarium
C. Hegar's sign
D. Subclinical jaundice

Q.5 First Movements of the baby felt by the mother are known as?

A. Lightening **B.** Engagement
C. Quickening **D.** Ballottement

Q.6 Why does bed rest is essential in pre-eclampsia?

A. Prevents eclampsia
B. Mobilizes tissue fluid circulations and decreases edema
C. Prevents premature labor
D. It improves blood circulation and decreases edema

Q.7 Which time is the most difficult to control diabetes during the maternity cycle?

A. First trimester **B.** Last trimester
C. Labour and delivery **D.** Puerperium

Q.8 At what point in a pregnancy is preeclampsia most likely to develop?

A. After 32 weeks **B.** 12-24 weeks
C. 0-12 weeks **D.** 20-32 weeks

Q.9 What is LDRP?

A. Labor, delivery, recovery and postpartum
B. labor, delivery, recovery and patients
C. labor, delivery, rate and patients
D. Labor, delivery, rest and period

Q.10 Road to health card is used for:

A. Measuring the size of road
B. Growth monitoring in children
C. Growth monitoring in adults
D. All of these

Q.11 Which of the following would be the best way to determine the health of a community?

A. Ask a firefighter which neighborhoods have the fewest fires.
B. Ask a realtor which neighborhoods have the most expensive houses.
C. Ask people living in the neighborhood if they are happy with where they live.
D. Ask the police department which neighborhoods have the lowest crime rates.

Q.12 A patient who has been diagnosed with the vasospastic disorder (Raynaud's disease) complains of cold and stiffness in the fingers. Which of the following descriptions is most likely to fit the patient?

A. An adolescent male **B.** An elderly woman
C. A young woman **D.** An elderly man

Q.13 According to C.E. Winslow, which of the following is the goal of public health?

A. For people to attain their birthrights of health and longevity
B. For promotion of health and prevention of disease
C. For people to have access to basic health services
D. For people to be organized in their health efforts

Q.14 A client is scheduled for a percutaneous transluminal coronary angioplasty (PTCA). The nurse knows that a PTCA is the

A. Surgical repair of a diseased coronary artery.
B. Placement of an automatic internal cardiac defibrillator.
C. Procedure that compresses plaque against the wall of the diseased coronary artery to improve blood flow.
D. Non-invasive radiographic examination of the heart.

Q.15 What sporting activities should the nurse organize for a small group of 7-year-old hospitalized children?

A. Sports with rules
B. Finger paints and water play
C. "Dress-up" clothes and props
D. Chess and television programs

Q.16 A patient with a spinal cord injury at level C3-4 is being cared for in the ED. What is the priority assessment?

A. Determine the level at which the patient has intact sensation.

B. Assess the level at which the patient has retained mobility.

C. Check blood pressure and pulse for signs of spinal shock.

D. Monitor respiratory effort and oxygen saturation level.

Q.17 The patient with multiple sclerosis tells the nursing assistant that after physical therapy she is too tired to take a bath. What is your priority nursing diagnosis at this time?

A. Fatigue related to disease state

B. Activity Intolerance due to generalized weakness

C. Impaired Physical Mobility related to neuromuscular impairment

D. Self-care Deficit related to fatigue and neuromuscular weakness

Q.18 Which of the following groups of symptoms indicates a ruptured abdominal aortic aneurysm?

A. Lower back pain, increased blood pressure, decreased red blood cell (RBC) count, increased white blood (WBC) count

B. Severe lower back pain, decreased blood pressure, decreased RBC count, increased WBC count

C. Severe lower back pain, decreased blood pressure, decreased RBC count, decreased RBC count, decreased WBC count

D. Intermittent lower back pain, decreased blood pressure, decreased RBC count, increased WBC count

Q.19 Mr. Bikas has renal calculus, age 35. He is believed to have a small stone that will pass spontaneously. To increase the chance of renal stone passing, the nurse would instruct the client to force fluids and to-

A. Ambulate

B. Remain on bed rest

C. Strain all urine

D. Ask for medications to relax him

Q.20 The client has severe rectal bleeding with 16 diarrheal stools a day, severe abdominal pain, dehydration, tenesmus. Due to these symptoms, the nurse should be alert for the other problems associated with what disease?

A. Diverticulitis **B.** Chrons disease

C. Ulcerative colitis **D.** Peritonitis

Q.21 What instruction should the client be given before undergoing a paracentesis?

A. NPO 12 hours before procedure

B. Empty bladder before procedure

C. Strict bed rest following procedure

D. Empty bowel before procedure

Q.22 Another name for stem cell transplantation is:

A. Bone marrow transplant

B. Spleen transplantation

C. Biopsy

D. Chemotherapy

Q.23 Varicosities are usually examined:

A. With the patient standing

B. With the patient lying flat

C. With the patient in the left lateral position

D. After the patient has had a hot bath

Q.24 Pneumocephalus occurs when:

A. Air enters the cranium

B. The patient also has pneumonia

C. The head is tilted below heart level

D. There is raised intracranial pressure

Q.25 Reasons for craniotomy include:

A. Biopsy of tissue

B. Evacuation of haematoma

C. Clipping of aneurysm

D. All of the above

Q.26 An aneurysm is a bulging in the weak wall of a ______________.

A. Artery **B.** Vein

C. Heart **D.** Pleural cavity

Q.27 The signs and symptoms of raised intracranial pressure include:

A. Hypotension and tachycardia

B. Hypertension and tachycardia

C. Hypertension and bradycardia

D. Hypotension and bradycardia

Q.28 ________is a teaching aid which consists of a series cards.

A. Flannel graph **B.** Flash card

C. Booklet **D.** None of these

Q.29 __________ is didactic method of group teaching.

A. Syposium **B.** Work shop

C. Role play **D.** Flannel graph

Q.30 In which one of the following year, the Central Advisory Board of Physical Education and Recreation was established?

A. 1959 **B.** 1939 **C.** 1950 **D.** 1954

Q.31 __________ is a series of speeches on the selected subject by experts.

A. Panel discussion **B.** Symposium

C. Lecture **D.** None of these

Q.32 _____________ is a type of communication which uses accepted form, rule or custom.

A. Formal communication

B. Informal communication

C. Non-verbal communication

D. None of these

Q.33 Which of the following is/are didactic methods of health communication?

A. Group discussion **B.** Workshop

C. Demonstration **D.** Lecture

Q.34 A type of communication in which the receiver has the chance of asking questions and clearing doubts-

A. One-way communication
B. Two–way communication
C. Non-verbal communication
D. None of these

Q.35 ___________communication takes place between two or three people or in small groups such as a family.
A. Face-to-face **B.** Mass
C. Both **D.** None of these

Q.36 How many types of amino acids are commonly found in proteins?
A. 25 **B.** 20 **C.** 15 **D.** 30

Q.37 Protein is one of the ______ nutrients that provide calories.
A. Four **B.** Three **C.** Two **D.** Five

Q.38 Which disease occurs due to the lack of nutrients in the diet for a longer period of time?
A. Deficiency disease **B.** Night blindness
C. Scurvy **D.** Anemia

Q.39 Most abundant Protein is found in:
A. Cytoplasm **B.** Liver
C. Mitochondria **D.** Brain

Q.40 Which of the following is a digestive enzyme that works in the stomach to break down the food?
A. Lactase **B.** Pepsin **C.** Keratin **D.** Collagen

Q.41 Which enzymes break down sugar lactose found in milk?
A. Keratin **B.** Collagen **C.** Lactase **D.** Pepsin

Q.42 Which is not a symptom of a heart attack?
A. Chest pain
B. Red, hot or dry skin
C. Pale or bluish in color
D. Profuse sweating

Q.43 When should you give rescue breathing?
A. Conscious choking victim
B. Unconscious choking victim
C. Unconscious, no pulse, not breathing
D. Unconscious, not breathing, but has a pulse

Q.44 Signals of an allergic reaction to a bee sting are:
A. Feeling of tightness in the chest and throat
B. Swelling of the face neck and tongue
C. Rash, dizziness, or confusion
D. All of the above

Q.45 When caring for a student who is allergic to bees and has just been stung, you should:
A. Give them an injection with their Epi-pen
B. Apply a heat pack to ease pain
C. Apply a cold pack
D. Both (A) and (C)

Q.46 Soft tissue wounds should be cared by:
A. Heat and elastic bandages
B. Ice and elevation
C. Apply direct pressure on the area to cut down on bleeding under the skin
D. Both (B) and (C)

Q.47 Internal bleeding can be caused by:
A. Injury **B.** Illness
C. Medication **D.** All of the above

Q.48 A first aid responder should move a victim when:
A. It would make it easier to administer first aid
B. The victim is in a dangerous position
C. Never
D. Both (A) and (B)

Q.49 Which of the following organelles shows similarity to a prokaryotic cell?
A. Only mitochondria **B.** Only chloroplast
C. Both (A) and (B) **D.** None of these

Q.50 Which of the following is NOT correct for the cerebellum?
A. It lies in the posterior region of the brain
B. It controls movements, speech, sight, smell, taste, hearing, intelligence etc
C. It is a part of hind brain
D. It maintains equilibrium of the body

Q.51 _____ controls involuntary activities like coughing and sneezing.
A. Medulla **B.** Brain
C. Pons **D.** Cerebellum

Q.52 What is the largest part of the human brain?
A. Midbrain **B.** Medulla Oblongata
C. Cerebrum **D.** Cerebellum

Q.53 The brain is a part of the _______ system.
A. Circulatory **B.** Digestive
C. Endocrine **D.** Nervous

Q.54 The Spinal cord is made up of ________.
A. Nervous tissue **B.** Muscle tissue
C. Epithelial tissue **D.** Connective tissue

Q.55 ______ are a connective tissue that connect two bones to each other.
A. Tendons **B.** Muscles
C. Cartilages **D.** Ligaments

Q.56 Ideally, nursing case management planning identifies goals that are:
A. Anticipated, acceptable and appropriate
B. Challenging and timely
C. Patient focused and cost effective
D. Realistic, measurable and specific

Q.57 Which healthcare provider at a rehabilitation facility addresses the cognitive, behavioral, and psychological problems that result following a patient's traumatic brain injury?
A. Medical social worker

B. Neuropsychiatrist
C. Neurosurgeon
D. Psychologist

Q.58 The nurse ratio in paediatric ward according to Staff Inspection Unit (SIU) norms is:
A. 1 : 3 **B.** 1 : 8 **C.** 1 : 4 **D.** 1 : 6

Q.59 Which ethical principle is grounded in truth with patients?
A. Autonomy **B.** Beneficence
C. Fairness **D.** Veracity

Q.60 When developing a program offering for patients who are newly diagnosed with diabetes, the nursing case manager demonstrates an understanding of learning styles by:
A. Administering a pre- and post-test assessment.
B. Allowing attendees time to voice their opinions.
C. Providing a snack with a low glycemic index.
D. Utilizing a variety of educational materials.

Q.61 Which primary resource guides the nursing case manager's practice?
A. American Case Management Association Member Code of Conduct.
B. Case Management Society of America's Standards of Practice.
C. Nursing: Scope and Standards of Practice.
D. Nursing's Social Policy Statement: The Essence of the Profession.

Q.62 The nursing case manager, who refers a 67-year-old patient to a skilled nursing facility for rehabilitative care, knows that it will be billed under which component of Medicare?
A. Medicare Part A **B.** Medicare Part B
C. Medicare Part D **D.** Medigap

Q.63 Medication errors, orders for unnecessary tests, and omission of standard tests or procedures are classified as which type of variance?
A. Community **B.** Operational
C. Patient **D.** Practitioner

Q.64 What are the tasks that should not be delegated to a non-professional employee?
A. Doing the vital signs
B. Turning the client every two hours
C. Grooming and bathing the client
D. Assessment of neurologicaldeficits

Q.65 A male patient has a soft wrist-safety device. Which assessment finding should the nurse consider abnormal?
A. A palpable radial pulse
B. A palpable ulnar pulse
C. Cool, pale fingers
D. Pink nail beds

Q.66 A nurse is preparing to hang a fat emulsion (lipids) and observes some visible fat globules at the top of the solution. The nurse ensures to do which of the following actions?
A. Take another bottle of solution.
B. Run the bottle solution under warm water.
C. Roll the bottle solution gently.
D. Shake the bottle solution vigorously.

Q.67 A female patient with a terminal illness is in denial. Indicators of denial include ___________.
A. shock dismay **B.** numbness
C. stoicism **D.** preparatory grief

Q.68 The nurse in charge is transferring a patient from the bed to a chair. Which action does the nurse take during this patient transfer?
A. Position the head of the bed flat.
B. Helps the patient dangle the legs.
C. Stands behind the patient.
D. Place the chair facing away from the bed.

Q.69 A clinical nurse specialist is a nurse who has:
A. Been certified by the National League for Nursing.
B. Received credentials from the American Nurses' Association.
C. Graduated from an associate degree program and is a registered professional nurse.
D. Completed a master's degree in the prescribed clinical area and is a registered professional nurse.

Q.70 Before administering the evening dose of prescribed medication, the nurse on the evening shift finds an unlabeled, filled syringe in the patient's medication drawer. What should the nurse in charge do?
A. Discard the syringe to avoid a medication error.
B. Obtain a label for the syringe from the pharmacy.
C. Use the syringe because it looks like it contains the same medication the nurse was prepared to give.
D. Call the day nurse to verify the contents of the syringe.

Q.71 When administering drug therapy to a male geriatric patient, the nurse must stay especially alert for adverse effects. Which factor makes geriatric patients have adverse drug effects?
A. Faster drug clearance
B. Aging-related physiological changes
C. Increased amount of neurons
D. Enhanced blood flow to the GI tract

Q.72 A female patient is being discharged after cataract surgery. After providing medication teaching, the nurse asks the patient to repeat the instructions. The nurse is performing which professional role?
A. Manager **B.** Educator
C. Caregiver **D.** Patient advocate

Q.73 A female patient exhibits signs of heightened anxiety. Which response by the nurse is most likely to reduce the patient's anxiety?
A. "Everything will be fine. Don't worry."
B. "Read this manual and then ask me any questions you may have."
C. "Why don't you listen to the radio?"
D. "Let's talk about what's bothering you."

Q.74 Which of the following is not considered in APGAR score?

A. Heart rate **B.** Respiratory rate
C. Skin colour **D.** Temperature

Q.75 Bronze baby syndrome is caused due to _________.

A. renal dysfunction
B. hepatic dysfunction
C. respiratory dysfunction
D. skin disease

Q.76 Tonsillectomy is not recommended in children below 4 years of age because:

A. It is a life threatening process.
B. It causes bleeding.
C. Tonsils are a part of the immune system.
D. Tonsils are not fully formed.

Q.77 Which of the following is an expected assessment finding in an 8 month old infant with severe diarrhoea?

A. Depressed posterior fontanelle
B. Normal skin elasticity
C. Depressed anterior fontanelle
D. Absence of bowel sounds

Q.78 Which of the following sites would be best to administer an intramuscular injection to a four month old infant?

A. Ventrogluteal **B.** Lateral deltoid
C. Rectus femoris **D.** Vastus lateralis

Q.79 What test or sign should a nurse look for in a 3 week old infant with developmental dysplasia of the hip?

A. Babinski's sign
B. Moro reflex
C. Ortolani's maneuver
D. Palmar-plantar grasp

Q.80 A child who is admitted to the hospital with persistent vomiting should be monitored closely for ____________________.

A. diarrhoea
B. metabolic acidosis
C. metabolic alkalosis
D. hyperactive bowel sounds

General Aptitude / Reasoning / General Awareness / Basic Computer knowledge

Q.81 Evan travelled 16 km from his residence towards the north. He then turned 90 degrees towards the left and travelled 12 km. He turned 90 degrees left again and travelled 16 km and stopped. How far is Evan from his residence?

A. 28 km **B.** 12 km **C.** 4 km **D.** 16 km

Q.82 A bag contains 4 red balls, 6 blue balls and 8 pink balls. One ball is drawn at random and replaced with 3 pink balls. A probability that the first ball drawn was either red or blue in colour and the second drawn was pink in colour:

A. $\frac{12}{21}$ **B.** $\frac{13}{17}$
C. $\frac{11}{30}$ **D.** None of these

Q.83 Three numbers are in the ratio $8:7:5$ and their average is 40. The largest number is:

A. 28 **B.** 32 **C.** 48 **D.** 42

Q.84 The sides of a triangle are 6.5 cm, 10 cm and x cm, where x is a positive number. What is the smallest possible value of x among the following?

[CTET Paper-II (Science & Mathematics), 2015]

A. 4.5 **B.** 2.8 **C.** 3.5 **D.** 4

Q.85 A person bought some eggs at a rate Rs. 5 for 3 and sold them at a rate Rs. 12 for 5. If he got Rs. 143, the number of eggs was:

A. 210 **B.** 200 **C.** 193 **D.** 195

Q.86 By increasing his speed by 15 km/h, a person reduced his travel time from 10 hours to 8 hours. How much time does he take to cover 375 km with his new speed?

A. 4 hours **B.** 6 hours
C. 6.5 hours **D.** 5 hours

Q.87 If 30th January 2003 was Thursday, what was the day on 2nd March, 2003?

[Sainik School Entrance Class IX, 2020]

A. Sunday **B.** Monday **C.** Saturday **D.** Tuesday

Q.88 At what time between 7 to 8 o' clock will the hands of a clock points coincide with each other?

A. $38\frac{2}{11}$ minutes past 8
B. $32\frac{8}{11}$ minutes past 7
C. $38\frac{2}{11}$ minutes past 7
D. $11\frac{2}{38}$ minutes past 7

Q.89 Direction: Study the following information carefully to answer the given question.

M 1 E & D 2 G 9 $ F @ 4 N Z W © 8 C Y A * 6

Four of following five are alike in a certain way based on their positions in the above arrangement and so form a group. Which is the one that does not belong to that group?

A. ME2 **B.** G$4 **C.** NWC **D.** YA6

Q.90 A man said to a lady, "The son of your only brother is the brother of my wife." What is the lady related to the man?

A. Mother
B. Sister
C. Sister of father-in-law
D. Grandfather

Q.91 Which division is considered as the hub of the world's finest carpet industries?

[UPSSSC Rajasva Lekhpal, 2015]

A. Devipatan **B.** Aligarh
C. Azamgarh **D.** Mirzapur

Q.92 In India, political parties are given 'recognition' by:

A. The President
B. Parliament
C. Election Commission
D. All Party Parliamentary Committee

Q.93 Megasthenes has given the description of the administration of which of the following Mauryan cities?

A. Pataliputra
B. Prayag
C. Tosali
D. Ujjayini

Q.94 Which among the following is not a block mountain?

A. Black Forest Mountain Range
B. Salt Range
C. Satpura Range
D. Ural Mountain

Q.95 Badminton player PV Sindhu has defeated whom to win swiss open women's singles title 2022?

A. Pornpawee Chochuwong
B. Sapsiree Taerattanachai
C. Busanan Ongbamrungpha
D. Rawinda Prajongjai

Q.96 Microsoft first introduced an operating system named Windows in which year?

A. 1977
B. 1980
C. 1985
D. 1990

Q.97 Which program is used by web clients to view the web pages?

A. Web browser
B. Protocol
C. Web server
D. Search engine

Q.98 Which of the following website is used to search other website by typing a keyword?

A. Search engine
B. Social networks
C. Routers
D. None of the above

Q.99 Which among the following can store a large amount of data?

A. CD
B. Hard disk
C. RAM
D. Floppy disk

Q.100 Which of the following is a type of virus that consists of self-replicating software that damages files and systems?

A. Viruses
B. Trojan horses
C. Bots
D. Worms

// Smart Answer Sheet //

Correct Indicates percentage of students who answered questions correctly.

Skipped Indicates percentage of students who skipped questions.

Q.	Ans.	Correct	Skipped
1	C	51.26 %	1.02 %
2	D	76.74 %	0.0 %
3	D	89.02 %	0.0 %
4	C	65.96 %	1.66 %
5	C	56.47 %	1.98 %
6	D	25.29 %	3.91 %
7	C	68.4 %	1.85 %
8	A	48.54 %	1.32 %
9	A	58.07 %	1.54 %
10	B	40.89 %	1.74 %
11	C	66.78 %	1.81 %
12	C	54.11 %	1.42 %
13	A	83.54 %	0.0 %
14	C	48.73 %	1.63 %
15	A	56.78 %	1.2 %
16	D	63.23 %	1.55 %
17	D	50.14 %	1.83 %
18	B	57.86 %	1.05 %
19	A	12.74 %	4.99 %
20	C	21.8 %	3.74 %
21	B	67.02 %	1.44 %
22	A	49.75 %	1.52 %
23	A	79.63 %	0.0 %
24	A	89.66 %	0.0 %
25	D	69.89 %	1.14 %
26	A	77.21 %	0.0 %
27	C	67.08 %	1.89 %
28	B	54.03 %	1.27 %
29	D	59.33 %	1.13 %
30	D	68.41 %	1.55 %
31	B	53.82 %	1.87 %
32	A	57.39 %	1.46 %
33	D	60.85 %	1.41 %
34	B	17.95 %	4.95 %
35	A	47.33 %	1.93 %
36	B	89.07 %	0.0 %
37	A	40.36 %	1.73 %
38	A	54.34 %	1.62 %
39	A	51.65 %	1.68 %
40	B	42.05 %	1.3 %
41	C	56.49 %	1.39 %
42	B	60.3 %	1.21 %
43	D	59.16 %	1.27 %
44	D	81.26 %	0.0 %
45	C	89.4 %	0.0 %
46	D	68.99 %	1.78 %
47	D	44.93 %	1.17 %
48	D	58.91 %	1.63 %
49	C	64.6 %	1.94 %
50	B	43.42 %	1.77 %
51	A	61.87 %	1.35 %
52	C	40.2 %	1.58 %
53	D	82.53 %	0.0 %
54	A	69.39 %	1.07 %
55	D	69.68 %	1.92 %
56	D	78.75 %	0.0 %
57	B	52.02 %	1.67 %
58	C	52.16 %	1.35 %
59	D	76.49 %	0.0 %
60	D	19.09 %	4.9 %
61	B	89.92 %	0.0 %
62	A	21.65 %	3.92 %
63	D	47.63 %	1.74 %
64	D	45.15 %	1.7 %
65	C	53.9 %	1.11 %
66	A	89.89 %	0.0 %
67	A	67.22 %	1.55 %
68	B	77.27 %	0.0 %
69	D	54.78 %	1.71 %
70	A	68.09 %	1.59 %
71	B	57.34 %	1.48 %
72	B	65.93 %	1.77 %
73	D	43.07 %	1.27 %
74	D	42.16 %	1.3 %
75	B	44.59 %	1.88 %
76	C	76.19 %	0.0 %
77	C	19.95 %	3.53 %
78	D	68.53 %	1.62 %
79	C	11.36 %	4.78 %
80	C	49.39 %	1.86 %

Q.	Ans.	Correct	Skipped
81	B	55.08 %	1.19 %
82	D	79.79 %	0.0 %
83	C	89.97 %	0.0 %
84	D	77.95 %	0.0 %

Q.	Ans.	Correct	Skipped
85	D	78.82 %	0.0 %
86	D	87.65 %	0.0 %
87	A	81.21 %	0.0 %
88	C	58.1 %	1.51 %

Q.	Ans.	Correct	Skipped
89	D	84.19 %	0.0 %
90	C	44.69 %	1.37 %
91	D	85.69 %	0.0 %
92	C	41.48 %	1.67 %

Q.	Ans.	Correct	Skipped
93	A	44.35 %	1.16 %
94	D	44.91 %	1.21 %
95	C	42.81 %	1.39 %
96	C	43.19 %	1.47 %

Q.	Ans.	Correct	Skipped
97	A	65.74 %	1.6 %
98	A	77.22 %	0.0 %
99	B	78.43 %	0.0 %
100	D	45.25 %	1.27 %

Performance Analysis	
Avg. Score (%)	59.0%
Toppers Score (%)	67.0%
Your Score	

//Hints and Solutions//

1. Antidiuretic hormone best categorizes this particular drug.

Oxytocin is often used to help augment labor by inducing contractions. Antidiuretic hormone is naturally made in the body and works as an anti-diuretic hormone (thus promotes the excretion of water). In labor, this hormone also works to stimulate uterine contractiity.

Hence, the correct option is (C).

2. Basal body temperature is determined by taking the temperature before rising.

The basal body temperature is a method many women use to determine when ovulation occurs. To take a basal body temperature, one must use a basal thermometer (which is more sensitive) and take their body temperature before getting out of bed (or even sitting up) each morning. This method is utilized the best if a woman wakes up and takes her temperature at the same time daily.

Hence, the correct option is (D).

3. Increased urination symptom is not a danger sign of pregnancy.

It is important for the obstetric registered nurse to recognize the following danger signs of pregnancy: profuse vaginal bleeding, severe headaches/visual disturbances/abdominal pain, persistent vomiting, fever, chills, or swelling in the face or fingers. These may be signs of placental abnormalities, hypertensive disorders of pregnancy, maternal infection, or hyperemesis.

Increased urination may be concerning to some women, but during pregnancy, the increased mass of the uterus induces pressure upon the bladder.

Hence, the correct option is (D).

4. All of the following are skin changes associated with pregnancy except Hegar's sign.

Hegar's sign is indicated by a softening of the portion of the uterus between the uterus and a portion of the cervix. The remaining choices are all examples of various skin discolorations commonly associated with pregnancy.

Hence, the correct option is (C).

5. The first Movements of the baby felt by the mother are known as Quickening.

Quickening is defined as the first movements of the fetus felt in utero. It occurs from the eighteenth to the twentieth week of pregnancy. Movements have been felt as early as the tenth week and in rare cases are not felt during the entire pregnancy.

Hence, the correct option is (C).

6. Bed rest is essential in pre-eclampsia because it improves blood circulation and decreases edema.

If the woman is far from the end of her pregnancy and her symptoms are mild, the doctor may advise her to rest in bed. Resting helps bring the blood pressure down, which in turn increases the flow of blood to the placenta, which benefits the baby.

Hence, the correct option is (D).

7. Labour and delivery time is the most difficult to control diabetes during the maternity cycle.

Between 32 – 36 weeks are what we know to be the toughest time for gestational diabetes. It's around this point that we typically see insulin resistance worsen.

Hence, the correct option is (C).

8. After 32 weeks in a pregnancy is preeclampsia most likely to develop.

Pregnancy lasts for about 280 days or 40 weeks. Preeclampsia occurs more frequently in the last 8 weeks or after 32 weeks of pregnancy. An occurrence at an earlier gestational age is associated with increased severity and poorer outcomes for both mother and fetus.

Hence, the correct option is (A).

9. LDRP room stands for labor, delivery, recovery and postpartum room. These rooms are equipped with the necessary tools and supplies to care for mother and baby before, during and after the birth. Most of the time, the baby will get to remain in the room with the mother instead of being taken to the nursery.

Hence, the correct option is (A).

10. Road to health card is used for growth monitoring in children. Growth monitoring is defined as the process of following the growth rate of a child in comparison to a standard by periodic, frequent anthropometric measurements in order to assess growth adequacy and identify faltering early.

Hence, the correct option is (B).

11. A healthy community is one in which residents are happy with their choice of location and exhibit characteristics that would draw others to the location. Thus, the best way to determine the health of the community is to talk to those living in it.

Hence, the correct option is (C).

12. Raynaud's disease is most common in young women and is frequently associated with rheumatologic disorders, such as lupus and rheumatoid arthritis. Vasospasm of the arteries reduces blood flow to the fingers and toes. In people who have Raynaud's, the disorder usually affects the fingers. In about 40 percent of people who have Raynaud's, it affects the toes.

Hence, the correct option is (C).

13. According to Winslow, all public health efforts are for people to realize their birthrights of health and longevity. According to him Public health is the science and art of preventing disease, prolonging life, and promoting health through the organized efforts and informed choices of society, organizations, public and private communities, and individuals.

Hence, the correct option is (A).

14. A client is scheduled for a percutaneous transluminal coronary angioplasty (PTCA). The nurse knows that a PTCA is the procedure that compresses plaque against the wall of the diseased coronary artery to improve blood flow.

PTCA is performed to improve coronary artery blood flow in a diseased artery. It is performed during a cardiac catheterization. Aorta coronary bypass graft is the surgical procedure to repair a diseased coronary artery.

Hence, the correct option is (C).

15. For a small group of 7-year-old hospitalized children, the nurse should organize activities with game rules. Logical reasoning and social skills are developed through play. Various sports help to investigate issues related to the child's experiences in the hospital and reduce the intensity of negative feelings accompanying a child's admission to hospital and hospitalization.

Hence, the correct option is (A).

16. A patient with a spinal cord injury at level C3-4 is being cared for in the ED. The priority assessment is monitor respiratory effort and oxygen saturation level.

The first priority for the patient with an SCI is assessing respiratory patterns and ensuring an adequate airway. The patient with a high cervical injury is at risk for respiratory compromise because the spinal nerves (C3-4) innervate the phrenic nerve, which controls the diaphragm.

Hence, the correct option is (D).

17. The patient with multiple sclerosis tells the nursing assistant that after physical therapy she is too tired to take a bath. At this time, based on the patient's statement, the priority is Self-Care Deficit related to fatigue after physical therapy. Fatigue is described as an overwhelming feeling of lassitude or lack of physical or mental energy that interferes with activities.

Hence, the correct option is (D).

18. Severe lower back pain, decreased blood pressure, decreased RBC count, increased WBC count groups of symptoms indicate a ruptured abdominal aortic aneurysm.

Severe lower back pain indicates an aneurysm rupture, secondary to pressure being applied within the abdominal cavity. When rupture occurs, the pain is constant because it can't be alleviated until the aneurysm is repaired. Blood pressure decreases due to the loss of blood. After the aneurysm ruptures, the vasculature is interrupted and blood volume is lost, so blood pressure wouldn't increase. For the same reason, the RBC count has decreased – not increased. The WBC count increases as cells migrate to the site of injury.

Hence, the correct option is (B).

19. Mr. Bikas has renal calculus, age 35. He is believed to have a small stone that will pass spontaneously. To increase the chance of renal stone passing, the nurse would instruct the client to force fluids and to Ambulate.

Unattached stones in the urinary tract can be passed out with the urine by ambulation which can mobilize the stone and by increased fluid intake which will flush out the stone during urination.

Hence, the correct option is (A).

20. The client has severe rectal bleeding with 16 diarrheal stools a day, severe abdominal pain, dehydration, tenesmus. Due to these symptoms the nurse should be alert for the other problems associated with Ulcerative colitis.

The symptoms may be associated with ulcerative colitis. It is a chronic inflammatory condition producing edema and ulceration that may affect the entire colon. Ulcerations lead to sloughing that causes stools as many as 20 times a day which is filled with blood, mucous and pus. The other symptoms are mentioned accompany the problem.

Hence, the correct option is (C).

21. Empty bladder before procedure instruction should the client be given before undergoing a paracentesis.

Paracentesis involves the removal of ascitic fluid from the peritoneal cavity through a puncture made below the umblicus. The client needs to void before the procedure to prevent accidental puncture of a distended bladder during the procedure.

Hence, the correct option is (B).

22. Another name for stem cell transplantation is a bone marrow transplant. A bone marrow transplant is a medical treatment that replaces your bone marrow with healthy cells. The replacement cells can either come from your own body or from a donor. A bone marrow transplant is also called a stem cell transplant or, more specifically, a hematopoietic stem cell transplant. Transplantation can be used to treat certain types of cancer, such as leukemia, myeloma, and lymphoma, and other blood and immune system diseases that affect the bone marrow.

Hence, the correct option is (A).

23. Varicosities are usually examined with the patient standing. A varicosity or varicose vein is a dilated vein that primarily occurs in the lower limbs particularly in the legs. Varicose veins are caused by increased blood pressure in the veins. Varicose veins happen in the veins near the surface of the skin (superficial). The blood moves towards the heart by one-way valves in the veins. When the valves become weakened or damaged, blood can collect in the veins.

Hence, the correct option is (A).

24. Pneumocephalus occurs when air enters the cranium. Pneumocephalus is the presence of air or gas within the cranial cavity. It is usually associated with disruption of the skull: after head and facial trauma, tumors of the skull base, after neurosurgery or otorhinolaryngology, and rarely, spontaneously.

Hence, the correct option is (A).

25. Reasons for craniotomy include all of the above options. A craniotomy is the surgical removal of part of the bone from the skull to expose the brain. Specialized tools are used to remove the section of bone called the bone flap. The bone flap is temporarily removed, then replaced after the brain surgery has been done.

Hence, the correct option is (D).

26. An aneurysm is a bulging in the weak wall of an artery. An aneurysm is a bulge in a blood vessel caused by a weakness in the blood vessel wall, usually where it branches. As blood passes through the weakened blood vessel, the blood pressure causes a small area to bulge outwards like a balloon.

Hence, the correct option is (A).

27. The signs and symptoms of intracranial pressure include Hypertension and bradycardia. Increased intracranial pressure can result from bleeding in the brain, a tumor, stroke, aneurysm, high blood pressure, or brain infection. Treatment focuses on lowering increased intracranial pressure around the brain. Increased intracranial pressure has serious complications, including long-term (permanent) brain damage and death.

Hence, the correct option is (C).

28. Flash card is a teaching aid that consists of a series cards.

Flash card consist of a series of cards, approximately 10 x 12 inches – each with an illustration pertaining to a story or talk to be given. Each card is "flashed" or displayed before a group as the talk is in progress. The message on the cards must be brief and to the point.

They are pictures arranged in sequence, which illustrate a story support the cards in front of the chest and practice in order to make the teaching effective. Use a Pointer so that the picture is not covered by your hand.

Hence, the correct option is (B).

29. Flannel graph is the didactic method of group teaching.

A flannel graph consists of a wooden board over which is pasted or fixed a piece of rough flannel cloth or khadi. It provides an excellent background for displaying cut out pictures and other illustrations. These illustrations and cut out pictures are provided with a rough surface at the back by pasting pieces of sand-paper, felt or rough cloth, and they adhere at once, put on the flannel. Flannel graph is a very chief medium, easy to transport and promotes thought and criticism. The pictures must be arranged in proper sequence based on the talk to be given.

Hence, the correct option is (D).

30. The Central Advisory Board of Physical Education and Recreation was established in the year 1954.

In 1954, Central Advisory Board of Physical Education and Recreation was established by the Government of India to advise the Government on the coordination of all programmes and activities in the field of physical education and Recreation in the country. its aim was to make every child physically, mentally and constitutionally fit.

Hence, the correct option is (D).

31. Symposium method of group teaching there is no discussion by experts.

Symposium is a series of speeches on a selected subject. Each expert presents one aspect of the subject briefly. There is no discussion among the experts unlike panel discussion. In the end, the audience may raise questions. The chairman makes a comprehensive summary at the end of the entire session.

Hence, the correct option is (B).

32. Formal communication is a type of communication that uses an accepted form, rule, or custom.

Formal communication refers to the flow of official information through proper, predefined channels and routes. Employees are bound to follow formal communication channels while performing their duties. Formal communication is considered effective as it is a timely and systematic flow of communication.

Hence, the correct option is (A).

33. Lecture is a didactic methods of health communication. Lectures are the most popular method of health teaching. In this, communication is mostly one-way, i.e., the people are only passive listeners; there is no active participation on their part in learning. The impressive and effective lecture is depends upon the personality and reputation of the speaker.

Hence, the correct option is (D).

34. A Two–way communication is a type of communication in which receiver has the chance of asking questions and clearing doubts.

Two-way communication involves feedback from the receiver to the sender. This allows the sender to know the message was received accurately by the receiver. Communication is also negotiated which means that the sender and receiver listen to each other, the messages then gathers information to respond.

Hence, the correct option is (B).

35. Face-to-face communication takes place between two or three people or in small groups such as a family.

Face-to-face communication refers to the interaction between two or three people where everyone is in direct contact with each other. It is also known as personal communication because people through this type of communication process can send and receive key information one-on-one.

Hence, the correct option is (A).

36. Proteins are made up of hundreds or thousands of smaller units called amino acids, which are attached to one another in long chains. There are 20 different types of amino acids that can be combined to make a protein.

Hence, the correct option is (B).

37. Protein is one of four nutrients that provide calories. Protein provides 4 calories per gram. A calorie is a unit used to measure the energy-producing value of food. Technically, a calorie is defined as the amount of heat required to raise the temperature of one gram of water by one degree centigrade.

Hence, the correct option is (A).

38. Deficiency disease occurs due to a lack of nutrients in food for a long time. The deficiency of one or more nutrients can cause diseases or disorders in the body.

For example, if a person does not get enough protein in his diet for a long time, he is likely to have stunted growth, facial swelling, discoloration of hair, skin diseases, and diarrhea. If the diet lacks both carbohydrates and protein for a long period of time, growth can stop completely. Such a person becomes very thin and so weak that he cannot even move.

Hence, the correct option is (A).

39. Most abundant Protein is found in Cytoplasm. Cytoplasm consists of a meshlike structure because of the presence of actin filaments, microtubules, and intermediate filaments. These filaments, together with actin- and tubulin-binding proteins and several enzymes, constitute the cytoplasm and maintain the cell structure.

Hence, the correct option is (A).

40. Pepsin is a digestive enzyme that works in the stomach to break down the food. Pepsin is a stomach enzyme that serves to digest proteins found in ingested food. Gastric chief cells secrete pepsin as an inactive zymogen called pepsinogen. Parietal cells within the stomach lining secrete hydrochloric acid that lowers the pH of the stomach. A low pH (1.5 to 2) activates pepsin.

Hence, the correct option is (B).

41. Lactase enzymes break down sugar lactose found in milk. Lactose is a sugar found in milk and milk products. Lactose intolerance happens when your small intestine does not make enough of a digestive enzyme called lactase. Lactase breaks down the lactose in food so your body can absorb it.

Hence, the correct option is (C).

42. Red, hot or dry skin is not a symptom of a heart attack. It may be the symptons of any allergic conditions.

symptoms of heart attack:

- Chest pain or discomfort
- Feeling weak, light-headed, or faint
- Pain or discomfort in the jaw, neck, or back
- Pain or discomfort in one or both arms or shoulders
- Shortness of breath

Hence, the correct option is (B).

43. Rescue breathing should be given when there is Unconscious, not breathing, but has a pulse.

If the person is not breathing but has a pulse, give 1 rescue breath every 5 to 6 seconds or about 10 to 12 breaths per minute. If the person is not breathing and has no pulse and you are not trained in CPR, give hands-only chest compression CPR without rescue breaths.

Hence, the correct option is (D).

44. Signals of an allergic reaction to a bee sting are Feeling of tightness in the chest and throat, Swelling of the face neck and tongue, and Rash, dizziness, or confusion.

Anaphylactic reaction to a bee sting can start within two hours of the incident and rapidly progress. Hives will develop on the face and body, followed by other symptoms, such as headache, dizziness, fainting, nausea, vomiting, and difficulty breathing and swallowing.

Hence, the correct option is (D).

45. When caring for a student who is allergic to bees and has just been stung, you should apply a cold pack.

Also apply hydrocortisone cream or calamine lotion to ease redness, itching or swelling. Avoid scratching the sting area. This will worsen itching and swelling and increase your risk of infection.

Hence, the correct option is (C).

46. Soft tissue wounds should be cared by Ice and elevation, and apply direct pressure on the area to cut down on bleeding under skin. Treatment involves healing the inflamed area with rest, compression, elevation, and anti-inflammatory medicine. Ice may be used in the acute phase of injury. Stretching and strengthening exercises can gradually be added to help avoid further injury.

A soft tissue injury is the damage of muscles, ligaments and tendons throughout the body. Common soft tissue injuries usually occur from a sprain, strain, a one off blow resulting in a contusion or overuse of a particular part of the body.

Hence, the correct option is (D).

47. Internal bleeding can be caused by Injury, Illness, and Medication. The tearing of the muscle can also damage small blood vessels, causing local bleeding, or bruising, and pain caused by irritation of the nerve endings in the area.

Internal bleeding in the gastrointestinal tract may be caused as a side effect of medications (most often from nonsteroidal anti-inflammatory drugs such as ibuprofen and aspirin) and alcohol.

Hence, the correct option is (D).

48. A first aid responder should move a victim when it would make it easier to administer first aid and the victim is in a dangerous position.

The two situations would allow us to move a victim, these could include:

- When they are faced with immediate danger, such as an unsafe accident scene or traffic hazards, fire, lack of oxygen, risk of explosion, or a collapsing structure.
- When we have to get to another person who may have more serious injuries.

Hence, the correct option is (D).

49. Both mitochondria and chloroplast are similar to a prokaryotic cell.

Prokaryotic cells are single-celled microorganisms that are the earliest known on Earth. Prokaryotes include bacteria and archaea.

A prokaryotic cell has a membrane and hence, all reactions take place within the cytoplasm. They can be free-living or parasitic.

Hence, the correct option is (C).

50. The cerebellum does not controls movements, speech, sight, smell, taste, hearing, intelligence etc.

- The activities like walking in a straight line, riding a bicycle, picking up a pencil are possible due to a part of the hindbrain called the cerebellum.
- It is responsible for the precision of voluntary actions and maintaining the posture and balance of the body.
- It is a part of the hind brain.

Hence, the correct option is (B).

51. The medulla is the lowest part of the brain and the lowest portion of the brainstem.

The medulla is connected by the pons to the midbrain and is continuous posteriorly with the spinal cord.

The medulla plays a critical role in transmitting signals between the spinal cord and the higher parts of the brain and in controlling autonomic activities, such as heartbeat and respiration.

Hence, the correct option is (A).

52. The cerebrum is the largest part of the human brain. The cerebrum is the main part of the brain in humans and other vertebrates.

It is located in the upper part of the cranial cavity, which is a space inside the top of the skull.

Hence, the correct option is (C).

53. Nervous System: The nervous system of the human body is divided into three parts:

1. **Central Nervous System:** It is a part of the nervous system which keeps control of the whole body and on the nervous system itself. It is made up of two parts - Brain and Spinal Cord.
2. **Peripheral Nervous System:** It is made up of the nerves arising from the brain and spinal cord called cranial and spinal nerves respectively.
3. **Autonomic Nervous System:** It is made up of some brain nerves and some spinal cord nerves.

Hence, the correct option is (D).

54. The spinal cord is protected by a flexible chain of bones. The bones house a thick bundle of nerves that stimulate reflex reactions.

The nervous system monitors and regulates body functions and behavior, and consists of two parts:

- **The central nervous system (CNS)** comprises the brain and spinal cord.
- **The peripheral nervous system (PNS)** comprises the branching peripheral nerves.

Nervous tissue consists of various types of nerve cells all of which have an axon.

Muscle tissue is composed of cells that have the special ability to shorten or contract to produce body parts movement.

Epithelial tissues are widespread throughout the body. They form the covering of all body surfaces, line body cavities and hollow organs, and are the major tissue in glands. Opposite the free surface, the cells are attached to underlying connective tissue by a non-cellular basement membrane.

Connective tissue is group of tissues in the body that maintain the form of the body and its organs and provide cohesion and internal support.

Hence, the correct option is (A).

55. Ligaments are the connective tissue that connects two bones to each other.

- Ligaments are a short band of tough flexible connective tissues which connect two bones.
- Ligaments connect bones to other bones.
- Tendons are made up of collagen.
- Tendons connect bones to muscles.
- There are 11 major organ systems in humans.
- Cartilage is an important structural component of the body. It is a firm tissue but is softer and much more flexible than bone.

Hence, the correct option is (D).

56. Ideally, nursing case management planning identifies goals that are realistic, measurable, and specific.

Realistic means able to see things as they really are and to deal with them in a practical way.

Measurable to be described in specific terms (as of size, amount, duration, or mass) usually expressed as a quantity Science is the study of facts that is, things that are measurable, testable, repeatable, verifiable.

Specific means clear and exactly presented or stated, precise or exact. Relating to a particular person, situation.

Hence, the correct option is (D).

57. Neuropsychiatrist at a rehabilitation facility addresses the cognitive, behavioral, and psychological problems that result following a patient's traumatic brain injury.

Neuropsychiatry is the assessment and treatment of patients with psychiatric illnesses or symptoms associated with brain abnormalities.

Hence, the correct option is (B).

58. Pediatrics also spelled pediatrics or pediatrics is the branch of medicine that includes the medical care of infants, children, adolescents, and young adults.

Recommendations of Nursing Staffing Norms by staff inspection unit:

- **Normal Wards:** 1 Staff Nurse/Nursing Sister for every 6 beds.
- **Special Wards:** 1 Staff Nurse/Nursing Sister for every 4 beds (1 : 4). That is,

1. Pediatrics
2. Burns/Burns Plastic
3. Neuro Surgery

4. Cardiac Thoracic
5. Neuro Medicine
6. Nursing Home
7. Tetanus
8. Spinal Injury
9. Emergency Wards attached to casual

Hence, the correct option is (C).

59. Veracity ethical principle is grounded in truth with patients. Nurses must not withhold the whole truth from clients even when it may lead to patient distress. For example, if a patient was starting chemotherapy and asked about the side effects, a nurse practicing veracity would be honest about the side effects they could expect with chemotherapy.

Hence, the correct option is (D).

60. When developing a program offering for patients who are newly diagnosed with diabetes, the nursing case manager demonstrates an understanding of learning styles by utilizing a variety of educational materials. Learning how to control your diabetes will save money and time, and help you have fewer emergency and hospital visits. Knowing how and when to take your medication, how to monitor your blood sugar (glucose), and how to take care of yourself, helps you manage your diabetes better.

Hence, the correct option is (D).

61. Case Management Society of America's Standards of Practice guides the nursing case manager's practice.

The basic concept of case management involves the timely coordination of quality services to address a client's specific needs in a cost-effective manner in order to promote positive outcomes. This can occur in a single health care setting or during the client's tran- sitions of care throughout the care continuum.

Hence, the correct option is (B).

62. The nursing case manager, who refers a 67-year-old patient to a skilled nursing facility for rehabilitative care, knows that it will be billed under the Medicare Part A component of Medicare.

Medicare Part A is hospital insurance. Part A generally covers inpatient hospital stays, skilled nursing care, hospice care, and limited home health-care services. We typically pay a deductible and coinsurance and/or copayments.

Hence, the correct option is (A).

63. Medication errors, orders for unnecessary tests, and omission of standard tests or procedures are classified as Practitioner type of variance.

A health care practitioner, licensed health care practitioner, licensed practitioner, or practitioner, as used in this Guidebook, is defined as an individual who is licensed or otherwise authorized by a state to provide health care services.

Hence, the correct option is (D).

64. Assessment of neurologicaldeficits task that should not be delegated to a non-professional employee.

A neurologic deficit refers to abnormal function of a body area. This altered function is due to injury of the brain, spinal cord, muscles, or nerves. Examples includes abnormal reflexes and inability to speak.

Hence, the correct option is (D).

65. A male patient has a soft wrist-safety device. Cool, pale fingers assessment finding the nurse should consider abnormal.

A safety device on the wrist may impair circulation and restrict blood supply to body tissues. Therefore, the nurse should assess the patient for signs of impaired circulation, such as cool, pale fingers. A palpable radial or lunar pulse and pink nail beds are normal findings.

Hence, the correct option is (C).

66. The nurse ensures to take another bottle of solution.

Fat emulsions are used as dietary supplements for patients who are unable to get enough fat in their diet, usually because of certain illnesses or recent surgery. The nurse should examine the bottle of fat emulsion for separation of emulsion into layers or fat globules or the accumulation of froth. The nurse should not hang a fat emulsion if any of these are observed and should return the solution to the pharmacy.

Hence, the correct option is (A).

67. A female patient with a terminal illness is in denial. Indicators of denial include shock dismay.

Shock and dismay are early signs of denial-the first stage of grief. Denial is a common defense mechanism used to protect oneself from the hardship of considering an upsetting reality. Kubler-Ross noted that after the initial shock of receiving a terminal diagnosis, patients would often reject the reality of the new information. The other options are associated with depression—a later stage of grief.

Hence, the correct option is (A).

68. The nurse in charge is transferring a patient from the bed to a chair. The nurse helps the patient dangle the legs during his transfer.

After placing the patient in High Fowler's position and moving the patient to the side of the bed, the nurse helps the patient sit on the edge of the bed and dangle the legs; the nurse then faces the patient and places the chair next to and facing the head of the bed.

Hence, the correct option is (B).

69. A clinical nurse specialist is a nurse who has completed a master's degree in the prescribed clinical area and is a registered professional nurse.

A clinical nurse specialist (CNS) is a graduate-level registered nurse who is certified in a specialty of choice. Obtaining specialty certification demonstrates an advanced level of knowledge as well as advanced clinical skills in a niche area of nursing. There are differences between a nurse practitioner (NP) and CNS.

Hence, the correct option is (D).

70. Before administering the evening dose of prescribed medication, the nurse on the evening shift finds an unlabeled, filled syringe in the patient's medication drawer. The nurse in charge should discard the syringe to avoid a medication error.

As a safety precaution, the nurse should discard an unlabeled syringe that contains the medication. The other options are considered unsafe because they promote error.

Hence, the correct option is (A).

71. When administering drug therapy to a male geriatric patient, the nurse must stay especially alert for adverse effects. Aging-related physiological changes make geriatric patients have adverse drug effects.

Aging-related physiological changes account for the increased frequency of adverse drug reactions in geriatric patients. ADEs are estimated to be indicated in 5% to 28% of acute geriatric medical admissions. Preventable ADEs is among one the serious consequences of inappropriate medication use in older adults.

Hence, the correct option is (B).

72. A female patient is being discharged after cataract surgery. After providing medication teaching, the nurse asks the patient to repeat the instructions. The nurse is performing the educator role.

When teaching a patient about medications before discharge, the nurse is acting as an educator. They provide educational leadership to patients and care providers to enhance specialized patient care within established healthcare settings. Assists patients and caregivers with educational needs, problem resolution, and health management across the continuum of care.

Hence, the correct option is (B).

73. A female patient exhibits signs of heightened anxiety. "Let's talk about what's bothering you." response by the nurse is most likely to reduce the patient's anxiety.

Anxiety may result from feelings of helplessness, isolation, or insecurity. This response helps reduce anxiety by encouraging the patient to express feelings. The nurse should be supportive and develop goals together with the patient to give the patient some control over an anxiety-inducing situation. Because the other options ignore the patient's feelings and block communication, they would not reduce anxiety.

Hence, the correct option is (D).

74. The APGAR score is a method to quickly summarize the health of newborn children against infant mortality.
APGAR stands for Appearance, Pulse, Grimace, Activity, and Respiration. Medical teams use this scoring system to make sure babies are healthy right after birth.

Thus, temperature is not considered in APGAR score.

Hence, the correct option is (D).

75. "Bronze baby" syndrome is a rare complication of phototherapy for neonatal jaundice occurring due to modified liver function, particularly cholestasis, of various origins. This is a case which occurred in a premature infant who developed a grey-brown coloration during phototherapy. The infant had haemolytic jaundice due to Rhesus incompatibility complicated by cholestasis of thick bile fluid.

When our liver is damaged, we may develop liver failure, also known as hepatic failure.

Hence, the correct option is (B).

76. A tonsillectomy was once a common procedure to treat infection and inflammation of the tonsils (tonsillitis). So, it is not recommended in children below 4 years of age because tonsils are a part of the immune system. Because of their location at the throat and palate, they can stop germs entering the body through the mouth or the nose.

Hence, the correct option is (C).

77. Depressed anterior fontanelle is an expected assessment finding in an 8 month old infant with severe diarrhoea. Dehydration is the primary cause of a sunken fontanel. Dehydration occurs when an infant does not have sufficient fluid in their body to maintain normal functioning. A noticeably sunken fontanelle is a sign that the infant does not have enough fluid in its body.

Hence, the correct option is (C).

78. Vastus lateralis is the best site to administer an intramuscular injection to a four month old infant.

Intramuscular (IM) injections in neonates may be required to administer medications or vaccines. The anterolateral thigh is the preferred site for IM injection in infants under 12 months of age. Medications are injected into the bulkiest part of the vastus lateralis thigh muscle, which is the junction of the upper and middle thirds of this muscle.

Hence, the correct option is (D).

79. The Ortolani maneuver identifies a dislocated hip that can be reduced. The infant is positioned in the same manner as for the Barlow maneuver, in a supine position with the hip flexed to 90°.

The Barlow maneuver is a test used to identify an unstable hip that can be passively dislocated. The infant is placed in a supine position with the hip flexed to 90° and in neutral rotation.

Thus, we can conclude that, Ortolani's maneuver is a test or sign should a nurse look for in a 3 week old infant with developmental dysplasia of the hip.

Hence, the correct option is (C).

80. A child who is admitted to the hospital with persistent vomiting should be monitored closely for metabolic alkalosis. It is a metabolic condition in which the pH of tissue is elevated beyond the normal range (7.35 – 7.45). Metabolic alkalosis is a condition that occurs when our blood becomes overly alkaline.

Hence, the correct option is (C).

81. According to given conditions,

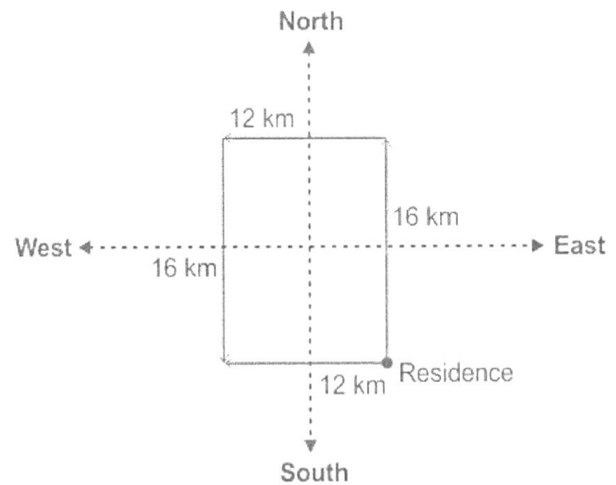

Clearly, Evan is 12 km far from his residence.

Hence, the correct option is (B).

82. Number of Red balls $= 4$

Number of Blue balls $= 6$

Number of Pink balls $= 8$

Total number of balls $= 4 + 6 + 8 = 18$

Required probability $= \frac{4}{18} \times \frac{11}{20} + \frac{6}{18} \times \frac{11}{20}$

$= \frac{11}{20}\left[\frac{4}{18} + \frac{6}{18}\right]$

$= \frac{11}{20} \times \frac{10}{18}$

$= \frac{11}{36}$

Hence, the correct option is (D).

83. Let the numbers be $8x, 7x$ and $5x$.

According to question,

$$\frac{(8x+7x+5x)}{3} = 40$$

$$\Rightarrow 20x = 120$$

$$\Rightarrow x = 6$$

Largest number $= 8x = 48$

Hence, the correct option is (C).

84. For a triangle the sum of any two sides should be greater than the third side.

Using this rule,

(1) 4.5

⇒ if third side is 4.5 cm, then 6.5 + 4.5 > 10 correct. But is 4.5 the smallest possible value.

Let's check more.

(2) 2.8

⇒ 2.8 + 6.5 = 9.3 < 10. Not a triangle

(3) 3.5

⇒ 6.5 + 3.5 = 10 = 10. Not possible

(4) 4

⇒ 4 + 6.5 = 10.5 >10. Correct and since 4 < 4.5 this is the smallest possible number among the options and hence it is the right answer.

Hence, the correct option is (D).

85. Let the number of eggs be x.

Cost of 3 eggs = Rs. 5

Cost of 1 egg = $\frac{5}{3} \times x$

So, CP = $\frac{5}{3} \times x$

Eggs sold = 5

Price at which eggs are sold = Rs. 12

So, SP = $\frac{12}{5x}$

Profit = SP - CP

$$143 = \frac{12}{5x} - \frac{5}{3x}$$

(For Solving, take the LCM of 3 and 5 and solve through it)

x = 195

Thus, he purchased 195 eggs.

Hence, the correct option is (D).

86. Suppose his original speed = x km/h

∴ Speed after increase = (x + 15) km/h

According to problem,

⇒ x × 10 = (x + 15) × 8

⇒ 10x = 8x + 120

⇒ x = 60

∴ His new speed = (60 + 15) = 75 km/h

∴ Time required to cover 375 km = $\frac{375}{75}$=5 hours

Hence, the correct option is (D).

87. Given,

30th January 2003= Thursday

∴ 6th, 13th, 20th and 27th February = Thursday

∴ 28th February = Friday

∴ 1st March = Saturday

∴ 2nd March = Sunday

Hence, the correct option is (A).

88. Given,

$H = 7$

Angle $= 0°$

As we know that, the angle between the hour hand and minutes hand.

$$\theta = \left(30\,H - 11\frac{M}{2}\right)$$

When minute and hour hands coincide, then $\theta = 0$

$\Rightarrow 0 = 30 \times 7 - 11\frac{M}{2}$

$\Rightarrow 0 = 210 - 11\frac{M}{2}$

$\Rightarrow 210 = 11\frac{M}{2}$

$\Rightarrow 420 = 11M$

$\Rightarrow M = \frac{420}{11}$

$\Rightarrow M = 38\frac{2}{11}$ minutes

Hence, the correct option is (C).

89. Given series:

Left Side M 1 E & D 2 G 9 $ F @ 4 N Z W © 8 C Y A * 6 Right Side.

Here the group is formed in which second element is to the second next of the first element and the third element is third next to the second.

Therefore, YA6 does not belong to the group.

Hence, the correct option is (D).

90. Since, the son of the only brother of the lady is the nephew of the lady, Therefore, the wife of the man is the niece of the lady. Hence, the lady is the sister of the father-in-law of the man.

Hence, the correct option is (C).

91. Mirzapur division is considered as the hub of the world's finest carpet industries.

Mirzapur Division: The hub of the world's finest carpet Industries, a very popular tourist destination for its natural beauties and one of the fastest-growing regions of Uttar Pradesh. It consists of vindhyachal shaktipeeth.

Hence, the correct option is (D).

92. In India, political parties are given 'recognition' by Election Commission.

- The Election Commission of India is an autonomous constitutional authority responsible for administering Union and State election processes in India.
- The body administers elections to the Lok Sabha, Rajya Sabha, and State Legislative Assemblies in India, and the offices of the President and Vice President in the country.
- Part XV of the Indian constitution deals with elections and establishes a commission for these matters.

Hence, the correct option is (C).

93. The description of the administration of Patliputra is available in the book "Indica" by Megasthenes, an ambassador to Chandra Gupta Maurya in Patliputra by Greek ruler Seleucus Nicator I.

Megasthenese described that Pataliputra city was administered by a city council comprising 30 members and these 30 members were divided into a board of 5 members each.

Hence, the correct option is (A).

94. Ural Mountain is not a block mountain.

Block mountains are the type of mountains in which the middle part of the mountain is lower and the parts on both sides are higher. The middle part is known as the rift valley. Black Forest (Germany), Salt Range (Pakistan), Vindhya and Satpura (India) are examples of block mountains.

The Ural is a fold mountain. Fold mountains are formed because of folds in the rocks due to the internal movements of the earth.

Hence, the correct option is (D).

95. Badminton player PV Sindhu has won the Swiss Open women's singles title 2022 by defeating Busanan Ongbamrungfa. After this win, PV Sindhu notched up her second women's singles title of the season. Sindhu had won her first title of 2022 in the Syed Modi International Super 300 in Lucknow.

Hence, the correct option is (C).

96. Microsoft introduced an operating system named Windows on November 20, 1985. It is a graphical operating system shell for MS-DOS in response to the growing interest in graphical user interfaces (GUIs). Windows is the most popular desktop operating system in the world, with 75% market share as of April 2022, according to StatCounter.

Hence, the correct option is (C).

97. A web browser, or simply "browser," is an program used to access and view websites. Web browser is a program used by web clients to view the web pages.

Protocol: A protocol is a set of rules for formatting and processing data.

Web server: A web server is a computer that runs websites.

Search engine: A search engine is a web-based tool that enables users to locate information on the World Wide Web.

Hence, the correct option is (A).

98. Search engine is used to search other website by typing a keyword. Nowadays, there are billions of websites online, there is a lot of information on the Internet. Search engines make this information easier to find. There are many different search engines we can use, but some of the most popular include Google, Yahoo!, and Bing.

Hence, the correct option is (A).

99. Hard disk can store a large amount of data.

- The hard disk is a spindle of magnetic disks, called platters.
- The hard disk is used to record and store information.
- Inside the hard disk, the data is stored magnetically and information is recorded even after the computer is shut down.
- This is an important difference between the hard disk and RAM, or memory, it is reset when the computer's power is turned off.
- The hard disk is housed inside the hard drive which is used to read and write data to the disk.
- The hard drive sends information to and fro between the CPU and the disk.

Hence, the correct option is (B).

100. A worm is a type of virus that spreads through your computer by creating duplicates of itself on other drives, systems, and networks. Computer worms replicate functional copies of themselves and can cause the same type of damage. In contrast to viruses, which require the spreading of an infected host file, worms are standalone software and do not require a host program or human help to propagate (Self-Replicate).

Hence, the correct option is (D).

Mock Test 05

Discipline

Q.1 Minimally invasive surgery is also known as:

A. Constructive surgery
B. Keyhole surgery
C. Ablative surgery
D. Palliative surgery

Q.2 Antiembolic stockings can help to reduce:

A. Thromboembolism **B.** Pain
C. Pressure sores **D.** Contractures

Q.3 Segmentectomy refers to:

A. A type of chemotherapy
B. Concerns the spleen
C. Involves removal of part of one of the lobes of the lung
D. Involves bilateral pneumonectomy

Q.4 The term tachypnoea refers to:

A. Cessation of breathing
B. Cheyne–Stokes breathing
C. A reduction in respiratory rate
D. An increase in respiratory rate

Q.5 Most coronary artery bypass grafts are performed on:

A. Women aged 60 years and over
B. Men with lung cancer
C. Women with lung cancer
D. Men who are aged 60 years and over

Q.6 Varicose veins are more prevalent:

A. In women **B.** In men
C. In white men **D.** In older people

Q.7 The circle of Willis is located:

A. At the base of the brain
B. In the spinal column
C. Within the dura mater
D. None of these

Q.8 What are the causes of thoracic aortic aneurysms?

A. Atherosclerosis
B. Genetic conditions
C. Blood vessel inflammation
D. All of the above

Q.9 In bariatric surgery, gastric stimulation involves:

A. External abdominal massage
B. The insertion of an inflatable gastric balloon
C. The insertion of a pacemaker device
D. The application of TENS

Q.10 In___________method of group teaching, may fail to change the health practice of people.

A. Lecture **B.** Group discussion
C. Symposium **D.** Role play

Q.11 ________are generally more effective in changing human behaviour during health education programme.

A. Group discussions **B.** Mass media
C. Work shops **D.** None of these

Q.12 Health exhibitions are conducted in connection with_________

A. Fairs **B.** Festivals
C. Mass campaigns **D.** All of these

Q.13 Discussion group is an example of________pattern of communication.

A. Wheel **B.** Chain
C. All-channel **D.** None of these

Q.14 Which of the following is a general term used to refer to the application of digital information and communication technology to health care?

A. Digi-health **B.** E-health
C. I-health **D.** Tech-health

Q.15 Which of the following refers to a programme that aims to enable patients to make better use of information and communication technology for health and health care?

A. Patient informatics **B.** ICT health
C. Health-tech **D.** None of these

Q.16 What is effective communication?

A. The process of exchanging ideas, thoughts, opinions, knowledge, and data so that the message is received and understood with clarity and purpose by writing.
B. A style of speaking that is used professionally to be understood by the majority of people and expressed in a way that is considered acceptable and respectful by the majority.
C. The process of exchanging ideas, thoughts, opinions, knowledge, and data so that the message is received and understood with clarity and purpose.
D. Both (A) and (B)

Q.17 Which of the following is not true about generational differences in the workplace?

A. It is highly probable that a workplace could have up to 4 different generations working closely together.
B. Generational differences can result in frequent misunderstandings and misconceptions
C. Recognizing the variation in generational perspective is a tool to improve communication
D. Although different generations vary in age, they all approach their job in the same manner

Q.18 A pediatric patient who is ventilator-dependent and has a gastrostomy button is scheduled to be discharged to home with visits from a home health nurse. Prior to discharge, the nursing case manager's most critical action is to:

A. Assess the patient's long-term home care needs.
B. Procure the required home medical equipment.
C. Secure funding sources for home health care.
D. Verify that the patient is being discharged to a safe environment.

Q.19 To avoid hospital readmission, a patient requires services at a specialty clinic. Because the services are not covered under the patient's healthcare plan, the nursing case manager intercedes with the patient's insurance company. In this situation, the nurse is acting in the role of:

A. Broker **B.** Consultant
C. Negotiator **D.** Provider

Q.20 The nursing case manager meets with a 15-year-old patient with type 1 diabetes, who has a recent A1C of 8%. The patient reports smoking two to three cigarettes per day denies using alcohol, and states, "I hate having diabetes; I just want to be like my friends." Which referral will benefit this patient's immediate needs?

A. A smoking cessation group for adolescents.
B. A support group for adolescents with diabetes.
C. An education session about insulin, aimed at adolescents.
D. Family counseling

Q.21 What makes you think is the most effective leadership style that can be used during emergency situations?

A. Democratic **B.** Laissez-faire
C. Autocratic **D.** Supportive

Q.22 A learning objective that is based on the cognitive domain includes asking participants to:

A. Demonstrate drawing blood from acentral line catheter
B. Explain how they feel about caringfor patients with terminal illness
C. Identify two risk factors forheart disease
D. Remove a colostomy pouchcorrectly.

Q.23 Which one of the following is not the aim of Nursing Practice?

A. Promote Health **B.** Prevent Illness
C. Disease Process **D.** Restore Health

Q.24 There are _______ periods of Nursing History.

A. 3 **B.** 5 **C.** 4 **D.** 6

Q.25 Research on nurse retention has indicated that many nurses leave nursing after what period of time?

A. Before the end of the first year
B. 5 years or less
C. 7 years or less
D. 10 years

Q.26 You have been identified as a Millennial Generation nurse. You are working with a team of three LVNs, two of whom are Baby Boomers and one is a Generation X nurse. You also are working with two CNAs both of who are from the Baby Boomers Generation. What should you focus on when working with your team?

A. Communication and teamwork among the staff of all generations is critical in assuring a positive work milieu that can affect safe patient care and good working relationships
B. All of the staff members will resent you because you are much younger and more educated than any of them
C. Your reputation is dependent on whether the team members acknowledge your authority and provide you with respect even if you are the youngest person on the team
D. Providing the LVNs with additional responsibilities and have then supervise the CNAs in whatever manner they choose

Q.27 A scrub nurse in the operating room has which responsibility?

A. Positioning the patient
B. Assisting with gowning and gloving
C. Handling surgical instruments to the surgeon
D. Applying surgical drapes

Q.28 A patient is in the bathroom when the nurse enters to give prescribed medication. What should the nurse in charge do?

A. Leave the medication at the patient's bedside.
B. Tell the patient to be sure to take the medication. And then leave it at the bedside.
C. Return shortly to the patient's room and remain there until the patient takes the medication.
D. Wait for the patient to return to bed, and then leave the medication at the bedside.

Q.29 To evaluate a patient for hypoxia, the physician is most likely to order a nurse which laboratory test?

A. Red blood cell count
B. Sputum culture
C. Total hemoglobin
D. Arterial blood gas (ABG) analysis

Q.30 A male patient is to be discharged with a prescription for an analgesic that is a controlled substance. During discharge teaching, the nurse should explain that the patient must fill this prescription how soon after the date on which it was written?

A. Within 1 month **B.** Within 3 months
C. Within 6 months **D.** Within 12 months

Q.31 Which human element considered by the nurse in charge during assessment can affect drug administration?

A. The patient's ability to recover
B. The patient's occupational hazards
C. The patient's socioeconomic status
D. The patient's cognitive abilities

Q.32 An employer establishes a physical exercise area in the workplace and encourages all employees to use it. This is an example of which level of health promotion?

A. Primary prevention
B. Secondary prevention
C. Tertiary prevention
D. Passive prevention

Q.33 When helping a person through grief work, the nurse knows:

A. Coping mechanisms that were effective in the past are often disregarded in response to the pain of a loss
B. A person's perception of a loss has little to do with the grieving process
C. The sequencing of stages of grief may occur in order, they may be skipped, or they may recur
D. Most clients want to be left alone

Q.34 Nurse Mackey is monitoring a patient for adverse reactions during barbiturate therapy. What is the major disadvantage of barbiturate use?

A. Prolonged half-life
B. Poor absorption
C. Potential for drug dependence
D. Potential for hepatotoxicity

Q.35 Which nursing action is essential when providing continuous enteral feeding?

A. Elevating the head of the bed
B. Positioning the patient on the left side
C. Attach the feeding bag to the current tubing
D. Cold the formula before administering

Q.36 The elements present in the proteins are:

A. Carbon, hydrogen, nitrogen, and oxygen
B. Carbon, hydrogen, and oxygen
C. Hydrogen, nitrogen, and oxygen
D. Carbon and hydrogen

Q.37 Which vitamin has a metallic component?

A. Vitamin E **B.** Vitamin A
C. Vitamin C **D.** Vitamin B12

Q.38 Which of the following proteins increases the rate of chemical reaction in the body?

A. Enzymes **B.** Antibody
C. Structural proteins **D.** Transport proteins

Q.39 Which protein helps to protect from infection, bacteria, virus, illness, and diseases in the body?

A. Antibodies **B.** Enzymes
C. Storage proteins **D.** Transport proteins

Q.40 Which proteins are called transport proteins?

A. Ovalbumin **B.** Hemoglobin
C. Keratin **D.** Enzymes

Q.41 Which protein stores the iron in the transport protein?

A. Ferritin **B.** Keratins
C. Elastin **D.** None of these

Q.42 Proteins are synthesized in the body through a process called:

A. Translation **B.** Transcription
C. Transport **D.** None of these

Q.43 Food hygiene is called:

A. Cleaning of food
B. Improvement of sanitation
C. Making food clean chain
D. All of the above

Q.44 How much B.M.I. or Body mass index score for obesity?

A. 20 to 25 **B.** More than 15
C. More than 30 **D.** Less than 18

Q.45 Meditation is an example of pain management by?

A. NSAIDs
B. Pharmacological measures
C. Opioids
D. Non-pharmacological measures

Q.46 A victim of a car accident has just vomited and now appears to be coughing up blood. He is breathing very quickly and his pulse is weak and fast. What is most likely wrong?

A. He is having a seizure.
B. He has internal bleeding.
C. He is having a heart attack.
D. He is having a diabetic emergency.

Q.47 Which of the following should be done for a person experiencing a heat-related illness?

A. Keep the victim warm
B. Force the victim to drink fluids
C. Apply cool wet cloths
D. Place the victim in warm water

Q.48 A boy is shot with an arrow through the chest and out the back, what would be the best course of action?

A. Remove the arrow and apply sterile gauze to the wound
B. Do not remove the arrow, place several dressing around the arrow to keep it from moving, bandage the dressings in place around the arrow
C. Do not remove the arrow; break off the part out the back, bandage with dressing around the arrow to hold it in place
D. Remove the arrow, wash the area, and bandage with sterile gauze

Q.49 A boy with frostbite on his feet, what should you do?

A. Rub his feet vigorously until feeling and color return
B. Apply hot moist towels to feet and massage gently
C. Soak feet in warm water, not more than 105 degrees, bandage with a dry sterile dressing
D. Soak feet in warm water not more than 90 degrees; rub feet gently until feeling and color return, then wrap with a sterile dressing

Q.50 You suspect that a person has been poisoned. She is conscious. Your first call should be to:

A. The Poison Control Center or your local emergency phone number
B. The victim's physician
C. The hospital emergency department
D. The local pharmacy

Q.51 Shock is a condition where:

A. The respiratory system fails to deliver air to the lungs.
B. The cardiovascular system fails to deliver blood to the heart.

C. The circulatory system fails to deliver blood to all parts of the body.
D. All of the above

Q.52 Snakebites can be very serious. When caring for a snakebite victim, which should you not do?
A. Wash wounds
B. Apply ice
C. Keep bitten part still and below the heart
D. Get professional medical care within 30 minutes

Q.53 What is the chromosome Number of pairs in a human ovum?
A. 47 **B.** 23
C. 48 **D.** None of these

Q.54 In the menstrual cycle, lowering of which hormone causes menstruation?
A. Progesterone
B. Thyroxine
C. Estrogen
D. Follicle stimulating hormone

Q.55 Where does the process of fertilization take place in the human body?
A. Uterus **B.** Fallopian tube
C. Ovary **D.** Vagina

Q.56 The structural and functional unit of lung is:
A. Alveoli **B.** Trachea
C. Bronchiole **D.** Bronchus

Q.57 Sperm are temporarily kept in ________.
A. Epididymis **B.** Vas-deferens
C. Bladder **D.** Vas Aference

Q.58 The muscular tube through which the stored urine is passed out of the body is called:
A. Kidney **B.** Ureter
C. Urinary bladder **D.** Urethra

Q.59 The hormones of the endocrine glands are released into the _______.
A. Blood **B.** Spinal fluid
C. Arteries of the heart **D.** Ducts

Q.60 What is the primary function of the eccrine glands?
A. To produce body hair
B. To produce colour of the skin
C. To produce sweat
D. To produce growth hormones

Q.61 Which of the following is a possible complication of amniocentesis?
A. Miscarriage **B.** RH sensitization
C. Needle injury **D.** All of these

Q.62 A woman who is 20 weeks pregnant calls the clinic because she is experiencing pink-tinged discharge for the first time. The nurse should advise the patient to ________.
A. Call back if she experiences an increase in pelvic pressure
B. Seek medical attention immediately
C. Decrease her activity level
D. Call back if the symptoms have not subsided in 24 hours

Q.63 While monitoring a laboring patient, the nurse notices that the fetal heart rate at baseline varies from 110-145 beats per minute. The nurse's first action would be which of the following?
A. Turn the mother on her left side
B. Decrease IV fluids
C. No action is required
D. Have the mother bear down

Q.64 Which of the following is not a risk factor for gestational diabetes?
A. Obesity
B. Previous macrosomic infant
C. Poor diet
D. Previous stillbirth

Q.65 Kegel exercise used after delivery to:
A. Strengthening urinary muscles and rectal muscles.
B. Strengthening of abdominal muscles
C. Subinvolution
D. Prevent PPH

Q.66 Pregnant individuals with gestational hypertension, proteinuria, and signs of liver or kidney dysfunction should be evaluated for what potentially life-threatening condition?
A. Preeclampsia **B.** Gestational diabetes
C. Ectopic pregnancy **D.** Placenta previa

Q.67 Sudden increase in occurrences of a disease in a particular time and place is known as:
A. Outbreak **B.** Inbreak
C. Disease crisis **D.** All of these

Q.68 The most important indicator of health status in India is:
A. MMR **B.** IMR **C.** NMR **D.** PMR

Q.69 Which among the following person is overall responsible for rural health services at district level?
A. District Health Officer
B. Medical Health Officer
C. Chief Medical Officer
D. None of the Above

Q.70 What is the role of a nurse in a care home?
A. Pivotal role in supporting the person and their family transition process.
B. Nursing care for children and young people with health needs in their own homes or the community.
C. The application of psychiatric nursing knowledge to prevent mental illness and promote and maintain people's mental health.
D. Nurses work with adults (aged 18 or over) who have a learning disability and additional health needs which require the support of a specialist learning disability nurse.

Q.71 The nurse should visit which of the following patient first?
A. The patient, which have diabetes with a blood glucose of

95mg/dL
- **B.** The patient with hypertension
- **C.** The patient with chest pain and a history of angina
- **D.** The patient with Raynaud's disease

Q.72 If a mother carry her 18 months old baby in the hospital who has not been immunized even with a single vaccine. At this time which vaccine can be given to the except:

A. DPT-Ist **B.** OPV-Ist **C.** Measles **D.** BCG

Q.73 The normal resting heart rate for a newborn is:

A. 75 to 115 bpm **B.** 85 to 125 bpm
C. 110 to 150 bpm **D.** 140 to 200 bpm

Q.74 An infant breathes, about ____ in a minute.

A. 26 times **B.** 52 times **C.** 72 times **D.** 13 times

Q.75 Height of the neonate doubles by:

A. 4 Years **B.** 3 Years **C.** 2 Years **D.** 1 Year

Q.76 Which of the following is correct concerning fetal hemoglobin (HbF)?

- **A.** HbF is composed of two alpha and two gamma subunits
- **B.** HbF has decreased oxygen carrying capacity
- **C.** HbF is composed of two alpha and two beta subunits
- **D.** HbF is present only in fetal life

Q.77 The temporary accumulation of epithelial cells formed on the hard palate in a neonate are called:

- **A.** Sucking callosities
- **B.** Epstein pearls
- **C.** Supernumerary teeth
- **D.** Retention cysts

Q.78 How much Vitamin C should a baby get per day?

A. 10 mg per day **B.** 30 mg per day
C. 50 mg per day **D.** 60 mg per day

Q.79 The condition of a newborn is considered normal if the Apgar score is:

A. 4-7 **B.** more than 10
C. more than 8 **D.** between 5-8

Q.80 By assessment, one can assign a developmental quotient (DQ) for any developmental sphere. It is calculated as the:

- **A.** average age at attainment by obtained age at attainment
- **B.** average age at attainment + obtained age at attainment × 100
- **C.** average age at attainment by obtained age at attainment × 100
- **D.** average age at attainment - obtained age at attainment × 100

General Aptitude / Reasoning / General Awareness / Basic Computer knowledge

Q.81 In a code language, if 'MOON' is coded as '5229', 'FILM' is coded as '6315', 'ARE' is coded as '487', then in the same language How will 'INFORMER' be coded?

A. 39611578 **B.** 39162258
C. 79627578 **D.** 39628578

Q.82 Direction: Read the given statement(s) and conclusions carefully and select which of the conclusions logically follow(s) from the statement(s).

Statement:

I. Some bells are golden

II. Some bells are red.

Conclusion:

I. Some red are golden

II. No golden is red

- **A.** Only conclusion I follows
- **B.** Both conclusions I and II follow
- **C.** Only conclusion II follows
- **D.** Either conclusion I or II follow

Q.83 Direction: In the following question, identify the pair of words which has a relationship similar to the pair in the question.

Lawyer : Court

- **A.** Chemist : Laboratory
- **B.** Businessman : Office
- **C.** Labour : Factory
- **D.** Athlete : Olympics

Q.84 Direction: In the question below a statement is given followed by two conclusions, I and II. You have to consider the statement to be true, even if it seems to be at variance from commonly known facts. You have to decide which of the given conclusions definitely is drawn from the given statement.

Statement: Aerated drinks are harmful for health.

Conclusions:

I. Leads to increase in amount of fat.

II. Leads to insulin resistance.

- **A.** If only conclusion I follows
- **B.** If only conclusion II follows
- **C.** If either I or II follows
- **D.** If both I and II follow

Q.85 Three of the following four words are alike in a certain way and one is different.

- **A.** Akbar
- **B.** Shahjahan
- **C.** Jahangir
- **D.** Chandragupta Maurya-I

Q.86 Which of the following is the full form of OPC?

[Allahabad High Court ARO, 2020]

- **A.** Optical Code Reading
- **B.** Optical Program Counter
- **C.** Operating Computer Resource
- **D.** Open Platform Communication

Q.87 A miniature graphical representation of files, folders, programs or other items in a GUI based operating system is called:

[Rajasthan Police Constable, 2020]

A. icon **B.** symbol **C.** tabs **D.** ribbon

Q.88 In which method we can connect to internet.

A. Dial-up **B.** SLIP
C. PPP **D.** All of these

Q.89 Which is the most common 'input device' used today?
[Uttarakhand Public Service Commission (UKPSC), 2011]

A. Mother board
B. Central Processing Unit
C. Keyboard
D. Semi-conductor

Q.90 A critical section is a program segment:

A. Which should run in a certain specified amount of time.
B. Which avoids deadlocks.
C. Where shared resources are accessed.
D. Which must be enclosed by a pair of semaphore operations, P and V.

Q.91 The Government has approved an Electronics Manufacturing Cluster (EMC) in which city?

A. Chennai **B.** Pune
C. New Delhi **D.** Bengaluru

Q.92 'Matki' is a popular folk dance of which of the following?

A. Assam **B.** Madhya Pradesh
C. Bihar **D.** Rajasthan

Q.93 Which among the following can be amended only by a special majority in India?

A. Admission of New State
B. Salaries and allowances of Members of Parliament
C. Allowances of the President
D. Amendment of the Constitution via Article 368

Q.94 Which of the following district of Uttar Pradesh is a major Bauxite Reserve of the state?

A. Banda **B.** Allahabad
C. Mirzapur **D.** Lalitpur

Q.95 Rulers of which of the following dynasty were known as Lords of the Dakshinapatha?

A. Pandyas **B.** Satavahanas
C. Cheras **D.** Cholas

Q.96 Nikita takes as much time in running 18 meters as a car takes in covering 48 meters. What will be the distance covered by Nikita during the time the car covers 1.6 km?

A. 480 m **B.** 520 m **C.** 600 m **D.** 800 m

Q.97 What is the fourth proportional to 9, 21 and 123?

A. 728 **B.** 278 **C.** 287 **D.** 246

Q.98 Find the value of k, if 18% of 450 = 30% of k.

A. 270 **B.** 750 **C.** 250 **D.** 320

Q.99 If seven persons can build a house in 30 days, how long will it take three persons to build the same house, provided that they all work at the same rate?

A. 100 days **B.** 70 days **C.** 30 days **D.** 210 days

Q.100 If $a^3 - b^3 = 253$, $a - b = 7$, then the value of ab is:

A. $-\frac{25}{7}$ **B.** -4 **C.** $\frac{25}{7}$ **D.** $-\frac{30}{7}$

// Smart Answer Sheet //

Correct Indicates percentage of students who answered questions correctly.

Skipped Indicates percentage of students who skipped questions.

Q.	Ans.	Correct	Skipped
1	B	59.19 %	1.52 %
2	A	58.81 %	1.71 %
3	C	82.62 %	0.0 %
4	D	60.49 %	1.24 %
5	D	67.61 %	1.84 %
6	D	57.6 %	1.19 %
7	A	78.75 %	0.0 %
8	D	80.69 %	0.0 %
9	C	43.61 %	1.91 %
10	A	43.05 %	1.07 %
11	B	12.07 %	4.29 %
12	D	64.54 %	1.27 %
13	C	63.84 %	1.52 %
14	B	18.48 %	3.94 %
15	A	54.68 %	1.71 %
16	C	83.7 %	0.0 %
17	D	64.83 %	1.11 %
18	D	44.48 %	1.91 %
19	C	78.15 %	0.0 %
20	B	50.59 %	1.54 %
21	C	44.58 %	1.18 %
22	A	42.42 %	1.23 %
23	C	76.43 %	0.0 %
24	C	61.92 %	1.52 %
25	B	40.69 %	1.7 %
26	A	30.99 %	4.69 %
27	C	64.33 %	1.49 %
28	C	79.22 %	0.0 %
29	D	27.54 %	4.4 %
30	C	61.09 %	1.83 %
31	D	48.39 %	1.86 %
32	A	41.47 %	1.91 %
33	C	65.37 %	1.61 %
34	C	59.8 %	1.12 %
35	A	48.66 %	1.52 %
36	A	57.23 %	1.81 %
37	D	61.11 %	1.33 %
38	A	30.79 %	3.96 %
39	A	64.83 %	1.12 %
40	B	46.69 %	1.79 %
41	A	63.67 %	1.88 %
42	A	46.63 %	1.97 %
43	B	80.88 %	0.0 %
44	C	59.62 %	1.18 %
45	D	81.71 %	0.0 %
46	B	30.3 %	4.01 %
47	C	56.25 %	1.05 %
48	B	23.66 %	3.93 %
49	C	49.8 %	1.38 %
50	A	76.27 %	0.0 %
51	C	50.97 %	1.92 %
52	B	49.94 %	1.3 %
53	B	53.62 %	1.2 %
54	A	66.75 %	1.39 %
55	B	46.64 %	1.07 %
56	A	41.23 %	1.74 %
57	A	47.97 %	1.43 %
58	D	61.52 %	1.14 %
59	A	62.68 %	1.68 %
60	C	63.24 %	1.75 %
61	D	82.73 %	0.0 %
62	B	48.22 %	1.72 %
63	A	50.54 %	1.83 %
64	C	54.23 %	1.56 %
65	A	47.8 %	1.87 %
66	A	60.3 %	1.57 %
67	A	43.69 %	1.64 %
68	B	64.69 %	1.98 %
69	C	50.92 %	1.28 %
70	A	63.66 %	1.23 %
71	C	68.95 %	1.2 %
72	D	45.1 %	1.63 %
73	C	62.56 %	1.76 %
74	B	77.49 %	0.0 %
75	A	69.01 %	1.97 %
76	A	68.73 %	1.21 %
77	B	69.62 %	1.52 %
78	B	47.29 %	1.21 %
79	C	58.07 %	1.35 %
80	C	48.35 %	1.15 %

Q.	Ans.	Correct	Skipped
81	D	89.29 %	0.0 %
82	D	82.9 %	0.0 %
83	A	66.98 %	1.92 %
84	D	57.54 %	1.71 %
85	D	79.12 %	0.0 %
86	D	51.15 %	1.24 %
87	A	65.46 %	1.99 %
88	D	56.62 %	1.16 %
89	C	81.31 %	0.0 %
90	C	46.9 %	1.23 %
91	B	64.15 %	1.61 %
92	B	85.36 %	0.0 %
93	D	56.43 %	1.27 %
94	A	59.46 %	1.38 %
95	B	61.51 %	1.43 %
96	C	46.01 %	1.36 %
97	C	43.43 %	1.89 %
98	A	59.55 %	1.61 %
99	B	53.16 %	1.93 %
100	D	57.91 %	1.74 %

Performance Analysis	
Avg. Score (%)	69.0%
Toppers Score (%)	69.0%
Your Score	

//Hints and Solutions//

1. Minimally invasive surgery is also known as keyhole surgery. Minimally invasive surgery refers to any surgical procedure that is performed through tiny incisions instead of a large opening. Because your surgeon will make smaller incisions, you will likely have a quicker recovery time and less pain than traditional open surgery but with the same benefits as traditional surgery.

Hence, the correct option is (B).

2. Antiembolic stockings can help to reduce thromboembolism. Antiembolic stockings, also known as TED hose, are designed specifically for non-mobile patients or those confined to a bed. They are low cost temporary solutions commonly used for patients in nursing homes and post-surgery to prevent deep vein thrombosis (DVT).

Hence, the correct option is (A).

3. Segmentectomy involves the removal of part of one of the lobes of the lung. A segmentectomy, or segment resection, is a surgical treatment that can be an option to treat early-stage, non-small cell lung cancer (NSCLC). It involves the removal of part of one of the lobes of the lung to entirely remove a cancerous tumor.

Hence, the correct option is (C).

4. The term tachypnoea refers to an increase in respiratory rate. Tachypnea is a condition that refers to rapid breathing. The normal breathing rate for an average adult is 12 to 20 breaths per minute. In children, the number of breaths per minute can be a higher resting rate than seen in adults.

Hence, the correct option is (D).

5. Most coronary artery bypass grafts are performed on men who are aged 60 years and over. Most coronary bypass surgeries are done through a long incision in the chest while a heart-lung machine keeps blood and oxygen flowing through your body. This is called on-pump coronary bypass surgery. The surgeon cuts down the center of the chest along the breastbone and spreads open the rib cage to expose the heart.

Hence, the correct option is (D).

6. Varicose veins are more prevalent in older people. Varicose veins are enlarged, swollen, twisted veins often caused by damaged or faulty valves that allow blood to travel in the wrong direction.

Hence, the correct option is (D).

7. The circle of Willis is located at the base of the brain. The Circle of Willis is the joining area of several arteries at the bottom (inferior) side of the brain. At the Circle of Willis, the internal carotid arteries branch into smaller arteries that supply oxygenated blood to over 80% of the cerebrum.

Hence, the correct option is (A).

8. An aneurysm is an abnormal bulge or ballooning in the wall of a blood vessel. "A proportion of these patients will go on to have a rupture. And the challenge with rupture is that it's unpredictable."

Causes of thoracic aortic aneurysms may include:

Hardening of the arteries (atherosclerosis): Plaque buildup on the artery walls causes the arteries to become less flexible. Additional pressure can cause the arteries to weaken and widen (dilate). High blood pressure and high cholesterol increase the risk of atherosclerosis. This is more common in older people.

Genetic conditions: Aortic aneurysms in younger people often have a genetic cause. Marfan syndrome, a genetic condition that affects the connective tissue in the body, may cause weakness in the wall of the aorta.

Other genetic conditions linked to aortic aneurysms and dissection and rupture include vascular Ehlers-Danlos, Loeys-Dietz, and Turner syndromes.

Blood vessel inflammation: Conditions that involve blood vessel inflammation, such as giant cell arteritis and Takayasu arteritis, are associated with thoracic aortic aneurysms.

Hence, the correct option is (D).

9. In bariatric surgery, gastric stimulation involves the insertion of a pacemaker device. The implantable Enterra gastric electrical stimulation device works by sending low energy, high frequency electrical pulses to the nerves in the stomach that lead to decreased symptoms of nausea and vomiting.

Hence, the correct option is (C).

10. In Lecture method of group teaching, may fail to change the health practice of people.

A lecture does provide basic information on the subject, but it may fail to change the health behaviour of the people. Nevertheless lectures have an important place in the health education of small groups.

Steps of lecture method of teaching:

Step 1: Opening- State the purpose of the lecture.

Step 2: Presentation- Elaboration Multi-media resources.

Step 3: Learner-Instructor two-way Interaction. Encouraging active learning Multi-media streaming.

Step 4: Formative Assessment.

Step 5: Conclusions

Hence, the correct option is (A).

11. Mass media are generally more effective in changing human behaviour during health education programme.

Mass media campaigns are widely used to expose high proportions of large populations to messages through routine uses of existing media, such as television, radio, and newspapers. Exposure to such messages is, therefore, generally passive. Such campaigns are frequently competing with factors, such as pervasive product marketing, powerful social norms, and behaviours driven by addiction or habit.

In this Review we discuss the outcomes of mass media campaigns in the context of various health-risk behaviours (eg, use of tobacco, alcohol, and other drugs, heart disease risk factors, sex-related behaviours, road safety, cancer screening and prevention, child survival, and organ or blood donation).

We conclude that mass media campaigns can produce positive changes or prevent negative changes in health-related behaviours across large populations. We assess what contributes to these outcomes, such as concurrent availability of required services and products, availability of community-based programmes, and policies that support behaviour change.

Hence, the correct option is (B).

12. Health exhibitions are conducted in connection with Fairs, Festivals, and Mass campaigns.

A health fair is an educational and interactive event designed for outreach to provide basic preventive medicine and medical screening to people in the community or employees at work in conjunction with workplace wellness.

Health campaigns are generally designed both to increase awareness of health threats and to move target audiences to action in support of public health. For example, public health campaigns often encourage target audience members to engage in healthy behaviors that provide resistance to serious health threats.

Hence, the correct option is (D).

13. A discussion group is an example of an All-channel pattern of communication.

In an all-channel network, communications flow upward, downward and laterally among all members of the group. This pattern of communication supports an egalitarian, (equal, unrestricted) participative culture and fosters (promote, cultivate) cross-functional efforts.

Hence, the correct option is (C).

14. E-health is a general term used to refer to the application of digital information and communication technology to health care.

E-health is a relatively recent term for health care practice supported by electronic processes and communication. It can also include health applications and links on mobile phones, referred to as m-health.

Hence, the correct option is (B).

15. Patient informatics refers to a programme that aims to enable patients to make better use of information and communication technology for health and health care.

Patient informatics may appear to have much in common with participatory medicine, which has been defined as a movement in which patients and health professionals actively collaborate and encourage one another as full partners in care.

Hence, the correct option is (A).

16. Effective communication is the process of exchanging ideas, thoughts, opinions, knowledge, and data so that the message is received and understood with clarity and purpose. When we communicate effectively, both the sender and receiver feel satisfied.

Effective communication is used to:

- Improve care services.
- Enhance patient experience.
- Create more transparency and openness.
- Reduce complaints.
- Build trust on the health and social care system.
- Reduce stress.
- Create a better working environment for carers.
- Increase self-confidence, professional standing, career prospects, and job satisfaction.

Hence, the correct option is (C).

17. Although different generations vary in age, they all approach their job, in the same manner, is not true about generational differences in the workplace.

Today's savvy healthcare organizations recognize that they can elevate patient outcomes, boost productivity and even reduce the cost of care by developing generational diversity to create a robust organizational culture.

Each generation has unique expectations, experiences, generational history, lifestyles, values, and demographics that influence their buying behaviors. Accordingly, many companies are reaching out to multi-generational consumers and trying to understand and gain the attention of these diverse buyers.

Hence, the correct option is (D).

18. Prior to discharge, the nursing case manager's most critical action is to verify that the patient is being discharged to a safe environment.

Essentially, the discharge planning nurse serves as a connection between in-patient care and follow-up or out-patient care. They help to make sure that the patient and their family understand exactly what to do after discharge to prevent injury and encourage healing. They are a crucial part of proper patient care. They help to make sure that the patient is moving to a safe environment.

Hence, the correct option is (D).

19. In this situation, the nurse is acting in the role of negotiator.

A negotiator is a person who either comes to an agreement with someone else, or one who helps other people reach such an agreement.

Hence, the correct option is (C).

20. A support group for adolescents with diabetes referral will benefit this patient's immediate needs. Support groups can provide a wealth of information and ideas on ways to make managing diabetes easier, such as diabetes-friendly recipes the whole family can enjoy, tips for eating right at holiday parties and work events, and local resources for people with diabetes.

Hence, the correct option is (B).

21. Autocratic is the most effective leadership style that can be used during emergency situations.

Autocratic leadership, often used in the past but less popular these days, involves the nurse leader making all decisions about the nursing unit, typically not consulting staff. Autocratic leadership is a command-and-control style, where leaders use negative reinforcement and punishment to ensure compliance with rules.

Hence, the correct option is (C).

22. A learning objective that is based on the cognitive domain includes asking participants to demonstrate drawing blood from a central line catheter.

A central line (or central venous catheter) is like an intravenous (IV) line. But it is much longer than a regular IV and goes all the way up to a vein near the heart or just inside the heart. A patient can get medicine, fluids, blood, or nutrition through a central line. It also can be used to draw blood.

Hence, the correct option is (A).

23. Disease Process is not the aim of Nursing Practice.

The Seven Goals of Nursing Caring for patients with acute and chronic illnesses; facilitating discharge planning; providing palliative care; and offering patient education; illness prevention services, and health maintenance care.

Hence, the correct option is (C).

24. There are 4 periods of Nursing History.

Although the origins of nursing predate the mid-19th century, the history of professional nursing traditionally begins with Florence Nightingale.

Florence Nightingale, the First Professional Nurse divided nursing history into four periods: Intuitive, Apprentice, Educative, and Contemporary, while Tomey and Alligood (2002), divided the history of professional nursing into the curriculum era, the research era, the graduate education era, and the theory era.

Hence, the correct option is (C).

25. Research on nurse retention has indicated that many nurses leave nursing after 5 years or less period of time. Nurse retention rates have shown a dramatic increase with the use of NRPs with most studies showing a retention rate of over 90% after the first year of hire.

Hence, the correct option is (B).

26. You should focus on that Communication and teamwork among the staff of all generations is critical in assuring a positive work milieu that can affect safe patient care and good working relationships when working with your team.

Effective communication within a team will build a common purpose among team members that will allow them to reach their goals. Frequent friendly communication can help team members develop a sense of belonging and strengthen relationships.

Hence, the correct option is (A).

27. A scrub nurse in the operating room has the responsibility of handling surgical instruments to the surgeon.

The scrub nurse assists the surgeon by providing appropriate surgical instruments and supplies, maintaining strict surgical asepsis, and with the circulating nurse, accounting for all gauze, sponges, needles, and instruments. The circulating nurse assists the surgeon and scrub nurse, positions the patient, applies appropriate equipment and surgical drapes, assists with gowning and gloving, and provides the surgeon and scrub nurse with supplies.

Hence, the correct option is (C).

28. The nurse should return shortly to the patient's room and remain there until the patient takes the medication to verify that it was taken as directed. With the growing reliance on medication therapy as the primary intervention for most illnesses, patients receiving medication interventions are exposed to potential harm as well as benefits. Benefits are effective management of the illness/disease, slowed progression of the disease, and improved patient outcomes with few if any errors. Harm from medications can arise from unintended consequences as well as medication errors (wrong medication, wrong time, wrong dose, etc.).

Hence, the correct option is (C).

29. To evaluate a patient for hypoxia, the physician is most likely to order Arterial blood gas (ABG) analysis test to the nurse.

Arterial blood gas (ABG) analysis is the only test that evaluates gas exchange in the lungs, providing information about a patient's oxygenation status. Hypoxia is a condition in which the body or a region of the body is deprived of adequate oxygen supply at the tissue level. Hypoxia may be classified as either generalized, affecting the whole body, or local, affecting a region of the body.

Hence, the correct option is (D).

30. During discharge teaching, the nurse should explain that the patient must fill this prescription within 6 months after the date on which it was written.

In most cases, an outpatient must fill a prescription for a controlled substance within 6 months of the date on which the prescription was written. A common reason people seek the care of medical professionals is pain relief. While many categories of pain medications are available, opioid analgesics are FDA-approved for moderate to severe pain. As such, they are a common choice for patients with acute, cancer-related, neurologic, and end-of-life pain. The prescribing of opioid analgesics for chronic pain is controversial and fraught with inconclusive standards.

Hence, the correct option is (C).

31. The patient's cognitive abilities are considered by the nurse in charge during assessment can affect drug administration.

The nurse must consider the patient's cognitive abilities to understand drug instructions. If not, the nurse must find a family member or significant other to take on the responsibility of administering medications in the home setting. The patient's ability to recover, occupational hazards, and socioeconomic status do not affect drug administration.

Hence, the correct option is (D).

32. An employer establishes a physical exercise area in the workplace and encourages all employees to use it. This is an example of the primary prevention level of health promotion.

Primary prevention precedes disease and applies to healthy patients. Primary prevention includes those preventive measures that come before the onset of illness or injury and before the disease process begins. Examples include immunization and taking regular exercise to prevent health problems from developing in the future.

Hence, the correct option is (A).

33. When helping a person through grief work, the nurse knows the sequencing of stages of grief may occur in order, they may be skipped, or they may recur.

Grief is manifested in a variety of ways that are unique to an individual and based on personal experiences, cultural expectations, and spiritual beliefs. The sequencing of stages or behaviors of grief may occur in order, they may be skipped, or they may recur. The amount of time to resolve grief also varies among individuals.

Hence, the correct option is (C).

34. Nurse Mackey is monitoring a patient for adverse reactions during barbiturate therapy. Potential for drug dependence is the major disadvantage of barbiturate use.

Patients can become dependent on barbiturates, especially with prolonged use. Due to the abuse potential of barbiturates, restricted access started with the passage of the Federal Comprehensive Drug Abuse and Control Act of 1970. Barbiturates classify as Schedule II-IV based on their abuse potential.

Hence, the correct option is (C).

35. Elevating the head of the bed is essential when providing continuous enteral feedings.

Elevating the head of the bed during enteral feeding minimizes the risk of aspiration and allows the formula to flow in the patient's intestines. Lying prone/supine during feeding increases the risk of aspiration and therefore where clinically possible the patient should be placed in an upright position. If unable to sit up for a bolus feed or if receiving continuous feeding, the head of the bed should be elevated 30-45 degrees during feeding and for at least 30 minutes after the feed to reduce the risk of aspiration.

Hence, the correct option is (A).

36. The elements present in the proteins are carbon, hydrogen, nitrogen, and oxygen. In addition to carbon, hydrogen, and oxygen atoms, all proteins contain nitrogen and sulfur atoms, and many also contain phosphorus atoms and traces of other elements. Proteins serve a variety of roles in living organisms and are often classified by these biological roles.

Hence, the correct option is (A).

37. Vitamin B12 has a metallic component. Vitamin B12 is also known as cobalamin. It is found naturally in animal foods, including meats, fish, poultry, eggs and dairy. It is required for the formation and maturation of RBCs. Anemia is a vitamin B12 deficiency disease.

Hence, the correct option is (D).

38. Enzymes are the proteins which act catalyst in the body and speed up the chemical reactions. Enzymes are proteins that have a specific function. They speed up the rate of chemical reactions in a cell or outside a cell. Enzymes act as catalysts; they do not get consumed in the chemical reactions that they accelerate.

Hence, the correct option is (A).

39. Antibodies help to protect from infection, bacteria, virus, illness, and diseases in the body. These are proteins which defend the body from antigens. They travel through the bloodstream. Antibodies are utilized by the immune system to identify and defend bacteria, viruses and other foreign intruders.

Hence, the correct option is (A).

40. Transport proteins are carrier proteins which move molecules from one place to another around the body.

Examples: Hemoglobin

Hemoglobin is responsible for transporting oxygen through the blood via red blood cell and transport the oxygen through the body.

Hence, the correct option is (B).

41. Ferritin protein stores the iron in the transport protein. Ferritin is a type of protein that combines with iron for storage in the liver. Ferritin has the shape of a hollow sphere. Inside the sphere, iron is stored in the Fe(III) oxidation state. To release iron when the body needs it, the iron must be changed from the Fe(III) to the Fe(II) oxidation state.

Hence, the correct option is (A).

42. Proteins are synthesized in the body through a process called Translation. Translation is the process of translating the sequence of a messenger RNA (mRNA) molecule to a sequence of amino acids during protein synthesis. The genetic code describes the relationship between the sequence of base pairs in a gene and the corresponding amino acid sequence that it encodes.

Hence, the correct option is (A).

43. Food hygiene is called improvement of sanitation. Food hygiene is the process of cleaning an environment from all sickness factors which may cause health problem. Hygiene process involves all the precautions to be taken in order to reduce microorganisms. Under this, the food is protected from getting infected. Cleanliness is taken care of at every level.

Hence, the correct option is (B).

44. More than 30 B.M.I. or Body mass index score for obesity. The higher the BMI, the greater the risk of developing additional health problems. A healthy weight is considered to be a BMI of 24 or less. A BMI of 25 to 29.9 is considered overweight. A BMI of less than 18.5 means that a person is underweight. A BMI of between 18.5 and 24.9 is ideal. A BMI of between 25 and 29.9 is overweight. A BMI over 30 indicates obesity.

Hence, the correct option is (C).

45. Meditation for Pain: Evidence exists that meditation does help some people with pain. Research shows that meditation uses neural pathways that make the brain less sensitive to pain. Meditation helps to increase the use of the brain's own pain-reducing opioids.

Other Non-pharmacological methods for pain management

Non-pharmacological pain management is the management of pain without medications. This method utilizes ways to alter thoughts and focus concentration to better manage and reduce pain. They are;

- Education and psychological conditioning
- Hypnosis
- Companionship
- Exercise
- Heat/cold application
- Lotions/massage therapy
- Meditation
- Music, art, or drama therapy
- Pastoral counselling
- Positioning
- Aqua therapy
- Massage therapy

Hence, the correct option is (D).

46. A victim of a car accident has just vomited and now appears to be coughing up blood. He is breathing very quickly and his pulse is weak and fast. Most likely he has internal bleeding.

Internal bleeding is one of the most serious consequences of trauma. Internal bleeding may occur in many areas of the body and may cause significant local inflammation and pain. If enough bleeding occurs, the person may go into shock.

Hence, the correct option is (B).

47. Apply cool wet cloths for a person experiencing a heat-related illness. It will make the person feel relaxed. Also give him to drink cool water or other nonalcoholic beverage without caffeine.

Hence, the correct option is (C).

48. A boy is shot with an arrow through the chest and out the back, the best course of action would be do not remove the arrow, place several dressing around the arrow to keep it from moving,bandage the dressings in place around the arrow and take the boy to nearby hospital immediately.

Hence, the correct option is (B).

49. For a boy with frostbite on his feet, you should soak his feet in warm water not more than 105 degrees, bandage with a dry sterile dressing.

Frostbite is an injury caused by freezing of the skin and underlying tissues. First your skin becomes very cold and red, then numb, hard and pale. Frostbite is most common on the fingers, toes, nose, ears, cheeks and chin. Exposed skin in cold, windy weather is most vulnerable to frostbite.

Hence, the correct option is (C).

50. You suspect that a person has been poisoned. She is conscious. Your first call should be to the Poison Control Center or your local emergency phone number.

A poison control center is a medical service that is able to provide immediate, free, and expert treatment advice and assistance over the telephone in case of exposure to poisonous or hazardous substances. Poison control centers answer questions about potential poisons in addition to providing treatment management advice about household products, medicines, pesticides, plants, bites and stings, food poisoning, and fumes.

Hence, the correct option is (A).

51. Shock is a condition where the circulatory system fails to deliver blood to all parts of the body.

Circulatory shock is the term used when inadequate blood flow results in damage to body tissues. Provided that sympathetic reflexes are intact, about 10% of the blood volume can be lost with little change in either arterial pressure or cardiac output.

Hence, the correct option is (C).

52. Snakebites can be very serious. When caring for a snakebite victim, you should not apply ice.

Dont apply a cold pack. Long-term application of cold makes the injury worse by reducing healthy circulation to the area. Even short-term exposure could be risky: Ice won't neutralize the venom, but some experts think snake venom increases vulnerability to frostbite.

Hence, the correct option is (B).

53. The chromosome Number of pairs in a human ovum is 23 in which 22 pairs of numbered chromosomes, called autosomes, and one pair of sex chromosomes, X and Y. Each parent contributes one chromosome to each pair so that offspring get half of their chromosomes from their mother and half from their father.

Hence, the correct option is (B).

54. During the ovulatory phase, at about the 14th day of the cycle, there is a rupture of the graffian follicle and the ovum gets released.

The ruptured Graffian follicle soon gets transformed into the Corpus luteum.

The Corpus luteum gets stimulated by the rising levels of LH and starts secreting the Progesterone hormone.

Progesterone hormone is required for the maintenance of the endometrium lining of the uterus.

In case if pregnancy does not occur after ovulation the levels of progesterone start to fall down and this leads to the disintegration of the endometrium lining causing menstruation.

Thus, lowering of progesterone hormone causes menstruation, as it is required for the maintenance of the endometrium lining, and for this reason, only progesterone is also called the pregnancy hormone.

Hence, the correct option is (A).

55. Fertilization is the biological process in which the fusion of gametes of two different sexes, i.e., male and female takes place.

Internal fertilization occurs in human beings. One egg is released from the ovary and is transferred to the fallopian tube during each ovulation cycle. The sperm travels to the egg through the fallopian tube. Fertilization also takes place in the fallopian tube.

Hence, the correct option is (B).

56. The structural and functional unit of lung is alveoli. The alveoli are where the lungs and the blood exchange oxygen and carbon dioxide during the process of breathing in and breathing out. Oxygen breathed in from the air passes through the alveoli and into the blood and travels to the tissues throughout the body.

Hence, the correct option is (A).

57. Sperm are temporarily kept in Epididymis. Each sperm cell takes between 65-75 days to form and around 300 million are produced every day. Inside the testes, sperm is made in structures called the seminiferous tubules. At the top and to the back of each testicle (testis) is the epididymis, which stores sperm.

Hence, the correct option is (A).

58. The muscular tube through which the stored urine is passed out of the body is called Urethra.

The urethra is a thin, fibromuscular tube that begins at the lower opening of the bladder and extends through the pelvic and urogenital diaphragms to the outside of the body. The length of the urethra is much shorter in women than in men. Due to the anatomical gender differences in the area. In males, it extends approximately 20 cm as it must traverse the length of the penis, whereas it is only 4 cm in length in females. The urethra serves a double purpose in men as it is a passage for semen during an ejaculation when partaking in sexual activities.

Hence, the correct option is (D).

59. Endocrine glands are glands which secrete their hormones directly into the bloodstream whereas exocrine glands are the type of glands which secrete their products into ducts.

The endocrine system includes pituitary gland, pineal gland, thyroid, parathyroid, pancreas, adrenal glands, testes, and ovaries.

Hence, the correct option is (A).

60. The primary function of the eccrine glands is to produce sweat. These glands stabilize the body temperature and help maintain homeostasis. These glands are found on the skin, mainly on the soles and palms. Endocrine glands have no arteries for transport and hence this body mixed with blood.

Hence, the correct option is (C).

61. Miscarriage, RH sensitization, and Needle injury all of these are a possible complication of amniocentesis.

There are several risks to amniocentesis, including (but not limited to) miscarriage, infection, needle injury, and RH sensitization. The rate of miscarriage due to amniocentesis is between 1 in 300 and 1 in 500. The other complications listed are relatively rare.

Miscarriage is when a baby dies in the womb before 20 weeks of pregnancy. Some women have a miscarriage before they know they're pregnant.

Rh sensitization can occur when a person with Rh-negative blood is exposed to Rh-positive blood. Most women who become sensitized do so during childbirth, when their blood mixes with the Rh-positive blood of their fetus.

Needlestick injuries are wounds caused by needles that accidentally puncture the skin.

Hence, the correct option is (D).

62. The nurse should advise the patient to seek medical attention immediately.

This woman could be experiencing pre-term labor. A 20-week pregnancy is not considered viable. She should be seen immediately to determine if there is a cause such as cervical insufficiency (premature dilation of the cervix).

Hence, the correct option is (B).

63. The nurse's first action would be to turn the mother on her left side.

Marked fetal heart rate baseline variability of 25 beats per minute or more may be cause for concern. Similar findings may indicate that there is poor oxygenation of the fetus. Turn the mother to her left side (to increase perfusion) and notify the physician. Note that this is still in the normal range for fetal heart rate for a laboring patient (about 130 beats per minute) and that the low end of this spectrum is of slightly more concern.

Hence, the correct option is (A).

64. Poor diet is not a risk factor for gestational diabetes.

Risk factors for gestational diabetes include obesity, family history of diabetes, history of gestational diabetes, hypertension, pre-eclampsia/eclampsia, recurrent urinary tract infections, vaginitis, polyhydramnios, previous large infants (9lbs or greater than 4000g), glycosuria or proteinuria on two or more occasions. While poor diet may contribute to diabetic concerns, it is not directly associated with a higher risk of gestation diabetes as the other risk factors are. During the prenatal period, nurses are responsible for educating their patients on all of these risk factors as well as a proper prenatal diet.

Hence, the correct option is (C).

65. Kegel exercise is used after delivery to strengthen urinary muscles and rectal muscles.

Exercises that strengthen the pelvic floor muscles can help hold urine inside the bladder, preventing leakage. These pelvic floor muscle exercises are commonly called "Kegel" exercises, named after the doctor who developed them.

Hence, the correct option is (A).

66. Preeclampsia is a potentially life-threatening disorder that generally includes gestational hypertension, proteinuria, edema, red-blood-cell dysfunction, and signs of liver or kidney dysfunction. It is more common in weeks 32-40 and develops in 2-8% of pregnancies worldwide.

Hence, the correct option is (A).

67. An outbreak is an increase in the occurrence of cases (HAI) above what is expected in that population in that area over a particular period of time. The occurrence of an outbreak always signals some significant shift in the existing balance between the agent, host, and environment. The outbreak can be detected through health personnel, laboratories official disease notification systems, newspapers, and media village health volunteers.

Hence, the correct option is (A).

68. The most important indicator of health status in India is IMR (Infant mortality Rate). Infant mortality represents an important component of under-five mortality. Like under-five mortality, infant mortality rates measure child survival. They also reflect the social, economic and environmental conditions in which children (and others in society) live, including their health care.

Hence, the correct option is (B).

69. On the lines of the State Health Mission, for healthcare of the public, every district has a District Health Mission headed by Chief medical Officer. It has the Chief Medical Officer as the Mission Director. Mission Director or CMO are responsible for the health of that area. Many health care programs are run under their supervision.

Hence, the correct option is (C).

70. During admission to a care home, the nurse plays a pivotal role in supporting the transition process for the person and their family. The nurse's role will include practical interventions such as assessing the new resident's needs, planning care and managing medicines.

Community nursing is nursing care delivered outside acute hospitals, for example in the home, within General Practice facilities, in community hospitals, in police custody, at a school, or in a care home. In the UK, a community nurse needs a degree approved by the Nursing and Midwifery Council and 1–2 years experience as a qualified Adult Nurse.

There 4 types of community health nursing:

- Care, Home Nurse
- Community Children's Nurse
- Community Mental Health Nurse (CMHN)
- Community Learning Disability Nurse

Hence, the correct option is (A).

71. The patient with chest pain should be seen first because this could indicate a myocardial infarction. The overall prognosis depends on the extent of heart muscle damage and ejection fraction.

Angina is a type of chest pain caused by reduced blood flow to the heart. Angina is a symptom of coronary artery disease. Angina, also called angina pectoris, is often described as squeezing, pressure, heaviness, tightness or pain in chest.

Hence, the correct option is (C).

72. A mother carries her 18 months old baby in the hospital who has not been immunized even with a single vaccine. At this time all vaccines can be given to the child except BCG vaccine.

BCG vaccine has a documented protective effect against meningitis and disseminated TB in children. It does not prevent primary infection and, more importantly, does not prevent reactivation of latent pulmonary infection, the principal source of bacillary spread in the community.

Hence, the correct option is (D).

73. The normal heart rate for a newborn that is sleeping is approximately 100 beats per minute. If the newborn was awake, the normal heart rate would range from 120-160 beats per minute. A heart rate of 130 to 150 beats per minute is normal for a newborn infant if the Heart rate is less than 80 bpm that is considered bradycardia.

Hence, the correct option is (C).

74. An infant breathes, about 52 times in a minute.

An infant's breathing rate is the number of breaths they take per minute. The normal breathing rate in infants: 30–60/mint.

The breathing rate of different age groups:

Group	**Age**	**Breath/min**
Newborn	Newborn to 6 weeks	30 - 60
Infant	6 weeks to 1 year	40 to 60
Toddler	1 to 3 years	20 - 30
Young Children	3 to 6 years	20 - 25
Older Children	10 to 14 years	15 - 20
Adults	Adults	12 - 20

Hence, the correct option is (B).

75. The height doubles between the age of 4 years old.

- Neonatal Height triples by 13 years old (based on height at birth).
- Physical growth is especially very fast during the first 2 years. Usually, an infant's birth weight generally doubles within 5 months and triples by the infant's first birthday.
- Also baby grows between 10 and 12 inches in length (or height), and the baby's proportions change during the first 2 years.
- A baby's length is measured usually from the top of their head to the bottom of one of their heels. It's the same as their height, but height is measured standing up, whereas length is measured when the baby is lying down.
- The average length at birth for a full-term baby is 19 to 20 inches or 50 cm.

Hence, the correct option is (A).

76. Fetal hemoglobin or HbF is the form of hemoglobin that is dominant during fetal life and also significantly increases in concentration for several weeks after birth.

HbF has a greater affinity for oxygen than Hb as the fetal hemoglobin must be able to bind oxygen with greater attraction than the maternal hemoglobin. Hence it transports O_2 from placental vasculature to the fetus.

HbF is present in fetal life, and its production ceases in the period just after the delivery. Like the adult Hb, the HbF is made of four-unit which comprise two alpha and two gamma subunits.

Hence, the correct option is (A).

77. Epstein pearls: Epstein's pearls are epithelial remnants of palatal fusion located along the mid-palatal raphe of the hard palate. It is a small white cyst that contains keratin. Frequently found on either side of the median raphe of the palate. Resolves in 1-2 months.

Cause of Epstein pearls: During the development process when the skin of the baby's mouth gets trapped then, Epstein pearls happen. This trapped skin fills with the protein known as keratin. When the mouth starts to develop and takes shape.

- Sucking callosities: it is described as a combination of intracellular edema and hyperkeratotic thickening of the lips.
- Supernumerary teeth: it may closely resemble the teeth of the group to which it belongs, i.e. molars, premolars, or anterior possibly from the splitting of the permanent bud itself.
- Retention cysts: it is an accumulation of a secretion formed when the outlet of a secreting gland is obstructed.

Hence, the correct option is (B).

78. Vitamin C is a vital nutrient that supports immunity and collagen production. It also acts as an antioxidant and babies need 30-40 mg of vitamin C per day depending on their age.

It is also known as ascorbic acid, is a water-soluble nutrient that plays a vital role in most of a baby's bodily functions. To maintain a healthy immune system it is necessary to increase the absorption of iron and produce collagen, which is the most abundant protein in the human body. It is an essential nutrient, which means a baby's body cannot make it on its own. Therefore, they get it from the foods they eat every day.

Hence, the correct option is (B).

79. APGAR SCORE is an assessment tool used to assess the overall health status of a newborn baby after birth and after 5 minutes of birth.

A low Apgar score determines any significant problem with the baby which needs immediate attention and action.

- A total of 7 to 10 scores is a reassuring score.
- A total of 4 to 6 score is moderately abnormal.
- A total 0 to 3 score is concerning.

The Apgar score consists of 5 features and each feature is assessed by the pediatrician and they need to give a score from 0 to 2.

The 5 features of the Apgar score are:

1. ACTIVITY/MUSCLE TONE
   - 0 score: - floppy tone
   - 1 score: - arm and legs flexed with little movement
   - 2 score: - active/spontaneous movement
2. PULSE/HEART RATE
   - 0 score: - absent (no pulse)
   - 1 score: - less than 100 beats per minute
   - 2 score: - greater than 100 beats per minute
3. GRIMACE (RESPONSE TO STIMULATION)
   - 0 score: - absent
   - 1 score: - facial movement with stimulation
   - 2 score: - prompt response to stimulation
4. APPEARANCE (colour of the skin)
   - 0 score: - blue, bluish-grey, or pale all over
   - 1 score: - body pink but extremities blue
   - 2 score: - pink all over
5. RESPIRATION/BREATHING
   - 0 score: - absent
   - 1 score: - irregular, weak crying
   - 2 score: - good, strong cry

Hence, the correct option is (C).

80. Development Quotient (DQ): It is the ratio of Functional age to Chronological age calculated as DQ = (Average age at attainment / obtained age at attainment) × 100

It is used to simply express a development delay.

Development Quotient in Infants

- It is the most widely used infant test
- Used for infants from 1 to 42 months
- Motor scale – it measures the infant's ability to do such things as grasps an object and throw a ball.
- Mental Scale – it measures adaptive behaviors such as reaching an object.
- Behavior rating scale – it measures behaviors such as goal-directedness, emotional regulation, and social responsibility.

The infant's development Quotient summarizes how the infant performs in comparison with the large norm group of age-peer infants.

Hence, the correct option is (C).

81. In a certain code language,

M	O	O	N
5	2	2	9

F	I	L	M
6	3	1	5

A	R	E
4	8	7

From above, the code for 'INFORMER' would be:

I	N	F	O	R	M	E	R
3	9	6	2	8	5	7	8

So, INFORMER is coded as '39628578'.

Hence, the correct option is (D).

82. The least possible Venn Diagram for the given statements will be as follows:

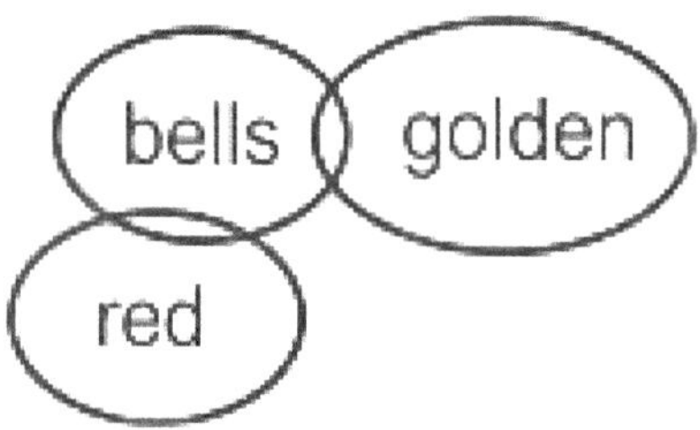

I. Some red are golden. (False, it can be true but not definite.)

II. No golden is red. (False, it can be true but not definite.)

So,Either conclusion I or II follow.

Hence, the correct option is (D).

83. As the working field of lawyer is Court, similarly the working field of chemist is laboratory.

Hence, the correct option is (A).

84. According to the given statement:

Conclusion I: This follows, because aerated drinks contain more sugar, which leads to an increase in the amount of fat.

Conclusion II: This follows, because aerated drinks contain more sugar.

So, both I and II follow.

Hence, the correct option is (D).

85. The logic follows here is:

Names	Name of Empire/Dynasty
Akbar	Mughal Empire
Shahjahan	Mughal Empire
Jahangir	Mughal Empire
Chandra Gupta Maurya-I	**Maurya Dynasty**

Akbar, Shahjahan & Mumtaz Mahal belongs to Mughal Empire except Chandragupta Maurya-I, who belongs to Maurya Dynasty.

Hence, the correct option is (D).

86. Open Platform Communication is the full form of OPC.

Open Platform Communication(OPC):

- OPC is a software interface interoperability standard that allows a secure and reliable exchange of data between Windows programs and industrial hardware devices.
- It is platform-independent and ensures the continuous flow of information across multiple vendor devices.

Hence, the correct option is (D).

87. A miniature graphical representation of files, folders, programs or other items in a GUI based operating system is called an icon.

Icon:

- A miniature graphical representation of files, folders, programs or other items in a GUI based operating system is called an icon.
- It is basically a pictogram or ideogram displayed on a computer screen in order to help the user navigate a computer system.
- The icon itself is a quickly understandable symbol of a software tool, function, or data file, accessible on the system and a detailed illustration of the actual entity it represents.

Hence, the correct option is (A).

88. Dial-up Internet access is a form of Internet access that uses the facilities of the public switched telephone network to establish a connection to an Internet service provider by dialing a telephone number on a conventional telephone line.

SLIP (Serial Line Internet Protocol) is the result of the integration of modem protocols prior to the suite of TCP/IP protocols.

Point-to-Point Protocol (PPP) is a data link layer communications protocol used to establish a direct connection between two nodes.

Hence, the correct option is (D).

89. Keyboard is the most common 'input device' used today.

An input device is a piece of equipment used to provide data and control signals to an information processing system, such as a computer or information appliance. Examples of input devices include keyboards, mouse, scanners, cameras, joysticks, and microphones.

A 'keyboard' is a human interface device which is represented as a layout of buttons. Each button, or key, can be used to either input an alphanumeric character to a computer, or to call upon a particular function of the computer. It acts as the main text entry interface for most users.

Hence, the correct option is (C).

90. A critical section is a program segment where shared resources are accessed. A critical section is a section of code belonging to a process in a. concurrent program that accesses a shared resource, e.g., a shared variable, shared. communication channel, shared file, etc. and for correct behavior of the program, only one process may access the.

Hence, the correct option is (C).

91. The government has approved an Electronics Manufacturing Cluster (EMC) in Pune at a cost of Rs 500 crore.

The proposal, approved by the Ministry of Electronics and Information Technology, is expected to attract investments of up to Rs 2,000 crore. The cluster will be set up over an area of 297 acres.

Hence, the correct option is (B).

92. 'Matki' is a popular folk dance of Madhya Pradesh.

- Matki dance form has been developed by nomadic tribes in Madhya Pradesh.
- Performed using a small pitcher is a folk dance originating from central India known as the "Matki Dance".
- This "pitcher dance" belongs to the state of Madhya Pradesh, and is mainly performed in the Malwa region.

Hence, the correct option is (B).

93. Amending the Constitution of India (Article 368) is the process of making changes to the nation's fundamental law or supreme law.

It provides for 2 types of amendments:

- by a special majority of the Parliament, and
- by a special majority of the Parliament and consent by at least half the states by a simple majority.

Hence, the correct option is (D).

94. Banda district of Uttar Pradesh is a major Bauxite Reserve of the state.

The minerals found in Uttar Pradesh include-

- Limestone is found in Guruma-Kanach-Bapuhari in the Mirzapur district and Kajrahat in the Sonebhadra district;
- Dolomite in Mirzapur, Sonebhadra, and Banda, glass-sand in Karchhana of Allahabad district,
- Karwi in Banda district and Mau district; marble in Mirzapur and Sonebhadra;
- Bauxite in Rajhgewan in Banda district;
- Non-plastic fireclay in Bansi and Makri-Khoh area of Mirzapur district;
- Uranium in Lalitpur district.
- Besides, Barytes and Edalusite are found in the districts of Mirzapur and Sonebhadra.
- Sandstone, pebbles, reh, salt punter, maurang, sand, and other minor minerals are also found in the State.

Hence, the correct option is (A).

95. The Satavahana rulers were known as lords of the Dakshinapatha.

- Gautamiputra Shri Satakarni and other Satavahana rulers were known as lords of the Dakshinapatha.
- Dakshinapatha was the route leading to the south, which was also used as a name for the entire southern region.
- To control the coasts, he sent his army to the eastern, western, and southern coasts.
- The Sunga dynasty came to an end around 73 BCE when their ruler Devabhuti was killed by Vasudeva Kanva.
- The Kanva dynasty then ruled over Magadha for about 45 years.
- Around this time, another powerful dynasty, the Satavahanas came to power in the Deccan area.
- The term "Satvahana" originated from the Prakrit which means " driven by seven" which is an implication of the Sun God's chariot that is driven by seven horses as per Hindu mythology.
- The Satavahanas (natives) succeeded the Mauryas in Deccan and Central India.

Hence, the correct option is (B).

96. Given:

Nikita takes as much time in running 18 meters as a car takes in covering 48 meters.

Calculation:

Time taken by Nikita = Time taken by Car

Time $= \frac{Distance}{Speed}$

$\Rightarrow \frac{d_1}{s_{\text{Nikita}}} = \frac{d_2}{s_{\text{Car}}}$

$\Rightarrow \frac{18}{s_{\text{Nikita}}} = \frac{48}{s_{\text{Car}}}$

$\Rightarrow \frac{s_{\text{Nikita}}}{s_{\text{Car}}} = \frac{18}{48} = \frac{d}{1600}$

⇒ Distance = 600 m

Hence, the correct option is (C).

97. Given:

9, 21, and 123

Concept:

If A : B :: C : D then (B × C) = (A × D)

Calculation:

Let the fourth proportion be F.

The proportion becomes = 9 : 21 :: 123 : F

According to the concept,

21 × 123 = 9 × F

$\Rightarrow F = \frac{21 \times 123}{9}$

⇒ F = 287

∴ The fourth proportion is 287.

Hence, the correct option is (C).

98. Given:

18% of 450 = 30% of k

⇒ 0.18 × 450 = 0.3 × k

⇒ 81 = 0.3k

$\Rightarrow k = \frac{81}{0.3}$

⇒ k = 270

∴ The value of k is 270.

Hence, the correct option is (A).

99. Given:

Seven persons can build a house = 30 days

Formula:

Total work = Number of people × Number of days

Calculation:

Total Work = 30 × 7 = 210 units

⇒ Number of days $= \frac{210}{3} = 70$ days

∴ 70 days they all work at the same rate.

Hence, the correct option is (B).

100. Given:

$a^3 - b^3 = 253$

a - b = 7

Formula:

$(a - b)^3 = a^3 - b^3 - 3ab(a - b)$

Calculation:

$\Rightarrow (7)^3 = 253 - 3ab(7)$

⇒ 343 = 253 - 21ab

⇒ 21ab = - 90

⇒ ab $= -\frac{30}{7}$

∴ The value of ab is $-\frac{30}{7}$.

Hence, the correct option is (D).

Mock Test 06

Discipline

Q.1 Which of the following is the definition of gestational hypertension?

A. Blood pressure over 130/85 mmHg or rise of more than 35 mmHg systolic or 20 mmHg diastolic over baseline
B. Blood pressure over 160/95 mmHg or rise of more than 30 mmHg systolic or 15 mmHg diastolic over baseline
C. Blood pressure over 140/90 mmHg or rise of more than 40 mmHg systolic or 25 mmHg diastolic over baseline
D. Blood pressure over 140/90 mmHg or rise of more than 30 mmHg systolic or 15 mmHg diastolic over baseline

Q.2 What treatment can prevent the development of sensitization to Rh-D antigen in an Rh negative mother carrying an Rh positive fetus?

A. Therapeutic abortion
B. Short-course immunosuppressant treatment
C. Rho(D) immune globulin
D. Rh (D) fetal serum injections

Q.3 The term placenta previa describes which of the following conditions?

A. All or part of the placenta is positioned between the fetus and the cervix
B. The fetus is inferior to the placental position
C. The placenta separates from the uterine wall
D. The placenta develops before the uterine lining is mature

Q.4 During Pregnancy, deficiency of which of the following leads to neural tube defects?

A. Folic acid **B.** Iron
C. Calcium **D.** Zinc

Q.5 During which stage of labor, the placenta is delivered?

A. Stage 1 **B.** Stage 2 **C.** Stage 3 **D.** Stage 4

Q.6 Which abdominal grip is used to assess the descent of the head in a pregnant woman?

A. Fundal **B.** Lateral **C.** Pelvic-1 **D.** Pelvic-2

Q.7 How much additional the amount of calories that should be taken by a pregnant women as per W.H.O?

A. 300 K. Calorie **B.** 500 K. Calorie
C. 1000 K. Calorie **D.** 100 K. Calorie

Q.8 Which of the following vaccine commonly given to pregnant mothers?

A. Measles **B.** B.C.G **C.** Tetanus **D.** D.P.T

Q.9 What is the expected weight gain of antenatal mothers during the first 20 weeks?

A. 0.5 to 1 kilogram **B.** 2 to 3 kilogram
C. 3 to 4 kilogram **D.** 4 to 5 kilogram

Q.10 A patient with a history of diabetes mellitus is on the second postoperative day following cholecystectomy. She has complained of nausea and isn't able to eat solid foods. The nurse enters the room to find the patient confused and shaky. Which of the following is the most likely explanation for the patient's symptoms?

A. Anesthesia reaction
B. Hyperglycemia
C. Hypoglycemia
D. Diabetic ketoacidosis

Q.11 Which of the following complications is of greatest concern when a nurse caring for a preoperative abdominal aneurysm person?

A. HPN
B. Aneurysm rupture
C. Cardiac arrhythmias
D. Diminished pedal pulses

Q.12 Which of the following classes of drugs is most widely used in the treatment of cardiomyopathy?

A. Antihypertensive
B. Beta-adrenergic blockers
C. Calcium channel blockers
D. Nitrates

Q.13 The nurse is aware the early indicator of hypoxia in the unconscious person is:

A. Cyanosis
B. Increased respirations
C. Hypertension
D. Restlessness

Q.14 While performing a physical assessment of a male patient with gout of the great toe, Nurse should assess for additional tophi (urate deposits) on the:

A. Buttocks **B.** Ears
C. Face **D.** Abdomen

Q.15 A male patient left tibia was fractured in an automobile accident, and a cast is applied. To assess for damage to major blood vessels from the fracture tibia, the nurse in charge should monitor the patient for:

A. Swelling of the left thigh
B. Increased skin temperature of the foot
C. Prolonged reperfusion of the toes after blanching
D. Increased blood pressure

Q.16 Which of the following signs and symptoms would Nurse include in her teaching plan as an early manifestation of laryngeal cancer?

A. Stomatitis **B.** Airway obstruction
C. Hoarseness **D.** Dysphagia

Q.17 Lydia is scheduled for elective splenectomy. Before the patient goes to surgery, the nurse in charge final assessment would be:

A. Signed consent **B.** Vital signs
C. Name band **D.** Empty bladder

Q.18 A person has aplastic anemia. Changes in which bodily function should the nurse monitor?

A. Bowel function **B.** Peripheral sensation
C. Bleeding tendencies **D.** Intake and output

Q.19 Phrase, 100 days cough is used for which disease?
[UPPSC Staff Nurse, 2021]

A. Tuberculosis **B.** Measles
C. Diphtheria **D.** Diphtheria

Q.20 A bleeding disorder characterized by deficiency of factor VIII and IX is termed as:
[UPPSC Staff Nurse, 2021]

A. Purpura **B.** Hemophilia
C. Thrombocytopenia **D.** Leukemia

Q.21 Which one is the most important drug in the management of Anaphylactic shock?
[UPPSC Staff Nurse, 2021]

A. Atropin **B.** Adrenalin
C. Deriphyllin **D.** Aminophyllin

Q.22 Spinal anesthesia is given usually at which level of spinal cord?
[UPPSC Staff Nurse, 2021]

A. L_2 - L_4 **B.** L_3 - L_4 **C.** L_5 - L_6 **D.** L_1 - L_2

Q.23 Rh factor incompatibility can produce:
[UPPSC Staff Nurse, 2021]

A. AIDS
B. Sickle Cell Anemia
C. Erythroblastosis foetalis
D. Turner's syndrome

Q.24 All the statements in relation to Halitosis is correct, except:
[UPPSC Staff Nurse, 2021]

A. Bad Breath
B. Odour producing bacteria
C. Carbon compound producing bacteria
D. Sulfur compound producing bacteria

Q.25 In which health problem phototherapy may be useful?
[UPPSC Staff Nurse, 2021]

A. Eczema **B.** Psoriasis
C. Neonatal Jaundice **D.** Burn

Q.26 Macewen's sign is found in which disease?
[UPPSC Staff Nurse, 2021]

A. Hydrocephalus **B.** Meningitis
C. Appendicitis **D.** Cerebral Palsy

Q.27 Normally which drug is used to dilate the pupil of eye?
[UPPSC Staff Nurse, 2021]

A. Gentamycin **B.** Tropicamide
C. Levofloxacin **D.** Betamethasone

Q.28 _______ is an essential tool of community health.

A. Health education **B.** Philosophy
C. Psychology **D.** None of these

Q.29 Health education help in desirable change in________.

A. Knowledge **B.** Attitude
C. Practice change **D.** All of these

Q.30 Which of the following are alternative methods of communication for ventilator-dependent patients?

A. Signal system
B. Pen and paper
C. Communication board
D. All of these

Q.31 A mother rescues two of her four children from a house fire. In the emergency department, she cries, "I should have gone back in to get them. I should have died, not them." What is the nurse's best response?

A. "The smoke was too thick. You couldn't have gone back in."
B. "You're feeling guilty because you weren't able to save your children."
C. "Focus on the fact that you could have lost all four of your children."
D. "It's best if you try not to think about what happened. Try to move on."

Q.32 A newly admitted client diagnosed with obsessive-compulsive disorder (OCD) washes hands continually. This behavior prevents unit activity attendance. Which nursing statement best addresses this situation?

A. "Everyone diagnosed with OCD needs to control their ritualistic behaviors."
B. "It is important for you to discontinue these ritualistic behaviors."
C. "Why are you asking for help if you won't participate in unit therapy?"
D. "Let's figure out a way for you to attend unit activities and still wash your hands."

Q.33 Which example of a therapeutic communication skill would be effective in the planning phase of the nursing process?

A. "We've discussed past coping skills. Let's see if these coping skills can be effective now."
B. "Please tell me in your own words what brought you to the hospital."
C. "This new approach worked for you. Keep it up."
D. "I notice that you seem to be responding to voices that I do not hear."

Q.34 Which of the following health communication style makes use of the person's knowledge and experience?

A. Doctor-centered communication
B. Patient-centered communication

C. Practitioner-centered communication
D. None of these

Q.35 A student nurse tells the instructor, "I'm concerned that when a client asks me for advice I won't have a good solution." Which should be the nursing instructor's best response?
A. "It's scary to feel put on the spot by a client. Nurses don't always have the answer."
B. "Remember, clients, not nurses, are responsible for their own choices and decisions."
C. "Just keep the client's best interests in mind and do the best that you can."
D. "Set a goal to continue to work on this aspect of your practice."

Q.36 The primary structure of the protein represents:
A. Linear sequence of amino acids joined by peptide bond
B. The 3-dimensional structure of protein
C. The helical structure of protein
D. Subunit structure of protein

Q.37 Which is not a source of carbohydrates?
A. High tide B. Rice
C. Gram D. Millet

Q.38 Which proteins are called messenger protein?
A. Enzymes B. Hormonal
C. Storage D. Antibodies

Q.39 The meal supplements in the mid-day meal plan should provide at least ______.
A. 300 calories with 8 to 12 grams of protein
B. 300 calories with 5 grams of protein
C. 250 calories with 8 to 12 grams of protein
D. 250 calories with 5 to 12 grams of protein

Q.40 Malnutrition comprises of following forms except:
A. Undernutrition B. Overnutrition
C. Imbalance D. Micronutrition

Q.41 Which of the following are "ammonic bacteria"?
A. Nitrosomonas B. Bacillus mycoides
C. Clostridium D. Rhizobium

Q.42 Which is the correct ratio of chest compressions to rescue breaths for use in CPR of an adult casualty?
A. 2 compressions : 30 rescue breaths
B. 5 compressions : 1 rescue breath
C. 15 compressions : 2 rescue breaths
D. 30 compressions : 2 rescue breaths

Q.43 What names are given to the three different depths of burns?
A. Small, medium, and large.
B. First, second and third
C. Minor, medium, and severe.
D. Superficial, partial thickness, full thickness.

Q.44 What is a fainting?
A. A response to fear
B. An unexpected collapse
C. A brief loss of consciousness
D. A sign of flu

Q.45 What happens with the carbon dioxide (CO_2) produced by the human body?
A. It remains in the body cells.
B. It is transferred to the heart muscle.
C. It is exhausted via the blood and breathing system.
D. It is transferred to the brain muscle.

Q.46 Where do you position the knot at the end of the bandages of an emergency bandage?
A. Always on top of the bandage
B. Crossed over the wound
C. Clearly away from the wound
D. Middle of the wound

Q.47 What do you do for a small cut?
A. Wash with soap and water, cover with a sterile bandage
B. Only cover with a sterile bandage
C. Clean the wound with cotton wool
D. None of these

Q.48 What is included in the CPR procedure?
A. Rescue breathings only
B. Compression of the chest only
C. Giving medicines
D. Rescue breathing and chest compressions

Q.49 Synapsis, in which stage does meiosis occur?
A. Leptotene B. Pachiten
C. Zygotene D. Metaphase I

Q.50 During which stage of mitosis, spindle fibers are formed and attached to chromosomes?
A. Middle age B. Hiatus
C. Prophase D. End stage

Q.51 In-plant tissue, the cell walls of ____ are coordinated by 'suberins' which make them impervious to gas and water molecules.
A. Epidermis B. Cork
C. Foramen D. Phloem Fiber

Q.52 The outermost covering of a plant cell is formed by ____.
A. Cellulose B. Lignin
C. Chitin D. Glycocalyx

Q.53 Which of the following organelles is known as the 'suicidal bag' of a cell?
A. Lysosomes
B. Plastid
C. Endoplasmic reticulum
D. Mitochondria

Q.54 Ribosomes are the workplace for which of the following?
A. Protein synthesis B. Photosynthesis
C. Fat synthesis D. Respiration

Q.55 The yellow color of urine is due to the presence of:

A. Gall
B. Lymphatic
C. Cholesterol
D. Urobilin or Urochrome

Q.56 Factors influencing core variables are:
A. Motivation
B. Mobility
C. Decentrilisation
D. Autonomy

Q.57 What are the different types of wards in a hospital?
A. Casuality ward
B. General ward
C. ICCU
D. All of the above

Q.58 The COPP had concluded that an OPD doctor examines:
A. 10-20 Patients per Day
B. 25-40 Patients per Day
C. 50-75 Patients per Day
D. 75-90 Patients per Day

Q.59 COPP had advocated the following as reasons for overcrowding in OPD's except:
A. Restricted Registration Time
B. Absence of Appointment System
C. Shortage of Medical Staff
D. Ineffective Public Relations

Q.60 Effective air conditioning in the OT complex decreases the chances of air-borne infection. HEPA filters are?
A. 0.1 to 0.2 micron in dimension
B. 0.2 to 0.3 micron in dimension
C. 0.3 to 0.4 micron in dimension
D. 0.4 to 0.5 micron in dimension

Q.61 HEPA provides an atmosphere which is:
A. 70% Particulate free
B. 80% Particulate free
C. 90% Particulate free
D. 100% Particulate free

Q.62 For effective air changes in Operation Theater the best of the following is:
A. High Turbulence displacement airflow
B. Low Turbulence displacement airflow
C. Mechanical extract of Air
D. Low to high displacement airflow

Q.63 Most commonly used model of care in ICUs:
A. Functional nursing
B. Team nursing
C. Primary nursing
D. Total patient care

Q.64 What form must be filled in before starting a surgery?
A. SF 520
B. SF 521
C. SF 522
D. SF 523

Q.65 When teaching a female patient how to take a sublingual tablet, the nurse should instruct the patient to place the tablet on the:
A. Top of the tongue
B. Roof of the mouth
C. Floor of the mouth
D. Inside of the cheek

Q.66 Which action by the nurse in charge is essential when cleaning the area around a Jackson-Pratt wound drain?
A. Cleaning from the center outward in a circular motion.
B. Removing the drain before cleaning the skin.
C. Cleaning briskly around the site with alcohol.
D. Wearing sterile gloves and a mask.

Q.67 A female patient undergoes a total abdominal hysterectomy. When assessing the patient 10 hours later, the nurse identifies which finding as an early sign of shock?
A. Restlessness
B. Pale, warm, dry skin
C. Heart rate of 110 beats/minute
D. Urine output of 30 ml/hour

Q.68 Which pulse should the nurse palpate during a rapid assessment of an unconscious male adult?
A. Radial
B. Brachial
C. Femoral
D. Carotid

Q.69 A patient is scheduled for a colonoscopy. The nurse will provide information to the patient about which type of enema?
A. Oil retention
B. Return flow
C. High large volume
D. Low, small volume

Q.70 The nurse is most likely to report which finding to the primary care provider for a patient who has an established colostomy?
A. The stoma extends 1/2 inch above the abdomen.
B. The skin under the appliance looks red briefly after removing the appliance.
C. The stoma color is a deep red purple.
D. An ascending colostomy just delivers liquid feces.

Q.71 A patient with a new stoma who has not had a bowel movement since surgery last week reports feeling nauseous. What is the appropriate nursing action?
A. Prepare to irrigate the colostomy.
B. After assessing the stoma and surrounding skin, notify the surgeon.
C. Assess bowel sounds and administer antiemetic.
D. Administer a bulk forming laxative, and encourage increased fluids and exercise.

Q.72 The nurse assesses a patient's abdomen several days after abdominal surgery. It is firm, distended, and painful to palpate. The patient reports feeling "bloated" . The nurse consults with the surgeon, who orders an enema. The nurse prepares to give what kind of enema?
A. Soapsuds
B. Retention
C. Return flow
D. Oil retention

Q.73 When caring for a terminally ill patient, it is important for the nurse to maintain the patient's dignity. This can be facilitated by:
A. Spending time to let patients share their life experiences
B. Decreasing emphasis on attending to the patient's appearance because it only increases their fatigue
C. Making decisions for patients so they do not have to make them
D. Placing the patient in a private room to provide privacy at

all times

Q.74 A child with thalassemia was given deferoxamine (Desferal); which of the following should alert the nurse to notify the physician?

A. Decreased hearing **B.** Hypertension
C. Red urine **D.** Vomiting

Q.75 Hydrocortisone cream of 1% is given to a child with eczema. The nurse gives instructions to the mother to apply the cream by?

A. Apply a thin layer of cream and spread it into the area thoroughly.
B. Avoid cleansing the area before the application.
C. Apply a thick layer of the cream to affected areas only.
D. Apply the cream to other areas to avoid occurrence.

Q.76 When a child injures the epiphyseal plate from a fracture, the damage may result in which of the following?

A. Rheumatoid arthritis
B. Permanent nerve damage
C. Osteomyelitis
D. Bone growth disruption

Q.77 Which of the following should the nurse include in the insulin administration instruction for the parents of a child being discharged on insulin?

A. Insert the needle and aspirate prior to injecting
B. Inject insulin into the extremity to be exercised to enhance absorption
C. The muscles in the abdomen and thigh are the easiest to use for self-administration
D. Clean the site of injection with soap and water and avoid alcohol

Q.78 Nurse Dorothy is caring for a child with Category A Near Drowning; she should do which of the following?

A. Plan for discharge in 12 to 24 hours.
B. Check for electrolyte imbalances.
C. Provide oxygen as ordered.
D. All of the above

Q.79 Reye's syndrome is a rare and severe illness affecting children and teenagers. Its development has been linked with the use of aspirin and which of the following?

A. Meningitis **B.** Encephalitis
C. Strep throat **D.** Varicella

Q.80 Niklaus was born with hypospadias; which of the following should be avoided when a child has such condition?

A. Surgery
B. Circumcision
C. Intravenous pyelography (IVP)
D. Catheterization

General Aptitude / Reasoning / General Awareness / Basic Computer knowledge

Q.81 A alone can complete a work in 12 days and B alone can complete the same work in 15 days. If they finish the work together and received Rs. 3600. Then find the share of A:

A. Rs. 1200 **B.** Rs. 3000 **C.** Rs. 1500 **D.** Rs. 2000

Q.82 From a pack of a well-shuffled decks of cards, two cards are drawn together at random. What is the probability of both the cards being Ace?

A. $\frac{1}{221}$ **B.** $\frac{2}{221}$ **C.** $\frac{2}{121}$ **D.** $\frac{1}{121}$

Q.83 The radius of two right circular cylinders are in the ratio $3:2$ and the of their volumes is $27:16$. What is the ratio of their heights?

[SSC CGL, 2020]

A. $4:3$ **B.** $9:8$ **C.** $3:4$ **D.** $8:9$

Q.84 In an election, there were two candidates Arvind and Manoj. If 20% of votes were declared invalid and Arvind got 20% more votes than Manoj. Then find the total number of people who voted if Arvind won by 480 votes.

A. 3000 **B.** 30000 **C.** 2400 **D.** 9600

Q.85 If $a - b = 3$ and $a^3 - b^3 = 279$, then what is the value of $a^3 + b^3$?

A. 317 **B.** 407 **C.** 297 **D.** 502

Q.86 A is standing North to B and B is standing East to C. In which direction will A come to meet C?

A. North-West **B.** South-West
C. North-East **D.** South-East

Q.87 Saniya remembers her friend's marriage is after 19th November. While her sister remembers the marriage is before 21st November. On which day of November is the marriage of Saniya's friend?

A. 17 **B.** 20 **C.** 23 **D.** 24

Q.88 If looking in a mirror shows that the time in the clock is 1 hour 30 minutes, then what was the right time in the actual clock?

[UPSSSC Forest Guard, 2015]

A. 6 hours 30 minutes **B.** 4 hours 30 minutes
C. 2 hours 30 minutes **D.** 10 hours 30 minutes

Q.89 Direction: Follow the given series to answer the question.

J U & 5 R 3 1 7 @ & M I 6 R 2 F S @ I M $ 9 L 7 1 6 A # 9 B Z $

How many such symbols are there in the above arrangement, each of which is immediately preceded by a symbol and immediately followed by a letter?

A. 2 **B.** 1 **C.** 4 **D.** 0

Q.90 Pointing towards a girl at wedding party, Ramu told Shamu that She is wife of my brother's son.
How is Ramu related to husband of that girl?

A. Aunt **B.** Grandmother
C. Uncle **D.** Either uncle or aunt

Q.91 Which Uttar Pradesh district is also known as 'Pital Nagari'?

[UP Police Constable, 2019]

A. Fatehpur **B.** Muzaffarnagar
C. Mirzapur **D.** Moradabad

Q.92 On 13th December 1946 ______ moved the Objective Resolution in the Constituent Assembly of India.

A. Sucheta Kripalani
B. Sarojini Naidu
C. Dr. Rajendra Prasad
D. Pandit Jawaharlal Nehru

Q.93 The first newspaper published in India was:

A. The Calcutta Gazette
B. The Calcutta Chronicle
C. The Bombay Herald
D. The Bengal Gazette

Q.94 Which of the following passes cuts through Pir Panjal range and links Manali and Leh by road?

A. Banihal Pass **B.** Baralachala Pass
C. Rohtang Pass **D.** Nathula Pass

Q.95 The pavilion of which of the following Ministries has been awarded for "Outstanding Contribution towards Public Communication and Outreach" at the 41st India International Trade Fair 2022?

A. Ministry of Home Affairs
B. Ministry of Health and Family Welfare
C. Ministry of Commerce
D. Ministry of Education

Q.96 What is the name of the software that is used for the maintenance and configuration of Computer Systems?

A. Device Driver
B. System Utilities
C. Operating System
D. General Purpose Software

Q.97 Which key combination is pressed simultaneously to minimize all the currently open windows on your desktop ?

[HTET PGT - Computer Science, 2020]

A. Alt+M **B.** Shift + M
C. Windows Key + M **D.** Ctrl + D

Q.98 What is the length and width of an A4 sheet in MS Word 2007?

A. 8.27 × 11.69 **B.** 8.27 × 12.69
C. 9.27 × 12.69 **D.** 9.27 × 11.69

Q.99 What is the output of the following MS-Excel function?
=FLOOR(34, 5)

A. 40 **B.** 35 **C.** 30 **D.** 33

Q.100 In PowerPoint, the dotted areas in an empty slide are called:

A. Template **B.** Placard
C. Placeholders **D.** Themes

// Smart Answer Sheet //

Correct Indicates percentage of students who answered questions correctly.

Skipped Indicates percentage of students who skipped questions.

Q.	Ans.	Correct	Skipped
1	D	41.0 %	1.65 %
2	C	25.72 %	4.7 %
3	A	65.1 %	1.68 %
4	A	41.91 %	1.34 %
5	C	59.47 %	1.45 %
6	D	41.28 %	1.94 %
7	A	61.93 %	1.37 %
8	C	53.8 %	1.63 %
9	B	69.76 %	1.62 %
10	C	60.64 %	1.55 %
11	B	30.65 %	3.71 %
12	B	60.65 %	1.59 %
13	D	83.16 %	0.0 %
14	B	68.93 %	1.68 %
15	C	69.34 %	1.53 %
16	C	32.86 %	4.38 %
17	B	59.36 %	1.18 %
18	C	85.2 %	0.0 %
19	D	51.63 %	1.55 %
20	B	41.36 %	1.79 %
21	B	62.67 %	1.64 %
22	B	80.23 %	0.0 %
23	B	43.35 %	1.21 %
24	C	81.95 %	0.0 %
25	C	40.29 %	1.85 %
26	A	69.84 %	1.64 %
27	B	56.87 %	1.34 %
28	A	43.08 %	1.05 %
29	D	49.29 %	1.92 %
30	D	49.29 %	1.4 %
31	B	25.52 %	4.08 %
32	D	76.09 %	0.0 %
33	A	84.2 %	0.0 %
34	B	52.51 %	1.58 %
35	B	46.89 %	1.17 %
36	A	46.62 %	1.16 %
37	C	42.83 %	1.46 %
38	B	66.39 %	1.26 %
39	A	64.49 %	1.73 %
40	C	40.24 %	1.15 %
41	B	41.12 %	1.3 %
42	D	56.73 %	1.26 %
43	D	42.21 %	1.73 %
44	C	85.22 %	0.0 %
45	C	59.55 %	1.06 %
46	C	78.91 %	0.0 %
47	A	61.9 %	1.81 %
48	D	40.28 %	1.99 %
49	C	60.41 %	1.72 %
50	A	48.2 %	1.67 %
51	B	53.1 %	1.24 %
52	A	42.79 %	1.29 %
53	A	88.99 %	0.0 %
54	A	43.64 %	1.63 %
55	D	43.06 %	1.86 %
56	B	44.11 %	1.45 %
57	D	57.66 %	1.89 %
58	B	60.01 %	1.01 %
59	D	62.36 %	1.63 %
60	C	50.09 %	1.47 %
61	C	85.71 %	0.0 %
62	B	29.56 %	3.66 %
63	D	60.84 %	1.82 %
64	C	44.77 %	1.54 %
65	C	84.95 %	0.0 %
66	A	26.24 %	3.47 %
67	A	61.06 %	1.68 %
68	D	48.53 %	1.15 %
69	D	55.07 %	1.74 %
70	C	18.37 %	3.66 %
71	B	61.84 %	1.1 %
72	C	26.68 %	3.81 %
73	A	40.8 %	1.94 %
74	A	85.43 %	0.0 %
75	A	49.5 %	1.01 %
76	D	61.72 %	1.11 %
77	D	54.48 %	1.97 %
78	D	55.8 %	1.64 %
79	D	61.62 %	1.06 %
80	B	44.11 %	1.78 %

Q.	Ans.	Correct / Skipped
81	D	46.47 % / 1.59 %
82	A	83.42 % / 0.0 %
83	C	81.29 % / 0.0 %
84	A	30.4 % / 3.39 %

Q.	Ans.	Correct / Skipped
85	B	63.21 % / 1.19 %
86	B	80.18 % / 0.0 %
87	B	88.9 % / 0.0 %
88	D	81.24 % / 0.0 %

Q.	Ans.	Correct / Skipped
89	B	80.71 % / 0.0 %
90	D	86.96 % / 0.0 %
91	D	80.66 % / 0.0 %
92	D	66.45 % / 1.29 %

Q.	Ans.	Correct / Skipped
93	D	64.81 % / 1.22 %
94	C	89.51 % / 0.0 %
95	B	67.95 % / 1.22 %
96	B	45.7 % / 1.55 %

Q.	Ans.	Correct / Skipped
97	C	88.41 % / 0.0 %
98	A	46.5 % / 1.52 %
99	C	50.24 % / 1.58 %
100	C	42.01 % / 1.81 %

Performance Analysis	
Avg. Score (%)	49.0%
Toppers Score (%)	66.0%
Your Score	

//Hints and Solutions//

1. Gestational hypertension is defined as blood pressure over 140/90 mmHg or the rise of more than 30 mmHg systolic or 15 mmHg diastolic over baseline. It generally develops after week 20 of pregnancy and returns to normal after delivery.

Gestational hypertension is high blood pressure in pregnancy. This condition is different from chronic hypertension.

Blood pressure is measured using two numbers: The first number, called systolic blood pressure, measures the pressure in your arteries when your heart beats. The second number, called diastolic blood pressure, measures the pressure in your arteries when your heart rests between beats.

Hence, the correct option is (D).

2. Rho(D) immune globulin treatment can prevent the development of sensitization to Rh-D antigen in an Rh negative mother carrying an Rh positive fetus.

Rh sensitization can be prevented by treatment of an Rh negative mother with Rho(D) immunoglobulin at 28 weeks, then again within 72 hours of delivery.

Rho(D) immune globulin is used to treat immune thrombocytopenic purpura (ITP) in patients with Rh-positive blood.

Hence, the correct option is (C).

3. The term placenta previa describes all or part of the placenta is positioned between the fetus and the cervix.

In placenta previa, the placenta develops in such a way that all or part of it is positioned in the lower one-third of the uterus, placing it between the fetus and the cervix. This can cause the placenta to tear and bleed. The most common sign is painless vaginal bleeding in the third trimester (generally after week 32).

Hence, the correct option is (A).

4. During Pregnancy, deficiency of Folic acid leads to neural tube defects.

Inadequate levels of folate (vitamin B9) and vitamin B12 during pregnancy have been found to lead to an increased risk of neural tube defects. Although both are part of the same biopathway, folate deficiency is much more common and therefore more of a concern.

Hence, the correct option is (A).

5. During Stage 3 of labor, the placenta is delivered.

The third stage of labor commences when the fetus is delivered and concludes with the delivery of the placenta. Separation of the placenta from the uterine interface is hallmarked by three cardinal signs, including a gush of blood at the vagina, lengthening of the umbilical cord, and a globular shaped uterine fundus on palpation.

Hence, the correct option is (C).

6. The pelvic-2 abdominal grip is used to assess the descent of the head in a pregnant woman.

The fingers of both hands are used to apply deep pressure in thedirection of the axis of the pelvic outlet down the sides of the uterustoward the pubis.The cephalic prominence is located on the side where the greatestresistance is felt.

If the prominence is located on the opposite side from the fetal back, thehead is said to be well flexed. If the prominence is located on the same side as the back, the head issaid to be extended (face presentation).

Hence, the correct option is (D).

7. 300 K. Calorie additional the amount of calories that should be taken by pregnant women as per W.H.O.

Eating for two does not mean eating twice as much food. Pregnant women need about 300 extra calories a day. But, where these calories come from matters. If you eat sweets or junk food, the extra calories do not provide the nutrients your baby needs. As a result, your growing baby will get the vitamins and minerals it needs from your own body. Your health could suffer.

Hence, the correct option is (A).

8. Tetanus vaccine is commonly given to pregnant mothers.

Obstetric care providers should administer the tetanus toxoid, reduced diphtheria toxoid, and acellular pertussis (Tdap) vaccine to all pregnant patients during each pregnancy, as early in the 27–36-weeks-of-gestation as possible.

Tetanus is an infection caused by bacteria called Clostridium tetani. When the bacteria invade the body, they produce a poison (toxin) that causes painful muscle contractions. Another name for tetanus is "lockjaw". It often causes a person's neck and jaw muscles to lock, making it hard to open the mouth or swallow.

Hence, the correct option is (C).

9. 2 to 3 kilogram is the expected weight gain of antenatal mothers during the first 20 weeks.

As you near the end of your first trimester, and begin the second, weight gain is expected to increase. Some providers like to see women with a "healthy" BMI prior to pregnancy, gain 2 to 3 kilogram by 20 weeks. During the second and third trimesters, guidelines often suggest gaining 0.2 to 0.4 kilogram per week.

Hence, the correct option is (B).

10. A postoperative diabetic patient who is unable to eat is likely to be suffering from hypoglycemia. Confusion and shakiness are common symptoms. Reduction in cerebral glucose availability (ie, neuroglycopenia) can manifest as confusion, difficulty with concentration, irritability, hallucinations, focal impairments (eg, hemiplegia), and, eventually, coma and death.

Hypoglycemia is a condition in which your blood sugar (glucose) level is lower than normal. Glucose is the main energy source of body. Hypoglycemia is often related to diabetes treatment.

Hence, the correct option is (C)

11. Rupture of an aneurysm is a life-threatening emergency and is of the greatest concern for the nurse caring for this type of person. The layers of the aortic wall can also separate (aortic dissection). This produces severe, tearing pain in the chest, back or abdomen. The potential for rupture is the most serious risk associated with an aortic aneurysm. A ruptured aortic aneurysm can cause life-threatening internal bleeding and/or a stroke.

Hence, the correct option is (B).

12. By decreasing the heart rate and contractility, beta-adrenergic blockers improve myocardial filling and cardiac output, which are primary goals in the treatment of cardiomyopathy. Cardiomyopathy is a disease of the heart muscle that makes it harder for your heart to pump blood to the rest of your body. Cardiomyopathy can lead to heart failure. The main types of cardiomyopathy include dilated, hypertrophic and restrictive cardiomyopathy.

Hence, the correct option is (B).

13. Restlessness is an early indicator of hypoxia. The nurse should suspect hypoxia in an unconscious client who suddenly becomes restless. When oxygen delivery is severely compromised, organ function will start to deteriorate. Neurologic manifestations include restlessness, headache, and confusion with moderate hypoxia. In severe cases, altered mentation and coma can occur, and if not corrected quickly may lead to death.

Hence, the correct option is (D).

14. While performing a physical assessment of a male patient with a gout of the great toe, the Nurse should assess for additional tophi (urate deposits) on the ears.

Uric acid has low solubility, it tends to precipitate and form deposits at various sites where blood flow is least active, including cartilaginous tissue such as the ears. Tophi, which are subcutaneous depositions of urate that form nodules, can also be found in patients with persistent hyperuricemia. Tophi typically occur in the joints, ears, finger pads, tendons, and bursae.

Hence, the correct option is (B).

15. Damage to blood vessels may decrease the circulatory perfusion of the toes, this would indicate the lack of blood supply to the extremity. If the intracompartmental pressure becomes higher than arterial pressure, a decrease in arterial inflow will also occur. The reduction of venous outflow and arterial inflow result in decreased oxygenation of tissues causing ischemia. If the deficit of oxygenation becomes high enough, irreversible necrosis may occur.

Hence, the correct option is (C).

16. Early warning signs of laryngeal cancer can vary depending on tumor location. Hoarseness lasting 2 weeks should be evaluated because it is one of the most common warning signs. Patients are typically male with a history of current or past tobacco smoking. Hoarseness is often an early presenting symptom of glottic cancers due to vocal cord immobility or fixation, with pain with swallowing and referred ear pain indicating advanced disease.

Hence, the correct option is (C).

17. An elective procedure is scheduled in advance so that all preparations can be completed ahead of time. The vital signs are the final check that must be completed before the patient leaves the room so that continuity of care and assessment is provided for.

Hence, the correct option is (B).

18. Aplastic anemia decreases the bone marrow production of RBCs, white blood cells, and platelets. The person is at risk for bruising and bleeding tendencies. Aplastic anemia refers to the syndrome of chronic primary hematopoietic failure from injury leading to diminished or absent hematopoietic precursors in the bone marrow and attendant pancytopenia.

Hence, the correct option is (C).

19. Phrase, 100 days cough is used for Pertussis.

Pertussis:

- The 100 days cough is a highly contagious bacterial upper respiratory tract infection caused by Bordetella Pertussis.
- It is commonly known as whooping cough.
- Bordetella Pertussis is a gram-negative, aerobic and encapsulated cocco-bacilli.
- The disease Pertussis was primarily described by a French physician Guillaume de Baillou after the epidemic in 1578 and the pathogen is isolated by Jules Bordet and Octave Gengau in 1906.
- Pertussis is an airborne disease, spreading through droplets from an infected person.
- The average incubation period is about 7-14 days.
- After inhalation, the bacteria primarily adhere to the ciliary epithelium of the nasopharynx and produces toxins.
- Tracheal cytotoxin destroys the ciliated epithelial cells and inhibits mucociliary function.
- The pertussis toxin (PTx) causes disturbances in the cellular signaling mechanism by affecting the ATP-cAMP pathways resulting in immune suppression.
- The classical symptoms include Paroxysmal cough (sudden recurrence and intensification of symptoms), inspiratory whoop, fainting, or vomiting after coughing.

Hence, the correct option is (D).

20. A bleeding disorder characterized by deficiency of factor VIII and IX is termed as hemophilia.

- Hemophilia is an inherited genetic disorder that impairs coagulation.
- There are mainly two types of hemophilia.
- Hemophilia A results from a deficiency of clotting factor 8 and Hemophilia B results from the deficiency of clotting factor 10.
- Factor 8 is known as an anti-hemophilic factor and factor 10 is known as the eponym Stuart–Prower factor.
- In hemophilia B (factor IX deficiency), the body doesn't make enough factor IX (factor 9), one of the substances the body needs to form a clot.

Hence, the correct option is (B).

21. Adrenalin is the most important drug in the management of Anaphylactic shock.

- Anaphylaxis is described as an acute systemic reaction with symptoms of an immediate-type allergic reaction that can involve the whole organism and is potentially life-threatening.
- It typically causes localized symptoms to organ system symptoms.

Adrenaline:

- The most important drug in the acute therapy of anaphylaxis is adrenaline (epinephrine).
- Through the activation of α- and β-adrenergic receptors, adrenaline functionally antagonizes all of the important pathomechanisms of anaphylaxis by vasoconstriction, reduction of vascular permeability, bronchodilatation, edema reduction, and positive inotropy in the heart.
- Administered intravenously, it shows the fastest onset of action of all anaphylaxis drugs.

Hence, the correct option is (B).

22. Spinal anesthesia is usually at L_3 - L_4 of spinal cord.

- Spinal anaesthesia is a type of neuraxial regional anaesthesia.
- Spinal anaesthesia involves the injection of a local anaesthetic or opioid into the subarachnoid space.
- It is done using a spinal needle.
- It is safe, easy, and effective when compared to general and other forms of anaesthesia.

Hence, the correct option is (B).

23. Rh factor incompatibility can produce sickle cell anemia.

- Rh incompatibility occurs when a pregnant woman has Rh-negative blood and the fetus has Rh-positive blood.
- Rh incompatibility can result in the destruction of the fetus's red blood cells, sometimes causing anaemia that can be severe.
- The fetus is checked periodically for evidence of anaemia.
- Sickle cell anaemia is one of a group of disorders known as sickle cell disease.
- Sickle cell anaemia is an inherited red blood cell disorder in which there aren't enough healthy red blood cells to carry oxygen throughout your body.
- Normally, the flexible, round red blood cells move easily through blood vessels.

Hence, the correct option is (B).

24. All the statements in relation to Halitosis is correct, except carbon compound producing bacteria.

- Halitosis is a health problem characterized by bad-smelling breath.
- Halitosis is commonly caused by sulfur-producing bacteria that are seen in the tongue and throat.
- The number of bacterial species, found in the oral cavity is about 500, and most of them are capable to produce odorous compounds which can cause halitosis.

Hence, the correct option is (C).

25. In Neonatal jaundice, phototherapy may be useful.

- Neonatal jaundice is a yellowish discoloration of the skin, and eyes from elevated serum bilirubin in the newborn period
- Neonatal jaundice in most newborns is a mild and transient event.
- Neonatal jaundice can arise due to physiological and pathological causes
- Physiologic jaundice is also known as non-pathologic jaundice and it is mild.
- Physiologic jaundice occurs on 2 to 4 days of birth and usually resolves in 2two weeks.

The causes of pathologic neonatal jaundice are :

- Increased bilirubin production.
- Decreased bilirubin clearance.
- Increased enterohepatic circulation.

Hence, the correct option is (C).

26. Macewen's sign is found in hydrocephalus disease.

- When an infant suffered from hydrocephalus, physicians use percussion as the tool for physical examination and tap the skull area over the junction between frontal, temporal, and parietal bones.
- If that will produce the sound of a cracked pot that will indicate increased intracranial pressure and increased intracranial pressure is a major clinical feature of hydrocephalus.
- This positive sign is known as Macewen's sign or the cracked pot sound.

Hence, the correct option is (A).

27. Normally tropicamide drug is used to dilate the pupil of eye.

- Drug name- Tropicacyl
- Generic name: Tropicamide ophthalmic
- Drug class: Mydriatics
- Mydriatics, such as tropicamide is a medication used to dilate the pupil and help the ophthalmic examination of the eye.

Hence, the correct option is (B).

28. Health education is an essential tool of community health.

Health education is a social science that draws from the biological, environmental, psychological, physical and medical sciences to promote health and prevent disease, disability and premature death through education-driven voluntary behavior change activities.

Hence, the correct option is (A).

29. Health education helps in a desirable change in knowledge, attitude, and practice change.

Health education is any combination of learning experiences designed to facilitate voluntary actions conducive to health. Health promotion is the combination of educational and environmental supports for actions and conditions of living conducive to health, thereby including health education.

Hence, the correct option is (D).

30. Signal system, Pen and paper, and Communication board are alternative methods of communication for ventilator-dependent patients.

Patients are unable to vocalize during mechanical ventilation due to the breathing tube. Also, ventilated patients may be sedated or have fluctuating consciousness; their ability to comprehend or attend to communications may also fluctuate. Patients often have other pre-existing communication impairments – many will be hard of hearing and approximately 80% will be glasses wearers, however, most will not have glasses or hearing aids readily available at the bedside. Writing may be impaired due to swollen hands/fingers, muscle weakness or lack of coordination.

Hence, the correct option is (D).

31. The best response by the nurse is, "You're feeling guilty because you weren't able to save your children." This response utilizes the therapeutic communication technique of reflection which identifies a patient's emotional response and reflects these feelings back to the patient so that they may be recognized and accepted.

Hence, the correct option is (B).

32. The most appropriate statement by the nurse is, "Let's figure out a way for you to attend unit activities and still wash your hands." This statement reflects the therapeutic communication technique of formulating a plan of action. The nurse attempts to work with the client to develop a plan without damaging the therapeutic relationship or increasing the client's anxiety.

Hence, the correct option is (D).

33. "We've discussed past coping skills. Let's see if these coping skills can be effective now." This statement by the nurse is an example of the therapeutic communication skill of formulating a plan of action. By the use of this skill, the nurse can help the client plan in advance to deal with a stressful situation which may prevent anger and/or anxiety from escalating to an unmanageable level.

Hence, the correct option is (A).

34. Patient-centered communication style makes use of the person's knowledge and experience.

Patient-centered communication, also known as person-centered communication or client-centered communication, is defined as a process that invites and encourages patients and their families to actively participate and negotiate in decision-making about their care needs. Patient-centered communication is crucial in promoting patient-centered care and requires that patients and their caregivers engage in the care process.

Hence, the correct option is (B).

35. "Remember, clients, not nurses, are responsible for their own choices and decisions." should be the nursing instructor's best response.

Giving advice tells the client what to do or how to behave. It implies that the nurse knows what is best and that the client is incapable of any self-direction. It discourages independent thinking. It implies that the client cannot handle life decisions and only the nurse knows what is best for the client.

Hence, the correct option is (B).

36. The primary structure of the protein represents linear sequence of amino acids joined by peptide bond. The amino acids are the monomeric units of proteins that are linked together by covalent bonds known as the peptide bonds which are a type of amide bond.

Hence, the correct option is (A).

37. Gram is not a source of carbohydrates, it is a source of protein. Carbohydrates are the main source of energy for our bodies. There are two types of carbohydrates - simple and complex.

Simple Carbohydrates – These are quick-energy foods, such as sugar. Sources of simple carbohydrates are natural fruits, milk and milk products, and vegetables including potatoes and carrots.

Complex Carbohydrates – These are better sources of energy than sugar as they are released slowly. The sources of complex carbohydrates are bread, cereals (rice, wheat, bajra, maize, barley, ragi, jowar, etc).

Hence, the correct option is (C).

38. Hormonal proteins are the messenger proteins which help to transmit the signals to coordinate the biological processes between different cells, tissues, and organs.

Examples are insulin, oxytocin, and somatotropin.

Hence, the correct option is (C).

39. Meal supplements in the midday meal plan should provide 300 calories with a minimum of 8 to 12 grams of protein. The food norms have been revised to ensure a balanced and nutritious diet by reducing the amount of pulses from 65 to 75 grams, oil and fat from 10 grams to 7.5 grams for upper primary group children from 25 to 30 grams.

Hence, the correct option is (A).

40. Malnutrition comprises undernutrition, overnutrition, and micronutrition forms except Imbalance. Malnutrition refers to deficiencies, excesses or imbalances in a person's intake of energy and/or nutrients. The term malnutrition covers 2 broad groups of conditions.

Undernutrition is a deficiency of calories or of one or more essential nutrients. Undernutrition may develop because people cannot obtain or prepare food, have a disorder that makes eating or absorbing food difficult, or have a greatly increased need for calories.

Overnutrition is a form of malnutrition in which the intake of nutrients is oversupplied. The amount of nutrients exceeds the amount required for normal growth, development, and metabolism.

Micronutrients are one of the major groups of nutrients your body needs. They include vitamins and minerals. Vitamins are necessary for energy production, immune function, blood clotting and other functions.

Hence, the correct option is (C).

41. Bacillus mycoides is an "ammonic bacteria". Ammonizing bacteria convert amino acids into ammonium compounds. Bacillus mycoides is a Gram-positive, non-motile, spore-forming bacteria that forms rhizoid colonies. It is found in soils throughout the world.

Hence, the correct option is (B).

42. The correct ratio of chest compressions to rescue breaths for use in CPR of an adult casualty is 30 compressions : 2 rescue breaths.

Place your palm on the center of the person's chest, then place the other hand on top and press down by 5 to 6cm (2 to 2.5 inches) at a steady rate of 100 to 120 compressions a minute. After every 30 chest compressions, give 2 rescue breaths.

Hence, the correct option is (D).

43. Superficial, partial thickness, full thickness are the name given to the three different depths of burns.

Burns are classified as first-, second-, third-degree, or fourth-degree depending on how deeply and severely they penetrate the skin's surface.

First-degree (superficial) burns. First-degree burns affect only the outer layer of skin, the epidermis. The burn site is red, painful, dry, and with no blisters. Mild sunburn is an example. Long-term tissue damage is rare and often consists of an increase or decrease in the skin color.

Second-degree (partial thickness) burns. Second-degree burns involve the epidermis and part of the lower layer of skin, the dermis. The burn site looks red, blistered, and may be swollen and painful.

Third-degree (full thickness) burns. Third-degree burns destroy the epidermis and dermis. They may go into the innermost layer of skin, the subcutaneous tissue. The burn site may look white or blackened and charred.

Fourth-degree burns. Fourth-degree burns go through both layers of the skin and underlying tissue as well as deeper tissue, possibly involving muscle and bone. There is no feeling in the area since the nerve endings are destroyed.

Hence, the correct option is (D).

44. A brief loss of consciousness is fainting.

Fainting happens when you lose consciousness for a short amount of time because your brain isn't getting enough oxygen. The medical term for fainting is syncope, but it's more commonly known as "passing out." A fainting spell generally lasts from a few seconds to a few minutes. Feeling lightheaded, weak, or nauseous sometimes happens before you faint.

Hence, the correct option is (C).

45. The carbon dioxide (CO_2) produced by the human body is exhausted by the blood and breathing system.

In the human body, carbon dioxide is formed intracellularly as a byproduct of metabolism. CO_2 is transported in the bloodstream to the lungs where it is ultimately removed from the body through exhalation.

Hence, the correct option is (C).

46. The knot should be positioned clearly away from the wound at the end of the bandages of an emergency bandage.

Apply the bandage firmly, but not tightly, and secure the end by folding it over and tying a knot in the end. You can also use a safety pin, tape, or a bandage clip. as soon as the bandage is on, ask if it feels too tight and checks the circulation by pressing on a fingernail or a piece of skin until it turns pale.

Hence, the correct option is (C).

47. Wash with soap and water, cover with a sterile bandage for a small cut.

These guidelines can help you care for minor cuts and scrapes:

- Wash your hands.
- Stop the bleeding.
- Clean the wound.
- Apply an antibiotic or petroleum jelly.
- Cover the wound.
- Change the dressing.
- Get a tetanus shot.
- Watch for signs of infection.

Hence, the correct option is (A).

48. CPR procedure includes Rescue breathing and chest compressions.

Rescue breathing is a type of first aid that's given to people who have stopped breathing. During rescue breathing, you blow air into a person's mouth to supply them with vital oxygen.

Chest compressions means you'll use your hands to push down hard and fast in a specific way on the person's chest. Chest compressions are the most important step in CPR.

Hence, the correct option is (D).

49. Synapsis, meiosis occurs in the zygotene stage. Prophase I of Meiosis I has 5 sub-stages:

1. Leptotene
2. Zygotene
3. Pachetin

4. Diplotene
5. Diakinesis

The zygotene stage is characterized by the pairing of homologous chromosomes called 'synapsis'. The pair of homologous chromosomes is called bivalent. There develops a structure between homologous chromosomes called the synaptonemal complex. It is a tripartite structure i.e., it is made up of 3 thick lines of DNA and protein.

Hence, the correct option is (C).

50. During the middle of mitosis, spindle fibers are formed and attached to the chromosomes. Mitosis is divided into 4 sub-stages:

1. Prophase
2. Middle age
3. Hiatus
4. End state

Middle age is characterized by:

- Complete disruption of the nuclear envelope, so chromosomes are spread throughout the cytoplasm
- Completion of the condensation of chromosomes, so chromosomes are clearly visible and their morphology is best studied.
- Spinal fibers are formed and attached to the chromosomes on the locus disc.

Hence, the correct option is (A).

51. The cell walls of in-plant tissues, 'corks', are coordinated by 'suberins' which make them impervious to water and gas molecules.

Protective tissue:

- These tissues provide strength to the plant.
- They consist of two basic things known as 'epidermis and cork'.

Cork cells lack intercellular gaps and be lifeless. The cell wall of cork is coordinated by suberin which makes them impermeable to water molecules and gas molecules.

Hence, the correct option is (B).

52. Cellulose constitutes the outermost covering of the plant cell. Epidermis is the protective outer layer of clonally related cells that resides in all plant organs. It is made up of cellulose, hemicellulose and pectin.

Functions of cell wall in plant:

- Regulates and controls the direction of cell growth.
- Providing strength, structural support and maintaining the shape of the cell.
- It helps in the entry of freely moving small molecules.

Hence, the correct option is (A).

53. Lysosomes are known as the suicidal bag of the cell because it is capable of destroying its own cell in which it is present. It contains many hydrolytic enzymes which are responsible for the destruction process. This happens. when either the cell is aged or gets infected by external agents like any bacteria or virus.

Plastids are double membrane organelles found in plant cells and contain pigments that help the plant in photosynthesis. They are responsible for storing and manufacturing food.

The endoplasmic reticulum usually contains ribosomes that are involved in lipid and protein synthesis.

Mitochondria are known as the powerhouse of the cell.

Hence, the correct option is (A).

54. Ribosomes are membranous granular structures present in the cytoplasm. They were first observed under an electron microscope in the year 1953 by George Palade as dense particles. Ribosomes are the site for "protein synthesis", hence they are also called "protein synthesis" of the cell.

There are two types of ribosomes:

- The eukaryotic ribosome - the 80s - is in the cytoplasm of the eukaryotic cell.
- Prokaryotic ribosomes - the 70s - are in the cytoplasm as well as attached to the cell membrane of the prokaryotic cell.

Hence, the correct option is (A).

55. The yellow color of urine is due to the presence of the pigment urochrome, which is a denatured product of hemoglobin from waste RBCs.

Normal urine color ranges from pale yellow to dark amber - a result of the pigment of the urine called urochrome and how to dilute or concentrated the urine is.

Pigments and other compounds in certain foods and medicines can change the color of your urine. Beets, berries, and fava beans are among the foods that affect the color.

Hence, the correct option is (D).

56. Factors influencing core variables are all except mobility.

Mobility has turned into a necessity, rather than a trend, in the modern world. Mobile apps have enhanced business in various sectors and had become essential in the fields of healthcare and hospital management.

Hence, the correct option is (B).

57. All of the above are different types of wards in a hospital.

Casualty ward is the part of a hospital where people who have severe injuries or sudden illnesses are taken for emergency treatment.

People are transferred from the intensive care unit to a general ward when medical staff decide that they no longer need such close observation and one-to-one care.

ICCU – Intermediate Cardiac Care Unit – This unit provides specialized cardiac care to patients who do not require the intensive level of care, but who do require cardiac monitoring and a more intensive nursing care than provided in most ward areas.

Hence, the correct option is (D).

58. The COPP had concluded that an OPD doctor examines 25-40 Patients per day.

In order to see more patients, usually 25-40 per day or more, they must no longer visit inpatients in the hospital nor see their patients in the emergency room. And they have shortened most visits to about 15-20 minutes which means 8-12 minutes of "face time." Too little time for someone with multiple chronic illnesses on 5-7 prescription medications and possibly impaired by age with reduced vision, hearing and memory.

Hence, the correct option is (B).

59. Ineffective public relations is not a reason for overcrowding in OPD's.

Hospitals require public relations activities to distinguish them from competitors, provide bidirectional communication between the society and the hospital, and assist to create of a strong hospital image and culture.

Hence, the correct option is (D).

60. Effective air conditioning in the OT complex decreases the chances of air-borne infection. HEPA filters are 0.3 to 0.4 micron in dimension.

The smaller the micron, the harder it is to filter out of the air. To put it into perspective the human eye can detect a particle that is approximately 10 microns. Bacteria can be as small as 0.3 microns, which is why 0.3 micron industrial HEPA filters are used in pharma companies.

Hence, the correct option is (C).

61. HEPA provides an atmosphere that is 90% Particulate free.

HEPA is a type of pleated mechanical air filter. It is an acronym for "high efficiency particulate air. Particles that are larger or smaller are trapped with even higher efficiency. This type of air filter can theoretically remove at least 99.97% of dust, pollen, mold, bacteria, and any airborne particles with a size of 0.3 microns (μm).

Hence, the correct option is (C).

62. For effective air changes in Operation Theater, the best of the following is Low Turbulence displacement airflow.

To meet the demands of highest degree air purity, the principle of low-turbulence displacement flow (UDAF) is being utilized in class A clean rooms. In doing so, a low-turbulence unidirectional displacement air flow (UDAF) is generated over the entire profile of a usually demarcated area. The speed of the airflow is uniform and pours into the cleanroom in close to parallel streamlines. It is the objective of our studies to record the magnitude of the flow velocity and the evenness of the flow by using measurement methods

Hence, the correct option is (B).

63. The most commonly used model of care in ICUs is Total patient care.

Total patient care is a model of care designed around a registered nurse overseeing personal care to one patient during a specific period of time. RNs can assist with medical, home care and care management needs, such as oversight of health services.

Hence, the correct option is (D).

64. SF 522 stands for Standard Form 522 which is to be filled out before starting surgery. This form is a record where the patient and the family know about the operation, the procedure, the risk involved, etc. They give consent for surgery, anesthesia, etc. The patient's vitals before the surgery are also mentioned in this form.

Hence, the correct option is (C).

65. When teaching a female patient how to take a sublingual tablet, the nurse should instruct the patient to place the tablet on the floor of the mouth.

The nurse should instruct the patient to touch the tip of the tongue to the roof of the mouth and then place the sublingual tablet on the floor of the mouth. Sublingual medications are absorbed directly into the bloodstream from the oral mucosa, bypassing the GI and hepatic systems. No drug is administered on top of the tongue or on the roof of the mouth.

Hence, the correct option is (C).

66. Cleaning from the center outward in a circular motion action by the nurse in charge is essential when cleaning the area around a Jackson-Pratt wound drain.

The nurse always should clean around a wound drain, moving from the center outward in ever-larger circles, because the skin near the drain site is more contaminated than the site itself. A Jackson-Pratt (JP) drain is used to remove fluids that build up in an area of the body after surgery. The Jackson-Pratt drain is a bulb-shaped device connected to a tube. One end of the tube is placed inside the patient during surgery. The other end comes out through a small cut in the skin. The bulb is connected to this end. The patient may have a stitch to hold the tube in place.

Hence, the correct option is (A).

67. A female patient undergoes a total abdominal hysterectomy. When assessing the patient 10 hours later, the nurse identifies restlessness as an early sign of shock.

Early in shock, hyperactivity of the sympathetic nervous system causes increased epinephrine secretion, which typically makes the patient restless, anxious, nervous, and irritable. It also decreases tissue perfusion to the skin, causing pale, cool clammy skin. Shock is characterized by decreased oxygen delivery and/or increased oxygen consumption or inadequate oxygen utilization leading to cellular and tissue hypoxia. It is a life-threatening condition of circulatory failure and most commonly manifested as hypotension (systolic blood pressure less than 90 mm Hg or MAP less than 65 mmHg).

Hence, the correct option is (A).

68. Carotid pulse the nurse should palpate during the rapid assessment of an unconscious male adult.

During a rapid assessment, the nurse's first priority is to check the patient's vital functions by assessing his airway, breathing, and circulation. To check a patient's circulation, the nurse must assess his heart and vascular network function. This is done by checking his skin color, temperature, mental status, and most importantly, his pulse. The nurse should use the carotid artery to check a patient's circulation.

Hence, the correct option is (D).

69. A patient is scheduled for a colonoscopy. The nurse will provide information to the patient about low, small volume type of enema.

Small volume enemas along with other preparations are used to prepare the patient for this procedure. The small volume enema is used to clean the lower portion of the colon or the sigmoid. This type of cleansing enema is often used for the patient who is constipated but does not need cleansing of the higher colon. The amount used is less than 500 ml and the bag is raised no higher than 12 inches.

Hence, the correct option is (D).

70. The nurse is most likely to report that the stoma color is a deep red-purple to the primary care provider for a patient who has an established colostomy.

An established stoma should be dark pink like the color of the buccal mucosa and is slightly raised above the abdomen. A stoma is the exteriorization of a loop of bowel from the anterior abdominal wall, done during a surgical procedure. It is done for diversion or decompression of the remaining bowel. It may be temporary or permanent, depending on the indication for which it was performed. Most stomas are incontinent, which means that there is no voluntary control over the passage of flatus and feces from the stoma.

Hence, the correct option is (C).

71. After assessing the stoma and surrounding skin, notify the surgeon this is the appropriate nursing action.

The patient has assessment findings consistent with complications of surgery. Providers and nurses should monitor stomas at regular intervals to look for the multiple complications of colostomies as an integrated team approach. Some complications are extremely troublesome to patients, and they come to the hospital with these presentations, but others may be more occult and have to be looked for.

Hence, the correct option is (B).

72. The nurse prepares to give a return flow kind of enema.

This provides relief of postoperative flatus, stimulating bowel motility. Options one, two, and four manage constipation and do not provide flatus relief. A return-flow enema, or Harris flush, is used to remove intestinal gas and stimulate peristalsis. A large volume fluid is used but the fluid is instilled in 100-200 ml increments. Then, the fluid is drawn out by lowering the container below the level of the bowel. This brings the flatus out with the fluid.

Hence, the correct option is (C).

73. When caring for a terminally ill patient, it is important for the nurse to maintain the patient's dignity. This can be facilitated by Spending time to let clients share their life experiences.

Spending time to let patients share their life experiences enables the nurse to know patients better. Knowing patients then facilitates the choice of therapies that promote patient decision-making and autonomy, thus promoting a patient's self-esteem and dignity. Regarding emotional needs, a review found that important actions for healthcare professionals providing end-of-life care include communicating, listening, conveying empathy, and involving patients in decision-making. Furthermore, good communication between the patient and their partner about their feelings should be promoted.

Hence, the correct option is (A).

74. A child with thalassemia was given deferoxamine (Desferal); Decreased hearing should alert the nurse to notify the physician.

Deferoxamine is ototoxic. Thus, any hearing problem should be immediately addressed to the physician. Chronic deferoxamine therapy can lead to sensorineural hearing loss and retinopathy. Hearing and vision loss can be reversible if the patient discontinues DFO early in the course. A screening hearing exam should be performed in the clinic every six months and a formal audiogram every 12 months.

Hence, the correct option is (A).

75. Hydrocortisone cream of 1% is given to a child with eczema. The nurse gives instructions to the mother to apply a thin layer of cream and spread it into the area thoroughly.

Hydrocortisone is commonly used to treat eczema flare-ups. Topical hydrocortisone is applied directly to irritated skin and can reduce redness, swelling, and itching. Hydrocortisone is available as a cream, ointment, lotion, or gel. Topical corticosteroids are administered sparingly and rubbed into the area thoroughly. Topical steroid creams and ointments should be applied in a thin layer and massaged into the affected area.

Hence, the correct option is (A).

76. The epiphyseal plate is a significant region of bone growth. Hence, any disruption may result in limb shortening. Sometimes, changes in the growth plate from the fracture can cause problems later. For example, the bone could end up a little crooked or a bit longer or shorter than expected.

Hence, the correct option is (D).

77. Cleaning the site of injection with soap and water and avoiding alcohol the nurse should include this in the insulin administration instruction for the parents of a child being discharged on insulin.

Infection risk from insulin injections is negligible (at least in normal environments – some experts feel hospital environments are riskier), and an alcohol swab is a poor way to sanitize skin in the first place. Soap and hot water are actually more effective.

Hence, the correct option is (D).

78. Near-drowning is defined as survival for at least 24 hours from suffocation by submersion. Aspiration of water causes the plasma to be pulled into the lungs, resulting in hypoxemia, acidosis, and hypovolemia. Hypoxemia results from the decrease in pulmonary surfactant caused by the absorbed water that leads to damage of the pulmonary capillary membrane. Children with

Category A Near Drowning are awake with minimal injury. Care includes checking electrolyte status, administering oxygen and warming, and preparing for discharge in 12 to 24 hours.

Hence, the correct option is (D).

79. Reye's syndrome is a rare and severe illness affecting children and teenagers. Its development has been linked with the use of aspirin and varicella.

Reye's (Reye) syndrome is a rare but serious condition that causes swelling in the liver and brain. Reye's syndrome most often affects children and teenagers recovering from a viral infection, most commonly the flu or chickenpox. Aspirin and varicella have been linked with Reye's syndrome, so use caution when giving aspirin to children or teenagers for fever or pain. Though aspirin and varicella are approved for use in children older than age 3, children and teenagers recovering from chickenpox or flu-like symptoms should never take aspirin and varicella.

For the treatment of fever or pain, consider giving your child an infant's or children's over-the-counter fever and pain medications such as acetaminophen (Tylenol, others) or ibuprofen (Advil, Motrin, others) as a safer alternative to aspirin and varicella.

Hence, the correct option is (D).

80. Hypospadias refers to a condition in which the urethral opening is located below the glans penis or anywhere along the ventral surface (underside) of the penile shaft. The ventral foreskin is lacking, and the distal portion gives an appearance of a hood. Early recognition is important so that circumcision is avoided; the foreskin is used for surgical repair.

Hence, the correct option is (B).

81. Given,

A alone can complete a work in = 12 days

B alone can complete the same work in = 15 days

As we know,

Wages are distributed into efficiency ratio.

Efficiency is inversely proportional to time.

Time ratio of A and B = 12 : 15 = 4 : 5

Efficiency ratio of A and B = 5 : 4

According to the question,

5 + 4 = 9 units

⇒ 9 units = 3600

⇒ 1 unit = 400

⇒ 5 units = 5 × 400 = Rs. 2000

∴ Share of A is Rs. 2000.

Hence, the correct option is (D).

82. We know that,

Probability $= \frac{\text{Number of favorable outcomes}}{\text{Total outcomes}}$

Number of all combinations of n things, taken r at a time, is given by ${}^{n}C_{r} = \frac{n!}{(r)!(n-r)!}$

According to question,

Total outcomes $= {}^{52}C_2$

$= \frac{52!}{(2)!(50)!}$

$= \frac{52\times51}{2} = 1326$

Number of favorable outcomes $= {}^{4}C_2 = \frac{4!}{(2)!(2)!}$

$= \frac{4\times3\times2\times1}{2\times1\times2\times1} = 6$

∴ Probability $= \frac{6}{1326} = \frac{1}{221}$

Hence, the correct option is (A).

83. Given:

Ratio of radius of two right circular cylinders $= 3:2$

Ratio of their volumes $= 27:16$

As we know,

Volume of right circular cylinder $= \pi r^2 h$

let the height of both cylinder be h_1 and h_2

$\Rightarrow \frac{\pi 3^2 h_1}{\pi 2^2 h_2} = 27:16$

$\Rightarrow \frac{9h_1}{4h_2} = 27:16$

$\Rightarrow 4h_1 = 3h_2$

$\Rightarrow h_1:h_2 = 3:4$

∴ The ratio of their heights is $3:4$.

Hence, the correct option is (C).

84. Given:

Invalid votes $= 20\%$ of the total votes

Arvind won by 480 votes.

And Arvind got 20% more votes than Manoj.

Let total votes be x.

Invalid votes $= 20\%$ of $x = 0.2x$

Valid votes $= x - 0.2x = 0.8x$

Arvind and Manoj gets $0.8x$ votes.

Arvind got 20% more votes than Manoj.

⇒ Arvind gets 60% of valid votes and Manoj gets 40% of valid votes.

$\Rightarrow$ Votes received by Arvind $= 0.8x \times \frac{60}{100} = 0.48x$

$\Rightarrow$ Votes received by Manoj $= 0.8x - 0.48x = 0.32x$

Votes of Arvind - Votes of Manoj $= 480$

$\Rightarrow 0.48x - 0.32x = 480$

$\Rightarrow 0.16x = 480$

$\Rightarrow x = 3000$

$\therefore$ Total number of people who voted are 3000.

Hence, the correct option is (A).

85. From the identity:

$(a-b)^3 = a^3 - b^3 - 3ab(a-b)$

$\Rightarrow 3^3 = 279 - 3ab \times 3$

$\Rightarrow 9ab = 279 - 27 = 252$

$\Rightarrow ab = 28$

Now,

$(a+b)^2 = (a-b)^2 + 4ab$

$\Rightarrow (a+b)^2 = 3^2 + 4 \times 28 = 121$

$\Rightarrow (a+b) = 11$

Now,

$(a+b)^3 = a^3 + b^3 + 3ab(a+b)$

$\Rightarrow 11^3 = a^3 + b^3 + 3 \times 28 \times 11$

$\Rightarrow 1331 = a^3 + b^3 + 924$

$\Rightarrow a^3 + b^3 = 407$

Hence, the correct option is (B).

86. According to the question,

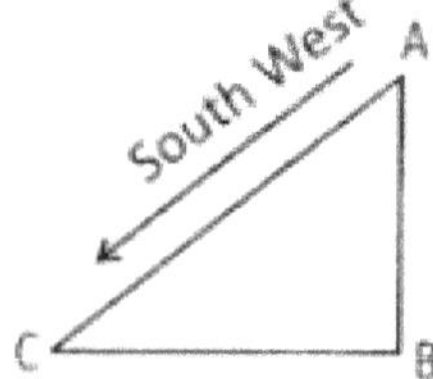

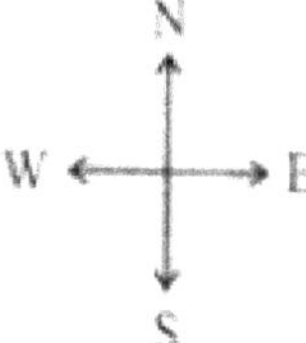

Clearly, A will come in South-West direction to meet C.

Hence, the correct option is (B).

87. Saniya remembers her friend's marriage is after 19th November (i,e., on 20th, 21st, 22nd, 23rd, etc.) while her sister remembers the marriage is before 21st November (i,e., on 20th, 19th, 18th, 17th, etc.)

Combining both the statements we get only one possible date which is 20th November.

Hence, the correct option is (B).

88. Here the mirror image is 1:30, the minutes are more than 00,

Therefore we need to subtract it from 11:60.

Thus, 11:60 - 1:30 = 10:30

The actual time shows 10:30 on the clock.

Hence, the correct option is (D).

89. Given series is:

J U & 5 R 3 I 7 @ & M I 6 R 2 F S @ I M $ 9 L 7 1 6 A # 9 B Z $

After finding such symbols are there in the above arrangement, each of which is immediately preceded by a symbol and immediately followed by a letter, we get

J U & 5 R 3 I 7 @ & M I 6 R 2 F S @ I M $ 9 L 7 1 6 A # 9 B Z $

So, there is only one such symbol.

Hence, the correct option is (B).

90. Based on given data, we can draw family tree:

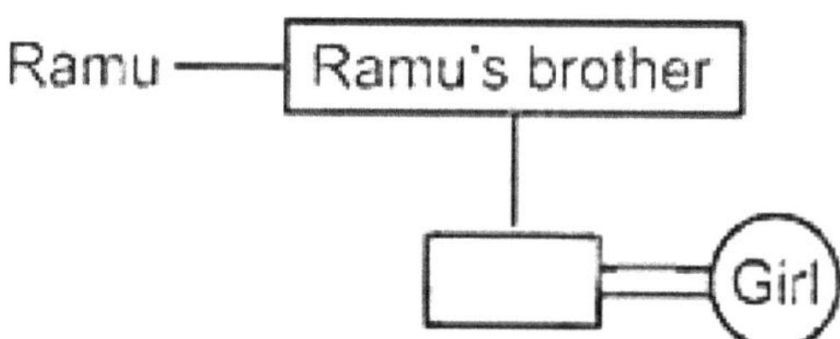

Here, the gender of Ramu is not sure.

Thus, 'Either uncle or aunt' is the correct alternative.

Hence, the correct option is (D).

91. Moradabad is situated on the banks of the Ramganga river, at a distance of 167 km (104 mi) from the national capital, New Delhi and 344 km north-west of the state capital Lucknow. The city is known as Pital Nagri, ("Brass City") for its famous brass handicrafts industry.

Hence, the correct option is (D).

92. On 13th December 1946, Pandit Jawaharlal Nehru moved the Objective Resolution in the Constituent Assembly of India.

Objective Resolution contained the basic ideology and philosophy upon which our Constitution is based. It defines the aim of the Constituent Assembly. The resolution was adopted by the Assembly unanimously on 22nd January 1947.

Hence, the correct option is (D).

93. The first newspaper published in India was The Bengal Gazette.

The Bengal Gazette was a weekly magazine. It was started in the year 1780 by James Augustus Hickey. It described itself as a commercial paper open to all, but influenced by none. Various other weekly magazines were published after Bengal Gazette. It was the first English newspaper published in the Indian Subcontinent.

Hence, the correct option is (D).

94. Rohtang Pass is a high mountain pass on the eastern end of the Pir Panjal Range of the Himalayas around $51\ km$ from Manali. It connects the Kullu Valley with the Lahaul and Spiti Valleys of Himachal Pradesh. It links Manali and Leh by road. Hence, the correct option is (C).

95. The pavilion of the Ministry of Health and Family Welfare has been awarded for "Outstanding Contribution towards Public Communication and Outreach" at the 41st India International Trade Fair 2022. As many as 37,887 screenings, investigations, counseling and trainings were conducted at the pavilion. Blood pressure and blood sugar had the highest number of screenings at 4990 and 4356, respectively.

Hence, the correct option is (B).

96. System Utilities is the name of the software that is used for the maintenance and configuration of Computer Systems. It is software designed to help analyze, configure, optimize or maintain a computer. Some system utilities may come embedded with OS and others may be added later on. System utility programs are used to list or change information that is related to data sets and volumes, such as data set names, catalog entries, and volume labels.

Hence, the correct option is (B).

97. Windows Key + M is pressed simultaneously to minimize all the currently open windows on your desktop.

Press this key	To do this
Windows logo key + Right arrow	Maximize the app or desktop window to the right side of the screen.
Windows logo key + Home	Minimize all except the active desktop window (restores all windows on second stroke).

Hence, the correct option is (C).

98. The length and width of an A4 sheet in MS Word 2007 is 8.27 × 11.69 inches.

Microsoft Word is a Microsoft computer software or application designed for document creation that allows users to easily prepare contracts, letters, agreements, and other types of documents. Microsoft Word is a user-friendly word-processing tool released by Microsoft back on October 25, 1983. It was developed by Charles Simonyi and Richard Brodie who are both former programmers of Xerox.

Hence, the correct option is (A).

99. The output of the function =FLOOR(34, 5) is 30.

The Floor command in MS Excel always passes two parameters. One is referred to as a number and the other one is significance. Here the significance is referred to as a factor. This factor will help to determine the value which is a closer multiple of the number.

=FLOOR(34,5): In this command, 34 represents the number, and 5 represents the significance. So, the result should be close to 34 and a multiple of 5. Also, it is to be remembered that the result always should be lower than the given number. So, the result is 30. which multiple of 5 and close to 34.

Hence, the correct option is (C).

100. In PowerPoint, the dotted areas in an empty slide are called Placeholders.

The layout is simply a collection of one or more placeholders, which set aside an area of the slide to hold information. PowerPoint includes a range of slide layouts, complete with placeholders that allow you to quickly and easily insert text, headings and pictures, and the like, onto a slide.

Hence, the correct option is (C).

Mock Test 07

Discipline

Q.1 Which nursing action is most important while caring for a client after cardiac catheterization?

A. Provide rest
B. Check the pulse distal to the puncture site
C. Monitor electrocardiogram every 15minutes
D. Administer oxygen

Q.2 If glaucoma is left untreated it leads to:

A. Conjunctivitis
B. Trachoma
C. Retrolental fibroplasias
D. Blindness

Q.3 Main clinical symptom of hiatal hernia:

A. Vomiting
B. Diarrhoea
C. Heartburn
D. Lower abdomen pain

Q.4 The most important aspect of management of burn injury in the first 24 hours is:

A. Dressing **B.** Antibiotic therapy
C. Fluid resuscitation **D.** Plastic surgery

Q.5 Nephrotic syndrome can be caused by:

A. Glomerulonephritis
B. Diabetes mellitus
C. Blood clotting in renal tubules
D. All of the above

Q.6 Treatment of the patient with appendicitis includes:

A. Transfusion to replace blood loss
B. Bowel prep for cleansing
C. Surgical removal of the appendix
D. Medications to lower pH within the stomach

Q.7 Joan has osteoporosis. She has an increased risk for:

A. Infection in the bone
B. Peripheral blood clot formation
C. Fracture formation
D. Painful joint inflammation

Q.8 Which deformity of the spine presents as an increased roundness of the thoracic curve?

A. Lordosis **B.** Kyphosis
C. Scoliosis **D.** Osteomyelitis

Q.9 The first technique in your physical assessment sequence is:

A. Palpation **B.** Auscultation
C. Inspection **D.** Percussion

Q.10 Hand rubbing time for Alcohol based hand washing is:

A. 10 to 15 sec **B.** 15 to 30 sec
C. 30 to 45 sec **D.** 60 sec

Q.11 Which of the following principle(s) is/are part of a patient-centered style of health communication?

A. Exploring both disease and experience
B. Understanding the whole experience
C. Incorporating prevention and health promotion
D. All of the above

Q.12 A culture of intimidation, which can be intimidating or condescending behavior, affects:

A. Nurses **B.** Patients
C. Physicians **D.** All of the Above

Q.13 It involves usage of manual communication and body language to convey meaning as opposed to acoustically conveyed sound patterns.

A. Lip reading **B.** Sign language
C. Human aids **D.** Technological aids

Q.14 Informed consent is:

A. The voluntary permission that a patient or patient's legal representative gives to the physician or authorized healthcare provider to do something to or for that patient after having been apprised of the risks, benefits and alternatives to the proposed test, medication or treatment.
B. The exchange of information, ideas, or opinions.
C. A barrier to effective communication.
D. A HIPAA violation.

Q.15 Breakdowns in communication can cause all of the following except:

A. Equipment failure
B. Medical errors
C. Malpractice lawsuits
D. HIPAA violations

Q.16 Health education is carried out by:

A. Individual Approach
B. Group Approach
C. Mass Approach
D. All of the above

Q.17 Assuring HIPAA compliance in electronic medical records is crucial because:

A. Patient information is stored and exchanged electronically through various technologies
B. Security breaches do happen
C. Unintentional distribution of e-mail addresses including sensitive patient information can happen
D. All of the above

Q.18 Which type of authorization is generated when services are rendered?

A. Concurrent **B.** Prospective

C. Retrospective
D. Subauthorization

Q.19 In a laboratory cultures most, human pathogens grow best at:

A. 30 to 37°C
B. 15 to 20°C
C. 38 to 50°C
D. 20 to 30°C

Q.20 Upon discharge from the hospital following total knee replacement surgery, a patient covered by Medicare with limited financial means will require six weeks of IV antibiotic therapy. The patient wants to go home. During the assessment, the nursing case manager discovers the patient lives alone, has no support at home, and lacks the dexterity to perform the infusion. What is the nurse's next step?

A. Collaborate with the insurance company to allow the patient to stay six weeks.
B. Explain to the patient about the barriers to going home and discuss other options.
C. Make a home infusion referral because this is what the patient has requested.
D. Order occupational therapy dexterity training for self-administration.

Q.21 The nurse manager generally uses a stepwise method to arrive at decisions that are logicaland that are used to maximize the achievement of the desired objective. Which decision-making model does this manager use?

A. Political decision-making model
B. Experimentation process
C. Rational decision-making model
D. Trial-and-error method

Q.22 As a new nursing professional development practitioner, the mastery of which skill ismostImportant?

A. Communicating effectively
B. Managing resources
C. Coordinating programs
D. Serving as facilitator

Q.23 During your transition from student nurse to your first position as a staff nurse, your general unit orientation is a key component of the transition. Which of the following questions would be most appropriate for you to ask about orientation?

A. How will I be paid for my time in orientation?
B. Do I have to attend every orientation session?
C. Will I be graded during the orientation?
D. How long should I expect to be in orientation?

Q.24 The provision of guidance, direction, evaluation, and follow-up by a licensed nurse for tasks provided by an CNA (certified nurses aide) is:

A. Delegation
B. Accountability
C. Supervision
D. Authority

Q.25 A student asks a nurse manager why they should use a SWOT analysis. The nurse manager explains that a SWOT analysis is:

A. A human resource process
B. Useful in strategic planning
C. A financial management term
D. An acronym for a type of quality improvement technique

Q.26 The nurse has just finished the change-of-shift report. Which patient should the nurse assess first?

A. An elderly client who has requested medication for pain
B. A client who is being discharged today
C. The patient who needs assistance transferring from the bed to the wheelchair
D. The client with COPD who is having difficulty breathing

Q.27 A nurse determines that a fracture bedpan should be used for the patient who __________.

A. has a spinal cord injury
B. is on bedrest
C. has dementia
D. is obese

Q.28 ________is the temperature for tepid sponging.

A. 15-18° C
B. 18-25° C
C. 27-37° C
D. 40-45° C

Q.29 All of the following are managerial functions of a community health nurse, except one:

[UPPSC Staff Nurse, 2017]

A. To assist in the training of nursing and health workers
B. Making plans
C. Monitoring
D. Assessment

Q.30 A practitioner orders a return flow enema (Harris flush drip) for an adult patient with flatulence. When preparing to administer this enema the nurse compares the steps of a return flow enema with cleansing enemas. What should the nurse do that is unique to a return flow enema?

A. Lubricate the last 2 inches of the rectal tube.
B. Insert the rectal tube about 4 inches into the anus.
C. Raise the solution container about 12 inches above the anus.
D. Lower the solution container after instilling about 150 ml of solution.

Q.31 A patient who had a "Do Not Resuscitate" order passed away. After verifying there is no pulse or respirations, the nurse should next:

A. Tell the family members say goodbye to the deceased
B. Call the transplant team to retrieve vital organs
C. Remove all tubes and equipment (unless organ donation is to take place), clean the body, and position appropriately
D. Call the funeral director to come and get the body

Q.32 A nurse is caring for a patient who will perform fecal occult blood testing at home. Which of the following information should the nurse include when explaining the procedure to the patient?

A. Eating more protein is optimal prior to testing.
B. One stool specimen is sufficient for testing.
C. A red color changes indicates a positive test.
D. The specimen cannot be contaminated with urine.

Q.33 A nurse is talking with a client who reports constipation. When the nurse discusses dietary changes that can help prevent constipation, which of the following foods should the nurse recommend?

A. Macaroni and cheese
B. Fresh food and whole-wheat toast
C. Rice pudding and ripe bananas
D. Roast chicken and white rice

Q.34 While a nurse is administering a cleansing enema, the patient reports abdominal cramping. Which of the following is the appropriate intervention?

A. Have a client hold his breath briefly.
B. Discontinue the fluid installation.
C. Remind the client that cramping is common at this time.
D. Lower the enema fluid container.

Q.35 A patient with the chronic pulmonary disease has a bluish tinge around the lips. The nurse charts which term to most accurately describe the patient's condition?

A. Hypoxia B. Hypoxemia
C. Dyspnea D. Cyanosis

Q.36 Plants obtain nutrients from ____.

A. Atmosphere B. Foliage
C. Soil D. Light

Q.37 Deficiency of which of the following nutrients causes slow growth in plants?

A. Iron B. Calcium
C. Magnesium D. Copper

Q.38 Which food component has the highest gross calorific value?

A. Carbohydrates B. Fats
C. Vitamins D. Proteins

Q.39 One of the following is not an energy yielding food:

A. Carbohydrate
B. Fat
C. Vitamins and minerals
D. Protein

Q.40 What type of nutrition does Euglena have to maintain its body cycle?

A. Autotrophic nutrition
B. Host nutrition
C. Both (A) and (B)
D. Neither (A) nor (B)

Q.41 Phytohormone is ______________.

A. They are regulators that are synthesized by plants influencing physiological processes
B. Substance handling diseases
C. Substances used for photosynthesis
D. Peeling chemicals

Q.42 The disease caused by the deficiency of iodine is:

A. Anaemia B. Goitre
C. Chicken pox D. Swine flu

Q.43 .... helps to maintain a constant body temperature in our body.

A. Roughage B. Vitamins
C. Energy giving food D. Water

Q.44 .... provide more than double the energy provided by carbohydrates or protiens in human body.

A. Vitamins B. Fats C. Minerals D. Starch

Q.45 What is the cause of angina?

A. Insufficient blood reaching the lungs
B. Insufficient blood reaching the brain
C. Insufficient blood reaching the heart muscles
D. Insufficient blood reaching the leg muscles

Q.46 What is your FIRST action when examining the condition of a patient?

A. Check for breathing
B. Check for insurance
C. Speak to the victim and shake his shoulders
D. Check for external injuries

Q.47 How do you check for breathing?

A. Listen
B. Look for rising chest
C. Feel with the cheek
D. Look, Listen and Feel

Q.48 What are the requirements for a cover bandage?

A. It may not absorb any fluids
B. It may not be older than 1 year
C. It must be sterile
D. None of these

Q.49 A passenger has been stung by a honey bee. The stinger is still under the skin and needs to be removed to prevent anaphylactic shock. What do you do next?

A. Remove the stinger using a pair of sterile tweezers
B. Remove the stinger using a pin
C. Use a knife to scrape it out
D. All of these

Q.50 For which of the following burn victims should you immediately call your local emergency phone number?

A. A 40-year-old man who has burned his hand with hot coffee
B. A 68-year-old woman who has a blistered grease burn on her hands and arms
C. A 26-year-old woman who has a sunburn on her shoulders
D. All of the above

Q.51 What you should suspect when a victim has head and spine injuries for:

A. An incident involving a lightning strike
B. A person found unconscious for unknown reasons
C. A fall from the height greater than the victim's height
D. All of the above

Q.52 After a dog bite, the wound should be cleaned with:

[UPPSC Staff Nurse, 2017]

A. Hydrogen peroxide **B.** Tincture iodine
C. Soap and water **D.** Chlorhexidine

Q.53 Breathing emergencies may be caused from:
A. Asthma or Allergic reaction
B. Hyperventilation
C. Injury to a muscle or bone in the chest
D. All of the above

Q.54 Which of the following glands in human beings secretes more than three hormones?
[CTET Paper-II (Science & Mathematics), 2021]

A. Pancreas **B.** Thyroid **C.** Adrenal **D.** Pituitary

Q.55 The nephrons are associated with ______.
A. Respiratory system **B.** The nervous system
C. Circulatory system **D.** Excretory system

Q.56 In which part of the excretory system of the human body is it stored before passing urine?
A. Urinary bladder **B.** Ureter
C. Bowman Capsule **D.** Urethra

Q.57 A sac is formed when a weak part of a blood vessel wall bulges out, what is it called?
[UPPSC Staff Nurse, 2017]

A. Atherosclerosis **B.** Aneurysm
C. Anastomosis **D.** Arteriosclerosis

Q.58 During respiration, the gaseous exchange takes place in ________.
A. Lungs and alveoli **B.** Trachea and larynx
C. Alveoli and throat **D.** Throat and lungs

Q.59 Centre for heat, touch, cold and pressure are in:
A. Frontal lobe
B. Occipital lobe
C. Parietal lobe
D. Frontal as well as occipital lobe both

Q.60 Central nervous system consists of:
A. Brain and spinal cord
B. Heart and lungs
C. Brain and heart
D. Heart and spinal chord

Q.61 Phases in cell division which include G1 phase, S phase, G2 phase:
A. Middle age **B.** Prephase
C. Hiatus **D.** Interstitial

Q.62 Animals in which cells are arranged in three embryonic layers are called _______.
A. Diploblastic **B.** Ectoderm
C. Tryoblastic **D.** Endoderms

Q.63 The nurse is assessing a woman in labor. He knows that fetal bradycardia occurs when the heart rate drops below ________.
A. 100 beats per minute
B. 120 beats per minute
C. 110 beats per minute
D. 130 beats per minute

Q.64 The nurse is assessing fetal heart rate in a pregnant patient. The nurse records a pulse of 82 beats per minute. The nurse should ________.
A. Try another doppler device
B. Add lubricant to the doppler's surface
C. Call the physician immediately
D. Move the doppler device

Q.65 The nurse completes a cervical exam on her laboring patient. She determines that her patient's cervix is 1cm in length. How would the nurse describe this length?
A. 30% effaced **B.** 25% effaced
C. 50% effaced **D.** 100% effaced

Q.66 The nurse helps the healthcare team to deliver a healthy baby girl. Upon delivery of the placenta, the nurse notices that it is not 100% intact. What is the nurse's first concern?
A. Pulmonary embolism
B. Deep vein thrombosis
C. Hemorrhage
D. Tissue perfusion

Q.67 Which of the following increases the risk of endometriosis?
A. Lack of exercise
B. Presence of an intrauterine device (IUD)
C. Family history of endometriosis
D. All of these

Q.68 A labor and delivery nurse is caring for a pregnant client that is experiencing contractions and has been on an external tocodynamometer to measure fetal heart tones as well as uterine contractions. The nurse notes that there are decreases in the fetal heart rate at different times of a contraction.
A. The third stage of labor
B. Fetal head compression during contraction
C. The effects of decreased pitosin infusion
D. A prolapsed umbilical cord or nuchal cord

Q.69 Which of the following clinical signs is not related to confirming the death status of the patient?
A. No evidence of pulse
B. Movements of limbs
C. Both (A) and (B)
D. None of these

Q.70 In a community, there is a child who have leg injury and it can't move. The nurse, assesting to the healthcare programme running in that community area sees swelling of the lower affected leg. Which of the following does the nurse suspect is the cause of the child's symptoms?
A. Possible fracture of the tibia
B. Bruising of the gastrocnemius muscle
C. Possible fracture of the radius
D. None of these

Q.71 Under NRHM one ASHA covers the population of:

A. 500 **B.** 1000 **C.** 2000 **D.** 4000

Q.72 Occurrence in the community of a number of cases of disease that is unusually large or unexpected:

A. Endemic **B.** Epidemic
C. Pandemic **D.** Infection

Q.73 What makes an effective public health campaign effective?

A. Grouping messages
B. Activities around a Single Overarching Communications Objective
C. Well-defined target audience
D. All of the above

Q.74 The main cause of mother's death in India is:

[UPPSC Staff Nurse, 2017]

A. Interrupted Birth Process
B. Anemia
C. Haemorrhage
D. None of these

Q.75 According to the World Health Organisation, the lowest birth weight means:

A. Less than 2.8 kg **B.** Less than 2.7 kg
C. Less than 2.5 kg **D.** Less than 2.3 kg

Q.76 First appearing teeth in a child is:

A. Premolar **B.** Incisors
C. Canines **D.** Third molar

Q.77 A child can copy a circle at:

A. 2 years **B.** 1.5 years **C.** 4 years **D.** 3 years

Q.78 A baby should be on the lookout for Bronze Baby Syndrome when she is getting:

[UPPSC Staff Nurse, 2017]

A. Immune therapy **B.** Chemotherapy
C. Photo therapy **D.** Radiation therapy

Q.79 What organ does Wilms' tumor affect in children?

[UPPSC Staff Nurse, 2017]

A. Lungs **B.** Kidney **C.** Brain **D.** Intestine

Q.80 The 'Rule of Ten' applies to:

[UPPSC Staff Nurse, 2017]

A. Cleft Lips **B.** Imperforate Anus
C. TEF **D.** CHD

General Aptitude / Reasoning / General Awareness / Basic Computer knowledge

Q.81 Perimeter of a square is $24\sqrt{2}cm$. Its diagonal is:

[HTET TGT Mathematics, 2020]

A. $6\sqrt{2}cm$ **B.** $8\sqrt{2}cm$ **C.** $8cm$ **D.** $12cm$

Q.82 The average marks obtained by the students in a class are 43. If the average marks obtained by 25 boys are 40 and average marks obtained by the girl students are 48, then what is the number of girl students in the class?

[Territorial Army Officer, 2019]

A. 20 **B.** 25 **C.** 15 **D.** 10

Q.83 Shopkeeper selling on article for Rs. 46 loses 8%. In order to gain of 6%, what should be the selling price of the article?

A. Rs. 65 **B.** Rs. 56 **C.** Rs. 53 **D.** Rs. 85

Q.84 Direction: What will come in the place of the question mark '?' in the following question?

$$\sqrt{324} + 9^2 - 7^2 = 2 \times (?)^2$$

A. 25 **B.** 5 **C.** 10 **D.** 125

Q.85 The sum of two positive numbers is 240 and their HCF is 15. Find the number of pairs of numbers satisfying the given condition.

A. 8 **B.** 2 **C.** 4 **D.** 5

Q.86 In a certain code language, "CARRYCOT" is written as "EYTPAAQR". How is "CALAMITY" written in that code language?

A. EYNYOGWV **B.** EYNYOGRW
C. EYNYORWG **D.** EYNYOGVW

Q.87 Direction: Read the given statement(s) and conclusions carefully and select which of the conclusions logically follow(s) from the statement(s).

Statements:

All Paint are Wall.

No Wall is Tall.

Conclusions:

I. No Paint are Tall.

II. Some Paint are Tall.

A. Only I follows
B. Only II follows
C. Both I and II follows
D. Neither I nor II follows

Q.88 'Bracelet' is related to 'Ornaments' in the same way as 'Clove' is related to '_____'.

[SSC CHSL (Combined Higher Secondary Level), 2021]

A. Taste **B.** Spices **C.** Cooking **D.** Kitchen

Q.89 Direction: In the question below a statement is given followed by two conclusions, I and II. You have to consider the statement to be true, even if it seems to be at variance from commonly known facts. You have to decide which of the given conclusions definitely is drawn from the given statement.

Statement: Eating nutritious food is the only way to keep the doctor away.

Conclusion:

I. Doctors will be out of job soon.

II. Nutritious food does not keep doctor away.

A. Only conclusion I follows
B. Both I and II follow
C. Neither I nor II follows
D. Only conclusion II follows

Q.90 Direction: Three of the following four-letter clusters are alike in a certain way and one is different. Pick the odd one out.

A. SUWY **B.** HJLN **C.** CEGI **D.** PRSU

Q.91 Kaziranga National Park is famous for _______.

A. One-horned Rhinos
B. Tigers
C. Swamp Dears (Barasingha)
D. Elephants

Q.92 The 2022 Nobel Prize in Chemistry has been jointly awarded to Carolyn Bertozzi, Morton Meldal Barry Sharpless for their work on snipping molecules. Who among these has also previously won the Noble Prize in Chemistry in 2001?

A. Carolyn Bertozzi **B.** Morton Meldal
C. Barry Sharpless **D.** None of these

Q.93 In which of the following sports, the words 'crawl', 'breaststroke', and 'butterfly' are used?

A. Swimming **B.** Shooting
C. Tennis **D.** Badminton

Q.94 Which Union Minister launched the 'Bal Raksha' mobile app at the All India Institute of Ayurveda (AIIA) on 24 July 2022?

A. Sarbananda Sonowal
B. Anurag Thakur
C. Amit Shah
D. Rajnath Singh

Q.95 Jhora folk dance belongs to which state?

A. Uttarakhand **B.** Karnataka
C. Assam **D.** Assam

Q.96 In Windows XP, what does XP stands for?

A. Extra-Powerful
B. Experience
C. Extended Platform
D. Experience Platform

Q.97 A ________ is a software program which allows us to access the Internet and view web pages on our computer.

A. Computer program **B.** Internet protocol
C. Web browser **D.** Website

Q.98 Whenever user opens any website then main page is called as:

A. Backend Page **B.** Dead End
C. Home Page **D.** None of these

Q.99 _____________ is also called auxiliary storage.

A. Secondary memory **B.** Tertiary memory
C. Primary memory **D.** Cache memory

Q.100 _______ are computer programs that are designed by attackers to gain root or administrative access to your computer.

A. Backdoors **B.** Rootkits
C. Malware **D.** Antiware

// Smart Answer Sheet //

Correct Indicates percentage of students who answered questions correctly.

Skipped Indicates percentage of students who skipped questions.

Q.	Ans.	Correct	Skipped
1	B	59.05 %	1.49 %
2	D	79.43 %	0.0 %
3	C	66.81 %	1.75 %
4	C	64.25 %	1.35 %
5	D	15.67 %	3.34 %
6	C	63.86 %	1.57 %
7	C	64.91 %	1.32 %
8	B	68.18 %	1.88 %
9	C	56.11 %	1.25 %
10	B	86.06 %	0.0 %
11	D	63.43 %	1.5 %
12	D	40.2 %	1.88 %
13	B	56.96 %	1.8 %
14	A	61.0 %	1.45 %
15	A	44.89 %	1.01 %
16	D	46.54 %	1.27 %

Q.	Ans.	Correct	Skipped
17	D	55.42 %	1.85 %
18	A	63.8 %	1.71 %
19	A	83.25 %	0.0 %
20	B	59.9 %	1.68 %
21	C	15.14 %	4.87 %
22	A	68.58 %	1.21 %
23	D	41.39 %	1.64 %
24	C	32.88 %	3.77 %
25	B	32.54 %	3.19 %
26	D	67.12 %	1.4 %
27	A	57.67 %	1.34 %
28	C	52.91 %	1.56 %
29	C	69.59 %	1.51 %
30	D	68.89 %	1.37 %
31	C	43.89 %	1.64 %
32	D	40.84 %	1.09 %

Q.	Ans.	Correct	Skipped
33	B	50.86 %	1.72 %
34	D	50.33 %	1.15 %
35	D	16.19 %	4.52 %
36	C	47.57 %	1.21 %
37	B	59.45 %	1.42 %
38	A	40.41 %	1.54 %
39	C	49.32 %	1.9 %
40	A	27.52 %	3.34 %
41	C	81.73 %	0.0 %
42	B	60.57 %	1.47 %
43	D	68.59 %	1.6 %
44	B	63.67 %	1.5 %
45	C	81.85 %	0.0 %
46	C	62.38 %	1.73 %
47	D	79.18 %	0.0 %
48	C	84.06 %	0.0 %

Q.	Ans.	Correct	Skipped
49	A	69.39 %	1.7 %
50	B	24.61 %	4.3 %
51	D	66.65 %	1.3 %
52	C	65.1 %	1.88 %
53	D	88.91 %	0.0 %
54	D	54.67 %	1.47 %
55	D	42.12 %	1.51 %
56	A	10.94 %	3.35 %
57	B	61.88 %	1.27 %
58	A	55.87 %	1.31 %
59	C	54.52 %	1.12 %
60	A	56.18 %	1.03 %
61	D	68.81 %	1.26 %
62	C	41.2 %	1.19 %
63	C	42.48 %	1.96 %
64	D	59.54 %	1.47 %

Q.	Ans.	Correct	Skipped
65	C	64.21 %	1.06 %
66	C	86.29 %	0.0 %
67	D	43.73 %	1.62 %
68	D	21.73 %	4.31 %
69	B	77.12 %	0.0 %
70	A	41.0 %	1.17 %
71	B	40.9 %	1.23 %
72	B	54.49 %	1.59 %
73	D	53.65 %	1.23 %
74	C	84.52 %	0.0 %
75	C	55.36 %	1.48 %
76	B	43.0 %	1.46 %
77	D	41.96 %	1.81 %
78	C	76.82 %	0.0 %
79	B	63.87 %	1.6 %
80	A	58.78 %	1.69 %

Q.	Ans.	Correct	Skipped
81	D	79.68 %	0.0 %
82	C	79.62 %	0.0 %
83	C	88.62 %	0.0 %
84	B	87.81 %	0.0 %

Q.	Ans.	Correct	Skipped
85	C	87.86 %	0.0 %
86	D	82.34 %	0.0 %
87	A	80.33 %	0.0 %
88	B	87.84 %	0.0 %

Q.	Ans.	Correct	Skipped
89	C	88.28 %	0.0 %
90	D	81.94 %	0.0 %
91	A	88.38 %	0.0 %
92	C	82.22 %	0.0 %

Q.	Ans.	Correct	Skipped
93	A	43.33 %	1.31 %
94	A	53.82 %	1.27 %
95	A	50.91 %	1.09 %
96	B	86.69 %	0.0 %

Q.	Ans.	Correct	Skipped
97	C	81.07 %	0.0 %
98	C	58.73 %	1.54 %
99	A	59.18 %	1.85 %
100	B	83.36 %	0.0 %

Performance Analysis	
Avg. Score (%)	51.0%
Toppers Score (%)	65.0%
Your Score	

//Hints and Solutions//

1. 'Check the pulse distal to the puncture site' is Most important while caring for a client after cardiac catheterization.

- Cardiac Catheterization is an invasive procedure used to visualize heart chambers, walls, and great vessels to diagnose and treat disease related to abnormalities of the coronary arteries.
- The procedure involves inserting a long, flexible, radio-opaque catheter into a peripheral vein/ artery and guiding it under fluoroscopy or angiography.
- Indications are to assess oxygen saturation, intra-cardiac pressure; ventricular function, valvular insufficiency and stenosis, septal defect, congenital abnormalities, and myocardial function.

Hence, the correct option is (B).

2. If glaucoma is left untreated it leads to blindness. Glaucoma is a group of eye conditions that damage the optic nerve, the health of which is vital for good vision. This damage is often caused by an abnormally high pressure in your eye. Glaucoma is one of the leading causes of blindness for people over the age of 60.

Hence, the correct option is (D).

3. Heartburn is the main clinical symptom of a hiatal hernia. A hiatal hernia is a condition where the top of your stomach bulges through an opening in your diaphragm. This can happen to people of any age and any gender. A hiatal hernia doesn't always have symptoms, but when it does they are similar to the symptoms of GERD.

Hence, the correct option is (C).

4. The most important aspect of management of burn injury in the first 24 hours is fluid resuscitation. The goals of fluid resuscitation include controlling bleeding, restoring lost blood volume, and regaining tissue perfusion and organ function.

Hence, the correct option is (C).

5. Nephrotic syndrome: It is a primary glomerular disease characterized by proteinuria, hypoproteinemia edema and hypercholesterolemia.

Caused of Nephrotic syndrome:

- Membranous nephropathy
- Glomerulonephritis
- Amyloidosis
- Blood clotting in renal tubules
- Diabetic kidney disease

symptoms:

- Weight gain
- Tired feeling
- Apnea
- Swelling in legs
- Frothy urine

Hence, the correct option is (D).

6. Treatment of the patient with appendicitis includes surgical removal of the appendix. And this process is called appendectomy. Appendectomy can be performed as open surgery using one abdominal incision about 2 to 4 inches (5 to 10 centimeters) long (laparotomy). Or the surgery can be done through a few small abdominal incisions (laparoscopic surgery). During a laparoscopic appendectomy, the surgeon inserts special surgical tools and a video camera into your abdomen to remove your appendix.

Hence, the correct option is (C).

7. Joan has osteoporosis. She has an increased risk for fracture formation. The word 'osteoporosis' means 'porous bone. ' It is a disease that weakens bones, and if you have it, you are at a greater risk for sudden and unexpected bone fractures. Osteoporosis means that you have less bone mass and strength.

Hence, the correct option is (C).

8. Kyphosis is an abnormal curve or rounding of the thoracic cavity.

- The spinal cord is reversed C-shape.
- The back appears to be curved.
- Symptoms of kyphosis:
- Back pain
- Stiffness in the upper back
- Noticeable curve

Hence, the correct option is (B).

9. The assessment of each body system begins with inspection. It's the most commonly used technique and it can reveal more than any other technique. Inspection is the visual examination, that is, assessing by using the sense of sight. Nurses frequently use visual inspection to assess moisture, colour, and texture of body surfaces, as well as shape, position, size, color, and symmetry of the body.

The other technique in your physical assessment are:

- Palpation
- Auscultation
- Percussion

Hence, the correct option is (C).

10. Hand rubbing time for Alcohol based hand washing is 15 to 30 sec.

- Hand washing is a basic procedure which is done by all the health care workers.
- 15 to 30 seconds we have to rub the hands to prevent the contamination.
- It differs with medical and surgical scrubbing.
- Surgical hand antisepsis takes 2 to 6 minutes.
- Medical scrubbing can be done with alcohols for 15 to 30 seconds.

Hence, the correct option is (B).

11. Insufficient expertise of the healthcare providers proved to be a major problem in the highly specialized treatment process of rare diseases. Here, the patient often becomes an expert in his disease. Therefore, we identified the patient-directed interaction as a widely experienced communication pattern among patients with rare diseases.

A patient-centered approach to communication is to acknowledge the whole person, their personality, life history, and social structure in order to develop a shared understanding of the problem, the goals of treatment, and the barriers to that treatment and wellness.

Hence, the correct option is (D).

12. A culture of intimidation, which can be intimidating or condescending behavior, affects Nurses, Patients, and Physicians.

Intimidation or harassment is a personalised form of anti-social behaviour, specifically aimed at particular individuals. People experience repeated incidents and problems of intimidation and harassment day after day.

Hence, the correct option is (D).

13. Sign language is a language that uses manual communication and body language to convey meaning, as opposed to acoustically transmitted sound patterns.

- This may involve stitching together the shape, orientation, and movement of the hands, arms, or body, and facial expressions to clearly convey the speaker's thoughts. Whereas those spoken languages mainly depend on sound.
- By using this language, a person is able to express his feelings without using words.
- To use sign language, the person explains his/her point of view with the help of hands, fingers, gestures, or facial expressions.
- This language is mostly used by people who are deaf in their mouths. Deaf children are trained differently so that they can use this language to build a better future.
- In sign languages, the same gesture has many meanings.

Hence, the correct option is (B).

14. Informed consent is the voluntary permission that a patient or patient's legal representative gives to the physician or authorized healthcare provider to do something to or for that patient after having been apprised of the risks, benefits, and alternatives to the proposed test, medication, or treatment.

Informed consent is a process of communication between you and your health care provider that often leads to agreement or permission for care, treatment, or services. Every patient has the right to get information and ask questions before procedures and treatments.

Hence, the correct option is (A).

15. Breakdowns in communication can cause Medical errors, malpractice lawsuits and HIPAA violations.

An equipment failure covers a piece of machinery when it stops working due to an internal malfunction or a broken part(s), requiring the repair or replacement of that equipment.

Hence, the correct option is (A).

16. Health education is carried out by individual Approach, group Approach and mass Approach.

- In order to teach individuals, we must develop skills and have sufficient knowledge to gain the confidence of the people (learners). First of all the nurse should set a good example by practicing principles of healthy living. Example is a good method of teaching.
- Group Health Education is an effective way of educating the community. The choice of subject is very important it must relate direct to the interest of the group health.
- For the education of the general public, we employ "mass media of communication' – Posters, health magazines, films, radio, television, health exhibitions and health museums.

Hence, the correct option is (D).

17. Assuring HIPAA compliance in electronic medical records is crucial because Patient information is stored and exchanged electronically through various technologies, Security breaches do happen, and Unintentional distribution of e-mail addresses including sensitive patient information can happen.

Hospitals, doctors, clinics, psychologists, dentists, chiropractors, nursing homes, and pharmacies are considered Healthcare Providers and need to be HIPAA compliant.

HIPAA Compliant Patient Communication-

- Mail: When sending PHI via mail, you must use either certified mail or a similar service that requires a signature.
- Phone: Similarly to email, you must have written consent from a patient before communicating PHI over the phone.

Hence, the correct option is (D).

18. Concurrent type of authorization is generated when services are rendered.

From a Medicare perspective, concurrent care exists "where more than one physician renders services more extensive than consultative services during a period of time."

Hence, the correct option is (A).

19. In a laboratory culture most, human pathogens grow best at 30 to 37°C.

- Temperature is a key physiochemical factor that affects the bacterial environment, making incubators indispensable in clinical laboratories. Human pathogens generally multiply best at temperatures similar to those of the human host i.e. 350C to 370C.

- Many pathogens are mesophiles as their preferred temperature is body temperature (370C).

Hence, the correct option is (A).

20. During the assessment, the nursing case manager discovers the patient lives alone, has no support at home, and lacks the dexterity to perform the infusion. The nurse's next step should be explain to the patient about the barriers to going home and discuss other options. Living alone at home may be dangerous for the patient. So nurse's duty is to explain the patient pros and cons of staying alone at home.

Hence, the correct option is (B).

21. The nurse manager generally uses a stepwise method to arrive at decisions that are logical and that are used to maximize the achievement of the desired objective. Rational decision-making model does this manager use.

Being the opposite of intuitive decision making, rational model of decision making is a model where individuals use facts and information, analysis, and a step-by-step procedure to come to a decision. The rational model of decision making is a more advanced type of decision-making model.

Hence, the correct option is (C).

22. As a new nursing professional development practitioner, the mastery of Communicating effectively skill ismostImportant.

Communication assists in the performance of accurate, consistent and easy nursing work, ensuring both the satisfaction of the patient and the protection of the health professional.

Hence, the correct option is (A).

23. How long should I expect to be in orientation? the question would be most appropriate for you to ask about orientation. Orientation checklists keep employees' first days organized and ensure new hires experience successful orientation days. These checklists require significant preparation and knowledge about the company. These checklists help new hires adjust to new environments quickly.

Hence, the correct option is (D).

24. The provision of guidance, direction, evaluation, and follow-up by a licensed nurse for tasks provided by a CNA (certified nurse's aide) is Supervision.

However, a key purpose of supervision is to assure the quality of the service being delivered and some means of being aware of how people who use services feel about what they are receiving from the organisation should be in place.

Hence, the correct option is (C).

25. A student asks a nurse manager why they should use a SWOT analysis. The nurse manager explains that a SWOT analysis is Useful in strategic planning.

A SWOT analysis will position you to seize opportunities and prepare effective strategies. Getting a clear and realistic view of your internal environment will help you identify ways to better satisfy clients, achieve your objectives and strengthen weaker areas that have an impact on your performance.

Hence, the correct option is (B).

26. The client with COPD who is having difficulty breathing should the nurse assess first.

The 3 major goals of the comprehensive management of COPD are the following: Lessen airflow limitation. Prevent and treat secondary medical complications (eg, hypoxemia, infection) Decrease respiratory symptoms and improve quality of life.

Hence, the correct option is (D).

27. A nurse determines that a fracture bedpan should be used for a patient who has a spinal cord injury.

A fracture bedpan has a low back that promotes the function of the patient's lower back while on the bedpan. The fracture pan has one flat end for ease of use with specific patient populations: i.e. hip fractures, hip replacements, or lower extremity fractures. Using the toilet may be a source of discomfort and embarrassment among all genders. Semi-private rooms or shared wards and hospital overcrowding are a challenge regarding patient privacy.

Hence, the correct option is (A).

28. 27-37° C is the temperature for tepid sponging.

- Tepid sponging refers to cold sponging of the body with tap water to reduce the temperature by evaporation is called tepid sponging.
- The temperature of water used for the Tepid sponge is 80 to 90°F/ or 27 to 37°C.

Hence, the correct option is (C).

29. Monitoring is not the managerial function of a community health nurse.

- Community-based monitoring is done to increase the accountability and quality of social services such as health, development aid, and better management of natural resources.
- It is done by the PHC monitoring committee

Role of community health nurse on the managerial level:

- coordinate and manage the environment
- responsible for nursing units and staffs
- assessing needs
- planning and implementing
- to assist in the training of nursing and health workers

Hence, the correct option is (C).

30. The nurse should lower the solution container after instilling about 150 ml of solution is unique to a return flow enema.

Lowering the container of solution creates a siphon effect that pulls the instilled fluid back out through the rectal tube into the solution container. The return flow promotes the evacuation of gas from the intestines. This technique is used only with a return flow enema. This action is appropriate for all types of enemas.

Hence, the correct option is (D).

31. A patient who had a "Do Not Resuscitate" order passed away. After verifying there is no pulse or respirations, the nurse should next Remove all tubes and equipment (unless organ donation is to take place), clean the body, and position appropriately.

The body of the deceased should be prepared before the family comes into view and says their goodbyes. This includes removing all equipment, tubes, supplies, and dirty linens according to protocol, bathing the patient, applying clean sheets, and removing trash from the room. In a home care, the nurse would ask the family if it was alright to remove any tubes or catheters from the patient, and if they would like to assist in bathing/preparing the patient for transport to the funeral home. The nurse would assist the family in removing any jewelry or other items from the patient.

Hence, the correct option is (C).

32. A nurse is caring for a patient who will perform fecal occult blood testing at home. The specimen cannot be contaminated with urine this is the information that nurse should include when explaining the procedure to the patient.

For fecal occult blood testing at home, the stool specimens cannot be contaminated with water or urine. The fecal occult blood test (FOBT) is a diagnostic test to assess for occult blood in the stool. This test has commonly been used for colorectal cancer screening, especially in developed nations. When used correctly for screening, this testing modality has established associations with decreased morbidity and mortality. When performing at home, the stool should be collected in a dry, clean container.

Hence, the correct option is (D).

33. When the nurse discusses dietary changes that can help prevent constipation, the nurse should recommend fresh food and whole-wheat toast.

A high fiber diet promotes normal bowel elimination. The choice of fruit and toast is the highest-fiber option. Most Americans consume only half the levels of recommended fiber per day, which is almost 15 grams per day. All existing definitions recognize fiber as "carbohydrate or lignin which bypasses digestion in the small intestine and is partially or completely fermented in the large intestine or colon."

Hence, the correct option is (B).

34. While a nurse is administering a cleansing enema, the patient reports abdominal cramping. Lowering the enema fluid container is the appropriate intervention.

To relieve the patient's discomfort, the nurse should slow the rate of installation by reducing the height of the enema solution container. An enema may be helpful when there is a problem forming or passing stool. The colon, also called the large intestine or large bowel is a long, hollow organ in the abdomen. It plays an important role in digestion by removing water from digested material and forming feces (stool). In some circumstances, due to diet, medical condition, or medication, among other possible causes, the bowel may form stool that is hard to pass easily resulting in constipation.

Hence, the correct option is (D).

35. A patient with the chronic pulmonary disease has a bluish tinge around the lips. The nurse charts cyanosis term to most accurately describe the patient's condition.

A bluish tinge to mucous membranes is called cyanosis. This is most accurate because it is what the nurse observes. Cyanosis refers to a bluish cast to the skin and mucous membranes. Peripheral cyanosis is when there is a bluish discoloration to the hands or feet. It's usually caused by low oxygen levels in the red blood cells or problems getting oxygenated blood to the body.

Hence, the correct option is (D).

36. Plants obtain nutrients from the soil. Soil is the main source of nutrients for plants. Plants obtain nitrogen, phosphorus, and potassium from the soil. These plants need a lot of it. These are called major nutrients. Plants absorb calcium, magnesium, and sulfur in small amounts.

Hence, the correct option is (C).

37. Lack of calcium causes slow growth in plants. Due to the lack of calcium in the plants, the primary leaves emerge late. The tip of the corn sticks apart from the top buds being spoiled. The unique source of water-soluble calcium acts as a carrier of nitrate-nitrogen within plants. Reduces calcium deficiency of plants and helps in the growth and vigor of crops.

Hence, the correct option is (B).

38. Fats have the highest gross calorific value. The digestion of fats starts from the small intestine. Bile from the liver makes the solution alkaline and breaks down the big fat globules into smaller ones. Lipase from the pancreas breaks down the fats further in the small intestine. Intestinal juice completes the process of digestion of fats and is absorbed. Fats are found in vegetable oils, animal, fats and other foods like nuts.

Hence, the correct option is (A).

39. Vitamins and minerals are not an energy yielding food. Carbohydrates (saccharides), proteins, vitamins, fats, minerals, fiber, water are different parts of a balanced diet. They play an important role in physical formation. Carbohydrates, fats, proteins are the long-term nutrients of the body, which participate in about 90% of the body's growth and energy. Carbohydrates and fats mainly give energy to the body, proteins help in the growth, repair and energy production of the body. Vitamins and minerals are helpful in other functions of the body like building bones, increasing immunity, etc.

Hence, the correct option is (C).

40. Euglena has autotrophic nutrition to maintain its body cycle. It is also known as autotrophic nutrition. It is the preparation of organic food by an organism from inorganic material, eg. All green plants, some unicellular organisms, such as Euglena, Chlamydomonas, and Volvox.

Hence, the correct option is (A).

41. Plant hormones are substances used for photosynthesis. Phytohormones are organic substances that are produced in plants. They are also called plant hormones. These hormones are the growth regulators of plants. Auxins, gibberellins, cytokinins, ethylene and abscisic acid are examples of phytohormones.

Hence, the correct option is (C).

42. The disease caused by the deficiency of iodine is Goitre. Iodine deficiency is the most common cause of goiter in the world. The goiter initially is diffuse, but it eventually becomes nodular. Some nodules may become autonomous and secrete thyroid hormone regardless of the TSH level.

Hence, the correct option is (B).

43. Water helps to maintain a constant body temperature in our body. Water has a large heat capacity which helps limit changes in body temperature in a warm or a cold environment. The body water has an important role as a thermoregulator, regulating the overall body temperature by helping dissipate heat. If the body becomes too hot, water is lost through sweat and the evaporation of this sweat from the skin surface removes heat from the body.

Hence, the correct option is (D).

44. Fat has more than twice as many calories per gram as carbohydrates and proteins. A gram of fat has about 9 calories, while a gram of carbohydrate or protein has about 4 calories. In other words, you could eat twice as much carbohydrates or proteins as fat for the same amount of calories.

Hence, the correct option is (B).

45. The cause of angina is insufficient blood reaching the heart muscle.

Angina is usually caused by the arteries supplying blood to the heart muscles become narrowed by a build-up of fatty substances. This is called atherosclerosis.

Hence, the correct option is (C).

46. Speak to the victim and shake his shoulders should be your FIRST action when examining the condition of a patient.

The framework presented here consists of the following sequence of steps: identifying the purpose of the assessment; taking a health history; choosing a comprehensive or focused approach; and examining the patient using the sequence of inspection, palpation, percussion and auscultation.

Hence, the correct option is (C).

47. To check for breathing you should Look, Listen and Feel.

To check if a person is still breathing:

- look to see if their chest is rising and falling.
- listen over their mouth and nose for breathing sounds.
- feel their breath against your cheek for 10 seconds.

Hence, the correct option is (D).

48. The requirement for a cover bandage is it must be sterile.

A dressing is used to protect a wound and prevent infection, but also to allow healing. A dressing should be large enough to totally cover the wound, with a safety margin of about 2.5 cm on all sides beyond the wound. A sterile dressing may be used to control bleeding from a major wound or to absorb any discharge from a minor wound.

Hence, the correct option is (C).

49. A passenger has been stung by a honey bee. The stinger is still under the skin and needs to be removed to prevent anaphylactic shock. You should remove the stinger using a pair of sterile tweezers.

Tweezers are small tools used for picking up objects too small to be easily handled with the human fingers. The tool is most likely derived from tongs, pincers, or scissors-like pliers used to grab or hold hot objects

Hence, the correct option is (A).

50. For a 68-year-old woman who has a blistered grease burn on her hands and arms, you should immediately call your local emergency phone number.

The first step in treating a major burn is to call 911 or seek emergency medical care. Steps to take until emergency arrives include: Make sure you and the person who's burned are safe and out of harm's way. Move them away from the source of the burn.

Hence, the correct option is (B).

51. You should suspect that a victim has head and spine injuries for An incident involving a lightning strike, A person found unconscious for unknown reasons, and A fall from a height greater than the victim's height.

A spinal injury should be suspected if the patient has: pain at or below site of injury. loss of sensation, or abnormal sensation such as tingling in hands or feet. loss of movement or impaired movement below site of injury.

Hence, the correct option is (D).

52. After a dog bite, the wound should be cleaned with soap and water.

- Very gently wash the bite wound with soap and water and pat dry.
- Use hydrogen peroxide, chlorhexidine or betadine to dab the wound in order to help kill germs.
- Use a clean dry gauze pad to dry the wound then apply an antibiotic ointment such as Neosporin.

Hence, the correct option is (C).

53. Breathing emergencies may be caused by Asthma or Allergic reaction, Hyperventilation, and Injury to a muscle or bone in the chest.

During an asthma attack the muscle wall contracts and the lining of the airways becomes swollen and inflamed.

Hyperventilation is breathing that is deeper and more rapid than normal. It causes a decrease in the amount of a gas in the blood (called carbon dioxide, or CO_2).

Injury to any of the layers of the muscles or bone of chest can cause pain and difficulty breathing. Muscle injury are a common cause of chest pain.

Hence, the correct option is (D).

54. Pituitary gland: It is a small pea-sized gland. It is often called the master gland as it controls several other hormone glands in our body. It is located in the brain between Hypothalamus and the Pineal gland.

Hormones produced by the pituitary gland:

- Adrenocorticotrophic hormone (ACTH)
- Thyroid-stimulating hormone (TSH)
- Luteinising hormone (LH)
- Follicle-stimulating hormone (FSH)
- Prolactin (PRL)
- Growth hormone (GH)
- Melanocyte-stimulating hormone (MSH)

Hence, the correct option is (D).

55. The kidneys are associated with the excretory system. A nephron is the basic unit of structure in the kidney. The nephron works through over-filtration.

Excretory system: The physiological process by which an organism disposes of its nitrogenous by-products is called excretion. The mechanisms for this process constitute the excretory system.

Hence, the correct option is (D).

56. Before passing urine, it is stored in the bladder of the excretory system of the human body.

The urethra is a tube that connects the urinary bladder to the urethral meatus. 91-96% of urine water consists of proteins, hormones and salts. Urine is pale yellow due to the result of a pigment called urochrome. The ureters carry urine from the kidney to the bladder. Bowman Capsule helps in the filtration of blood to form urine.

Hence, the correct option is (A).

57. A sac is formed when a weak part of a blood vessel wall bulges out, it is called aneurysm.

- Aneurysm, widening of an artery that develops from weakness or destruction of the medial layer of the blood vessel.
- With the constant pressure of the circulating blood within the artery, the weakened part of the arterial wall becomes enlarged.
- Enlargement leads ultimately to serious and even fatal complications from the compression of surrounding structures or from rupture and hemorrhage.
- Aneurysms may occur in any part of the aorta or major arteries.
- Atherosclerosis, sometimes called "hardening of the arteries," occurs when fat, cholesterol and other substances build up in the walls of arteries.

Hence, the correct option is (B).

58. In the respiratory process, the exchange of gases takes place in the lungs and alveoli. As a result of respiratory exhalation, air reaches the various alveoli of the lungs. A dense network of blood cells is present around the vasculature.

The transport of oxygen is mainly by the red pigment hemoglobin found in the blood. Gaseous exchange in the lungs is called external respiration. The trachea is an important part of the respiratory system that connects the nose and mouth to the lungs. The larynx is a respiratory organ present in the throat of humans and other mammalian organisms that helps in speaking.

The act of transporting oxygen and carbon dioxide from the lungs to the body cells and back to the lungs is called the transport of gases.

Hence, the correct option is (A).

59. There are four lobes in the human brain.

- Frontal lobe.
- Parietal lobe.
- Occipital lobe.
- Temporal lobe

Parietal lobe:

- Located behind the frontal lobe.
- Receive and transmit sensory information from the body and skin. Also connected other parts of the brain.
- Deals with many sensations including touch, pressure, pain, heat, cold, etc.

Hence, the correct option is (C).

60. The Nervous System:

- Human nervous system is the most complex and most developed of all living creatures.
- Though the nervous system functions as a whole, for ease of study, we can divide it into many parts depending on its location or functions.
- Based on location, the nervous system can be divided into two parts: the Central Nervous System (CNS) and the Peripheral Nervous System (PNS).

Central Nervous System (CNS):

- The central nervous system (CNS) is the center of all neural activity.
- It integrates all incoming sensory information, performs all kinds of cognitive activities, and issues motor commands to muscles and glands.
- The CNS comprises of the (a) brain and (b) spinal cord.

Hence, the correct option is (A).

61. Interphase in cell division includes G1 phase, S phase, G2 phase. Interphase is the period between the end of one cell division to the beginning of the next cell division. Interphase takes up about 95% of the total time of the cell cycle.

During interphase, the cell grows in size, preparing itself for the next division. Therefore the cell is most actively metabolized during the interphase.

Interphase is divided into 3 phases:

1. G1 phase
2. S-Phase
3. G2-Phase

Hence, the correct option is (D).

62. Animals in which cells are arranged in three embryonic layers are called tripoblastic.

Triploblastic: The triploblastic form of animals is that the embryos are arranged in a three-tiered structure. These layers are ectoderm, mesoderm and endoderm. Most multicellular animals are triploblastic except for sponges and coelenterates.

Hence, the correct option is (C).

63. The nurse is assessing a woman in labor. He knows that fetal bradycardia occurs when the heart rate drops below 110 beats per minute.

Fetal bradycardia is recognized when the fetal heart rate drops below 110 beats per minute for 10 minutes or longer. The normal fetal heart rate is between 120 beats per minute and 160 beats per minute. Fetal tachycardia is a heart rate above 160 beats per minute.

Hence, the correct option is (C).

64. The nurse is assessing fetal heart rate in a pregnant patient. The nurse records a pulse of 82 beats per minute. The nurse should move the doppler device.

An 82 beat per minute reading could be the mother's heart rate, indicating that the nurse does not have the doppler in the correct position. A normal fetal heart rate is between 120 and 160 beats per minute. The nurse must always remember to take the mother's pulse before assessing the fetal heart rate. Before calling the physician, it is important to determine that the data is accurate. To increase oxygen perfusion to the fetus, ask the mother to lay on her left side.

Hence, the correct option is (D).

65. The normal cervical canal is 2cm in length. Effacement is the thinning of the cervix as the body prepares for delivery. Thus, a 2cm cervix is 0% effaced and a 0cm cervix is 100% effaced. Thus patient's cervix is 1cm in length is 50% effaced.

Hence, the correct option is (C).

66. Hemorrhage is the nurse's first concern.

If the placenta is not whole upon delivery, a piece may still be present in the uterus. This inhibits the ability of the uterus to shrink in size and may cause hemorrhage. The missing piece needs to be located immediately.

Hence, the correct option is (C).

67. Lack of exercise, the Presence of an intrauterine device (IUD), and a Family history of endometriosis increases the risk of endometriosis.

The incidence of endometriosis increases significantly in individuals with a family history of the condition. Other contributing factors are sedentary lifestyle (lack of exercise), presence of an intrauterine device, a diet high in fat, the presence of estrogen dominance, and liver dysfunction (due to decreased estrogen metabolism).

Hence, the correct option is (D).

68. Variable decelerations can occur at any time during a contraction, or without a contraction. They are caused by the umbilical cord that is prolapsed or wrapped around the fetal neck also known as a nuchal cord. The compression of the cord can ultimately lead to fetal hypoxia and therefore an intervention will be required to alleviate the compression.

A nuchal cord is a complication that occurs when the umbilical cord wraps around the baby's neck one or more times. This is common and occurs in about 15 to 35 percent of pregnancies. Often, nuchal cords do not impact pregnancy outcomes. However, certain types of nuchal cords can pose a significant risk to the baby.

Hence, the correct option is (D).

69. Movements of limbs signs is not related to confirming the death status of the patient.

Clinical signs related to confirming the death status of the patient:

- No evidence of pulse
- Pupils fixed and dilated
- No evidence of respirations or blood pressure

Hence, the correct option is (B).

70. The nurse, assesting to the healthcare programme running in that community area will suspect Possible fracture of the tibia of that child's leg.

The child's refusal to walk, combined with swelling of the limb is suspicious for fracture . The severity of a fracture usually depends on the force that caused the break. If the bone's breaking point has been exceeded , then the bone may crack. Walking after a tibia fracture can make your injury worse and may cause further damage to the surrounding muscles, ligaments and skin. Walking on a fractured tibia is also likely to be extremely painful.

Hence, the correct option is (A).

71. There is one Community Health Volunteer i.e. ASHA (Accredited Social Health Activist) for every village with a population of 1000. In tribal, hilly, desert areas the norm could be relaxed to one ASHA per habitation, dependant on workload etc.

ASHA will provide information to the community on determinants of health such as nutrition, basic sanitation & hygienic practices, healthy living and working conditions, information on existing health services and the need for timely utilisation of health & family welfare services.

Hence, the correct option is (B).

72. Occurrence in the community of a number of cases of disease that is unusually large or unexpected epidemic.

An epidemic is the rapid spread of disease to a large number of people in a given population within a short period of time. For example, in meningococcal infections, an attack rate in excess of 15 cases per 100,000 people for two consecutive weeks is considered an epidemic.

Hence, the correct option is (B).

73. An effective public health campaign involves grouping messages and activities around a Single Overarching Communications Objective (SOCO), that identifies the change that you want to achieve, against actionable and measurable targets. It has a well-defined target audience, which is positioned to act upon the messages that you convey.

Hence, the correct option is (D).

74. The main cause of mother's death in India is Haemorrhage.

- An Indian woman dies from childbirth every 7 minute
- The maternal mortality ratio in India is approximately 200 per 100000 live births.
- Death of a woman who is pregnant or within 42 days of termination of pregnancy.
- It is irrespective of the site and duration of pregnancy.

4 major causes of maternal mortality:

- Hemorrhage
- Infection
- Eclampsia
- Obstructed labor

Hence, the correct option is (C).

75. According to the World Health Organisation, the lowest birth weight is Less than 2.5 kg.

Birth weight	Grade
>3500g	Obese
3500-2500 g	Normal birth weight babies
2500-2000 g	low birth weight baby
2000-1000 g	Very low birth weight baby
<1000 g	Extremely low birth weight babies

Hence, the correct option is (C).

76. The bottom incisors are the first teeth that tend to erupt in children at 6-8 months of age.

Type of teeth	Description
Incisors	The permanent teeth contain four incisors on the upper jaw and four incisors on the lower jaw. The eight incisors have the primary function of biting food as a result of their sharpness.
Canines	They are sharper than the canine and meant for ripping and tearing food. There are two canines on the upper jaw and two canines in the lower jaw.
Premolars	There are two premolars on the upper jaw and also two premolars on the lower jaw on either side of the mouth. The premolars are responsible for the chewing and grinding of food.
Molars	Molars develop in a child as part of the milk teeth between a year and 1.5 years.

Hence, the correct option is (B).

77. A child can copy a circle at 3 years.

Pictures at this age include the following shapes, combined in different ways:

- Circles and squares
- crosses
- dots
- The letters T, V and H. Similar Size

Hence, the correct option is (D).

78. A baby should be on the lookout for Bronze Baby Syndrome when she is getting photo therapy.

- "Bronze baby" syndrome is a rare complication of phototherapy for neonatal jaundice occurring due to modified liver function, particularly cholestasis, of various origins.
- Phototherapy is a type of medical treatment that involves exposure to fluorescent light bulbs or other sources of light like halogen lights, sunlight, and light-emitting diodes (LEDs) to treat certain medical conditions.

Hence, the correct option is (C).

79. Wilms tumor is a rare kidney cancer that mainly affects children.

- Wilms tumor known as nephroblastoma, it is the most common cancer of the kidney in children.
- Wilms' tumor most often affects children between the ages of 3 and 4 and becomes less common after the age of 5.
- Wilms tumor most often occurs in only one kidney, but it can sometimes occur in both kidneys at the same time.
- Wilms' tumor can spread to lymph nodes in the abdomen and lungs, and sometimes to the liver, but has not spread to the bones, bone marrow, or brain.

Hence, the correct option is (B).

80. The 'Rule of Ten' applies to Cleft Lips.

A cleft lip is a birth defect that results in a unilateral or bilateral opening in the upper lip between the mouse and nose.

Cleft lip development:

- Failure of fusion between median nasal process and maxillary process.
- Failure of mesodermal migration.
- Rupture of a cyst.

Rule of 10:

- 10 week old
- Weight of 10 pounds
- 10 grams of haemoglobin

Hence, the correct option is (A).

81. Given,

Perimeter of a square is $24\sqrt{2}cm$.

As we know,

Diagonal of square $= \sqrt{2} \times$ Side

The perimeter of square $= 4 \times$ Side

$\Rightarrow 24\sqrt{2}cm = 4 \times$ Side

$\Rightarrow$ Side $= 6\sqrt{2}cm$

Diagonal of square $= \sqrt{2} \times$ Side

$= \sqrt{2} \times 6\sqrt{2}cm$

$= 12cm$

∴ Diagonal of a square is $12cm$.

Hence, the correct option is (D).

82. Given,

Total average marks of class $= 43$

Number of boys $= 25$

Average marks of boys $= 40$

Average marks of girls $= 48$

As we know,

Means of the marks $= \left(\frac{Total\ marks}{number\ of\ students}\right)$

Let, the number of girls $= x$

$\Rightarrow (25 \times 40) + (48 \times x) = 43 \times (25 + x)$

$\Rightarrow 1000 + 48x = 1075 + 43x$

$\Rightarrow 5x = 75$

$\Rightarrow x = 15$

∴ The number of girls is 15.

Hence, the correct option is (C).

83. Given:

Shopkeeper selling on article for Rs. 46 loses 8%.

We know that,

Selling price = Cost price – Loss

Selling price = Cost price + profit

Let cost price of the article is 100%

Loss is 8%

Selling price $(100 - 8) = 92\%$

Accordingly,

$92\% = 46$

$\Rightarrow 100\% = \frac{46}{92} \times 100$

$\Rightarrow 100\% = 50$

Cost price of the article is Rs. 50

He has to gain 6%.

Selling price should be $(100 + 6) = 106\%$

$100\% = 50$

$\Rightarrow 106\% = \frac{50}{100} \times 106$

$\Rightarrow 106\% = 53$

∴ In order to gain of 6%, the selling price of the article should be Rs. 53.

Hence, the correct option is (C).

84. Given,

$\sqrt{324} + 9^2 - 7^2 = 2 \times (?)^2$

$\Rightarrow 18 + 81 - 49 = 2 \times (?)^2$

$\Rightarrow 50 = 2 \times (?)^2$

$\Rightarrow \frac{50}{2} = (?)^2$

$\Rightarrow 25 = (?)^2$

$\Rightarrow ? = \sqrt{25}$

$\Rightarrow ? = 5$

∴ The value of (?) is 5.

Hence, the correct option is (B).

85. Given:

The sum of the two positive numbers is 240 and their HCF is 15.

Now,

Let two positive number is $15x$ and $15y$ where x and y should be coprime which means x and y should have HCF as 1.

According to the question:

The sum of the number is,

$15x + 15y = 240$

$\Rightarrow x + y = 16$

Now, we have to find the number of pairs in which the sum of the two numbers is 16 but no common factor between them, such a pair is,

$$\Rightarrow (1,15)(3,13)(5,11)(7,9)$$

$\therefore$ Total possible pairs are 4.

Hence, the correct option is (C).

86. The pattern followed here is:

3	1	18	18	25	3	15	20
C	A	R	R	Y	C	O	T
+2↓	-2↓	+2↓	-2↓	+2↓	-2↓	+2↓	-2↓
E	Y	T	P	A	A	Q	R
5	25	20	16	1	1	17	18

The same pattern will be followed for "CALAMITY".

3	1	12	1	13	9	20	25
C	A	L	A	M	I	T	Y
+2↓	-2↓	+2↓	-2↓	+2↓	-2↓	+2↓	-2↓
E	Y	N	Y	O	G	V	W
5	25	14	25	15	7	22	23

So, the answer is 'EYNYOGVW'.

Hence, the correct option is (D).

87. The least possible Venn Diagram for the given statements will be as follows:

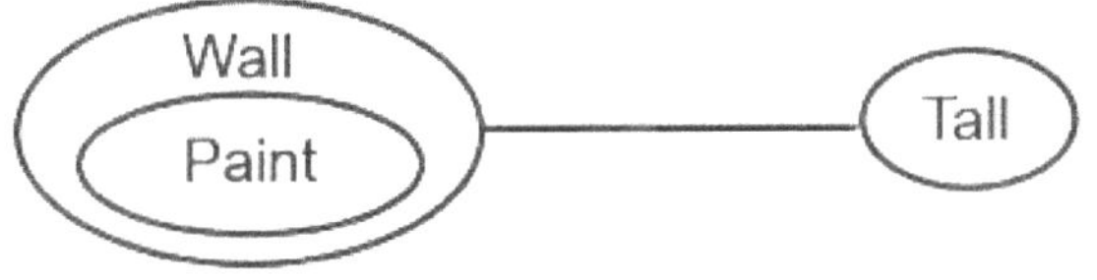

I. No Paint are Tall → True (As all paint are wall and no wall is tall. Thus, No paint are tall.)

II. Some Paint are Tall → False (This is definitely not true)

So,Only I follows.

Hence, the correct option is (A).

88. The logic followed here is:

Given:

'Bracelet' is related to 'Ornaments' = Bracelet is the type of ornaments.

Similarly,

'Clove' is related to 'Spices'= Clove is the type of spices.

Therefore, 'Spices' is the correct answer.

Hence, the correct option is (B).

89. The statement given here is:

Eating nutritious food will keep a person healthy so there will be no health issues so that it will keep doctor away.

I. Doctors will be out of job soon → False (There is no definite relation that eating nutritious food keeps doctor away but there is no information that doctors will be out of job soon).

II. Nutritious food does not keep doctor away → False (It is clear that from statement eating nutritious food keeps doctor away but from this conclusion eating Nutritious food does not keep doctor away).

So, Both conclusions are 1,2 are Complimentary pairs.

Thus, Neither I nor II follows.

Hence, the correct option is (C).

90. The pattern followed here is:

$$S \xrightarrow{+2} U \xrightarrow{+2} W \xrightarrow{+2} Y$$

$$H \xrightarrow{+2} J \xrightarrow{+2} L \xrightarrow{+2} N$$

$$C \xrightarrow{+2} E \xrightarrow{+2} G \xrightarrow{+2} I$$

$$P \xrightarrow{+2} R \xrightarrow{+1} S \xrightarrow{+2} U$$

Hence, 'PRSU' is the odd one among the following options.

Hence, the correct option is (D).

91. Kaziranga National Park is located at Assam, India. Designated with National Park status in 1968. Declared a UNESCO World Heritage Site in 1985. Kaziranga National Park hosts two-thirds of the world's great one-horned rhinoceroses.

- Kanha National Park in Madhya Pradesh is famous for Swamp Dears (Barasingha).
- Periyar National Park in Kerala is famous for Elephants.
- Sunderbans National Park in West Bengal is famous for The Royal Bengal Tiger.
- Gir National Park in Gujarat is famous for the Lions.
- Rann of Kutch Wild Ass Sanctuary in Gujarat is famous for Wild Ass.

Hence, the correct option is (A).

92. The 2022 Nobel Prize in Chemistry has been jointly awarded to Carolyn Bertozzi, Morton Meldal Barry Sharpless for their work on snipping molecules together, known as 'click chemistry'. Their work is used to explore cells track biological processes and can be applied in cancer treatment drugs. Barry Sharpless also won a Nobel Prize in 2001 for his work on chirally catalysed oxidation reactions.

Hence, the correct option is (C).

93. The words crawl, breaststroke, and butterfly are associated with the game of swimming.

In this game, the entire body of the person is moved through the water. In pools or open water, the sports take place. The events butterfly, breaststroke, freestyle, and individual medley are associated with swimming. A set of specific techniques is required by swimming. There are distinct regulations in competition.

Hence, the correct option is (A).

94. Union Minister of Ayush, Sarbananda Sonowal on 24 July 2022 launched Bal Raksha mobile app at the All India Institute of Ayurveda (AIIA).

The app aims to raise parental awareness of paediatric preventive healthcare through Ayurvedic intervention. Mr Sonowal also inaugurated the 'Vaccination Centre for Children' at the AIIA.

Hence, the correct option is (A).

95. Jhora dance originated in the Kumaon region of Uttarakhand. This is a magical folk dance form that binds people of all castes. Jhora dance is generally performed in the spring season. Jhora dance is usually seen in the evening at weddings or fairs. The men and women join hands and move in the circular formation. They bend their bodies smoothly.

Hence, the correct option is (A).

96. In Windows XP, XP stands for experience.

Windows XP is an operating system (OS) developed and exclusively distributed by Microsoft Corporation and targeted to owners of personal computers, laptops and media centers. The "XP" stands for eXPerience.

Hence, the correct option is (B).

97. A web browser is a software program that allows us to access the Internet and view web pages on our computer.

- A web browser, or simply "browser," is an application used to access and view websites.
- Common web browsers include Microsoft Internet Explorer, Google Chrome, Mozilla Firefox, and Apple Safari.
- The primary function of a web browser is to render HTML, the code used to design or "mark up" web pages.

Hence, the correct option is (C).

98. Whenever the user opens any website then main page is called as Home Page.

A home page (or homepage) is the main web page of a website. The term may also refer to the start page shown in a web browser when the application first opens.

Hence, the correct option is (C).

99. The secondary memory which allows us to store a large amount of data is often referred to as the auxiliary memory. It generally stores a large amount of data on a permanent basis.

Hence, the correct option is (A).

100. Rootkits are computer programs that are designed by attackers to gain root or administrative access to your computer. Once an attacker gains admin privilege, it becomes a cakewalk for him to exploit your system.

Unlike most viruses, it is not directly destructive and unlike worms, its objective is not to spread infection as wide as possible.

Hence, the correct option is (B).

Mock Test 08

Discipline

Q.1 The nurse is aware the procedure performed for an incompetent cervix is called ________.

A. Dilation and curettage
B. Colporrhaphy
C. Tubal ligation
D. Shirodkar procedure

Q.2 What is the proper management of atypical squamous cells of undetermined significance (ASC-US) or low-grade intraepithelial lesion (LSIL) in women age 21-24?

A. Repeat cytology in 6 months
B. Cervical conization
C. Repeat cytology in 1 year
D. LEEP (loop electrosurgical excision procedure)

Q.3 How is glomerular filtration rate (GFR) affected during a normal pregnancy?

A. No change **B.** Increases by 50%
C. Decreases by 15% **D.** Increases by 15%

Q.4 Which of the following assessments is not a focal point of the postpartum assessment?

A. Stool assessment, including consistency and color
B. Bonding, including maternal/fetal and family dynamics
C. Vital signs, including blood pressure and pulse
D. Fundus, including height, location, and consistency

Q.5 Which hormone is helpful in the growth of Ovarian follicles?

A. F.S.H **B.** L.H
C. Estrogen **D.** Progesterone

Q.6 What is the most common presentation of the foetus during labour?

A. Face **B.** Shoulder **C.** Vertex **D.** Breech

Q.7 When will the uterus normally reach the level of xiphisternum?

A. 32 weeks **B.** 36 weeks
C. 40 weeks **D.** 42 weeks

Q.8 What do you mean by fetal macrosomia?

A. Birth weight less than 1.5 kg
B. Large size head of a newborn
C. Fetal distress
D. Birth weight more than 4.5kg

Q.9 What is the most common complication associated with too rapid delivery in precipitate labor?

A. Pitting edema of the baby's scalp
B. Dural or subdural tears in fetal brain tissue
C. Premature separation of the placenta
D. Prolonged retention of the placenta

Q.10 Medical Termination of Pregnancy is considered safe up to how many weeks of pregnancy?

A. 6 weeks **B.** 8 weeks
C. 12 weeks **D.** 18 weeks

Q.11 The ___________ in the endometrial cycle is the phase that begins as spiral arteries leading to ischemia release blood into the uterus, and the endometrial lining begins to slough off.

A. Ischemic phase **B.** Proliferative phase
C. Secretory phase **D.** Menstrual phase

Q.12 The health personnel which acts as a link between ANM and Anganwari worker?

A. LHV **B.** ASHA
C. PHN **D.** Health guide

Q.13 A person having glaucoma have to put miotic eye drops instilled in both eyes. The nurse knows that the purpose of instilling miotic eye drops to the eyes is to:

A. Anesthetisation the cornea
B. Dilate the pupils of eyes
C. Constrict the pupils of eyes
D. Paralyze the muscles of accommodation

Q.14 An infected person is less likely to encounter a susceptible person when a large proportion of the members of the group are immune is called:

A. Active immunity **B.** Passive immunity
C. Herd immunity **D.** Specific immunity

Q.15 The proportion of cases of a specified disease or condition which are fatal within a specified time?

A. Morbidity rate
B. Case fatality rate
C. Proportionate mortality
D. Death rate

Q.16 Universal Immunisation Programme was started in India in:

A. 1974 **B.** 1963 **C.** 1984 **D.** 1985

Q.17 The National Vector Borne Disease Control Programme (NVBDCP) covers all of the following diseases except:

A. Malaria **B.** H1N1(Swine Flu)
C. Dengue fever **D.** None of the above

Q.18 All of the following are potential benefits of a randomized clinical trial, except:

A. The likelihood that the study groups will be comparable is increased
B. Self-selection for a particular treatment is eliminated
C. External validity of the study is increased
D. Assignment of the next subject cannot be predicted

Q.19 Match List - I with List-II and select the correct answer using the code given below the lists:

	List - I		List - II
A.	Soft tick	1.	Relapsing fever
B.	Hard tick	2.	Oriental sore
C.	Louse	3.	Tularaemia
D.	Sandfly	4.	Epidemic typhus

[UPPSC Staff Nurse, 2022]

A. A - 3, B - 4, C - 2, D - 1
B. A - 4, B - 2, C - 1, D - 3
C. A - 2, B - 1, C - 3, D - 4
D. A - 1, B - 3, C - 4, D - 2

Q.20 Match List - I with List-II and select the correct answer using the code given below:

	List - I		List - II
	(Body Part)		(Width of Bandage)
A.	Chest	1.	5 cm
B.	Thigh	2.	8 – 9 cm
C.	Head	3.	10 – 15 cm
D.	Wrist	4.	6 – 8 cm

[UPPSC Staff Nurse, 2022]

A. A - 3, B - 2, C - 4, D - 1
B. A - 1, B - 3, C - 2, D - 4
C. A - 2, B - 4, C - 1, D - 3
D. A - 4, B - 1, C - 3, D - 2

Q.21 The formula for calculating cardiac output is:
[UPPSC Staff Nurse, 2022]

A. Stroke volume × Respiratory rate
B. Respiratory rate × Reserve volume
C. Stroke volume × Blood pressure
D. Stroke volume × Heart rate

Q.22 Palpable pyloric tumour and projectile vomiting is found in:
[UPPSC Staff Nurse, 2022]

A. Pyloric stenosis **B.** Megacolon
C. Diarrhoea **D.** Omphalocele

Q.23 Match List - I with List - II and select the correct answer using the code given below:

	List - I		List - II
A.	Halitosis	1.	Cracking of lips
B.	Glossitis	2.	Inflammation of gums
C.	Gingivitis	3.	Inflammation of tongue
D.	Cheilosis	4.	Bad breath

[UPPSC Staff Nurse, 2022]

A. A - 1, B - 3, C - 4, D - 2
B. A - 2, B - 1, C - 3, D - 4
C. A - 3, B - 4, C - 1, D - 2
D. A - 4, B - 3, C - 2, D - 1

Q.24 The nurse Neeta had a needle stick injury with a hepatitis B infected needle, what is priority nursing action?

A. Wash puncture site with soap and water
B. Start PEP treatment immediately
C. Get a doctor appointment
D. Collect needle for laboratory check

Q.25 Which site of bleeding 'Haematomyelia' represents?
[UPPSC Staff Nurse, 2022]

A. Blood in stool
B. Bleeding from spinal cord
C. Bleeding per vagina
D. Bleeding from nose

Q.26 A client is hospitalized with signs of transplant rejection following a recent transplant. Assessment of the client would be expected to reveal:

A. A weight loss of 2 pounds in 1 day
B. A serum creatinine 1.25 mg/dl
C. Urinary output of 50ml /hr
D. Rising blood pressure

Q.27 Which one is the commonest cause of pleural effusion in young patients?
[UPPSC Staff Nurse, 2022]

A. Lung cancer
B. S.L.E.
C. Tuberculosis
D. Rheumatoid arthritis

Q.28 To promote the ingestion of which of the following, the hostess should motivate the patient for a low sodium diet?

A. Bread **B.** Vegetables
C. Milk **D.** Fruit

Q.29 What is the best exercise the nurse should educate a patient with cystocoele?

A. Abdomen exercise
B. Deep breathing exercise
C. Leg exercise
D. Kegel exercise

Q.30 The Nurse health educates the group of middle-aged women to undergo which of the following test for screening of cervical cancer?

A. Mantoux test
B. Ultrasonography
C. Fine needle aspiration cytology
D. Pap smear

Q.31 The nurse should teach the community that a minor burn injury could be caused by what common occurrence?

A. Chimney sweeping every year
B. Cooking with a microwave oven
C. Use of sunscreen agents
D. Use of space heaters

Q.32 Diet-related prenatal advice includes:

A. diet should be light and nutritious
B. there should be plenty of green vegetables and fruits in the diet
C. supplemental iron therapy is required for all pregnant

women

D. All of the above

Q.33 Minimum scrubbing time for surgical hand wash?

A. 1 min **B.** 2 min **C.** 3 min **D.** 5 min

Q.34 Which of the following would be considered a hand off point in hospitals?

A. Lunch time

B. The transfer of patient information and knowledge while nursing shift changes

C. Transfer from the emergency department to an in-patient setting

D. All of the above

Q.35 A patient says that he does not feel any pain at all, but he grimaces every time you touch his arm. What technique could validate the accuracy of what you see?

A. Stating observation

B. Offering medication

C. Asking question

D. Doing a head to toe assessment

Q.36 The component of food which help our body to fight against infections is:

A. Proteins **B.** Fats

C. Carbohydrates **D.** Starch

Q.37 Deficiency of proteins and carbohydrates in infants leads to:

A. Maramus **B.** Goitre

C. Obesity **D.** None of these

Q.38 Which nutrients live in the stomach for the longest time?

A. Lipids **B.** Proteins

C. Carbohydrates **D.** Fats

Q.39 Which of the following are the micronutrients?

A. Vitamins and Minerals

B. Proteins and Vitamins

C. Carbohydrates and Fats

D. Proteins and Minerals

Q.40 Which of the following nutrients is the energy producer?

A. Carbohydrates and Proteins

B. Proteins and Fats

C. Carbohydrates and Fats

D. Proteins and Vitamins

Q.41 Which of the following are the primary products of photosynthesis?

A. Proteins **B.** Carbohydrates

C. Minerals **D.** Water

Q.42 How should you open the airway of an unconscious casualty?

A. Head tilt and chin lift

B. Jaw thrust

C. Head tilt and jaw thrust

D. Lift the chin

Q.43 What should a person with a severe allergy carry at all times?

A. Insulin

B. Acetaminophen/Paracetamol

C. Adrenaline (Epipen)

D. Aspirin

Q.44 What can you do to avoid that a person experiences a short period of unconsciousness "Fainting"?

A. Speak to the victim and administer a pain stroke

B. Let the victim remain in their chair

C. Give fresh air, let the victim lay down and reassure the victim

D. Give the victim CPR

Q.45 What applies to a victim with a reduced consciousness?

A. The victim is still capable to speak

B. The victim is in shock

C. The victim does not react to speaking and shacking

D. The victim is still alert

Q.46 What can cause the blood circulation to stop?

A. A heart attack

B. A bleeding in the smaller veins

C. A head wound

D. A vein bleeding

Q.47 What is the best treatment for second degree burn?

A. Put Aloe vera lotion on it

B. Water

C. Put ice on the burn

D. None of these

Q.48 When performing chest compressions on an adult we press the chest:

A. 2 – 3 cm **B.** 2.5 – 3.5 cm

C. 4 – 5 cm **D.** 1- 2 cm

Q.49 Milk letdown hormone is _____.

A. Oestrogen **B.** Progesterone

C. Oxytocin **D.** Prolactin

Q.50 In mammals, the female secondary sexual characters are developed by the hormone?

A. Estrogens **B.** Relaxin

C. Progesterone **D.** Gonadotropins

Q.51 Which of the following hormone plays a major role during milk ejection in human beings?

A. Estrogen **B.** Prolactin

C. Oxytocin **D.** Progesterone

Q.52 Adrenaline hormone increases:

A. Heartbeat **B.** Blood pressure

C. Both (A) and (B) **D.** None of these

Q.53 Which is the longest muscle in the body?

A. Soleus **B.** Gracilis

C. Trapezius **D.** Sartorius

Q.54 Kidneys are helping to maintain pH balance by which of the following?

A. Adding hydrogen ions to the filter
B. Removal of hydrogen ions from the blood
C. Dissolving calcium and sodium ions in the blood
D. Removal of carbonate ions from the blood

Q.55 Excretory organs of Ascaris are:

A. Kidney **B.** Flame cell
C. Renette glands **D.** Nephridia

Q.56 Capability to identify who has the disease is done by measuring:

A. Validity **B.** Sensitivity
C. Specificity **D.** Repeatability

Q.57 All except ____ is the output indicator of hospital system.

A. Patient satisfaction **B.** Public relation
C. Quality of care **D.** Machines

Q.58 Supportive Services of the hospital includes all except:

A. Pharmacy services
B. Laboratory services
C. House-keeping services
D. Laundry services

Q.59 Care of disability includes all except:

A. Disability prevention
B. Disability limitation
C. Rehabilitation
D. Treatment of fracture

Q.60 The functions of the Out Patient Department Include :

A. Promotion of Health
B. Training of Medical and Nursing Personnel
C. Social Search
D. All of the Above

Q.61 The type of day care surgical units includes all except :

A. Hospital Integrated Unit
B. Hospital Autonomous Unit
C. Hospital Satellite Unit
D. Hospital Galaxy Unit

Q.62 What color code is used for a person suffering from cardiac arrest?

A. Red **B.** Blue **C.** Black **D.** Green

Q.63 What are the ISO standards for hospital equipment?

A. 9001 – product design, development, installation and servicing, 9002 – quality assurance at production and installation charges, 9003 – testing and inspections
B. 9001 – sterility in hospitals, 9002 – regulations to follow before surgery, 9003 – post operative regulations
C. 9001 – designing of hospitals, 9002 – maintenance of hospitals, 9003 – hospital procedures
D. 9001 – setting up of hospital labs, 9002 – maintenance of sterility in labs, 9003 – maintenance of hospital equipment

Q.64 What is AMC?

A. Annual Machine Calibration
B. Annual Maintenance Contract
C. Atomic Mass Calibration
D. Autonomous Machine Calibration

Q.65 Which of the following is the proper way to inject insulin?
[UPPSC Staff Nurse, 2017]

A. Intramuscular **B.** Intradermal
C. Subcutaneous **D.** Intravenous

Q.66 For a burn patient, the nurse should assess the following in the initial stage:
[UPPSC Staff Nurse, 2017]

A. Hyperkalaemia **B.** Hyponatremia
C. Hypernatremia **D.** Metabolic alkalosis

Q.67 Direction: Consider the following statements.

Assertion (A): Biochemical test to know the nutritional level is useful in the early detection of nutritional disease.

Reason (R): The disease can be caught indirectly by laboratory tests.
[UPPSC Staff Nurse, 2017]

A. (A) and (R) both are correct and (R) is the correct explanation of (A).
B. (A) is correct, but (R) is wrong.
C. (A) is wrong, but (R) is correct.
D. (A) and (R) both are not correct.

Q.68 What will you do when caring for a person with epileptic seizures?
[UPPSC Staff Nurse, 2017]

A. Anything that hurts in the vicinity will be removed.
B. Make a ball of cloth and place it between the teeth of the victim.
C. Will hold the person so that he does not move
D. All of the above

Q.69 In which disease morphine should not be given?
[UPPSC Staff Nurse, 2017]

A. Angina
B. Bronchial asthma
C. Pancreatitis
D. Myocardial infarction

Q.70 Important nursing interventions when caring for a patient with hyponatremia include:
[UPPSC Staff Nurse, 2017]

A. Fuid restriction
B. Provide isotonic saline
C. Giving potassium as ordered by the doctor
D. Provide N. G. feed

Q.71 Which of the following is not a symptom of heat stroke?
[UPPSC Staff Nurse, 2017]

A. 106°F body temperature
B. Rapid pulse rate
C. Hot and dry skin

D. Sweating profusely

Q.72 The Breteau index is often used to assess the density of the vector of:

[UPPSC Staff Nurse, 2017]

A. Yellow fever **B.** Dengue
C. Chikungunya **D.** Kala azar

Q.73 The International Council of Nurses (ICN) first adopted code of ethics in which year?

[UPPSC Staff Nurse, 2022]

A. 1953 **B.** 1971 **C.** 1951 **D.** 1942

Q.74 Size of suction catheter which is used for suctioning of mouth and nose in a new born baby?

A. 12 no. **B.** 10 no. **C.** 6 no. **D.** 20 no.

Q.75 Head control is possible in an infant by which month?

A. 1 **B.** 2 **C.** 3 **D.** 6

Q.76 A 1-month-old boy presents with failure to thrive. On examination, he shows features of congestive heart failure. The femoral pulses are feeble as compared to the brachial pulses. what is the most likely clinical diagnosis?

A. Congenital aortic stenosis
B. Coarctation of aorta
C. Patent ductus arteriosus
D. Congenital aortoiliac disease

Q.77 The nurse is aware that the most common assessment finding in a child with ulcerative colitis is __________.

A. Intense abdominal cramps
B. Profuse diarrhea
C. Anal fissures
D. Abdominal distention

Q.78 Which one is the most common cause of opthalmia neonatorum?

[UPPSC Staff Nurse, 2021]

A. Chlamydia trachomatis
B. Candida albicans
C. Streptococcus
D. Staphylococcus

Q.79 Which of the following should not be provided to the newborn in galactosemia?

A. Milk **B.** Starch
C. Gluten **D.** Glycogen

Q.80 A 10-year-old child with asthma is admitted to the ward. Which of the following observations needs immediate action by the nurse?

A. Breath rate 20/ min
B. Sitting upright and refusing to lie down
C. Refusing to eat food
D. Oxygen saturation 96%

General Aptitude / Reasoning / General Awareness / Basic Computer knowledge

Q.81 Ajeet and Bharni can complete a work in 12 days and 16 days. If they work together to complete the task and get Rs. 2100, then find the share of Bharni.

A. Rs. 850 **B.** Rs. 900 **C.** Rs. 1000 **D.** Rs. 1100

Q.82 Ajay, Alex, and Adyut are three friends appearing for an interview. Probabilities of their selection is $\frac{7}{10}, \frac{5}{6}$ and $\frac{3}{5}$ respectively. Find the probability that at most two of them get selected.

A. $\frac{7}{20}$ **B.** $\frac{13}{20}$ **C.** $\frac{9}{20}$ **D.** $\frac{11}{20}$

Q.83 The average salary of the entire staff in the office is Rs. 120 per month. The average salary of officers is Rs. 460 and that of non-officers is Rs. 110. If the number of officers is 15, then find the number of non-officers in the office.

A. 610 **B.** 510
C. 410 **D.** Can't be determined

Q.84 The length of sides of a triangle are in the ratio $3:4:5$ and its perimeter is 144 cm. The area of a triangle is:

[Joint Entrance Examination (Polytechnic), 2019]

A. 764 cm^2 **B.** 684 cm^2 **C.** 864 cm^2 **D.** 664 cm^2

Q.85 Navneet purchased a motorcycle with a marked price of Rs. 45,000 at a discount of 5%. If 10% sales tax is charged, find the net amount Navneet had to pay to purchase the motorcycle.

A. Rs. 47035 **B.** Rs. 47000
C. Rs. 47025 **D.** Rs. 47020

Q.86 Ananya walks east for a distance of 3 km, then turns to the right and walks for 1 km. Now in which direction is she from her initial position?

A. South-East **B.** North-East
C. South-West **D.** North-West

Q.87 If the water image of the clock shows 10:20 then what is the actual time?

A. 08:00 **B.** 08:10 **C.** 08:50 **D.** 09:30

Q.88 5th January 2018 was a Friday. Which of the following years will also have 5th January on a Friday?

[RRB/RRC Group D, 2018]

A. 2022 **B.** 2020 **C.** 2024 **D.** 2023

Q.89 Direction: Select the alphanumeric cluster from among the given options that can replace the question mark (?) in the following series.

KI12, JH11, IG10, ?

A. HG9 **B.** HF9 **C.** HM12 **D.** GF11

Q.90 Kitty is the wife of Raman. Dev is the only brother of Kitty. If Dolly is the daughter of Kitty, how is Dev related to Dolly?

A. Father **B.** Maternal Uncle
C. Paternal Uncle **D.** Grandfather

Q.91 Who presided over the session of the Indian National Congress held in Varanasi in the year 1905?

A. Acharya JB Kriplani
B. Pt. Jawaharlal Nehru
C. Gopalkrishna Gokhale
D. Romesh Chandra Dutt

Q.92 Who said, "A Government without a Constitution is a power without right"?

A. Thomas Paine **B.** Karl Deutsch
C. David Apter **D.** Walter Bagehot

Q.93 In which year Battle of Plassey was fought?

A. 1757 **B.** 1782 **C.** 1748 **D.** 1764

Q.94 With the separation of tectonic plates, there is the formation of ______.

A. Mid-ocean ridge **B.** Rift valley
C. Seamount **D.** Ocean trench

Q.95 India has sent a team to which of the following country to assess potential lithium deposits?

A. Australia **B.** Brazil
C. Argentina **D.** Egypt

Q.96 If you want to open "My Computer" on your computer, you will press ________.

A. Window + R **B.** Window + E
C. Window + K **D.** Window + C

Q.97 In MS PowerPoint, Page in a presentation is called:

A. Slide **B.** E-slide **C.** E-page **D.** Page

Q.98 Which is the slowest Internet connection service?

A. Land line
B. Dial up service
C. Digital subscriber line
D. Cable modem

Q.99 What cannot be done from the windows control panel?

A. Run Application
B. Printer configuration
C. Add fonts
D. Install Application

Q.100 Which among the following is not a type of Non-impact printer?

A. LED printer **B.** Inkjet
C. Laser **D.** Dot Matrix

// Smart Answer Sheet //

Correct Indicates percentage of students who answered questions correctly.

Skipped Indicates percentage of students who skipped questions.

Q.	Ans.	Correct	Skipped
1	D	42.59 %	1.63 %
2	C	18.96 %	3.72 %
3	B	61.67 %	1.8 %
4	A	48.06 %	1.53 %
5	A	47.93 %	1.03 %
6	C	53.25 %	1.65 %
7	B	43.41 %	1.38 %
8	D	44.25 %	1.73 %
9	B	47.68 %	1.88 %
10	C	63.16 %	1.85 %
11	D	49.23 %	1.52 %
12	B	63.31 %	1.46 %
13	C	55.45 %	1.67 %
14	C	56.02 %	1.36 %
15	B	69.3 %	1.89 %
16	A	61.08 %	1.12 %
17	B	46.78 %	1.01 %
18	C	65.92 %	1.6 %
19	D	48.33 %	1.45 %
20	C	79.22 %	0.0 %
21	D	56.28 %	1.74 %
22	A	59.76 %	1.75 %
23	D	30.28 %	4.68 %
24	A	66.6 %	1.87 %
25	B	78.4 %	0.0 %
26	D	40.93 %	1.28 %
27	A	79.86 %	0.0 %
28	D	53.6 %	1.14 %
29	D	53.12 %	1.5 %
30	D	62.36 %	1.67 %
31	D	79.08 %	0.0 %
32	D	58.35 %	1.56 %
33	D	82.25 %	0.0 %
34	B	22.49 %	3.53 %
35	A	50.48 %	1.91 %
36	A	53.67 %	1.58 %
37	A	55.66 %	1.79 %
38	D	66.39 %	1.17 %
39	A	50.47 %	1.96 %
40	C	48.98 %	1.33 %
41	B	65.77 %	1.5 %
42	A	54.16 %	1.4 %
43	C	63.5 %	1.63 %
44	C	77.86 %	0.0 %
45	A	59.12 %	1.73 %
46	A	64.0 %	1.77 %
47	B	54.21 %	1.16 %
48	C	44.24 %	1.56 %
49	C	41.43 %	1.69 %
50	A	66.47 %	1.32 %
51	C	57.0 %	1.3 %
52	C	49.1 %	1.7 %
53	D	46.38 %	1.65 %
54	B	61.6 %	1.35 %
55	C	47.46 %	1.93 %
56	B	82.82 %	0.0 %
57	C	50.31 %	1.62 %
58	C	42.59 %	1.79 %
59	D	55.68 %	1.64 %
60	D	63.53 %	1.98 %
61	D	50.83 %	1.21 %
62	B	49.62 %	1.15 %
63	A	61.58 %	1.37 %
64	B	51.04 %	1.23 %
65	C	45.77 %	1.99 %
66	B	63.85 %	1.79 %
67	A	76.27 %	0.0 %
68	D	50.62 %	1.8 %
69	B	62.52 %	1.56 %
70	B	53.99 %	1.42 %
71	D	56.68 %	1.81 %
72	B	49.13 %	1.52 %
73	A	85.25 %	0.0 %
74	C	41.88 %	1.16 %
75	C	67.75 %	1.61 %
76	B	52.79 %	1.85 %
77	B	54.88 %	1.91 %
78	A	66.04 %	1.23 %
79	A	62.14 %	1.03 %
80	B	40.29 %	1.02 %

Q.	Ans.	Correct	Skipped
81	B	79.05 %	0.0 %
82	B	80.67 %	0.0 %
83	B	76.82 %	0.0 %
84	C	81.92 %	0.0 %
85	C	89.17 %	0.0 %
86	A	82.77 %	0.0 %
87	B	84.41 %	0.0 %
88	C	77.99 %	0.0 %
89	B	76.09 %	0.0 %
90	B	82.3 %	0.0 %
91	C	80.67 %	0.0 %
92	A	44.63 %	1.06 %
93	A	52.93 %	1.32 %
94	B	53.93 %	1.61 %
95	C	88.44 %	0.0 %
96	B	83.45 %	0.0 %
97	A	83.19 %	0.0 %
98	B	62.38 %	1.36 %
99	A	60.49 %	1.16 %
100	D	44.59 %	1.09 %

Performance Analysis	
Avg. Score (%)	66.0%
Toppers Score (%)	73.0%
Your Score	

//Hints and Solutions//

1. The nurse is aware the procedure performed for an incompetent cervix is called a Shirodkar procedure.

A Shirodkar procedure involves sewing a suture in and around the cervix to hold it closed. This is usually performed within the first trimester and later removed when the risk of miscarriage has lessened.

Hence, the correct option is (D).

2. Repeat cytology in 1 year is the proper management of atypical squamous cells of undetermined significance (ASC-US) or low-grade intraepithelial lesion (LSIL) in women age 21-24.

ASC-US or LSIL in women age 21-24 should be managed by repeat cytology in one year.

Cytology is the exam of a single cell type, as often found in fluid specimens. It's mainly used to diagnose or screen for cancer. It's also used to screen for fetal abnormalities, for pap smears, to diagnose infectious organisms, and in other screening and diagnostic areas.

Hence, the correct option is (C).

3. Glomerular filtration rate (GFR) Increases by 50% during a normal pregnancy.

In the average normal pregnancy, the GFR increases by upwards of 50%. This correlates with an overall 50% increase in blood plasma volume.

Hence, the correct option is (B).

4. Stool assessment, including consistency and color, is not a focal point of the postpartum assessment.

The postpartum assessment includes vital signs (blood pressure, pulse), fundus (location, height, consistency), lochia (color, volume), urinary output (measure first void), and bonding between the mother and infant. The postpartum assessment is valuable because it allows for nursing interventions at warning signs of postpartum complications, including infection, hemorrhage, and uterine atony. Stool assessment is not a vital part of the postpartum assessment because it does not lend information to the assessment of potential danger signs.

Hence, the correct option is (A).

5. F.S.H hormone is helpful in the growth of ovarian follicles.

Follicle-stimulating hormone is one of the hormones essential to pubertal development and the function of women's ovaries and men's testes. In women, this hormone stimulates the growth of ovarian follicles in the ovary before the release of an egg from one follicle at ovulation.

Hence, the correct option is (A).

6. The fetal presentation refers to the part of the body of the fetus that comes out through the birth placenta which is also known as the presented part.

In normal delivery, the head comes out first, but sometimes the buttock or shoulder can also come out first. The summit or head is the most common fetal presentation in which the head comes out first in delivery.

The fetal presentation refers to the part of the fetus that is located above the maternal pelvis.

The fetus refers to the relationship between the mother's longitudinal axis in relation to the mother's longitudinal axis (longitudinal position, transverse position, oblique position).

General fetal presentations:

- The head first (called the peak or head presentation)
- Backward
- Face and body at right or left angle
- Neck
- Chin shrunk
- Arms bended across the chest

Hence, the correct option is (C).

7. The uterus normally reaches the level of xiphisternum in 36 weeks.

After 12 weeks of pregnancy, the fundus of the uterus is palpable above the symphysis pubis. It reaches the umbilicus by the 20-22 weeks and finally ceases to ascend at 36-38th week (uterine fundus at about the level of the xiphisternum).

Hence, the correct option is (B).

8. Fetal macrosomia means birth weight more than 4.5kg.

More than 9 out of 10 babies born at term (37 to 40 weeks) weigh between 2.5kg and 4.5kg. If your baby weighs 4.5kg or more at birth, they are considered larger than normal. This is also known as fetal macrosomia and large for gestational age (LGA).

Hence, the correct option is (D).

9. The most common complication associated with too rapid delivery in precipitate labor is dural or subdural tears in fetal brain tissue.

Precipitate delivery may cause intracranial hemorrhage resulting from a sudden change in pressure on the fetal head during rapid expulsion. It may cause aspiration of amniotic fluid, if unattended at or immediately following delivery.

Hence, the correct option is (B).

10. Medical Termination of Pregnancy is considered safe up to a period of 12 weeks of pregnancy.

Medical termination of pregnancy is also termed as MTPs. MTPs are used to get rid of unwanted pregnancies and the pregnancies which could be harmful or fatal to the mother or to the foetusor both. MTPs are safe upto 12 weeks i.e. the first trimester or pregnency. Government of India legalized MTP in 1971.

Hence, the correct option is (C).

11. The menstrual phase in the endometrial cycle is the phase that begins as spiral arteries leading to ischemia release blood into the uterus, and the endometrial lining begins to slough off.

Menstruation is the elimination of the thickened lining of the uterus (endometrium) from the body through the vagina. Menstrual fluid contains blood, cells from the lining of the uterus (endometrial cells) and mucus. The average length of a period is between three days and one week.

Hence, the correct option is (D).

12. ASHA acts as a link between ANM and Anganwari worker. One of the key components of the National Rural Health Mission / NHM is to provide every village in the country with a trained female community health activist called ASHA or Accredited Social Health Activist.

Hence, the correct option is (B).

13. Miotic eye drops constrict the pupil and allow aqueous thing to drain out of the corner of Schlemm. Pilocarpine is a muscarinic acetylcholine agonist that is effective in the treatment and management of acute angle-closure glaucoma and radiation-induced xerostomia. It is useful as an adjunct medication in the form of ophthalmic drops.

Hence, the correct option is (C).

14. An infected person is less likely to encounter a susceptible person when a large proportion of the members of the group are immune is called herd immunity.

Herd immunity is a form of indirect protection from infectious disease that can occur with some diseases when a sufficient percentage of a population has become immune to an infection, whether through previous infections or vaccination, thereby reducing the likelihood of infection for individuals who lack immunity.

Hence, the correct option is (C).

15. The proportion of cases of a specified disease or condition which are fatal within a specified time is case fatality rate.

Case fatality rate, also called case fatality risk in epidemiology, the proportion of people who die from a specified disease among all individuals diagnosed with the disease over a certain period of time. Case fatality rate typically is used as a measure of disease severity and is often used for prognosis (predicting disease course or outcome), where comparatively high rates are indicative of relatively poor outcomes. It also can be used to evaluate the effect of new treatments, with measures decreasing as treatments improve. Case fatality rates are not constant; they can vary between populations and over time, depending on the interplay between the causative agent of disease, the host, and the environment as well as available treatments and quality of patient care.

Hence, the correct option is (B).

16. Universal Immunisation Programme (UIP) is a vaccination programme launched by the Government of India in 1985. It became a part of Child Survival and Safe Motherhood Programme in 1992 and is currently one of the key areas under National Rural Health Mission since 2005.

Hence, the correct option is (A).

17. The National Vector Borne Disease Control Programme (NVBDCP) was launched in 2003-04 by merging National anti - malaria control programme ,National Filaria Control Programme and Kala Azar Control programmes .Japanese B Encephalitis and Dengue/DHF have also been included in this Program Directorate of NAMP is the nodal agency for prevention and control of major Vector Borne Diseases. This programme covers the diseases Kala - Azar, malaria, filaria, Japenese Encephilitis, dengue etc. H1N1 is not included in this programme. H1N1 (swine flu) is an influenza virus causing illness in people. This virus was first detected in people in the United States in April 2009.

Hence, the correct option is (B).

18. All of the following are potential benefits of a randomized clinical trial, except external validity of the study is increased.

Clinical trial randomization is the process of assigning patients to groups that receive different treatments. In the simplest trial design, the investigational group receives the new treatment and the control group receives standard therapy. Randomization helps prevent bias. Clinical trials do not increase external validity of a study or research.

Hence, the correct option is (C).

19. The correct match is: A - 1, B - 3, C - 4, D - 2.

	List - I		**List - II**
A.	Soft tick	1.	Relapsing fever
B.	Hard tick	3.	Tularaemia
C.	Louse	4.	Epidemic typhus
D.	Sandfly	2.	Oriental sore

Relapsing fever:

- Relapsing fever typically refers to malaria-like illnesses, characterized by recurrent fevers, chills, and malaise.
- It is caused by various spirochetes belonging to the Borrelia species.

Oriental sore:

- Cutaneous leishmaniasis (oriental sore) is characterized by slowly evolving inflammatory lesion(s) that are nodular, noduloulcerative, or ulcerative and that heal spontaneously with the scar in 3 to 12 months.

Tularaemia:

- Tularemia is a bacterial disease in humans, wild, and domestic animals.
- Francisella tularensis, the causative agent of the zoonotic disease tularemia, is characterized by high morbidity and mortality rates in over 190 different mammalian species, including humans

Epidemic typhus:

- Louse-borne typhus (epidemic typhus or exanthematic typhus) is a vector-borne disease caused by Rickettsia prowazekii and transmitted through infected feces of the body louse Pediculus humanus humans.

Hence, the correct option is (D).

20. The correct answer is: A - 2, B - 4, C - 1, D - 3

	List - I		List - II
	(Body Part)		(Width of Bandage)
A.	Chest	1.	8 – 9 cm
B.	Thigh	2.	6 – 8 cm
C.	Head	3.	5 cm
D.	Wrist	4.	10 – 15 cm

Bandaging: it is the process of covering a wound or an injured part.

- To prevent contamination of the wound by holding dressings in position.
- To provide support to the part that is injured, sprained, or dislocated joints.
- To provide rest to the part that is injured.
- To prevent and control hemorrhage.

Types of Bandages:

1- Triangular Bandage: It could be used on many parts of the body to support and immobilize.

2- Crape Bandage: Type of woven gauze which has the quality of stretching.

3- Gauze/Cotton Bandage: Lightly woven, cotton material. Frequently used to retain dressings on wounds of fingers, hands, toes, feet, ears, eyes, head.

4- Adhesive Bandage: Use to retain dressing and also used where application of pressure to an area is needed.

Hence, the correct option is (C).

21. The cardiac output is cardiac physiology term which describes the functioning of a human heart, and also about the total volume of blood (5 to 6 litres) being pumped every minute. Normal cardiac output is said when a person is resting.

- Cardiac output: the amount of blood pumped from the left and right ventricle per minute.
- For an average adult at rest, cardiac output is approx. 3.0 L PER sq. m of body surface area or a total of 5 liters each minute.
- Cardiac out is determined by multiplying the stroke volume by the heart rate.
- Cardiac output = stroke volume × heart rate
- Cardiac output = 70 × 72 = 5 liter

Hence, the correct option is (D).

22. Palpable pyloric tumour and projectile vomiting is found in Pyloric stenosis.

- Pyloric stenosis is an uncommon condition in infants that blocks food from entering the small intestine.
- Normally, a muscular valve (pylorus) between the stomach and small intestine holds food in the stomach until it is ready for the next stage in the digestive process. In pyloric stenosis, the pylorus muscles thicken and become abnormally large, blocking food from reaching the small intestine.
- Pyloric stenosis can lead to forceful vomiting, dehydration and weight loss. Babies with pyloric stenosis may seem to be hungry all the time.

Hence, the correct option is (A).

23. The correct match is:

	List - I		List - II
A.	Halitosis	1.	Bad breath
B.	Glossitis	2.	Inflammation of tongue
C.	Gingivitis	3.	Inflammation of gums
D.	Cheilosis	4.	Cracking of lips

A. Halitosis. The microscopic uneven surface of the tongue can trap bacteria that produce odors, contributing to bad breath. Bad breath, also called halitosis, can be embarrassing and in some cases may even cause anxiety.

B. Glossitis refers to inflammation of the tongue. The condition causes the tongue to swell in size, change in color, and develop a different appearance on the surface. The tongue is the small, muscular organ in the mouth that helps you chew and swallow food.

C. Gingivitis is a common and mild form of gum disease (periodontal disease) that causes irritation, redness and swelling (inflammation) of your gingiva, the part of your gum around the base of your teeth. It's important to take gingivitis seriously and treat it promptly.

D. Cheilosis is swelling and fissuring of the lips. It is painful and results in bleeding. Angular stomatitis is fissuring and ulceration at the angles of the mouth. Other symptoms include dermatitis and a rash on the scrotum or vulva.

Hence, the correct option is (D).

24. While doing any procedure it is basic responsibility of a nurse to protect her self.

In certain situations there may be chances of pricking in that time it must be washed with soap and water. The puncture site should be dried and then the staff should have self assessment of her health. All the medical investigations should be done and based on that she should take her post exposure prophylaxis for Hepatitis-B

Hence, the correct option is (A).

25. 'Haematomyelia' represents bleeding from spinal cord.

It is the haemorrhage in the spinal cord that occurs due to trauma. It causes severe back or neck pain and sometimes radicular pain.

Bleeding from spinal cord:

- It is caused by trauma, vascular malformations, or bleeding diatheses.
- It can cause pain, weakness, numbness, difficulty walking etc.
- MRI is a good choice for early diagnosis.
- It can be treated by giving medicines (phytonadione) or by surgery.

Hence, the correct option is (B).

26. Transplant rejection is the process in which a transplant recipient's immune system attacks the transplanted organ or tissue. Mismatched organs, or organs that are not matched closely enough, can trigger a blood transfusion reaction or transplant rejection.

Elevated blood pressure predicts the risk of acute rejection in patients. It occurs when the host immune system starts responding post-transplant. It helps to diagnose the transplant rejection. It helps the health care provider assess the sign of transplant rejection. When a person receives an organ from someone else during transplant surgery, that person's immune system may recognize that it is foreign and it causes the transplant rejection.

Hence, the correct option is (D).

27. Lung cancer is the commonest cause of pleural effusion in young patients.

Pleural effusion is the condition of accumulation of excess fluid around the lung. It causes due to the leaking of fluid from the organs, lung cancer, infections like pneumonia and tuberculosis, etc.

It can cause:

- Shortness of breath
- Chest pain, especially when breathing in deeply (This is called pleurisy or pleuritic pain.)
- Fever
- Cough

Hence, the correct option is (A).

28. Fruits have a lesser amount of sodium as compared to vegetables. Apples, guavas, avocado, papaya, mango, carambola, pineapple, banana, melons, and pears contain natural sodium ranging between 1-8 mg per 100 grams. So fruit intake is more recommended to maintain a low sodium diet.

Hence, the correct option is (D).

29. He is only when ligaments that keep your bladder in position, and weakens or stretch the tissue between the vagina and the bladder, raising the bladder in the vagina. The possibility of cystosle increases with age as muscles and tissues weaken.

Kegel exercise:

- Bladder control depends on muscles working together when the bladder is filling with urine.
- The bladder muscle should be relaxed and the muscles around the urethra (the tube that urine passes through), called the pelvic floor muscles, should be tight.
- Exercises that strengthen the pelvic floor muscles can help hold urine inside the bladder, preventing leakage. These pelvic floor muscle exercises are commonly called "Kegel" exercises, named after the doctor who developed them.

Hence, the correct option is (D).

30. Cervical Cancer is a disease in which cells in the body grow out of control within the cervix.

All women are at risk for cervical cancer. It occurs most often in women over age 30. Screening tests and the HPV vaccine can help prevent cervical cancer. When cervical cancer is found early, it is highly treatable and associated with long survival and good quality of life.

Hence, the correct option is (D).

31. A minor burning injury is a common phenomenon. If the space heater has clothes, beds and other flammable items, using it can cause fire. Be sure to keep any object at a distance of at least 3 feet from flammable substances or equipment that provides heat.

Most of the burning injuries are minor and patients can be treated in external patients or local hospitals. Sunscreen factors are recommended to prevent sunburn. The wide-spectrum sunscreen with at least 30 SPF should be applied 30 minutes before the sunlight and then every 90 minutes.

Hence, the correct option is (D).

32. Perinatal care: systemic supervision of a woman during pregnancy is called prenatal care.

Diet-related prenatal advice:

- The diet should be light and nutritious.
- there should be plenty of green vegetables and fruits in the diet.
- supplemental iron therapy is required for all pregnant women.
- approximately 300 extra calories are needed each day.
- calories should come from a balanced diet of protein, fruits, vegetables, and whole grains.
- Sweets and fats should be kept to a minimum.

Hence, the correct option is (D).

33. Surgical Hand Wash -> It is a hand washing process that includes complete disinfection, also known as aseptic handwashing. It is used especially in the operation room during surgery. This can be done for 5 - 8 minutes.

Medical hand washing includes rubbing hands with each other, dorsal part of hands, interlessing, inter -bonding, adornment of thumbs, adornings of fingers etc. The same happens in surgery but it is different. This can prevent infection from one person to another.

Hence, the correct option is (D).

34. In hospitals, handoffs points are episodes in which control of, or responsibility for, a patient passes from one health professional to another, and in which important information about the patient is also exchanged.

A handoff may be described as the transfer of patient information and knowledge, along with authority and responsibility, from one clinician or team of clinicians to another clinician or team of clinicians during transitions of care across the continuum.

Hence, the correct option is (B).

35. Stating the observation technique could validate the accuracy of what you see.

Observation research is a qualitative research technique where researchers observe participants' ongoing behavior in a natural situation. In other words, researchers can capture data on what participants do as opposed to what they say they do.

Hence, the correct option is (A).

36. The component of food which help our body to fight against infections is Proteins. Proteins are vitamin and minerals, that fight against germs. Protein is vital to build and repair body tissue and fight viral and bacterial infections. Immune system powerhouses such as antibodies and immune system cells rely on protein. Too little protein in the diet may lead to symptoms of weakness, fatigue, apathy, and poor immunity.

Hence, the correct option is (A).

37. Deficiency of proteins and carbohydrates in infants leads to maramus. Marasmus is a type of protein-energy malnutrition that can affect anyone but is mainly seen in children. You can get marasmus if you have a severe deficiency of nutrients like calories, proteins, carbohydrates, vitamins, and minerals.

ence, the correct option is (A).

38. The diet between the stomach gurusica and the small intestine is a stretched part of the placenta. The stomach serves as both a reservoir and digestive organ. It empties its content to small parts to continue in the small intestine. Carbohydrates spend the least time in the stomach, while the protein lasts longer in the stomach, and fat lasts for the longest.

Fat: micronutrients that provide energy sources centered to our body. Fats are found in blood and body cells in our fat tissue which storing energy. Protein and fat present in them are complex molecules that take more time to damage your body tissue. Conversely, fruits and vegetables, which have high fiber amounts, can rotate in your system in less than a day.

Hence, the correct option is (D).

39. Vitamins and Minerals are called micronutrients or protective principles of food. Micronutrients are one of the major groups of nutrients your body needs. They include vitamins and minerals. Vitamins are necessary for energy production, immune function, blood clotting and other functions. Meanwhile, minerals play an important role in growth, bone health, fluid balance and several other processes.

Hence, the correct option is (A).

40. Carbohydrates and Fats are the energy producer. Carbohydrates are the nutrients most frequently used as an energy source (containing 4kcal per gram), as they are fast-acting and turn into energy as soon as they are ingested. Fats are used for energy after they are broken into fatty acids. Protein can also be used for energy, but the first job is to help with making hormones, muscle, and other proteins.

Hence, the correct option is (C).

41. Carbohydrates are the primary products of photosynthesis. The main product of photosynthesis is glucose, which is the carbohydrate molecule that produces energy to run the processes of the cell. Oxygen is mainly a byproduct of the process of photosynthesis. Six molecules of carbon dioxide and six molecules of water are needed to produce one molecule of glucose.

Hence, the correct option is (B).

42. By doing Head tilt and chin lift you should open the airway of an unconscious casualty.

To open the airway, place 1 hand on the casualty's forehead and gently tilt their head back, lifting the tip of the chin using 2 fingers. This moves the tongue away from the back of the throat. Don't push on the floor of the mouth, as this will push the tongue upwards and obstruct the airway.

Hence, the correct option is (A).

43. A person with a severe allergy should carry Adrenaline (Epipen) at all times. If your doctor says you are at risk of a severe allergic reaction, be sure to carry a device to inject adrenaline (such as an EpiPen) and a mobile phone to call for help.

Adrenaline (Epipen) medication is used in emergencies to treat very serious allergic reactions to insect stings/bites, foods, drugs, or other substances. Epinephrine acts quickly to improve breathing, stimulate the heart, raise a dropping blood pressure, reverse hives, and reduce swelling of the face, lips, and throat.

Hence, the correct option is (C).

44. You can Give fresh air, let the victim lay down and reassure the victim to avoid when a person experiences a short period of unconsciousness "Fainting".

Fresh air can also help, especially if you are feeling hot. If it is not possible to lie down, put your head down as low as possible. If you do faint, remain lying down for ten minutes. Sit up slowly when you need to get up.

Hence, the correct option is (C).

45. The victim is still capable to speak applies to a victim with reduced consciousness.

An altered level of consciousness can result from a variety of factors, including alterations in the chemical environment of the brain (e.g. exposure to poisons or intoxicants), insufficient oxygen or blood flow in the brain, and excessive pressure within the skull.

Hence, the correct option is (A).

46. A heart attack can cause the blood circulation to stop.

During a heart attack, plaque can rupture and spill cholesterol and other substances into the bloodstream. A blood clot forms at the site of the rupture. If the clot is large, it can block blood flow through the coronary artery, starving the heart of oxygen and nutrients (ischemia).

Hence, the correct option is (A).

47. The best treatment for second degree burns is Water.

Rinse burned skin with cool water until the pain stops. Rinsing will usually stop the pain in 15 to 30 minutes.

Hence, the correct option is (B).

48. When performing chest compressions on an adult we press the chest 4 – 5 cm. Place your palm on the centre of the person's chest, then place the other hand on top and press down by 4 to 5cm (2 to 2.5 inches) at a steady rate of 100 to 120 compressions a minute. After every 30 chest compressions, give 2 rescue breaths.

Hence, the correct option is (C).

49. Milk letdown hormone is oxytocin.

Milk letdown means the ejection of a mother's milk from the alveoli of the breast into the mammary ducts and to the nipple. When the nipple is sucked the Prolactin acts on the milk-making tissues. The Oxytocin hormone causes the breast to push out or 'let down' the milk.

Hence, the correct option is (C).

50. In mammals, the female secondary sexual characters are developed by the estrogen hormone.

Estrogen and progesterone are the two groups of steroid hormones. It is produced by the ovary.

The estrogen is synthesized and secreted mainly by the growing ovarian follicles.

Hence, the correct option is (A).

51. Oxytocin: It is synthesized by the hypothalamus and is transported axonally to the neurohypophysis.

It has the following physiological functions:

- It acts on the smooth muscles of our body and stimulates their contraction. In women, it stimulates a vigorous contraction of the uterus at the time of childbirth.
- It stimulates the secretion of milk from the mammary gland.

Hence, the correct option is (C).

52. Adrenaline hormone is secreted by the adrenal gland.

The adrenaline hormone is rapidly secreted in response to stress during any type of stress and in emergency situations and is called the emergency hormone or the fight or flight hormone.

When we are angry or in a stressful situation, our heart beats faster, this raises blood pressure, this causes adrenaline to rise in the bloodstream.

Adrenaline prepares our body to face such distress.

Hence, the correct option is (C).

53.

Muscle	**Use**
Sartorius	The longest muscle in the human body. Helps flex, adduct, and rotate the hip.
Trapezius	Used to tilt and turn the head and neck, shrug, steady the shoulders, and twist the arms.
Gracilis	Responsible for assists knee flexion and hip adduction.
Soleus	They increase the angle between the foot and the leg. vital in walking, running, and keeping balance.

Note: gluteus maximus Largest muscle in the human body.

Hence, the correct option is (D).

54. Kidneys help maintain pH balance by removing hydrogen ions from the blood.

They are an essential part of our urinary system and also perform homeostatic functions such as electrolyte control, acid-base balance, and blood pressure control, etc. The kidneys perform these homeostatic functions both independently and in association with the organs of the endocrine system.

Hence, the correct option is (B).

55. Excretory organs of Ascaris are Renette glands. The function of Renette glands is believed to be something like an excretory system. Renette varies among the species. In many marine nematodes they excrete salt through a pore on the underside of the animal, close to the pharynx.

Hence, the correct option is (C).

56. Capability to identify who has the disease is done by measuring Sensitivity.

The sensitivity of a clinical test refers to the ability of the test to correctly identify those patients with the disease. A test with 100% sensitivity correctly identifies all patients with the disease.

Hence, the correct option is (B).

57. All except quality of care is the output indicator of the hospital system.

Quality of care is the degree to which health services for individuals and populations increase the likelihood of desired health outcomes. It is based on evidence-based professional knowledge and is critical for achieving universal health coverage.

Hence, the correct option is (C).

58. Supportive Services of the hospital include all except house-keeping services.

Support Services is a vital field in health care, and careers in this area help provide a welcoming and safe environment for patients and the public. The Support Services pathway encompasses both technical and professional careers.

Common hospital housekeeping duties include mopping, vacuuming and sweeping floors; cleaning windows and dusting furniture; washing and changing linens on patients' beds; and ensuring that all waste is disposed of properly.

Hence, the correct option is (C).

59. Care of disability includes all except treatment of fracture.

Disability care is simply practical help with anything from everyday tasks like housework and bathing, to assistance with complex needs like continence. Specially trained carers, experienced in working with people living with disabilities, can be employed to come into the home and lend a hand.

Treatment often involves resetting the bone in place and immobilising it in a cast or splint to give it time to heal. Sometimes, surgery with rods, plates and screws may be required so it need its specialist.

Hence, the correct option is (D).

60. The functions of the Out Patient Department Include promotion of health, training of medical and nursing personnel, and social search.

The outpatient department provides the initial diagnoses. Patient visits the OPD of hospitals for treatment. The patient is not required to be admitted to the hospital for treatment. Generally, OPD takes minor cases for treatment.

Health promotion is the process of enabling people to increase control over, and to improve, their health.

Medical training is education related to the practice of being a medical practitioner, including the initial training to become a physician (i.e., medical school and internship) and additional training thereafter (e.g., residency, fellowship and continuing medical education).

Nursing personnel includes professional nurses, auxiliary nurses, enrolled nurses and related occupations such as dental nurses and primary care nurses.

Hence, the correct option is (D).

61. The type of day care surgical units includes all except Hospital Galaxy Unit.

A day care surgery is defined as a procedure in which the patients undergo elective operation on the day of their admission and are discharged within 24 hours after surgery. Patients who fulfilled the criteria of day care surgery and had regular follow-up on 3rd and 7th days post surgery.

Hence, the correct option is (D).

62. A blue color code is used for a person suffering from cardiac arrest.

Places like hospitals use various color codes to quickly convey information. Since these codes mean the same thing all over the hospitals, a doctor, nurse, or medical staff is quickly able to understand the situation and take necessary action. Blue is for cardiac arrest, red is for fire, black is for a bomb threat and green is for evacuation.

Hence, the correct option is (B).

63. The ISO standards for hospital equipment are 9001 – product design, development, installation, and servicing, 9002 – quality assurance at production and installation charges, 9003 – testing and inspections.

Standards are sets of rules that have been accepted all over for the regulation and maintenance of a certain place, organization, machine, technology, etc. It helps provide uniformity. ISO 9000 is a list of standards related to quality management regarding products so the standards 9001, 9002, 9003 relating to the product are the solution.

Hence, the correct option is (A).

64. AMC means Annual Maintenance Contract.

This is the contract that is signed between the hospitals and the company when the hospital buys their machine. The contract states how and when the company will send in maintenance engineers, scheduling the next maintenance, duration of the contract, etc.

Hence, the correct option is (B).

65. Subcutaneous is the proper way to inject insulin.

- Insulin should be injected into the fatty tissue just below your skin.
- If you inject the insulin deeper into your muscle, your body will absorb it too quickly, it might not last as long, and the injection is usually more painful.

Hence, the correct option is (C).

66. For a burn patient, the nurse should assess the Hyponatremia in the initial stage.

Burn is the transfer of energy from one source to another which leads to tissue damage, destruction, protein denaturalization, and ionization of content.

- There is a loss of sodium in the burn patient therefore hyponatremia often occurs, hyperkalemia is also characterized by this period due to massive tissue necrosis.
- After a burn injury, sodium and water retention occurs in the kidneys, and potassium is lost in the urine.
- Hyponatremia in these cases rarely results from sodium deficiency but is usually from excess water retention and entry of sodium into cells.

Hence, the correct option is (B).

67. The nutritional status of an individual reflects the extent to which their physiological needs of nutrients have been covered at a particular life stage.

- Dietary assessment and nutritional status are traditionally measured by means of dietary intake data, such as 24-h dietary patterns.
- Biochemicals provide a more proximal measure of nutrient status than dietary intake. So by, Generally speaking, a nutritional biomarker is a characteristic that can be objectively measured in different biological samples and can be used as an indicator of nutritional status with respect to the intake or metabolism of dietary constituents.

Hence, the correct option is (A).

68. A seizure is a sudden disruption of the brain's normal electrical activity accompanied by altered consciousness and/or other neurological and behavioral manifestations. Epilepsy is a condition characterized by recurrent seizures that may include repetitive muscle jerking called convulsions.

Caring for a person with epileptic seizures:

- Make a ball of cloth and place it between the teeth of the victim.
- Do not force the tongue blade during an episode of the seizure (It may injure the tooth).
- Note prodromal signs and time of onset after a seizure occurs.
- Anything that hurts in the vicinity will be removed.

Hence, the correct option is (D).

69. If a person has any problem like asthma, COPD, liver disease, then he should not take morphine medicine.

Asthma is the difficulty in breathing due to lack of oxygen in the lungs. This is due to the shrinking of the air passages. Asthma is easily diagnosed. The patient breathes loudly with great effort. Breathing is often accompanied by a sound that can be heard from a distance.

Hence, the correct option is (B).

70. Important nursing interventions when caring for a patient with hyponatremia include provide isotonic saline.

- Hyponatremia is a condition where sodium levels in the blood are abnormally low.
- This causes nausea, vomiting, fatigue, headache, or confusion.
- Isotonic is a kind of solution that consists of the same salt concentration as the cells and the blood.
- A standard measuring agent is sodium chloride; a 0.9% solution of sodium chloride is considered isotonic with blood, although, in fact, its osmotic pressure is actually slightly higher.

Hence, the correct option is (B).

71. Sweating profusely is not a symptom of heat stroke.

- Heatstroke is a condition in the body heat rises rapidly.
- The body loses the ability to cool down.
- The body temperature rises to 106°F or higher within 10 to 15 minutes.
- The sweating mechanism of the body fails.

The symptoms of heatstroke are:

- Altered mental status; seizures
- Loss of consciousness (coma)
- Hot, dry skin
- Very high body temperature

Hence, the correct option is (D).

72. The Breteau index is often used to assess the density of the vector of Dengue.

- The Breteau index helps to detect the risk of dengue transmission.
- It helps to control the spread of dengue spread by Aedes aegypti.
- It is important for surveillance and control activities.
- It includes the number of positive containers per 100 houses inspected.
- These surveillances help to manage the environment to stop the spread.

Hence, the correct option is (B).

73. The International Council of Nurses (ICN) first adopted code of ethics in 1953.

The International Council of Nurses (ICN) is a federation of more than 130 national nurses associations. It was founded in 1899 and was the first international organization for health care professionals. It is headquartered in Geneva, Switzerland.

The organization's goals are to bring nurses' organizations together in a worldwide body, to advance the socio-economic status of nurses and the profession of nursing worldwide, and to influence global and domestic health policy.

Hence, the correct option is (A).

74. First suction with the mouth, then suit the baby's nose using the suction catheter size 6. The bulb should not do deep entertaining from the syringe as it can cause bradycardia. The bulb should not do deep entertaining from the syringe as it can cause bradycardia.

The following formula can be used to determine the appropriate size catheter:

- Suction catheter size (in French) = 2x
- For suction, the respiratoryway is blocked from the top of the thumb with the thumb of the indestructible hand and then the catheter is removed.
- Do not suit for more than 5 to 10 seconds.
- Let the baby rest for 15 to 20 seconds before suction again.
- If the mucous is thick, put 3 to 5 drops of ordinary salts in the nose before suction.

Hence, the correct option is (C).

75. Developmental achievements are a set of functional skills or age-specific tasks that most children can achieve within a certain age range.

By about four to 12 weeks, they may be able to lift their head when they're lying on their stomach, as if they're doing a small push-up.

Head and neck control is a prerequisite for many other important developments, such as sitting up and eventually walking. Around 3 months of age, most babies develop enough strength in their necks to hold their heads partially upright.

Hence, the correct option is (C).

76. Growth failure is diagnosed when the child is underweight or rare and the child is not growing as expected. The child may consume enough food, but may not be able to absorb enough nutrients and calories. Failure to thrive can result in short height, behavioral problems, and developmental delay.

A constriction of the heart is a narrowing of a large blood vessel that leads out of the heart. The exact cause of the constriction is unknown. It results from abnormalities in the development of the aorta before birth. It is diagnosed by electrocardiogram, CT, angiography. Coarctation of the aorta is more common in people with certain genetic disorders.

Hence, the correct option is (B).

77. The nurse is aware that the most common assessment finding in a child with ulcerative colitis is profuse diarrhea.

The most common assessment finding in a child with ulcerative colitis is profuse diarrhea. The main symptom of ulcerative colitis is bloody diarrhea, with or without mucus. Other symptoms include blood in the toilet, on toilet paper, or in the stool. Characteristically, it involves inflammation restricted to the mucosa and submucosa of the colon. Typically, the disease starts in the rectum and extends proximally in a continuous manner.

Hence, the correct option is (B).

78. Ophthalmia neonatorum (ON) refers to any conjunctivitis in newborns caused by gonococci. 0.5% erythromycin or 1% silver nitrate ointment is used for treatment.

- Candida albicans:- It is an opportunistic pathogen found in the gastrointestinal tract of humans. This can cause a disease known as candidiasis (oral and genital).
- Streptococcus:- It is a gram-positive bacilli that can cause many disorders like pharyngitis, pneumonia, wound and skin infections, sepsis, endocarditis, etc.
- Staphylococcus:- It is gram positive bacilli which can cause skin infections, pneumonia, endocarditis and osteomyelitis. It is mostly responsible for abscess formation.

Hence, the correct option is (A).

79. Galactosemia is a condition in which the body is unable to metabolize galactose (a simple sugar). So, milk should not be provided to the newborn in galactosemia.

If milk is given to a child with galactosemia, substances made of galactose accumulate in the child's system. These substances harm the brain, liver, kidney and eyes of the newborn. People with galactosemia cannot digest any type of milk (human or animal).

Hence, the correct option is (A).

80. In children, Asthma Attack Scale is used to determine the disease severity and it has four-level i.e.

1. Mild (no SOB at rest, mild SOB with walking, can talk normally, can lay down normally, wheezes not heard or mild)
2. Moderate (SOB at rest, speaks in the phrase, sitting upright and refusing to lie down, wheezing can be heard)
3. Severe (severe SOB at rest, can talk in single words, wheezing may be loud)
4. Peak flow rate tells how well a person can move air out of the lungs.

In the above scenario, nurses need to take immediate action because the child develops a moderate type of asthma attack.

Hence, the correct option is (B).

81. Given:

Ajeet can complete the work $= 12$ days

Bharni can complete the work $= 16$ days

We know that,

$W = E \times T$ (Where, $W =$ Work, $E =$ Efficiency, and $T =$ Time)

Let the share of Bharni be X.

According to the question,

The one day work of Ajeet $= \frac{1}{12}$

The one day work of Bharni $= \frac{1}{16}$

The one day work of together $= \frac{1}{12} + \frac{1}{16}$

$= \frac{4+3}{48}$

$= \frac{7}{48}$

The share of Bharni $= \frac{3}{7} \times 2100$

$= 3 \times 300$

$= 900$

∴ The required result will be 900.

Hence, the correct option is (B).

82. Given:

Passing probability of Ajay $= \frac{7}{10}$

Passing probability of Alex $= \frac{5}{6}$

Passing probability of Adyut $= \frac{3}{5}$

We know that,

Probability of at most two selection $= 1 -$ Probability of all three selections

Probability of all three selection $= \frac{7}{10} \times \frac{5}{6} \times \frac{3}{5} = \frac{7}{20}$

Probability of at most two selection $= 1 - \frac{7}{20} = \frac{13}{20}$

Hence, the correct option is (B).

83. Let the number of non-officers $= a$

Total number of officers $= 15$

The average salary of officers is Rs. 460

Then, total salary of officers $= 15 \times 460 = 6900$

Similarly, total salary of non-officers $= a \times 110$

Now we can obtain the total salary of all the employees as:

$\Rightarrow 120 \times (15 + a) = 6900 + 110a$

$\Rightarrow 1800 + 120a = 6900 + 110a$

$\Rightarrow 120a - 110a = 6900 - 1800$

$\Rightarrow 10a = 5100$

$\Rightarrow a = 510$

∴ The total number of non-officers is 510.

Hence, the correct option is (B).

84. Let Sides $= 3x, 4x$ and 5x

Then, $3x + 4x + 5x = 144$ cm

$12x = 144$

$\Rightarrow x = 12$

Area of triangle

$= \frac{1}{2} \times 4x \times 3x$

$= \frac{1}{2} \times 12x^2$

$= \frac{1}{2} \times 12 \times 12 \times 12$

$= 144 \times 6$

$= 864$ cm ^{2}

Hence, the correct option is (C).

85. According to the question,

MP of motorcycle = Rs. 45000

Discount = 5% of 45000

$\frac{5}{100} \times 45000$

= Rs. 2250

Now, the price = 45000 - 2250

= Rs. 42750

Sales tax = 10% of 42750

$\frac{10}{100} \times 42750$

= Rs. 4275

Net amount he has to pay = 42750 + 4275

= Rs. 47025

Hence, the correct option is (C).

86. According to the given information, we can draw the following diagram:

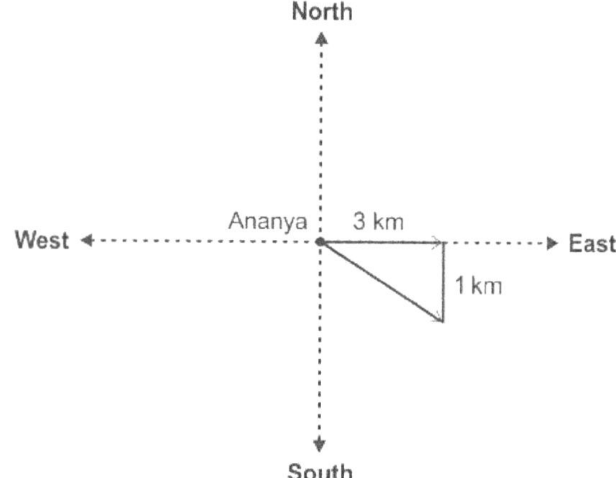

Thus, Ananya is to the South-East of her initial position.

Hence, the correct option is (A).

87. Here the water image is 10:20, the minutes are less than 30,

Therefore we need to subtract it from 18:30.

Thus, 18:30 - 10:20 = 08:10.

The actual time shows 08:10 on the clock.

Hence, the correct option is (B).

88. Number of odd days from 5th January 2018 till 5th January 2019 = 1

Number of odd days from 5th January 2019 till 5th January 2020= 1

Number of odd days from 5th January 2020 till 5th January 2021= 2

Number of odd days from 5th January 2021 till 5th January 2022= 1

Number of odd days from 5th January 2022 till 5th January 2023= 1

Number of odd days from 5th January 2023 till 5th January 2024= 1

Total odd days = 1 + 1 + 2 + 1 + 1 + 1 = 7 = 0 odd days

5th January 2024 is Friday.

Hence, the correct option is (C).

89. The pattern followed here is:

(Number = Numerical value of second letter + 3)

KI12 → K = 11, K – 2 = I, I = 9, 9 + 3 = 12

JH11 → J = 10, J – 2, H, H = 8, 8 + 3 = 11

IG10 → I = 9, I – 2 = G, G = 7, 7 + 3 = 10

Now, the first letter of the next term = First letter of the previous term (i.e., I) – 1 = H

H – 2 = F, F = 6, 6 + 3 = 9

Thus, the missing term is 'HF9'.

Hence, the correct option is (B).

Q.90 Preparing the family tree using the following symbols:

Symbol in Diagram	Meaning
○	Female
□	Male
═	Married Couple
—	Siblings
|	Difference of A Generation

Possible tree diagram will be:

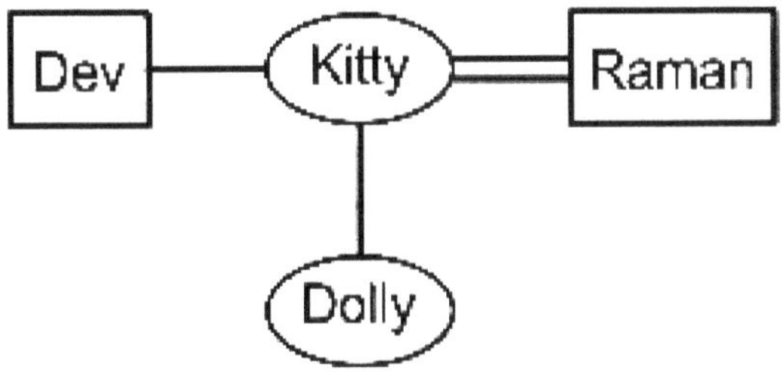

Therefore, Dev is the maternal uncle of Dolly.

Hence, the correct option is (B).

91. Gopalkrishna Gokhale presided over the session of the Indian National Congress held in Varanasi in the year 1905.

Prior to this, in the 1905 session of Banaras, a proposal was made (supported) to boycott British goods. In 1905, at the Banaras session of the Congress, Gopal Krishna Gokhale supported the Swadeshi and Bengal boycott movements.

The resolution of Swadeshi was adopted in the 1906 Calcutta session of the Indian National Congress. This session was presided over by Dadabhai Naoroji. Earlier, in the 1905 convention of Banaras, a proposal was made to boycott British goods. However, it was in the 1906 session in Calcutta that four resolutions were passed by the Congress on self-government, the boycott movement, Swadeshi, and national education.

Hence, the correct option is (C).

92. Thomas Paine said, "A Government without a Constitution is a power without right".

Thomas Paine was a debater, magazine writer, and international revolutionary. His work Common Sense (1776) was an important text in mobilizing the American freedmen against the United Kingdom. The Rights of Man (1791–2) was the most widely read pamphlet in the Reformation movement in Britain in the 1790s and the first decades of the nineteenth century.

He was a key figure in the emergence of claims to state responsibilities. He made it clear in his pamphlet Right of Man that "the constitution is not the function of the government, but of the people who form the government, and government without a constitution is power without authority."

Hence, the correct option is (A).

93. The Battle of Plassey took place on 23 June 1757 at a place called 'Plassey' on the banks of the river Ganges in Nadia district, 22 miles south of Murshidabad. In this war, on one side was the army of the British East India Company and on the other side was the army of the Nawab of Bengal. Nawab Siraj-ud-daulah was defeated by the Company's army under the leadership of Robert Clive.

Hence, the correct option is (A).

94. With the separation of tectonic plates, there is the formation of the rift valley.

A rift valley is a lowland region that forms where Earth's tectonic plates move apart or rift. Rift valleys are found both on land and at the bottom of the ocean, where they are created by the process of seafloor spreading.

Hence, the correct option is (B).

95. On November 20, 2022 India has sent a team of three geologists to Argentina to assess potential lithium deposits and possible acquisition opportunities in the country.

The team comprises of one geologist each from Mineral Exploration Corporation Ltd (MECL), KABIL (Khanij Bidesh India Ltd) and the Geological Survey of India (GSI). India does not have any lithium resource and the mineral is primarily imported. Lithium is the key component of rechargeable batteries used in EVs.

Hence, the correct option is (C).

96. If you want to open "My Computer" on your computer, you will press Window + E.

In all versions of Windows, on pressing Windows key + E opens My Computer. Your computer's drives are listed under the "This PC" section on the left.
Hence, the correct option is (B).

97. The page in a Microsoft PowerPoint presentation is called a slide.

A slide is a page of a presentation. Collectively, a group of slides may be known as a slide deck. In the digital age, a slide most commonly refers to a single page developed using a presentation program such as MS PowerPoint, Apple Keynote, Google Slides, Apache OpenOffice or LibreOffice.

Hence, the correct option is (A).

98. Dial-up is by far the slowest of all Internet connections available. Use of dial-up requires a separate phone line, since users must connect via the telephone to their Internet service provider. Speeds max out at about 56Kbps, which is only about a tenth of the speed of even the slowest broadband connections.

Hence, the correct option is (B).

99. Application Run method (Excel) Runs a macro or calls a function. This can be used to run a macro written in Visual Basic or the Microsoft Excel macro language or to run a function in a DLL or XLL. Syntax. expression A variable that represents an Application object.

Hence, the correct option is (A).

100. Dot Matrix is not a type of Non-impact printer.

- It prints each character as a combination of dots.
- They have a matrix of pins on the print head of the printer which form the character.
- The words get printed on the paper when the pin strikes the carbon.

Hence, the correct option is (D).

Previous Year Paper 01

General Aptitude / Reasoning / General Awareness / Basic Computer knowledge

Q.1 Five boys A, B, C, D and E are standing in a row. D is on the right of E. B is on the left of E but on the right of A. D in on the left of C, who is standing on the extreme right. Who is standing in the middle?

A. B **B.** C **C.** D **D.** E

Q.2 If 'T' means (x), 'U' means (-), 'X' means (÷) and W means (+), then will be the value of the following expression. (50 X 2) W (28 T 4)

A. 142 **B.** 158 **C.** 137 **D.** 163

Q.3 Barun is taller than Sanjay. Bipul is taller than Barun. Krishna is also not as tall as Bipul but is taller than Barun. Who is the tallest?

A. Barun **B.** Bipul **C.** Krishna **D.** Sanjay

Q.4 In a certain code language 'MADRAS' is written as 'DAMSAR', how can 'MUMBAI' be written in that code language?

A. BAIUMM **B.** MUMIAB
C. IABMUM **D.** MBIAUM

Q.5 If in a certain code language 'RAMESH' is written as 'HSEMAR', then how will 'CREATE' be written in that language?

A. TEACRE **B.** ETAECR
C. ETAERC **D.** ETACRE

Q.6 Arrange the following words according to English dictionary.

1. Episode 2. Epistle 3. Episcope 4. Epigraph

A. 1, 2, 3, 4 **B.** 4, 2, 1, 3 **C.** 3, 2, 1, 4 **D.** 4, 3, 1, 2

Q.7 A woman said to a man, "The daughter of your only sister is the sister of my husband." what is the relation of man's sister to the woman?

A. Mother **B.** Mother-in-law
C. Data inadequate **D.** None of these

Q.8 A man walks 6 km South, turns left and walks 4 km, again turns left and walks 5 km. which direction is he facing now?

A. South **B.** North **C.** East **D.** West

Q.9 Find the odd word that does not belong to the group?

A. I **B.** J **C.** K **D.** L

Q.10 Choose the correct answer having same relation of the following:

Austria : Vienna

A. Pakistan : Lahore **B.** Egypt : Cairo
C. USA : Orlando **D.** Germany : London

Q.11 The 'Cannes Award' is given for excellence in which field?

A. Films **B.** Journalism
C. Literature **D.** Economics

Q.12 Pulitzer prize is awarded for outstanding work in the field of:

A. Science and Technology
B. Environmental Studies
C. Literature and Journalism
D. International Understanding

Q.13 Which among the following is the smallest Human Chromosome?

A. Chromosome 10 **B.** Chromosome 16
C. Chromosome 20 **D.** Chromosome 21

Q.14 Headquarters of International Labour Organization (ILO) is situated at ________.

A. Paris **B.** Frankfurt
C. Geneva **D.** New York

Q.15 The Centre for Cellular and Molecular Biology is situated at:

A. Patna **B.** New Delhi
C. Hyderabad **D.** Mumbai

Q.16 The Chamera Dam is located in which State/UT?

A. Puducherry **B.** Uttar Pradesh
C. Himachal Pradesh **D.** Jharkhand

Q.17 Which port is known as Queen of Arabian Sea?

A. Vizag port **B.** Paradip port
C. Kochi Port **D.** Mumbai Port

Q.18 Who among the following has discovered X-rays?

A. Marie Curie **B.** J.J. Thomson
C. W.C. Roentgen **D.** James Chadwick

Q.19 Who among the following founded "National Herald"?

A. Bal Gangadhar Tilak
B. Mahatma Gandh
C. Jawahar Lal Nehru
D. Indira Gandhi

Q.20 Who among these has been honored with the 2020 Asia Game Changer Award?

A. Sonu Sood **B.** Virat Kohli
C. Vikas Khanna **D.** Narendra Modi

Q.21 Puskas Award is associated with the game of:

A. Football **B.** Cricket
C. Badminton **D.** Tennis

Q.22 Chetan Chauhan who has passed away recently was a former player of which sports?

A. Football **B.** Cricket **C.** Golf **D.** Hockey

Q.23 Which institute has developed the first ICMR-approved mobile RT-PCR lab?

A. AIIMS
B. IIT-Guwahati
C. IIT-Delhi
D. IISC-Bengaluru

Q.24 Who launched Operation Samudra Setu?

A. Indian Army
B. Indian Navy
C. Indian Air Force
D. NITI Aayog

Q.25 ANANDA is a digital application launched by which organization recently?

A. LIC
B. RBI
C. SEBI
D. SBI

Q.26 Which country has topped the Global Economic Freedom Index 2020?

A. Singapore
B. Hong Kong
C. Germany
D. Finland

Q.27 Which country has recently joined the IMF as its 190th member?

A. Andorra
B. Armenia
C. Iran
D. Madagascar

Q.28 Which country hosted the 12th BRICS Summit in 2020?

A. Russia
B. India
C. South Africa
D. Nepal

Q.29 The Ministry of Housing and Urban Affairs (MoHUA) has partnered with which foodtech company to take street vendors online?

A. Swiggy
B. Zomato
C. Uber Eats
D. Food Panda

Q.30 India's first sandalwood museum has been unveiled in which city?

A. Mysuru
B. Hyderabad
C. Chennai
D. Bhubaneswar

Discipline

Q.31 The various methods of intrapartum fetal monitoring includes all except:

A. Fetal scalp stimulation test
B. Fetal pulse oximetry
C. Fetal blood sampling
D. Braxton Hicks contractions

Q.32 During active management of labour injection ergometrine is contraindicated in which of the following conditions?

A. Primigravida
B. Severe eclampsia
C. Prolonged labour
D. None of the above

Q.33 The fetal movement felt by the mother is called:

A. Braxton Hicks contractions
B. Quickening
C. Goodell's sign
D. Hegar's sign

Q.34 Fetal tachycardia is caused due to all of the following factors except:

A. Maternal or fetal anemia
B. Maternal or fetal infection
C. Severe Fetal hypoxia
D. Fetal compromise

Q.35 Fetal blood sampling is contraindicated in which of the following conditions?

A. HIV positive women
B. Thick meconium stained liquor
C. Atypical and abnormal tracing on Electronic Fetal Monitoring
D. All the above

Q.36 A family planning measure of using a Diaphragm or Dutch Cap is called:

A. Natural method
B. Barrier method
C. Intra uterine contraceptive device
D. Calendar method

Q.37 Any bleeding from or into the genital tract after the period of viability but before the birth of the baby is called:

A. Antepartum haemorrhage
B. Intrapartum haemorrhage
C. Postpartum haemorrhage
D. All the above

Q.38 The clinical features of first stage of labour includes all except:

A. Effacement of cervix
B. Contractions every three to five minutes
C. Minimal descent of presenting part
D. Sudden gush of vaginal bleeding

Q.39 Crowning occurs in:

A. First stage of labour
B. Second stage of labour
C. Third stage of labour
D. Forth stage of labour

Q.40 The immunity an individual develops after acquiring an infection is called:

A. Active immunity
B. Passive immunity
C. Herd immunity
D. All the above

Q.41 The equipment used to carry small quantities of vaccines for out reach programme is called:

A. Walk in freezers
B. Walk in coolers
C. Vaccine carriers
D. Ice packs

Q.42 The major cause of nutritional blindness in children usually between the age of 1-3 years is called:

A. Xeropthalmia
B. Night blindness
C. Blindness
D. None of the above

Q.43 The poisoning caused due to ingestion of foods contaminated by living bacteria is all except:

A. Salmonella poisoning

B. Staphylococcal poisoning
C. Botulism
D. Chemical poisoning

Q.44 Varicella vaccine is a:
A. Killed vaccine
B. Live attenuated vaccine
C. Immunoglobulin
D. None of the above

Q.45 The route of administration of measles vaccine is:
A. Intradermal **B.** Subcutaneous
C. Intramuscular **D.** Oral

Q.46 The incubation period of mumps is:
A. 0 to 1 week **B.** 1 to 2 weeks
C. 2 to 4 weeks **D.** 5 to 8 weeks

Q.47 The antiviral drug used to treat influenza is:
A. Acyclovir **B.** Oseltamivir
C. Imunovir **D.** Zidovudine

Q.48 The vaccine-preventable diseases that are caused by droplet infection are all except:
A. Meningococcal meningitis
B. Whooping cough
C. Diptheria
D. Polio

Q.49 Which of the following is a blood borne disease?
A. Hepatitis A **B.** Hepatitis C
C. Hepatitis E **D.** All the above

Q.50 In children with diarrhea the main aim of ORS therapy is to:
A. Prevent dehydration
B. Reduce mortality
C. To correct water and electrolyte deficit
D. All the above

Q.51 In a person with cholera, diarrhea occurs due to a toxin produced by the virus on multiplication in the small intestine. The toxin produced by vibrio cholerae is:
A. Endotoxin **B.** Enterotoxin
C. Hepatotoxin **D.** None of the above

Q.52 The cancer arising from mesodermal cells constituting the various connecting tissues is called:
A. Carcinomas **B.** Sarcomas
C. Lymphomas **D.** Leukeamias

Q.53 Blood glucose values above normal but below those diagnostic diabetes, occurring during pregnancy is called:
A. Type 1 diabetes
B. Type 2 diabetes
C. Gestational diabetes
D. Insulin resistance syndrome

Q.54 In a patient with perinicious anaemia the primary purpose of schilling test is to determine:
A. Intake of vitamin B12
B. Absorption of vitamin B12
C. Excretion of vitamin B12
D. None of the above

Q.55 A type of fracture in which one fragment of the bone goes into another is called:
A. Spiral fracture **B.** Transverse fracture
C. Oblique fracture **D.** Impacted fracture

Q.56 Signs and symptoms of asthma include all except:
A. Shortness of breath **B.** Fever
C. Wheezing **D.** Chest pain

Q.57 The signs and symptoms of Parkinson's disease is:
A. Tremors
B. Impaired postures and balance
C. Speech changes
D. All the above

Q.58 Infection of the urinary bladder caused by Escherichia coli is a type of bacteria commonly found in gastro intestinal tract is called:
A. Pyelonephritis
B. Cystitis
C. Urethritis
D. Nephrotic syndrome

Q.59 The most essential fatty acid that serves as a basis for production of other fatty acids is:
A. Lineloic acid **B.** Transfatty acid
C. Butyric acid **D.** Caproic acid

Q.60 Vitamin D is largely stored in the body in:
A. Muscles **B.** Fatty tissues
C. Skin **D.** Gall bladder

Q.61 Fat soluble vitamins are all except:
A. Vitamin A **B.** Vitamin C
C. Vitamin E **D.** Vitamin K

Q.62 The clinical sign of Riboflavin deficiency is:
A. Angular stomatitis **B.** Keratitis
C. Pellagra **D.** Rickets

Q.63 The richest source of vitamin C is:
A. Lemon **B.** Orange **C.** Amla **D.** Tomato

Q.64 Thiamine deficiency results in:
A. Cardiac Beriberi **B.** Infantile Beriberi
C. Peripheral neuritis **D.** None of the above

Q.65 A thorough investigation made to evaluate the overall nursing care received by a patient is called:
A. Nursing process **B.** Nursing Audit
C. Medical Audit **D.** Nursing assessment

Q.66 Patient fall due to improper application of restraints in the ICU is an act of:
A. Assault **B.** Battery
C. Negligence **D.** Fraud

Q.67 While resuscitating a preterm baby, Positive Pressure Ventilation should be started with oxygen concentration of:

A. 21% **B.** 40% **C.** 75% **D.** 80%

Q.68 International Nurses Day is observed around the world on ______.

A. 12th May **B.** 16th May
C. 18th May **D.** 20th May

Q.69 The most central and accessible artery to check the pulse in children over one year of age is:

A. Brachial **B.** Carotid
C. Dorsalis pedis **D.** Popliteal

Q.70 A patient is diagnosed to have insomnia. The term insomnia means:

A. Inability to think **B.** Inability to move
C. Inability to eat **D.** Inability to sleep

Q.71 The ideal position to provide mouth care for an unconscious patient is:

A. Fowlers position **B.** Lateral Position
C. Supine position **D.** Knee chest position

Q.72 The most preferred site of administration of intramuscular injection in children under one year is:

A. Dorso Gluteal site **B.** Vastus Lateralis
C. Ventro gluteal site **D.** Deltoid site

Q.73 Major factors influencing an individuals blood pressure are all except:

A. Stroke volume
B. Venous return
C. Heart rate
D. Normal body weight

Q.74 The drugs administered to promote uterine contractions are:

A. Oxytocin **B.** Ergometrine
C. Misoprostol **D.** Duvadilan

Q.75 Medication appropriate to treat an acute anginal attack is:

A. Propranolol **B.** Nadolol
C. Atenolol **D.** Nitroglycerine

Q.76 An essential micronutrient iodine is required for synthesis of which of the following hormones?

A. Goitre, Cretinism
B. Thyroxine, Triiodothyronine
C. Tyrosine, Thyroxine
D. Trypsin, Thyroxine

Q.77 Drug used to treat hyperkalemia is:

A. Atenolol **B.** Predinosolone
C. Nitroglycerine **D.** Calcium gluconate

Q.78 Drugs used to treat nausea and vomiting are all except:

A. Dopamine antagonists
B. Serotonin receptor antagonists
C. Cannabinoids
D. Calcium channel blockers

Q.79 The function of state nursing council is all except:

A. Ensure proper training is given in the institutions
B. Approve training institutions
C. Register all trained nurses and provide license to practice
D. Provide employment to all trained nurses

Q.80 Hypoxia may be caused by all the following factors except:

A. Decreased Hemoglobin
B. A respiratory problem
C. A decrease in blood supply to an area
D. Increased haemoglobin

Q.81 A defensive reaction intended to neutralize, control or eliminate the offending agent and to prepare the site for repair is called:

A. Infection **B.** Inflammation
C. Induration **D.** Insult

Q.82 Movement of hands towards midline of the body is called:

A. Abduction **B.** Adduction
C. Inversion **D.** Eversion

Q.83 The first aid measure to be taken to stop bleeding due to epistaxis:

A. Make the person sit down, lean backward and pinch soft part of nose
B. Make the person sit down, lean forward and pinch soft part of the nose
C. Make the person lie down and pinch the soft part of nose
D. Make the person lie downand pinch the top part of nose

Q.84 According to the MTP act the following are indications for terminating a pregnancy before viability except:

A. Severe cardiac disease
B. Chromosomal abnormality
C. Pregnancy due to rape
D. Unplanned pregnancy

Q.85 Chemicals that reduce or inhibit the transmission or perception of pain is:

A. Prostaglandnins **B.** Leukotrienes
C. Endorphins **D.** Serotonins

Q.86 The factors that results in increasing the serum osmolality are all except:

A. Diabetes insipidus **B.** Uremia
C. Hyperglycemia **D.** Renal failure

Q.87 The characteristics of fluid volume deficit includes all except:

A. Decreased skin turgor
B. Postural hypotension
C. Increased temperature
D. Increased central venous pressure

Q.88 The systemic complications of intravenous therapy includes all except:

A. Fluid Overload **B.** Air Embolism
C. Infection **D.** Infiltration

Q.89 A 30-year-old man is brought to the emergency with a history of accident. Which of the following sign indicates skull fracture?

A. Fluid draining from ear or nose, periorbital ecchymosis
B. Blood from nose, blood from forehead
C. Battle sign, Kernigs sign
D. None of the above

Q.90 A type of presentation in which the fetal buttocks presents at the pelvic inlet and the denominator is sacrum is called as:

A. Vertex Presentation
B. Breech Presentation
C. Knee Presentation
D. Footling Presentation

Q.91 Which of the following is the most important nursing action that has to done for a patient who has undergone cardiac catheterization?

A. Check for pulse deficit
B. Elevate the head end of bed
C. Assess the catheterization site for bleeding
D. Provide a bed cradle

Q.92 A nurse is assigned to take of a patient with multiple sclerosis. The priority nursing diagnosis for the patient would be:

A. Impaired urinary elimination
B. Altered body temperature
C. Deficient knowledge
D. Impaired mobility

Q.93 The indication for a newborn to be given positive pressure ventilation soon after birth is when _______.

A. Heart rate < 100 beats/minute
B. Cyanosis in baby
C. SpO2 below 95%
D. Baby is not crying at birth

Q.94 In a restaurant a person suddenly collapses, choking while eating food. The ideal method to clear the airway is to use which of the following methods?

A. Jaw thrust manuevre
B. Head tilt chin lift manuevre
C. Heimlich manuevre
D. Valsalva manuevre

Q.95 The formula for calculating mean arterial pressure is:

A. Diastolic BP + systolic BP/3
B. Diastolic BP + 2(systolic BP)/4
C. Systolic BP + Diastolic BP/2
D. Systolic BP + 2(Diastolic BP)/3

Q.96 In the compensatory shock stage, the patient's blood pressure remains within normal limits. The factors that contribute to maintain adequate cardiac output are:

A. Increased contractility of the heart
B. Vasoconstriction
C. Increased heart rate
D. Increased movement of extremities

Q.97 The role of a nurse in treating a patient in the compensatory stage of shock is all except:

A. Monitor patient's hemodynamic status
B. Promote patient safety
C. Administer prescribed IV fluids and medications
D. Provide health education

Q.98 Unreversed hypovolemic shock progresses to which of the following types of shock?

A. Anaphylactic shock **B.** Cardiogenic shock
C. Septic shock **D.** Neurogenic shock

Q.99 The vaccine that is administered after exposure is:

A. Measles **B.** Typhoid **C.** Mumps **D.** Rabies

Q.100 The Complications that are associated with poor nutrition and growth restriction in postnatal life in a newborn include:

A. Stunting
B. Wasting
C. Adverse neurodevelopmental outcome
D. All the above

// Smart Answer Sheet //

Correct Indicates percentage of students who answered questions correctly.

Skipped Indicates percentage of students who skipped questions.

Q.	Ans.	Correct	Skipped
1	D	41.31 %	1.94 %
2	C	56.06 %	1.42 %
3	B	56.37 %	1.91 %
4	B	85.9 %	0.0 %
5	C	88.53 %	0.0 %
6	D	64.9 %	1.06 %
7	B	14.34 %	3.47 %
8	B	40.5 %	1.93 %
9	A	41.43 %	1.17 %
10	B	29.96 %	4.83 %
11	A	61.03 %	1.04 %
12	C	26.28 %	4.61 %
13	D	57.34 %	1.09 %
14	C	67.24 %	1.4 %
15	C	32.06 %	3.45 %
16	C	20.16 %	4.79 %
17	C	48.71 %	1.51 %
18	C	49.36 %	1.03 %
19	C	15.32 %	4.55 %
20	C	10.05 %	4.69 %
21	A	50.45 %	1.42 %
22	B	42.75 %	1.76 %
23	D	44.8 %	1.19 %
24	B	58.88 %	1.5 %
25	A	77.98 %	0.0 %
26	B	44.35 %	1.64 %
27	A	13.27 %	4.5 %
28	A	61.0 %	1.99 %
29	A	51.78 %	1.93 %
30	A	56.62 %	1.83 %
31	D	54.22 %	2.0 %
32	B	25.24 %	4.79 %
33	B	56.45 %	1.54 %
34	C	62.0 %	1.3 %
35	A	28.14 %	3.26 %
36	B	67.7 %	1.37 %
37	A	30.91 %	4.01 %
38	D	76.39 %	0.0 %
39	B	49.88 %	1.65 %
40	A	76.21 %	0.0 %
41	C	69.05 %	1.49 %
42	A	56.85 %	1.83 %
43	D	82.12 %	0.0 %
44	B	57.7 %	1.03 %
45	B	84.22 %	0.0 %
46	C	41.89 %	1.27 %
47	B	87.2 %	0.0 %
48	D	58.12 %	1.95 %
49	B	84.37 %	0.0 %
50	D	54.75 %	1.08 %
51	B	60.72 %	1.98 %
52	B	32.9 %	3.95 %
53	C	18.66 %	4.55 %
54	B	56.72 %	1.67 %
55	D	55.81 %	1.2 %
56	B	82.84 %	0.0 %
57	D	41.56 %	1.76 %
58	B	30.12 %	3.73 %
59	A	55.16 %	1.03 %
60	B	41.11 %	1.1 %
61	B	86.16 %	0.0 %
62	A	63.03 %	1.57 %
63	C	83.02 %	0.0 %
64	A	40.28 %	1.47 %
65	B	65.84 %	1.94 %
66	C	64.99 %	1.5 %
67	A	30.42 %	4.38 %
68	A	81.45 %	0.0 %
69	B	64.34 %	1.95 %
70	D	52.23 %	1.56 %
71	B	24.58 %	3.72 %
72	B	12.58 %	3.84 %
73	D	57.63 %	1.71 %
74	A	54.23 %	1.6 %
75	D	64.67 %	1.28 %
76	B	59.33 %	1.04 %
77	D	58.5 %	1.97 %
78	D	65.24 %	1.72 %
79	D	44.06 %	1.84 %
80	D	30.55 %	3.16 %

Q.	Ans.	Correct / Skipped
81	B	56.58 % / 1.3 %
82	B	28.05 % / 4.37 %
83	B	46.74 % / 1.11 %
84	D	56.84 % / 1.88 %

Q.	Ans.	Correct / Skipped
85	C	69.16 % / 1.92 %
86	D	58.76 % / 1.54 %
87	D	29.47 % / 4.78 %
88	D	17.62 % / 3.53 %

Q.	Ans.	Correct / Skipped
89	A	25.49 % / 3.3 %
90	B	63.54 % / 1.35 %
91	C	69.54 % / 1.74 %
92	A	60.57 % / 1.67 %

Q.	Ans.	Correct / Skipped
93	A	66.26 % / 1.15 %
94	C	12.81 % / 4.97 %
95	D	64.51 % / 1.7 %
96	D	66.34 % / 1.94 %

Q.	Ans.	Correct / Skipped
97	D	85.09 % / 0.0 %
98	B	41.0 % / 1.95 %
99	D	81.95 % / 0.0 %
100	D	56.81 % / 1.5 %

Performance Analysis	
Avg. Score (%)	44.0%
Toppers Score (%)	62.0%
Your Score	

//Hints and Solutions//

1. According to the question,

C is standing on the extreme right.

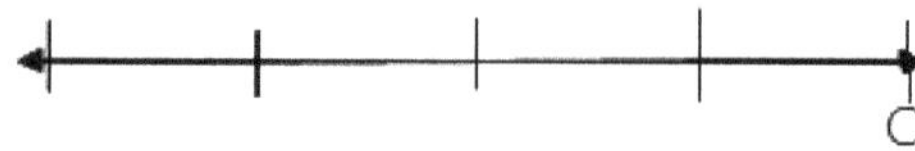

D is on the left of C

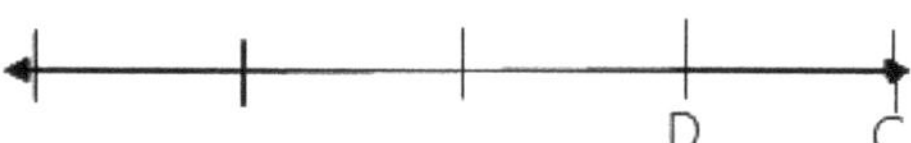

D is on the right of E

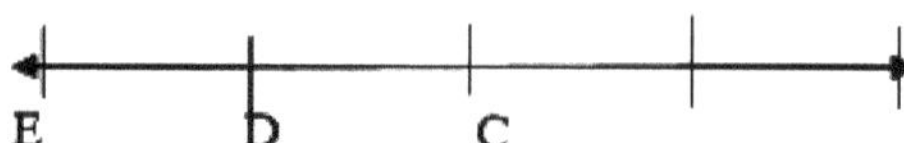

B is left of the E but the right of the A

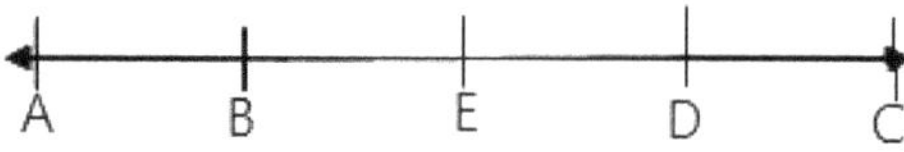

E is standing in the middle.

Hence, the correct option is (D).

2. T is replaced by 'x' (multiply)

U is replaced by '-' (Minus)

X is replaced by '÷' (Divide)

W is replaced by '+' (Plus)

⇒ (50 X 2) W (28 T 4)

⇒ (50 ÷ 2) + (28 x 4)

Applying the BODMAS rule

⇒ (25) + (112) = 137

Hence, the correct option is (C).

3. The information given in the question may be arranged as follows

- Barun is taller than Sanjay.
- Barun > Sanjay
- Krishna is also not as tall as Bipul but is taller than Barun.
- Bipul > Krishna > Barun

So according to the above explanation, the final arrangement is

- Bipul > Krishna > Barun > Sanjay

So, Bipul is the tallest person.

Hence, the correct option is (B).

4. The given image shows how 'MADRAS' is written as 'DAMSAR'.

Similarly,

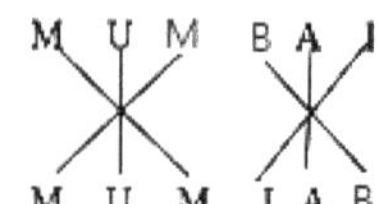

Hence, the correct option is (B).

5. The given image shows how 'RAMESH' is written as 'HSEMAR'.

Similarly,

Hence, the correct option is (C).

6. According to the English dictionary,

1. Episode 2. Epistle 3. Episcope 4. Epigraph

In these all 4 given words first three alphabets (EPI) are the same.

The fourth alphabet is S, S, S, and G, then G comes first than S so according to the English dictionary 4th word will place 1st.

In the remaining words, all three words will compare according to the 5th alphabet.

The 5th alphabet in the remaining words is O, T, and C.

In the placing order of the alphabet C will come first, then O, and then T.

So word 3rd will put in 2nd place

1st word will put on 3rd place and then 2nd word will put on last place so the order will be according to the English dictionary that is 4,3,1,2.

Hence, the correct option is (D).

7. The answer to the given question is as follows:

- The following statement, "the woman said to the man that the daughter of your only sister is the sister of my husband" indicates that man's sister is the woman's mother-in-law.

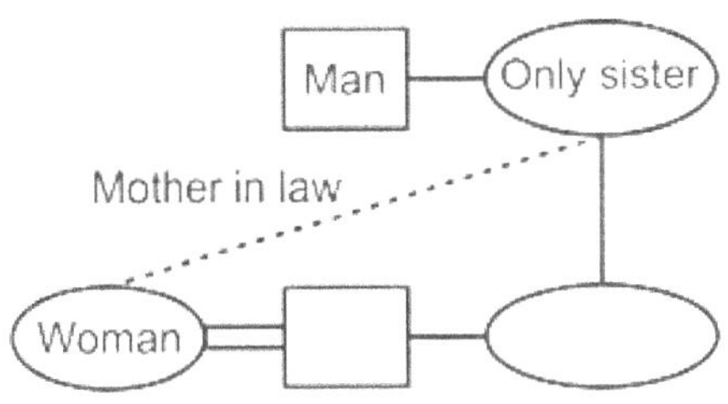

Hence, the correct option is (B).

8. With the help of a Direction graph and as per the given instruction in the question. It is clear from the diagram that the man is facing north.

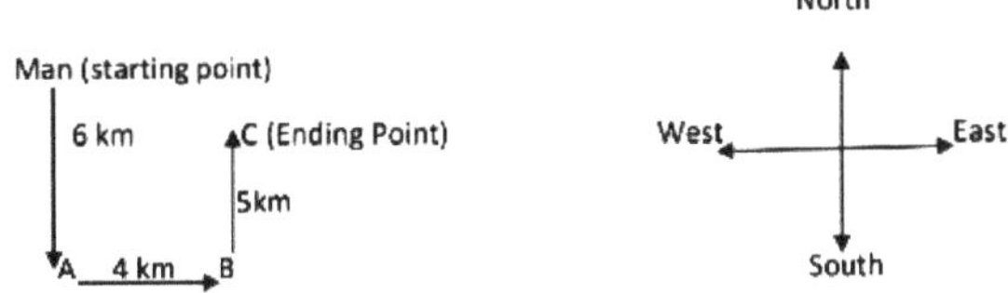

Hence, the correct option is (B).

9. Odd words mean word which does not match with other words of the group.

There are 21 consonants: B, C, D, F, G, H, J, K, L, M, N, P, Q, R, S, T, V, W, X, Y, and Z.

J, K, and L are consonants and 'I' is a vowel. So 'I' does not belong to the group.

Hence, the correct option is (A).

10. The given question having the relation of Country and Capital.

As Austria's capital is Vienna,

Similarly,

Egypt's capital is Cairo.

Hence, the correct option is (B).

11. The 'Cannes Award' is given for excellence in films field.

- Cannes Film Awards is an international film festival with a live screening for film distributors in the most popular city for the film industry, Cannes.
- The first winner of the Cannes was the short film DA YIE by Ghanaian director Anthony Nti, whose film was also on the Shortlist at the Academy Awards Oscar.

Hence, the correct option is (A).

12. The Pulitzer Prize is an award for achievements in newspaper, magazine, online journalism, literature, and musical composition within the United States.

- It was established in 1917 by provisions in the will of Joseph Pulitzer.
- Prizes are awarded annually in twenty-one categories.
- In twenty of the categories, each winner receives a certificate and a US$15,000 cash award (raised from $10,000 in 2017).
- The winner in the public service category is awarded a gold medal.

Hence, the correct option is (C).

13. Chromosomes are filamentous bodies found in the cells of all plants and animals, which are known to determine and transmit genetic properties. The chromosome is the microscopic thread-like part in the nucleus of the cell which is essential for inheritance.

- In humans, chromosome numbers 13, 15, 21, and 22 are similar chromosomes.
- Chromosome 21 is the smallest human chromosome, spanning approximately 48 million base pairs (the building blocks of DNA) and representing 1.5 to 2 percent of the total DNA in cells.

Hence, the correct option is (D).

14. Headquarters of International Labour Organization (ILO) is situated at Geneva.

- The headquarters of the International Labour Organization was founded in October 1919 under the league of nations, it is the first and oldest specialized agency of the UN.
- The Headquarters of the International Labour Organization has 187 member states: 186 out of 193 UN member states plus the cook-islands.
- The headquarters of the International Labour Organization is headquartered in Geneva, Switzerland, with around 40 field offices around the world and employs some 3381 staff across 107 nations.

Hence, the correct option is (C).

15. The Center for Cellular and Molecular Biology is situated in Hyderabad, Telangana, India.

Molecular biology is the field of biology that studies the structure, structure, and interactions of cellular molecules – such as nucleic acids and proteins – that carry out the biological processes necessary for the function and maintenance of a cell.

Hence, the correct option is (C).

16. The Chamera Dam impounds the River Ravi and supports the hydroelectricity project in the region. It is located near the town of Dalhousie, in the Chamba district in the state of Himachal Pradesh. The reservoir of the dam is Chamera Lake. A large part of its reservoir lies in the Salooni sub-division of Chamba.

Hence, the correct option is (C).

17. Kochi Port is known as Queen of Arabian Sea.

- It is one of the largest Ports in India. It is also the first transshipment port in India.
- It is operated by Cochin Port Authority and Dubai Ports World.

- It was established in 1928 and has completed over 90 years of active service.
- Kochi was an important spice trading center on India's west coast from the 14th century and maintained a trade network with Arab traders from the pre-Islamic era. Occupied by the Portuguese in 1503, Kochi was the first of the European colonies in colonial India.

Hence, the correct option is (C).

18. W.C. Roentgen on 8 November 1895 produced and detected electromagnetic radiation in a wavelength range known as X-Rays.

- An X-ray is a quick, painless test that produces images of the structures inside your body, especially the bones.
- X-ray beams pass through your body, and they are absorbed in varying amounts depending on the density of the material they pass through.
- W.C. Roentgen received Nobel Prize in Physics in 1901 for X-Rays production.

Hence, the correct option is (C).

19. National Herald was founded by India's first Prime Minister Jawaharlal Nehru in 1938 as a tool to win independence. The National Herald is an Indian newspaper published by The Associated Journals Ltd.

It was banned by the British government in 1942 during the Quit India movement. The newspaper has been linked to and controlled by members of the Indian National Congress political party.

Hence, the correct option is (C).

20. Vikas Khanna has been honored with the 2020 Asia Game Changer Award.

- The award will be given to him for feeding lakhs of people across India through his massive food distribution campaign 'Feed India' during the COVID-19 pandemic.
- He is the only Indian among the six honorees chosen by the leading organization.
- He successfully ran his massive food delivery campaign from his Manhattan home in New York, thousands of miles from India.

Hence, the correct option is (C).

21. Puskas Award is associated with the game of Football.

- The FIFA Puskas Prize was an award created in 2009 to award a football player who scored the most beautiful or aesthetically pleasing goal.
- The award is named in honor of Hungarian striker Ferenc Puskas, one of the most prolific strikers of the 1950s and 1960s.

Hence, the correct option is (A).

22. Former Indian cricketer Chetan Chauhan passed away in August 2020. He was infected with the coronavirus.

- His death was informed by his younger brother Pushpendra Chauhan.
- Chetan Chauhan breathed his last at Medanta Hospital in Gurugram.
- Chetan was also a minister in the UP government.

Hence, the correct option is (B).

23. India's first mobile RT-PCR testing lab was inaugurated in Bengaluru. The laboratory has been developed by the Indian Institute of Science (IISC-Bengaluru) and has the capacity to conduct 9000 tests a day.

- Inaugurated the country's first mobile RT-PCR (reverse transcription-polymerase chain reaction) testing lab in the capital of Karnataka.
- Karnataka's Medical Education Minister Dr. Sudhakar on Wednesday inaugurated this laboratory, which is the first of its kind. This lab is said to be the country's only mobile RT-PCR mobile lab approved by the Indian Council of Medical Research or ICMR.

Hence, the correct option is (D).

24. Indian Navy launched Operation Samudra Setu.

In support of the country's fight against COVID-19 and as part of Operation Samudra Setu, seven Indian Naval Ships namely Kolkata, Kochi, Talwar, Tabor, Trikand, Jalashwa, and Airavat were flown from various countries to liquid medical oxygen-filled cryogenic containers and Concerned medical equipment has been deployed for shipment.

Hence, the correct option is (B).

25. ANANDA is a digital application launched by LIC recently.

- ANANDA stands for Atma Nirbhar Agents New Business Digital Application. ANANDA is a paperless solution for new business processes.
- This digital application will help in the process of obtaining an insurance policy through a paperless module with the help of an agent or an intermediary.

Hence, the correct option is (A).

26. Hong Kong has topped the Global Economic Freedom Index 2020.

- India has slipped 26 places to 105th place in the annual comparative report 'Global Economic Freedom Index' 2020, published by a Canadian organization about the openness of the business environment in countries.
- In 2019 the country was ranked 79th. In this list, Hong Kong and Singapore are in first and second place, and China is in 124th place.

Hence, the correct option is (B).

27. Recently Andorra formally gained membership of the International Monetary Fund (IMF) and has become the 190th country to become a member of the International Monetary Fund. Andorra is a microstate located between France and Spain. However, it is the largest microstate in Europe.

The IMF said trade and tourism comprised close to 40% of Andorra's economic output, with about 8 million visitors to its ski slopes and mountainous routes in 2019.

Hence, the correct option is (A).

28. The 12th BRICS Summit hosted by Russia was held via video conference on November 17, 2020. The conference was held under the chairmanship of Russian President Vladimir Putin. The central theme of this summit was "Global Stability, Shared Security and Innovative Growth".

Hence, the correct option is (A).

29. The Ministry of Housing and Urban Affairs (MoHUA) has partnered with leading food delivery platform "Swiggy" to connect street food vendors with a large number of customers online on the e-commerce platform.

- The objective of this MoHUA is to provide street food vendors with online access to thousands of consumers and help them grow their businesses.
- This agreement has been done under the Prime Minister's Street Vendor Self-Reliant Fund PM Svanidhi Yojana.

Hence, the correct option is (A).

30. India's first sandalwood museum has been set up at Aranya Bhavan in Ashokapuram, Mysuru, Karnataka.

- The museum has been set up by the regional forest department to educate the farmers about the importance of sandalwood cultivation.
- It will also provide information on technical assistance, plant availability, marketing facilities, pest control measures, incentives, and schemes provided by the government for sandalwood growers.

Hence, the correct option is (A).

31. The various methods of intrapartum fetal monitoring includes all except Braxton Hicks contractions.

All other methods are used for intrapartum fetal monitoring. These methods are as follows:-

- Fetal scalp stimulation test
- Fetal Pulse Oximetry
- Fetal blood sample

Hence, the correct option is (D).

32. During active management of labour injection ergometrine is contraindicated in Severe eclampsia condition.

Ergometrine is an agopeptin, Which is part of the agontite family of alkaloids. It is structurally and biochemically related to 20102 many neurotransmission has a structural similarity to meters and is a vasoconstructor for biological functions.

Hence, the correct option is (B).

33. The first fetal movement felt by the mother is called Quickening. One function of these movements is to alert the pregnant woman that a fetus is growing in her uterus.

Quickening often occurs between the 16th and 22nd week of pregnancy. It is said to be a predictable sign of pregnancy because other movements of the woman's body can mimic early fetal movements such as flatus, peristalsis, and contractions of the abdominal muscles.

Hence, the correct option is (B).

34. Fetal tachycardia is caused due to all of the given factors except Severe Fetal hypoxia.

A fetal tachycardia can be associated with several maternal, as well as fetal conditions, including:

Maternal:

- Maternal hyperthyroidism
- Maternal medications
- Maternal anaemia
- Maternal tachycardia (eg systemic infection)

Fetal:

- In uterine infection
- In utero hypoxia
- Fetal anaemia
- Chromosomal anomalie

Hence, the correct option is (C).

35. Fetal blood sampling is contraindicated in HIV positive women condition.

- Fetal blood sampling is a procedure to remove a small amount of blood from the fetus during pregnancy.
- If the woman is 'HIV positive, then in that case a sample of fetal blood is taken.
- HIV, the virus that causes AIDS, is transmitted in utero with a 66% risk of infecting the fetus and may cause intrauterine growth retardation.
- HIV-positive women may be immunosuppressed so they should be offered termination of pregnancy.

Hence, the correct option is (A).

36. A family planning measure of using a Diaphragm or Dutch Cap is called Barrier method.

- Diaphragms and caps are barrier methods of contraception. These are fitted inside vagina and prevent sperm from entering through the entrance of the uterus (cervix).
- Diaphragms are soft, thin domed, and made of latex (rubber) or silicone. Caps are smaller and may also be made of latex or silicone. These come in different shapes and sizes.
- To be effective at preventing pregnancy, they need to be used in conjunction with spermicide, a chemical that destroys sperm.

Hence, the correct option is (B).

37. Any bleeding from or into the genital tract after the period of viability but before the birth of the baby is called Antepartum haemorrhage.

- Antepartum haemorrhage (APH) is usually defined as bleeding from the genital tract after the 24th week of pregnancy.
- Antepartum haemorrhage can occur at any time until the second stage of labor is complete and postpartum bleeding is bleeding after childbirth.

Hence, the correct option is (A).

38. The clinical features of first stage of labour includes all of the given except sudden gush of vaginal bleeding.

First Stage: The first stage of labor is usually the longest part of labor. This is where mothers are having contractions and their cervix is dilating. During the first stage of labor, the cervix dilates and effaces to allow the baby into the birth canal.

This phase is divided into three phases:

- Early stages
- Active Phase
- Transition stage

Hence, the correct option is (D).

39. Crowning occurs when the top part of the baby's head can be seen through the opening of the vagina. Crowning occurs during the second stage of labor when the newborns give birth by pushing.

It has two stages:

- The propulsive stage
- The phase of expulsion

Hence, the correct option is (B).

40. The immunity an individual develops after acquiring an infection is called active immunity.

Active immunity

- Active immunity results when exposure to a disease organism activates the immune system to produce antibodies against that disease.
- Active immunity can be achieved through natural immunity or vaccine-induced immunity.

Hence, the correct option is (A).

41. The equipment used to carry small quantities of vaccines for out reach programme is called Vaccine carriers.

- Vaccine carriers are containers that can be used during transportation.
- There are coolant packs lined to keep the vaccines and diluents cool that are within the temperature of the container. So that the vaccine does not get spoiled.

Hence, the correct option is (C).

42. The major cause of nutritional blindness in children usually between the age of 1-3 years is called Xeropthalmia.

- Xerophthalmia is an eye disease caused by a deficiency of vitamin A.
- There is a reason. Due to the deficiency of Vitamin A in the body, spots appear and the membranes present in the front part of the eyes start getting dry. It becomes thick and compact. For this reason, it is not visible in low light.

Hence, the correct option is (A).

43. The poisoning caused due to ingestion of foods contaminated by living bacteria is all except chemical poisoning.

All other types of poisoning are caused by ingestion of food contaminated by living bacteria which are as follows:-

- salmonella poisoning
- staphylococcal poisoning
- botulism

Chemical poisoning is caused by chemical substances.

Hence, the correct option is (D).

44. Varicella vaccine is a live attenuated vaccine.

- Varicella vaccine is a vaccine designed to provide protection against chicken pox.
- The varicella vaccine is a weakened, but live virus, that stimulates a response from the body's immune system which in turn provides lifelong protection against varicella infection. Although the varicella vaccine is 95% effective at preventing disease, health professionals argue that two doses are better than one for complete protection against the disease.

Hence, the correct option is (B).

45. The route of administration of measles vaccine is subcutaneous.

- Measles is an infectious disease caused by an infectious virus. It can spread easily from one person to another.
- In measles, a red rash appears all over the body. In the case of measles, this red rash initially occurs on the head and then gradually spreads all over the body. Measles disease is also called rubeola.
- Measles is caused by infection with a virus of the paramyxovirus family. These viruses are small parasitic microbes.

Hence, the correct option is (B).

46. The incubation period of mumps is 2 to 4 weeks.

- Mumps is a disease caused by the genus Rubella virus. This infection spreads through person-to-person contact.
- Mumps mainly affects the parotid gland. These glands make saliva. There are three groups of glands located behind and below the ears on all three sides of the mouth.

- Symptoms of mumps usually develop 12 to 25 days after being infected with the mumps virus (this delay is known as the incubation period).

Hence, the correct option is (C).

47. The antiviral drug used to treat influenza is Oseltamivir.

Influenza is a viral infection that affects our respiratory system. Oseltamivir drug can ease your illness and are also helpful in preventing serious complications. Oseltamivir is an oral medication.

Hence, the correct option is (B).

48. The vaccine-preventable diseases that are caused by droplet infection are all given except Polio.

The Polio virus is often spread by faeces orally to persons living in unhygienic and crowded conditions. Acute infection is caused by any of the three serotypes of poliovirus that initially replicate in the gastrointestinal tract.

Hence, the correct option is (D).

49. Hepatitis C is a blood borne disease.

Hepatitis is an inflammation of the liver caused by a variety of infectious viruses and non-infectious agents, causing a variety of health problems, some of which can be fatal.

Hence, the correct option is (B).

50. Diarrhea is often loose or watery bowel movements that deviate from the baby's normal pattern. ORS is a simple, proven intervention that can be used to prevent and treat diarrheal dehydration and reduce diarrheal mortality at the community and facility levels.

The purpose of ORS therapy in children suffering from diarrhoea is suitable for all:

- Prevent dehydration
- Reduce death rate
- Correcting water and electrolyte deficiencies.
- Reduce weakness

Hence, the correct option is (D).

51. In a person with cholera, diarrhea occurs due to a toxin produced by the virus on multiplication in the small intestine. The toxin produced by vibrio cholerae is Enterotoxin.

- Cholera toxin (CT) is an enterotoxin produced by Vibrio cholerae and responsible for the manifestations of the disease.
- A bacterium called Vibrio cholerae causes cholera infection. The lethal effects of the disease are the result of a toxin that the bacteria produce in the small intestine.
- The toxin causes the body to secrete large amounts of water, causing diarrhea and rapid loss of fluids and salts (electrolytes).

Hence, the correct option is (B).

52. The cancer arising from mesodermal cells constituting the various connecting tissues is called sarcomas.

Sarcomas arise from soft tissues and connective tissue covering organs such as cartilage, bone, or fascia, smooth or skeletal muscle, blood vessels, lymphatic vessels, and mesothelium which, in general, sarcomas consist of very large pulmonary spindle-shaped cells gets made.

Hence, the correct option is (B).

53. Blood glucose values above normal but below those diagnostic diabetes, occurring during pregnancy is called gestational diabetes.

Gestational diabetes sometimes occurs in pregnant women. Having gestational diabetes increases the risk of health problems for your baby. In most cases, gestational diabetes goes away after the baby is born. However, you also have an increased risk of developing type 2 diabetes later in life.

Hence, the correct option is (C).

54. In a patient with perinicious anaemia the primary purpose of schilling test is to determine absorption of vitamin B12.

- Anaemia is a medical condition in which the blood is low in normal red blood cells. Pernicious anaemia is one of the vitamin B-12 deficiency anaemias.
- It is caused by your body's inability to absorb the vitamin B-12 needed to make enough healthy red blood cells.
- This type of anaemia is called "pernicious" because it was once considered a pernicious disease. This was due to the lack of available treatment.
- The Schilling test is also known as the vitamin B12 absorption test. It was previously used to determine whether a person was absorbing vitamin B12 normally. If not, the test can find the cause of any vitamin B12 deficiency.

Hence, the correct option is (B).

55. A type of fracture in which one fragment of the bone goes into another is called impacted fracture.

An impacted fracture refers to a fracture in which bone fragments have been driven into each other. A compression fracture is similar to an impaction fracture, but the term is applied to describe a fracture in which cancellous bone collapses and compresses upon itself.

Hence, the correct option is (D).

56. Signs and symptoms of asthma include all of the given except fever.

Asthma signs and symptoms include:

- Shortness of breath.
- Chest tightness or pain.
- Wheezing when exhaling, which is a common sign of asthma in children.

- Trouble sleeping caused by shortness of breath, coughing or wheezing.
- Coughing or wheezing attacks that are worsened by a respiratory virus, such as a cold or the flu.

Hence, the correct option is (B).

57. In Parkinson's disease the cells of the nigra begin to die in this, while they cannot be replaced by any other cell, as a result, the level of dopamine starts falling and it is unable to convey the message properly to our brain. The control of our body gets exhausted from the body parts.

Parkinson's signs and symptoms may include:

- Tremor
- Slowed movement (bradykinesia)
- Rigid muscles
- Impaired posture and balance
- Loss of automatic movements
- Speech changes
- Writing changes

Hence, the correct option is (D).

58. Infection of the urinary bladder caused by Escherichia coli is a type of bacteria commonly found in gastro intestinal tract is called cystitis.

- Due to this, the bladder becomes inflamed and there is also redness and burning.
- Bladder infection is a painful and distressing condition and can become a serious problem if the infection spreads from the bladder to the kidneys.

Hence, the correct option is (B).

59. The most essential fatty acid that serves as a basis for production of other fatty acids is Lineloic acid.

Essential fatty acids:

- Fatty acids that the body cannot synthesize are called essential fatty acids.
- Fatty acids are carboxylic acids (or organic acids), often either saturated or unsaturated, with long aliphatic tails (long chains). For that particular animal, fatty acids that cannot be synthesized in the body are called essential fatty acids.
- The three fatty acids synthesized in the animal body are Linoleic, Linolenic, and Arachidonic acid and are examples of essential fatty acids.

Hence, the correct option is (A).

60. Vitamin D is largely stored in the body in fatty tissues.

- Vitamin D keeps our body healthy and makes bones strong. Strengthens the immunity of the body. Helps fight diseases like cancer.
- When vitamin D is absorbed through the skin or obtained from food or supplements, it is stored in the body's Fatty tissues. Here it remains dormant until it is needed.

Hence, the correct option is (B).

61. Fat soluble vitamins are all of the given except Vitamin C.

- There are two types of Vitamin: water-soluble and fat-soluble vitamins. The water-soluble vitamins are vitamins B and C.
- Fat-soluble vitamins are vitamins A, D, E, and K. They are present in foods containing fats.
- The body absorbs these vitamins as it does dietary fats.
- They do not dissolve in water.

Hence, the correct option is (B).

62. The clinical sign of Riboflavin deficiency is angular stomatitis.

The signs and symptoms of riboflavin deficiency (also known as ariboflavinosis) include skin disorders, hyperemia (excess blood), angular stomatitis, hair loss, reproductive problems, sore throat, etc.

Hence, the correct option is (A).

63. The richest source of vitamin C is amla.

- Vitamin C is also known as ascorbic acid. It is water-soluble vitamin.
- Vitamin C deficiency leads to scurvy disease.
- Vitamin C plays a role in controlling infections and healing wounds and is a powerful antioxidant that can neutralize harmful free radicals.

Hence, the correct option is (C).

64. Thiamine deficiency results in Cardiac Beriberi.

- Cardiac beriberi occurs as a result of decreased cardiac function from impaired cellular metabolism.
- Thiamine deficiency impairs the production of adenosine triphosphate (ATP), leading to the accumulation of adenosine.
- Wet beriberi causes right-sided heart failure and pulmonary hypertension with high cardiac output due to vasodilation.
- Most common symptoms of thiamine deficiency are loss of appetite, fatigue, irritability, nerve damage, blurry vision, etc.

Hence, the correct option is (A).

65. A thorough investigation made to evaluate the overall nursing care received by a patient is called nursing audit.

Purpose of the nursing audit is to evaluate nursing care given, and to achieve deserved and feasible quality of nursing care.

Types of Nursing Audits:

- Internal
- External

Hence, the correct option is (B).

66. Patient fall due to improper application of restraints in the ICU is an act of negligence.

- Restraints may be used to keep a person in proper position and prevent movement or falling during surgery or while on a stretcher.
- Restraints can also be used to control or prevent harmful behavior.
- There are three types of restraints: physical, chemical, and environmental.

Hence, the correct option is (C).

67. While resuscitating a preterm baby, Positive Pressure Ventilation should be started with oxygen concentration of 21%.

Newborn or neonatal resuscitation refers to emergency medical intervention techniques employed immediately after childbirth to assist babies who are not able to breathe independently after birth.

Premature (also known as preterm) birth is when a baby is born too early before 37 weeks of pregnancy have been completed. Newborns at least 35 weeks gestation, PPV (Positive Pressure Ventilation) should be started at 21% oxygen.

Hence, the correct option is (A).

68. International Nurses Day is observed around the world on 12th May to commemorate the anniversary of Florence Nightingale's birthday.

- This day also celebrates the contribution done by nurses to society around the world.
- Florence Nightingale, (12 May 1820 – 13 August 1910) was the founder of modern nursing.

Hence, the correct option is (A).

69. The most central and accessible artery to check the pulse in children over one year of age is carotid.

- The best spot to feel the pulse in a child is the wrist, called the radial pulse but If can't easily find the pulse on the wrist, can try the neck, which has the carotid pulse.
- The pulse rate in a child is affected by: Crying, Activity, Body temperature (fever), Dehydration, Illness, Anemia, Stress, and Congenital heart disease (CHD).

Hence, the correct option is (B).

70. A patient is diagnosed to have insomnia. The term insomnia means inability to sleep.

- Insomnia is a common sleep disorder that can make it hard to fall asleep, hard to stay asleep, or cause to wake up too early and not be able to get back to sleep.
- Common causes of insomnia include stress, an irregular sleep schedule, poor sleeping habits, mental health disorders like anxiety and depression, physical illnesses and pain, and specific sleep disorders.

Hence, the correct option is (D).

71. The ideal position to provide mouth care for an unconscious patient is lateral position.

- Unconsciousness is when a person is unable to respond to people and activities.
- Mouth care prevents infection, plaque, bleeding gums, mouth sores, and cavities.
- This position prevents the pooling of secretions at the back of the oral cavity, thereby reducing the risk of aspiration.

Hence, the correct option is (B).

72. The most preferred site of administration of intramuscular injection in children under one year is vastus lateralis.

- The intramuscular injection delivers medication into a muscle.
- The angle for giving an IM injection is 90 degrees.
- The anterolateral aspect of the thigh, or vastus lateralis muscle, is the preferred IM site of administration of intramuscular injection in children under one year old.

Hence, the correct option is (B).

73. Major factors influencing an individuals blood pressure are all except normal body weight.

- High blood pressure (hypertension) is a common condition in which the long-term force of the blood against artery walls.
- The normal range of systolic blood pressure (SBP) is 90-140mmHg.
- The normal range of diastolic blood pressure is (DBP) 60-90mmHg.
- Factors that can influence blood pressure are strike volume, venous return, heart rate, blood pressure resistance, blood viscosity, blood vessel diameter, etc.

Hence, the correct option is (D).

74. The drugs administered to promote uterine contractions are oxytocin.

Uterine contraction: The tightening and shortening of the uterine muscles.

Oxytocin is the most widely used uterotonic drug. The hormone oxytocin has been identified as inducing uterine contractions, and labor in general.

The two main physical functions of oxytocin are to stimulate uterine contractions in labor and childbirth and to stimulate contractions of breast tissue to aid in lactation after childbirth.

Hence, the correct option is (A).

75. Medication appropriate to treat an acute anginal attack is nitroglycerine.

- Anginal is often a symptom of coronary heart disease (CHD).
- The pain often spreads to the neck, jaw, arms, shoulders, throat, back, or teeth.
- Nitroglycerin is a vasodilatory drug used primarily to provide relief from anginal chest pain.

Hence, the correct option is (D).

76. Micronutrients, mostly iodine and selenium, are required for thyroid hormone synthesis and function.

Iodine is an essential component of thyroid hormones and its deficiency is considered the most common cause of preventable brain damage

Triiodothyronine (T3) and tetraiodothyronine (T4) or thyroxine require iodine for the synthesis in the thyroid gland. Swelling in the front of the neck is the most common symptom of an iodine deficiency.

Hence, the correct option is (B).

77. Drug used to treat hyperkalemia is calcium gluconate.

- High potassium (called "hyperkalemia") is a medical problem in which there is too much potassium in the blood.
- Calcium gluconate should be used as a first-line agent in patients with ECG changes or severe hyperkalemia to protect cardiomyocytes.
- Insulin and glucose combination is the fastest-acting drug that shifts potassium into the cells. B-agonists can be used in addition to insulin to decrease plasma potassium levels.

Hence, the correct option is (D).

78. Drugs used to treat nausea and vomiting are all except calcium channel blockers.

Drugs that can be used to treat nausea and vomiting are:

- A dopamine antagonist, also known as an anti-dopaminergic is a type of drug which blocks dopamine receptors by receptor antagonism. Dopamine antagonists are antiemetics used in the treatment of nausea and vomiting.
- Serotonin receptor blockers (antagonists) are highly effective for treating nausea and vomiting.
- Cannabinoids may be a useful therapeutic option for people with chemotherapy-induced nausea and vomiting that respond poorly to commonly used anti-emetic agents.

Calcium channel blockers are medications used to lower blood pressure. They work by preventing calcium from entering the cells of the heart and arteries.

Hence, the correct option is (D).

79. The function of state nursing council is all except provide employment to all trained nurses.

The main Functions of the State Nursing Council are as follows:

- Regulation of training program of the diploma, Graduate, and Postgraduate courses.
- Supervised the practice of the profession by its members.
- Granting recognition to the training institutions.
- Proscribing syllabus and curriculum for various nursing courses and conducting qualifying examinations.
- Registration and granting certificates to qualified persons to practice their profession.

Hence, the correct option is (D).

80. Hypoxia may be caused by all the given factors except increased haemoglobin.

- Hypoxia is when the tissues of the body don't have enough oxygen.
- Causes of hypoxia include anemia, Lung diseases such as chronic obstructive pulmonary disease (COPD), emphysema, bronchitis, pneumonia, pulmonary edema (fluid in the lungs), etc.

Hence, the correct option is (D).

81. A defensive reaction intended to neutralize, control or eliminate the offending agent and to prepare the site for repair is called inflammation.

- Inflammation is a defensive reaction intended to neutralize, control, or eliminate the offending agent and to prepare the site for repair.
- The innate immune system is the body's first line of defense against germs entering the body.

Hence, the correct option is (B).

82. Movement of hands towards midline of the body is called Adduction.

Synovial joints allow the body a tremendous range of movements. Each movement at the synovial joint results from the contraction or relaxation of the muscles that are attached to the bones on either side of the articulation. These actions are possible about an axis arranged in an anteroposterior direction through a joint.

Hence, the correct option is (B).

83. The first aid measure to be taken to stop bleeding due to epistaxis is to make the person sit down, lean forward and pinch soft part of the nose.

A nosebleed is the loss of blood from the tissue that lines the inside of your nose. Nosebleeds (also called epistaxis) are common. The most common cause of nosebleeds is dry air, Nose picking, etc.

Hence, the correct option is (B).

84. According to the MTP act the following are indications for terminating a pregnancy before viability except unplanned pregnancy.

- MTP Act (Medical Termination of Pregnancy) is Deliberate termination of pregnancy either by the medical & surgical method before the viability of the fetus is called induction of abortion.
- The abortion laws fall under the Medical Termination of Pregnancy (MTP) Act, which was enacted by the Indian Parliament in the year 1971.
- The MTP Act came into effect on 1 April 1972 and was amended in the years 1975 and 2002.

Hence, the correct option is (D).

85. Chemicals that reduce or inhibit the transmission or perception of pain is endorphins.

- Pain involves changing or inhibiting the transmission of pain impulses in the spinal cord.
- Descending inhibition involves the release of inhibitory neurotransmitters that block or partially block the transmission of pain impulses
- Endorphins are released by the hypothalamus and pituitary gland in response to pain or stress, this group of peptide hormones both relieves pain and creates a general feeling of well-being.

Hence, the correct option is (C).

86. The factors that results in increasing the serum osmolality are all except renal failure.

Osmolality tests measure the number of certain substances in blood, urine, or stool. A serum osmolality test looks for a chemical imbalance in the blood.

Conditions that increased osmolality:

- Diabetes mellitus (hyperglycemia)
- Diabetes insipidus
- Uremia
- Hypernatremia

Hence, the correct option is (D).

87. The characteristics of fluid volume deficit includes all except increased central venous pressure.

- Fluid Volume Deficit (FVD) also known as hypovolemia is a state or condition where the fluid output exceeds the fluid intake.
- It occurs when the body loses both water and electrolytes in similar proportions.
- Common sources of fluid loss are the gastrointestinal tract, polyuria, and increased perspiration.

Hence, the correct option is (D).

88. The systemic complications of intravenous therapy includes all except infiltration.

- Fluid overload: If too much fluid is given too quickly, you can experience headaches, high blood pressure, and trouble breathing. headaches.
- Air embolism: An air embolism, or gas embolism, occurs when an IV pushes too much air into the vein.
- Infection: If the area is not clean when the needle is inserted for giving medication there will be chances of infection.

IV or intravenous therapy is a way to give fluids, medicine, nutrition, or blood directly into the bloodstream through a vein. There are 2 main types of IV Therapy known IV Push and IV Drip.

Hence, the correct option is (D).

89. A 30-year-old man is brought to the emergency with a history of accident. Fluid draining from ear or nose and periorbital ecchymosis sign indicates skull fracture.

- Skull Fractures Linear skull fractures or simple breaks or "cracks" in the skull may accompany TBIs. Possible forces, strong enough to cause a skull fracture may damage the underlying brain.
- Periorbital ecchymosis (raccoon eye or panda sign) is a common clinical sign of skull base injury resulting from accidental injuries.

Hence, the correct option is (A).

90. A type of presentation in which the fetal buttocks presents at the pelvic inlet and the denominator is sacrum is called as breech presentation.

A breech presentation is when the baby is lying with its bottom or feet down. it's the most common type of malpresentation. Malpresentation may be caused by: having a low-lying placenta, having too much or too little amniotic fluid, and an abnormally shaped uterus.

Hence, the correct option is (B).

91. Assess the catheterization site for bleeding is the most important nursing action that has to done for a patient who has undergone cardiac catheterization.

Cardiac catheterization is a procedure in which a thin, flexible tube (catheter) is guided through a blood vessel to the heart to diagnose or treat certain heart conditions, such as clogged arteries or irregular heartbeats.

Hence, the correct option is (C).

92. A nurse is assigned to take of a patient with multiple sclerosis. The priority nursing diagnosis for the patient would be impaired urinary elimination.

Multiple sclerosis (MS) is a demyelinating disease of autoimmune etiology and is among the leading causes of nontraumatic neurological disability in young adults.

Hence, the correct option is (A).

93. The indication for a newborn to be given positive pressure ventilation soon after birth is when Heart rate < 100 beats/minute.

Neonatal resuscitation refers to emergency medical intervention techniques employed immediately after childbirth to assist babies who are not able to breathe independently after birth.

Hence, the correct option is (A).

94. In a restaurant a person suddenly collapses, choking while eating food. The ideal method to clear the airway is to use heimlich manuevre method.

- Choking occurs when a foreign object lodges in the throat or windpipe, blocking the flow of air.
- Choking cuts off oxygen to the brain.
- Heimlich maneuver is a first aid procedure used to treat upper airway obstructions by foreign objects.

Hence, the correct option is (C).

95. The formula for calculating mean arterial pressure is systolic BP + 2(Diastolic BP)/3.

- Arterial pressure is defined as the average pressure in a patient's arteries during one cardiac cycle.
- It is considered a better indicator of perfusion to vital organs than systolic blood pressure (SBP).
- Blood pressure is measured in millimetres of mercury (mm Hg).

Hence, the correct option is (D).

96. In the compensatory shock stage, the patient's blood pressure remains within normal limits. The factors that contribute to maintain adequate cardiac output are increased movement of extremities.

- Compensated shock, the body is experiencing a state of low blood volume but is still able to maintain blood pressure and organ perfusion by increasing the heart rate and constricting the blood vessels.
- The compensatory stage begins as the body's homeostatic mechanisms attempt to maintain CO, blood pressure, and tissue perfusion.

Hence, the correct option is (D).

97. The role of a nurse in treating a patient in the compensatory stage of shock is all except provide health education.

- Compensated shock is the phase of shock in which the body is still able to compensate for absolute or relative fluid loss.
- During this phase, the patient is still able to maintain adequate blood pressure as well as brain perfusion.

Hence, the correct option is (D).

98. Unreversed hypovolemic shock progresses to Cardiogenic shock.

- The most common cause of hypovolemic shock is blooded loss when a major blood vessel bursts or when seriously injured.
- Cardiogenic shock is a serious condition that happens when the heart can't supply enough oxygen-rich blood.

Hence, the correct option is (B).

99. The vaccine that is administered after exposure is Rabies.

- Rabies is a preventable viral disease most often transmitted through the bite of a rabid animal.
- The rabies virus infects the central nervous system of mammals, ultimately causing disease in the brain and death.

Hence, the correct option is (D).

100. The Complications that are associated with poor nutrition and growth restriction in postnatal life in a newborn includes Stunting, Wasting and Adverse neurodevelopmental outcome.

- Stunting is the impaired growth and development that children experience from poor nutrition, repeated infection, and inadequate psychosocial stimulation. Children are defined as stunted if their height-for-age is more than two standard deviations below the WHO Child Growth Standards median.
- Wasting is the most immediate, visible, and life-threatening form of malnutrition. It results from the failure to prevent malnutrition among the most vulnerable children. Children with wasting are too thin and their immune systems are weak, leaving them vulnerable to developmental delays, disease, and death.
- Neurodevelopmental outcomes include cerebral palsy, sensory impairments, and cognition, as well as behavioural difficulties and developmental coordination disorders.

Hence, the correct option is (D).

Previous Year Paper 02

General Aptitude / Reasoning / General Awareness / Basic Computer knowledge

Q.1 A man started walking West. He turned right, then right again and finally turned left. Towards which direction was he walking now?

A. North **B.** South **C.** West **D.** East

Q.2 There are five houses P, Q, R, S and T. P is right of Q and T is left of R and right of P. Q is right of S. Which house is in the middle?

A. P **B.** Q **C.** T **D.** R

Q.3 If A means '÷', B means '-' C means 'x', then find the value of following equation.

46 A 2 B 3 C 4 = ?

A. 34 **B.** 23 **C.** 17 **D.** 11

Q.4 Seema's younger brother Sohan is older than Seeta. Sweta in younger than Deepti but elder than Seema, who is the eldest?

A. Seema **B.** Sweta **C.** Seeta **D.** Deepti

Q.5 If 'MEAT' is written as 'TEAM', then 'BALE' is written as:

A. ELAB **B.** EABL **C.** EBLA **D.** EALB

Q.6 If an a certain code language 'SECTOR' is written as 'ESCTOR', then how will 'MOTHER' be written in that code?

A. MOHTER **B.** OMHTER
C. OMHTRE **D.** OMTHER

Q.7 Arrange the following words according to English dictionary.

1. Hepatitis 2. Cholera 3. Peptidoglycan 4. Chitin

A. 2, 3, 1, 4 **B.** 4, 2, 1, 3 **C.** 4, 1, 3, 2 **D.** 3, 1, 4, 2

Q.8 Introducing Alka to guests, Rakesh said, "Her father is the only son of my father". How is Alka related to Rakesh?

A. Daughter **B.** Mother
C. Sister **D.** Niece

Q.9 Arjuna Award is given for:

A. Exceptional service in emergency
B. Bravery on battlefield
C. Outstanding performance in sports
D. Exceptional service in slum dwellers

Q.10 The first Indian to receive Nobel Prize in Literature was:

A. Mother Teresa
B. C.V. Raman
C. Rabindranath Tagore
D. Sarojini Naidu

Q.11 Which of the following disease is not caused by bacteria?

A. Whooping Cough **B.** Typhoid
C. Malaria **D.** None of the above

Q.12 The famous Dilwara Temples are situated in:

A. Rajasthan **B.** Uttar Pradesh
C. Madhya Pradesh **D.** Assam

Q.13 B.C. Roy award is given in the field of:

A. Music **B.** Journalism
C. Medicine **D.** Sports

Q.14 Hirakud Dam is located on which river?

A. Yamuna **B.** Kaveri
C. Mahanadi **D.** Bhargavi

Q.15 Which of the following country is not larger than India in terms of geographical area?

A. Australia **B.** Brazil
C. Canada **D.** Indonesia

Q.16 Who is the father of Botany?

A. Adam Smith **B.** Greco-Roman
C. Theophrastus **D.** Carl Linnaeur

Q.17 Which of the following branch of Physics deal with study of Atomic Nuclei?

A. Nuclear Physics **B.** Bio Physics
C. Atomic Physics **D.** None of the above

Q.18 Which among the following books was authored by Mahatma Gandhi?

A. Hindu View of Life **B.** Hind Swaraj
C. Discovery of India **D.** My Truth

Q.19 Thomas Cup and Uber Cup are prestigious trophies of:

A. Badminton **B.** Lawn Tennis
C. Table Tennis **D.** Golf

Q.20 Sunita Lakra of India announced her retirement, she belongs to which sport?

A. Football **B.** Badminton
C. Cricket **D.** Hockey

Q.21 Veteran footballer Diego Armando Maradona who has passed away played for which country?

A. Portugal **B.** Argentina
C. Spain **D.** New Zealand

Q.22 Which Indian State has the highest number of nursing colleges?

A. Uttar Pradesh **B.** Madhya Pradesh
C. Andhra Pradesh **D.** Karnataka

Q.23 Which body has replaced Medical Council of India?

A. Medical Body of India

B. Indian Medical Council
C. National Medical Commission
D. Medical Confederation of India

Q.24 On which date, World Heart Day is celebrated every year?
A. September 23 **B.** September 25
C. September 27 **D.** September 29

Q.25 Which mobile application became the word's fastest app to reach 50 million downloads in just 13 days?
A. PRAGYAM **B.** Aarogya Setu
C. Covidgyan **D.** SarCov

Q.26 Which ministry launched the e-Governance platform, SAMARTH?
A. Human Resource Development
B. Science & Technology
C. Tourism
D. Culture

Q.27 Which city has topped the Swachh Survekshan 2020 ranking for being the cleanest city of India?
A. Surat **B.** Chennai
C. Indore **D.** Navi Mumbai

Q.28 Which ministry has recently linked an agreement with the ministry of AYUSH to control malnutrition?
A. Agriculture & Farmer's Walfare
B. Health & Family Welfare
C. Education
D. Women and Child Development

Q.29 Fine the odd one from the given options which is different from others.
A. 144 **B.** 169 **C.** 196 **D.** 210

Q.30 Choose the correct answer having same relation of the following:
Agra : Taj Mahal
A. Delhi : Hawa Mahal
B. Patna : Red Fort
C. Gaya : Golghar
D. Amritsar : Golden Temple

Discipline

Q.31 The symptoms of false labor are all of the following except:
A. Intervals between contractions remain longer
B. Heads remain free
C. Emptying of bowel may lead to relief of symptoms
D. Pain occurs at regular intervals

Q.32 The cause of pain in labor is due to all of the following factors except:
A. Myometrial ischemia during contractions
B. Inefficient sedation
C. Cervical stretching during dilatation
D. Peritoneal stretching over the fundus

Q.33 Disappearance of cervix during labor is called:
A. Dilatation **B.** Ripening
C. Effacement **D.** Letting down

Q.34 A graphical representation of the progress of labor in which cervical dilatation and descent of fetal head are plotted against time is called:
A. Electrocardiogram **B.** Partogram
C. Vitals graph **D.** Labour graph

Q.35 During active phase of labour head is delivered by:
A. Flexion **B.** Extension
C. Abduction **D.** None of these

Q.36 Estimated date of delivery is calculated using:
A. Mc Donald's rule **B.** Naegele's rule
C. Rule of nine **D.** Dawn's formula

Q.37 The nausea and vomiting which generally starts around 4 to 6 weeks of pregnancy is called:
A. Amenorrhoea **B.** Morning sickness
C. Galactopoiesis **D.** Early symptoms

Q.38 The first fetal movement felt by the mother is called:
A. Lightening **B.** Quickening
C. Chloasma **D.** Linea nigra

Q.39 The normal average range of fetal heart rate in utero is:
A. 80-120 beats/mt **B.** 100-200 beats/mt
C. 120-160 beats/mt **D.** 180-200 beats/mt

Q.40 A woman who has delivered once a fetus who reached the stage of viability is called:
A. Gravida **B.** Parity
C. Nullipara **D.** Primipara

Q.41 The nutritional supplement that is prescribed in early pregnancy is:
A. Vitamin A **B.** Calcium
C. Protein **D.** Folic acid

Q.42 The colour of lochia rubra is:
A. Brown **B.** Red **C.** Yellow **D.** White

Q.43 How many weeks post delivery is called puerperium period?
A. 4 weeks **B.** 6 weeks
C. 8 weeks **D.** 10 weeks

Q.44 The thin serous fluid secreted from breast during the 24 to 48 hours following delivery is called:
A. Fore milk **B.** Hind milk
C. Colostrum **D.** Mature milk

Q.45 Which of the following medicine can be used for suppression of lactation?
A. Inj. Methergine **B.** Inj. Oxytocin
C. Tab. Cabergoline **D.** Tab. Progesterone

Q.46 Keeping the baby with the mother, in the cot is called:
A. Caring **B.** Kangaroo care

C. Rooming in **D.** Neonatal care

Q.47 The colour of amniotic fluid in meconium stained liquor is:

A. Greenish **B.** Watery **C.** Watery **D.** Reddish

Q.48 The components of active management of third stage of labour includes all except:

A. Use of oxytocin **B.** Uterine massage
C. Delivery of placenta **D.** Rooming in

Q.49 During labour inj. Oxytocin has to be administered intravenously in which of the following ways?

A. Bolus
B. Intravenous infusion
C. Fast push
D. Intramuscular

Q.50 If the placenta is not delivered within 30 minutes of delivery of the baby, it is called:

A. Placenta praevia
B. Post partum haemorrhage
C. Retained placenta
D. Placental ischemia

Q.51 If the placenta is not delivered within 30 minutes of delivery then it can be removed ________.

A. By controlled traction
B. Manual method
C. Surgery
D. None of the above

Q.52 Episiotomy has to be done during:

A. Onset of labour
B. First stage of labour
C. Second stage of labour
D. Third stage of labour

Q.53 The normal birth weight of a newborn in India is ________.

A. 1.5 to 2.5 kg **B.** 2.5 to 3.5 kg
C. 1.5 to 3 kg **D.** 4.5 to 5 kg

Q.54 Wiping the amniotic and making the baby dry prevents heat loss from the infant as Heat loss in the first half hour is largely due to ________ of amniotic fluid.

A. Conduction **B.** Convection
C. Evaporation **D.** Radiation

Q.55 A newborn baby is delivered and has visible secretion, the method of suction to be followed:

A. Nose first then mouth
B. Mouth first then nose
C. Deep inside mouth up to larynx
D. Hold baby upside down and clean

Q.56 White cheesy material on the skin of newborn present at birth is called:

A. Lanugo **B.** Vernix caseosa
C. Amniotic fluid **D.** Brown fat

Q.57 The vaccine to be given at birth are:

A. BCG, Hepatitis B, DPT
B. BCG, OPV, Hepatitis B
C. BCG, DPT, MMR
D. DPT, MMR, Hepatitis B

Q.58 Adequacy of breast feeding can be assessed by all of the following signs except:

A. Passes urine 6-8 times per day
B. Sleeps for 2-3 hours after feed
C. Gains weight adequately
D. Crosses birth weight by 3 days

Q.59 Normal body temperature of newborn is ________.

A. 36 - 36.8 degree celsius
B. 36.5 - 37.4 degree celsius
C. 37 - 38 degree celsius
D. 37 - 40 degree Celsius

Q.60 While preparing for neonatal resuscitation, the bag and mask should be checked for all of the following except:

A. Appropriate size of the face mask
B. Bag for re-inflation
C. Adequate pressure
D. Suction catheter

Q.61 Preterm newborn is a baby born at:

A. < 37 completed weeks of gestation
B. < 38 completed weeks of gestation
C. < 39 completed weeks of gestation
D. < 40 completed weeks of gestation

Q.62 Failure of descent of one or both testes at birth in newborns is called ________.

A. Orchidopexy **B.** Phimosis
C. Cryptorchidism **D.** Hydrocele

Q.63 The available strength of epinephrine is:

A. 1:100 **B.** 1:500 **C.** 1:1000 **D.** 1:10,000

Q.64 A newborn is assessed for APGAR at five minutes after birth. The score is 8 . What does this indicate?

A. No depression
B. Mild depression
C. Moderate depression
D. Severe depression

Q.65 In the first day of life of a newborn, the possible causes of seizures are all except:

A. Hypoglycaemia
B. Tetanus
C. Asphyxia
D. Intraventricular bleeding

Q.66 While providing first aid, do not provide anything to eat or drink to all the following persons except:

A. Severely injured
B. Becoming sleepy
C. Falling unconscious

D. Diarrhea and fever leading to dehydration

Q.67 When the victim is 8 years old boy the appropriate method to provide CPR is ___________.

A. Thumb technique
B. Two finger technique
C. One hand technique
D. Two hand technique

Q.68 The compression ventilation ratio for providing CPR for an adult victim is:

A. 10:2 **B.** 15:2 **C.** 20:2 **D.** 30:2

Q.69 What help the heart to pump blood to all parts of the body?

A. Relaxation **B.** Contraction
C. Ejaculation **D.** Expansion

Q.70 The one which carries waste materials from different parts of the body to kidneys is:

A. Heart **B.** Lungs **C.** Blood **D.** Bone

Q.71 The system that is responsible for all the sensations of the body is called ________.

A. Skeletal system
B. Gastro intestinal system
C. Nervous system
D. Excretory system

Q.72 What gives shape and support to the human body?

A. Muscles **B.** Bones **C.** Heart **D.** Skin

Q.73 Largest sense organ of human body is:

A. Heart **B.** Lungs **C.** Skin **D.** Hands

Q.74 An hygienic measure to prevent spread of COVID 19 infection is:

A. Eating well
B. Brushing twice a day
C. Hand washing
D. Sleeping

Q.75 International Day of the Midwife is celebrated on:

A. 5th May **B.** 7th April
C. 1st May **D.** 12th May

Q.76 For an unconscious patient the method to remove excess secretions from mouth is:

A. Suction **B.** Bed bath
C. Early mobilization **D.** Isolation

Q.77 A person with anxiety disorder will have all the following symptoms except:

A. Increased heart rate **B.** Rapid breathing
C. Increased sleep **D.** Restlessness

Q.78 A state in which a person has strong emotions and behaves in an uncontrolled way is called:

A. Tension **B.** Hysteria
C. Chorea **D.** All the above

Q.79 Fear of closed spaces is called:

A. Acrophobia **B.** Claustrophobia
C. Arachnophobia **D.** Autophobia

Q.80 The signs and symptoms of hysteria includes all the following except:

A. Anxiety
B. Fainting
C. Seizure like movements
D. Appropriate thinking and decision making

Q.81 The essentials of primary health care are all of the following except:

A. Immunization against major infectious diseases
B. Promotion of food supply and proper nutrition
C. An adequate supply of safe water
D. Providing higher education for all

Q.82 Involvement of individuals and community in the promotion of their own health and welfare in primary health care is called:

A. Equitable distribution
B. Community participation
C. Appropriate technology
D. All the above

Q.83 As per Indian public health standards first antenatal visit should be done at:

A. 2 weeks of gestation
B. Within 12 weeks of gestation
C. Within 14 weeks of gestation
D. Within 20 weeks of gestation

Q.84 Antenatal care in a primary health centre includes all of the following except:

A. Lab investigations like haemoglobin and blood grouping
B. Nutrition and health counselling
C. Identification and management of high risk and alarming signs during pregnancy
D. Conducting high risk delivery

Q.85 The term initiation of early breast feeding means:

A. Initiating breast feeding within one minute after delivery
B. Initiating breast feeding within one hour of delivery
C. Initiating breast feeding within two hours of delivery
D. Initiating breast feeding with one day of delivery

Q.86 For emergency care of sick children at PHC the strategy to be followed is:

A. PALS guidelines **B.** NALS guidelines
C. IMNCI guidelines **D.** APA guidelines

Q.87 To maintain sanitation at community level the following measures have to be taken except:

A. Proper waste disposal
B. Avoid waste of water resource
C. Avoid high noise
D. Improper housing

Q.88 The diseases that are spread through unsafe water are all of the following except:

A. Cholera
B. Dysentery
C. Typhoid
D. Small pox

Q.89 Vaccine that is administered in children to prevent diarrhoea is:

A. Polio vaccine
B. Hepatitis B
C. Rota virus
D. Pneumococcal

Q.90 The route of administration of BCG vaccine is:

A. Oral
B. Intradermal
C. Subcutaneous
D. Intramuscular

Q.91 Vitamin A deficiency causes:

A. Beriberi
B. Anaemia
C. Night blindness
D. Marasmus

Q.92 Oral polio vaccine is a:

A. Killed vaccine
B. Immunoglobulin
C. Antiviral
D. Both A and B

Q.93 Scurvy is caused due to the deficiency of which of the following vitamin?

A. Vitamin A
B. Vitamin B
C. Vitamin C
D. Vitamin D

Q.94 The programme that has permitted to use drugs by ANM's in case of specific emergency situations to reduce maternal mortality is:

A. Janani Suraksha Yogana
B. Janani Shishu Suraksha Karyakram
C. RCH Phase I
D. RCH Phase II

Q.95 The three critical determinants for declaring a facility as first referral unit include 24 hours availability all of the following facilities except:

A. Surgical interventions
B. New Born Care
C. Blood storage facility
D. Immunization facility

Q.96 While providing feed to a bed ridden patient the ideal position the patient has to be kept is:

A. Supine position
B. Prone position
C. Fowler's position
D. Side lying position

Q.97 An infant attains head control by _______.

A. 15 days
B. 3-4 months
C. 6 months
D. 8 months

Q.98 The mode of transmission of Hepatitis C is __________.

A. Fecal oral route
B. Droplet nuclei
C. Contaminated Blood
D. None of these

Q.99 Which animal is amplifier of Japanese encephalitis?

A. Cow
B. Monkey
C. Pig
D. Cat

Q.100 Breast feeding week is celebrated in:

A. 1st week of July
B. 1st week of August
C. 1st week of September
D. 1st week of November

// Smart Answer Sheet //

Correct Indicates percentage of students who answered questions correctly.

Skipped Indicates percentage of students who skipped questions.

Q.	Ans.	Correct	Skipped
1	A	53.85 %	1.19 %
2	A	41.52 %	1.39 %
3	D	77.09 %	0.0 %
4	D	46.96 %	1.24 %
5	D	83.93 %	0.0 %
6	D	61.44 %	1.07 %
7	B	81.99 %	0.0 %
8	A	16.08 %	4.34 %
9	C	40.81 %	1.57 %
10	C	51.08 %	1.17 %
11	C	88.19 %	0.0 %
12	A	53.74 %	1.48 %
13	C	16.59 %	4.55 %
14	C	45.03 %	1.42 %
15	D	65.37 %	1.43 %
16	C	45.7 %	1.12 %

Q.	Ans.	Correct	Skipped
17	A	81.69 %	0.0 %
18	B	44.91 %	1.06 %
19	A	63.99 %	1.34 %
20	D	18.92 %	3.24 %
21	B	64.62 %	1.26 %
22	D	53.75 %	1.72 %
23	C	51.76 %	1.83 %
24	D	52.66 %	1.39 %
25	B	66.48 %	1.46 %
26	A	46.81 %	1.33 %
27	C	47.65 %	1.02 %
28	D	23.85 %	3.72 %
29	D	56.53 %	1.84 %
30	D	59.9 %	1.0 %
31	D	52.31 %	1.3 %
32	B	41.84 %	1.71 %

Q.	Ans.	Correct	Skipped
33	C	46.08 %	1.99 %
34	B	10.45 %	4.42 %
35	B	26.82 %	3.62 %
36	B	62.45 %	1.1 %
37	B	68.35 %	1.64 %
38	B	50.16 %	1.99 %
39	C	41.25 %	1.39 %
40	D	51.74 %	1.52 %
41	D	66.87 %	1.89 %
42	B	68.56 %	2.0 %
43	B	65.15 %	1.88 %
44	C	13.5 %	3.54 %
45	C	40.58 %	1.9 %
46	C	76.69 %	0.0 %
47	A	59.0 %	1.86 %
48	D	31.88 %	3.65 %

Q.	Ans.	Correct	Skipped
49	B	18.85 %	3.39 %
50	C	66.35 %	1.51 %
51	B	57.7 %	1.89 %
52	C	82.84 %	0.0 %
53	B	69.36 %	1.84 %
54	C	64.19 %	1.38 %
55	B	45.42 %	1.24 %
56	B	21.83 %	3.96 %
57	B	63.42 %	1.59 %
58	D	47.22 %	1.57 %
59	B	55.39 %	1.56 %
60	D	78.58 %	0.0 %
61	A	50.38 %	1.55 %
62	C	58.65 %	1.34 %
63	C	87.78 %	0.0 %
64	A	44.49 %	1.97 %

Q.	Ans.	Correct	Skipped
65	B	84.94 %	0.0 %
66	D	58.36 %	1.45 %
67	A	76.82 %	0.0 %
68	D	58.33 %	1.52 %
69	B	59.5 %	1.86 %
70	C	43.88 %	1.0 %
71	C	45.16 %	1.69 %
72	B	65.17 %	1.52 %
73	C	88.22 %	0.0 %
74	C	87.04 %	0.0 %
75	A	89.53 %	0.0 %
76	A	41.31 %	1.27 %
77	C	45.72 %	1.97 %
78	B	18.12 %	3.59 %
79	B	54.79 %	1.15 %
80	D	62.83 %	1.12 %

Q.	Ans.	Correct	Skipped
81	D	81.15 %	0.0 %
82	B	42.33 %	1.66 %
83	B	83.27 %	0.0 %
84	D	62.16 %	1.14 %

Q.	Ans.	Correct	Skipped
85	B	87.44 %	0.0 %
86	C	14.12 %	3.18 %
87	D	59.79 %	1.83 %
88	D	68.45 %	1.02 %

Q.	Ans.	Correct	Skipped
89	C	27.37 %	4.67 %
90	B	62.78 %	1.63 %
91	C	88.94 %	0.0 %
92	C	79.94 %	0.0 %

Q.	Ans.	Correct	Skipped
93	C	59.35 %	1.96 %
94	D	56.61 %	1.85 %
95	D	59.94 %	1.09 %
96	C	11.25 %	4.78 %

Q.	Ans.	Correct	Skipped
97	B	44.65 %	1.0 %
98	C	51.95 %	1.18 %
99	C	54.62 %	1.87 %
100	B	44.97 %	1.3 %

Performance Analysis	
Avg. Score (%)	51.0%
Toppers Score (%)	62.0%
Your Score	

//Hints and Solutions//

1. The man started moving towards the west, then turned to his right facing north. He turns right and again he turns right and then he turns left at last.

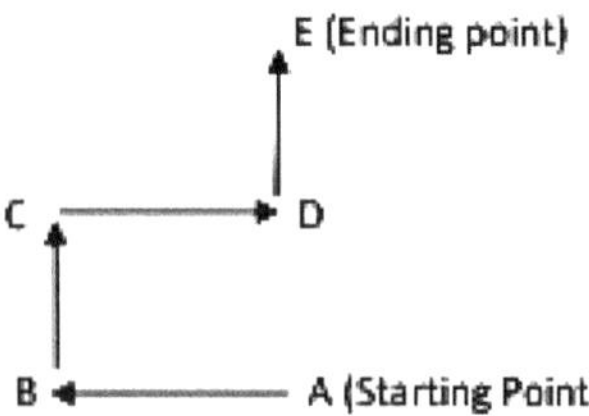

At the ending point, the man walks towards Northside.

Hence, the correct option is (A).

2. It is given that,

- P is to the right of Q ------ (1)
- T is to the left of R and is to the right of P------ (2)
- From (1) and (2), we have QPTR.
- Q is to the right of S ---------- (3)
- Combining these, we get- S Q P T R

P is precisely in the middle.

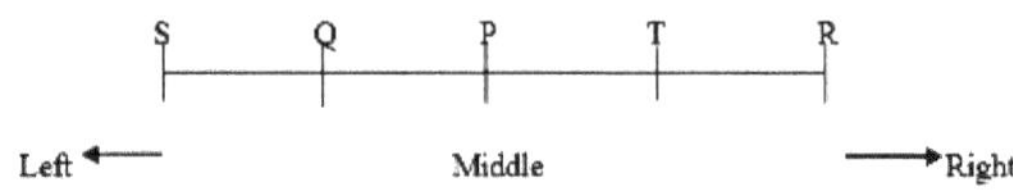

Hence, the correct option is (A).

3. Given, that 46 A 2 B 3 C 4=?

According to the question,

⇒ 46 ÷ 2 3 x 4 = ?

⇒ 23 - 3 x 4 = 23 - 12 = 11

Hence, the correct option is (D).

4. According to the question,

To arrange all the persons in decreasing order of age.

The decreasing order of age is

- Deepti > Sweta > Seema > Sohan > Seeta.
- So Deepti is the oldest person among all of them.

Hence, the correct option is (D).

5. As "MEAT" is written as "TEAM".

Similarly,

"BALE" is written as "EALB".

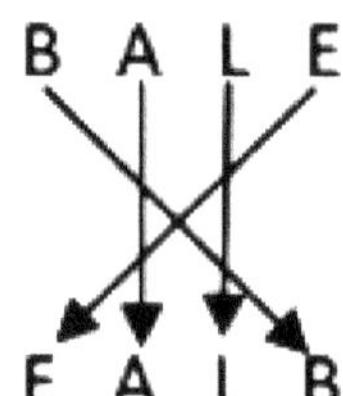

Hence, the correct option is (D).

6. As "SECTOR" is written as "ESCTOR".

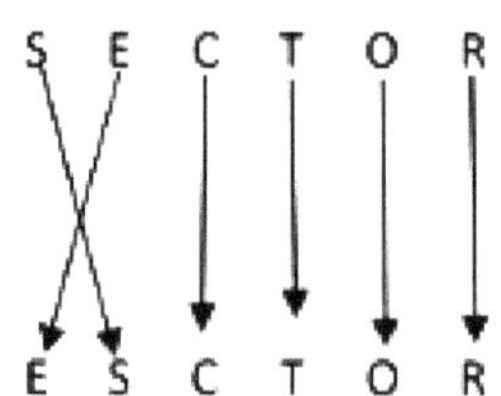

Similarly,

"MOTHER" is written as "OMTHER".

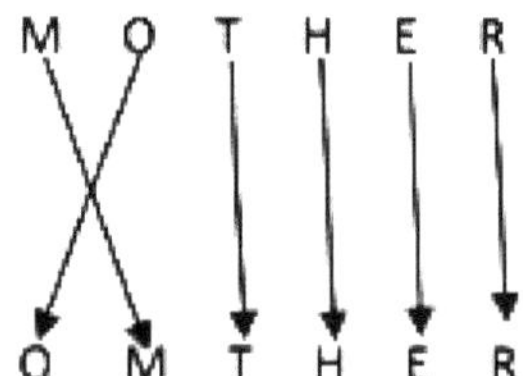

Hence, the correct option is (D).

7. According to the English dictionary, chitin comes first, followed by cholera, followed by hepatitis, and peptidoglycan last.

So, the correct sequential order of words is 4, 2, 1, 3 i.e., Chitin, Cholera, Hepatitis, Peptidoglycan.

Hence, the correct option is (B).

8. Rakesh says Alka's father is the only son of my father. Therefore, Alka and Rakesh are daughter and father respectively.

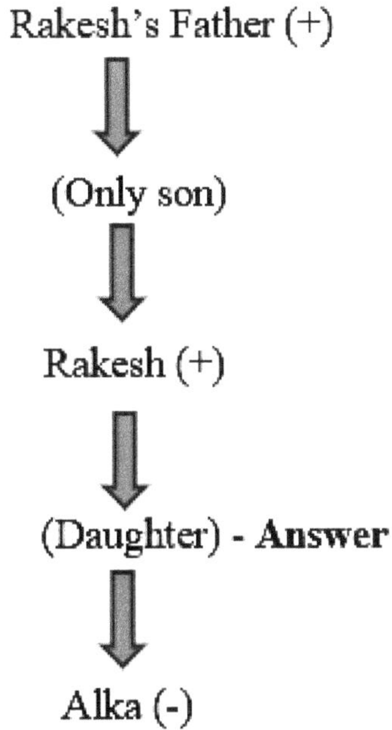

Hence, the correct option is (A).

9. Arjuna Award is given for outstanding performance in sports.

The system of conferring 'Arjuna Awards' to the best sports persons of the year was initiated by the Government of India in 1961 and is awarded to those who have consistently performed well at the international level in the last three years and have demonstrated qualities such as leadership, sportsmanship and discipline is given to the players.

The purpose of these awards was to reward the players and make them more enthusiastic about sports.

Hence, the correct option is (C).

10. The first Indian to receive Nobel Prize in Literature was Rabindranath Tagore.

He was awarded the 1913 Nobel Prize in Literature for his book of poems, Gitanjali. Tagore has also written many love songs. Gitanjali and Sadhana are his important works.

Hence, the correct option is (C).

11. Malaria is not caused by bacteria.

Bacteria are unicellular organisms that belong to the prokaryotic group where the organisms are few organelles and lack a true nucleus.

Malaria disease is caused by a Plasmodium parasite, which is transmitted through the bite of infected mosquitoes. The severity of the disease varies and is based on the species of Plasmodium-infected with it.

Hence, the correct option is (C).

12. Dilwara Jain Temple Temple is the most beautiful pilgrimage site of Jains situated amidst the Aravalli hills of Rajasthan.

This temple was built between the 11th and 13th centuries by Vastupala Tejpal. This temple is famous for its intricate carvings and is adorned with marble from every corner.

Hence, the correct option is (A).

13. B.C. Roy award is given in the field of medicine.

The BC Roy Award or the Vidhan Chandra Roy National Award was instituted in 1962 by the Medical Council of India.

This award is given by the President on 1 July every year on the occasion of National Doctor's Day, in the name of doctor and freedom fighter Vidhan Chandra Roy, on the occasion of National Doctor's Day.

Hence, the correct option is (C).

14. Hirakud Dam is one of the river valley projects of India. Hirakud Dam is built on the Mahanadi.

The construction of Hirakud Dam started in 1948 and it was completed in 1953. This dam was fully functional in the year 1957.

This dam is one of the longest dams in the world. The length of this dam is 4.8 km. and its total length including the embankment is 25.8 km.

Hence, the correct option is (C).

15. Indonesia is not larger than India in terms of geographical area.

Indonesia is the world's largest archipelagic state and the 14th-largest country by area, at 1,904,569 square kilometers (735,358 square miles). With over 275 million people, Indonesia is the world's fourth-most populous country. India is the seventh largest in the world geographically and in terms of population. It is the second country after China.

Hence, the correct option is (D).

16. Theophrastus is the father of Botany. Plants are studied in botany.

He was a scholar, botanist, biologist, and physicist. The most important of his books are two large botanical treatises, Enquiry into Plants, and On the Causes of Plants, which constitute the first systemization of the botanical world and were major sources for botanical knowledge during antiquity and the Middle Ages.

Hence, the correct option is (C).

17. Nuclear Physics deal with study of Atomic Nuclei.

This branch of physics deals with the structure of atomic nuclei and the radiation emitted from unstable nuclei.

Nuclear physics is the study of the protons and neutrons at the centre of an atom and the interactions that hold them together in a space just a few femtometres (10-15 metres) across.

Hence, the correct option is (A).

18. "Hind Swaraj" was authored by Mahatma Gandhi.

Hind Swaraj or Indian Home Rule is a book written by Gandhiji in his native language, Gujarati, during his travels from London to

South Africa in 1909. In the year 1910, it was banned by the British on the grounds of seditious text.

This included his views on Swaraj, modern civilization, mechanization, etc.

Hence, the correct option is (B).

19. Thomas Cup and Uber Cup are prestigious trophies of Badminton.

The 2022 Thomas and Uber Cup was the 32nd edition of the Thomas Cup and the 29th edition of the Uber Cup, the biennial international badminton championship contested by the men and women's national teams of the member associations of Badminton World Federation.

Hence, the correct option is (A).

20. Sunita Lakra belongs to Hockey.

Indian women's hockey team defender Sunita Lakra announced her retirement from international hockey due to a knee injury. She was part of the silver medal-winning team at the 2018 Asian Games.

Hence, the correct option is (D).

21. World-renowned Argentine football player Diego Maradona passed away on November 25, 2020, after suffering a heart attack. He was 60 years old.

Maradona represented Boca Juniors, Napoli, Barcelona, and Newell's Old Boys as a player. He was also considered a key player in helping Argentina win the country's second World Cup title in 1986.

Hence, the correct option is (B).

22. Karnataka has the highest number of nursing colleges in India.

It has a total of 314 colleges out of which 13 are government colleges and 301 are private colleges. Health is a state subject, so the opening of new nursing colleges comes under the purview of the respective state government.

Hence, the correct option is (D).

23. National Medical Commission has replaced Medical Council of India.

The NITI Aayog recommended the replacement of the Medical Council of India (MCI) with the National Medical Commission (NMC).

The National Medical Commission Bill was re-introduced in the Lok Sabha on 22 July 2019.

Hence, the correct option is (C).

24. World Heart Day is celebrated every year on 29 September.

World Heart Day is the perfect platform for the Cardiovascular disease community to unite in the fight against Cardiovascular disease and reduce the global disease burden.

World Heart Day is a global campaign during which individuals, families, communities, and governments around the world participate in activities to take charge of their heart health and that of others.

Hence, the correct option is (D).

25. Aarogya Setu, India's app to fight COVID-19 has reached 50 M users in just 13 days-fastest ever globally for an App. The proud development has been confirmed by Niti Aayog CEO Amitabh Kant.

Hence, the correct option is (B).

26. The Ministry of Human Resource Development (HRD) has developed an e-governance platform 'SAMARTH Enterprise Resource Planning (ERP)' under the National Mission of Education in Information and Communication Technology Scheme (NMEICT).

It is an Open Standard, Open Source Architecture, Secure, Scalable, and Evolutionary Process Automation Engine for Universities and Higher Educational Institutions.

Hence, the correct option is (A).

27. Indore has topped the Swachh Survekshan 2020 ranking for being the cleanest city of India.

According to the 2020 survey, Swachh Survekshan Results in 2020: Indore in Madhya Pradesh retained its position as the cleanest city in India for the fourth consecutive year, according to the Swachh Survekshan 2020 survey results.

Hence, the correct option is (C).

28. Women and Child Development has recently linked an agreement with the ministry of AYUSH to control malnutrition.

An MoU was signed between the Ministry of AYUSH and the Ministry of Women and Child Development in New Delhi to control malnutrition under the nutrition campaign. Under this, work will be done on timely and scientifically proven AYUSH-based solutions to control malnutrition.

Hence, the correct option is (D).

29. 210 is odd among this question because all the other numbers are squares of 12, 13, and 14 respectively.

- $(12)^2 = 144$
- $(14)^2 = 196$
- $(13)^2 = 169$
- 210 is not a square number

Hence, the correct option is (D).

30. Taj Mahal is located in Agra in the state of Uttar Pradesh.

Similarly,

The Golden Temple is a gurudwara located in Amritsar in the state of Punjab, India. It is the central spiritual place of Sikhism.

Hence, the correct option is (D).

31. The symptoms of false labor are all of the given options except pain occurs at regular intervals.

Labor means birth or giving birth to a child. After the completion of the prescribed period of pregnancy, the birth of the child without any obstruction is called simple birth.

Symptoms of False labor:

- Intervals between contractions remain longer
- Heads remain free
- Emptying of bowel may lead to relief of symptoms

Hence, the correct option is (D).

32. The cause of pain in labor is due to all of the following factors except Inefficient sedation.

Cause of pain in labor-

- Pain during labor is caused by the contraction of the uterine muscles and pressure on the cervix.
- This pain can be felt as a sensation of pain along with sharp cramps in the abdomen, groin, and back. Some women also experience pain in the arms or thighs.
- Other causes of pain during labor include pressure on the bladder and bowels by the baby's head and stretching of the Cervical canal and vagina during dilatation.

Hence, the correct option is (B).

33. Disappearance of cervix during labor is called Effacement.

- Effacement refers to the thinning of the cervix during labor.
- During labor, the cervix shortens, dilates, and almost disappears toward the uterus in preparation for childbirth.

Hence, the correct option is (C).

34. A graphical representation of the progress of labor in which cervical dilatation and descent of fetal head are plotted against time is called Partogram.

A partogram or partograph is a composite graphical record of key data (maternal and fetal) during labour entered against time on a single sheet of paper. Relevant measurements might include statistics such as cervical dilation, fetal heart rate, duration of labour and vital signs.

Hence, the correct option is (B).

35. During active phase of labour head is delivered by Extension.

Extension- At the time of delivery of the fetal head, this cardinal movement occurs as a result of the combined effect of uterine contractions and the pelvic floor.

Hence, the correct option is (B).

36. Estimated date of delivery is calculated using Naegele's rule.

Naegele's rule-

Naegele's law is a standard way to calculate the due date for a pregnancy. It is named after the German obstetrician Franz Karl Naegele (1778–1851), who formulated the rule.

The formula to calculate your Estimated Due Date using Naegele's rule: Date of Last Menstrual Period + 7 Days + 9 Calendar Months = Date of Estimated Date of Delivery.

Hence, the correct option is (B).

37. The nausea and vomiting which generally starts around 4 to 6 weeks of pregnancy is called Morning sickness.

Morning sickness is a common symptom of pregnancy and sometimes includes nausea or vomiting.

Pregnancy morning sickness is common during the first three months and usually begins around nine weeks after conception.

Hence, the correct option is (B).

38. Around the fifth month of pregnancy, women may begin to feel their baby move for the first time this is called quickening.

Mothers who have been pregnant before may feel it as early as 16 weeks.

Fetal movements refer to the muscle movements of the developing baby inside the mother's womb.

Hence, the correct option is (B).

39. The normal average range of fetal heart rate in utero is 120-160 beats/mt.

Fetal heart monitoring is usually done externally, often by placing electrodes on the skin of the mother's abdomen.

A normally developing fetus usually has a heart rate of anywhere from 120 to 180 bpm.

Hence, the correct option is (C).

40. A woman who has delivered once a fetus who reached the stage of viability is called Primipara.

Fetal viability is the ability of a human embryo to survive outside the uterus. Medical viability is usually considered between 23 and 24 weeks of gestational age.

Hence, the correct option is (D).

41. The nutritional supplement that is prescribed in early pregnancy is Folic acid.

Folic acid is a B vitamin that is needed by every cell in the body for healthy growth and development.

Nutritional supplements are substances you can use to add nutrients to your diet or reduce your risk of health problems.

Hence, the correct option is (D).

42. The colour of lochia rubra is Red.

Lochia is also called postpartum bleeding. It is referred to as vaginal discharge after childbirth that contains blood, mucus, uterine tissue, amniotic fluid, and remnants of the placenta.

Lochia Rubra:

- Dark or bright red blood.
- Lasts for 3 to 4 days.
- Flows like a heavy period.

- Small clots are normal.
- Mild, menstrual cramps.

Hence, the correct option is (B).

43. 6 weeks post delivery is called puerperium period.

The time after six months of delivery is called the postpartum period. Meanwhile, the recovery of the woman's body takes place, so special care for the body is needed.

During this, the woman needs a lot of care because in the meantime the recovery of her body takes place.

Hence, the correct option is (B).

44. The thin serous fluid secreted from breast during the 24 to 48 hours following delivery is called Colostrum.

- Colostrum is the first milk that comes into the breast of a new mother after delivery.
- It is very beneficial for the newborn. It is yellow or slightly orange in colour and is usually thick But sometimes it can be neat and thin too.

Hence, the correct option is (C).

45. Tab. Cabergoline medicine can be used for suppression of lactation.

Lactation is the process of making human milk. Human milk is secreted through the mammary glands, which are located in your breasts.

Cabergoline helps in the treatment of disorders that occur as a result of very high levels of the hormone prolactin in the body.

Hence, the correct option is (C).

46. Keeping the baby with the mother, in the cot is called Rooming in.

Rooming-in is provided as part of our family-centered care to help students learn how to relax and care for a newborn. Rooming-in helps prepare you to go home with your new baby.

Hence, the correct option is (C).

47. The colour of amniotic fluid in meconium stained liquor is Greenish.

Meconium is a medical term used to describe the first stool that occurs after childbirth.

Meconium gives green color to amniotic fluid. This is called meconium staining. If the meconium has been in the amniotic fluid for a long time, the baby's skin and nails may turn yellow, giving it a yellow-green appearance.

Hence, the correct option is (A).

48. The components of active management of third stage of labour includes all except Rooming in.

Active management of the third stage of labor:

- The uterus contracts very rapidly and the placenta detaches itself from the inner wall of the uterus.
- The mother can push the placenta out herself, or she cannot, so the nurse helps with the delivery of the placenta by placing one hand on the abdomen to protect the uterus and massaging the uterus while the placenta is held in a taut position with the other lives in.
- With the placenta released, the blood vessels attached to it close and stop the flow of blood (although some bleeding is normal).
- The hormone oxytocin is released by the act of feeding the baby or simply holding the baby there. It acts on your uterus which then contracts and expels the placenta and membranes. The placenta is cut off when it stops beating and usually when the placenta comes out.

Hence, the correct option is (D).

49. During labour inj. Oxytocin has to be administered intravenously in Intravenous infusion.

Intravenous is a term that means within a vein. An intravenous injection is the introduction of a substance into a vein using a needle.

Oxytocin is administered externally during pregnancy to induce labor and control postpartum hemorrhage.

Hence, the correct option is (B).

50. If the placenta is not delivered within 30 minutes of delivery of the baby, it is called Retained placenta.

Retained placenta:

- A retained placenta occurs when the placenta is not delivered within 30 minutes after the baby is born.
- Retained placenta refers to the inability of the placenta to come out.
- When a woman pushes during labour, the placenta is also delivered after the baby.
- When the placenta remains in the woman's body even after delivery, bleeding may occur in small amounts.

Hence, the correct option is (C).

51. If the placenta is not delivered within 30 minutes of delivery then it can be removed by Manual method.

Manual removal of the placenta is an alternative to the treatment of an intact placenta but carries risks of bleeding, infection, and trauma to the genital tract.

In an attempt to avoid manual removal of the placenta, intraumbilical vein injection of oxytocin (10–20 units of oxytocin in 20 mL of saline solution) has been proposed as an alternative to the management of retained placenta.

Hence, the correct option is (B).

52. Episiotomy has to be done during second stage of labour.

Episiotomy-

- Episiotomy is needed during delivery while the baby's head is taken out.

- Episiotomy is a procedure performed during delivery in which an incision is made in the tissue between the vagina and the anus.

Hence, the correct option is (C).

53. In an Indian newborn baby, the weight of the male child is 2.5 - 3.5 kg, while the weight of the female remains 2.7 - 3.1 kg.

Due to the good weight of the mother, the weight of the child is also good. Children who are 3.1, and 3.2 kg are considered healthy babies.

Hence, the correct option is (B).

54. Wiping the amniotic and making the baby dry prevents heat loss from the infant as Heat loss in the first half hour is largely due to Evaporation of amniotic fluid.

Evaporation-

- Evaporation occurs when wet surfaces come into contact with air. The heat is dissipated when the surface dries.
- At birth, the newborn is bathed with amniotic fluid. As the amniotic fluid dries up on the baby's skin (evaporates), the baby loses heat.

Hence, the correct option is (C).

55. A newborn baby is delivered and has visible secretion, the method of suction to be followed mouth first then nose.

Monitor the baby's vital signs before and after suctioning, as no procedure is without risk. Airway trauma, hypoxia, infection, and increased intracranial pressure are especially dangerous for newborns, so weigh the risks and benefits and know the baby's health history before proceeding. Wipe off visible secretions from the mouth and nose with a clean, dry cloth.

Hence, the correct option is (B).

56. White cheesy material on the skin of newborn present at birth is called Vernix caseosa.

Basically, vernix caseosa is a protective layer on your baby's skin. It appears as a white-colored substance.

This coating develops on the skin of the baby in the womb itself. Residues of this substance may be visible on the skin after birth.

Hence, the correct option is (B).

57. The vaccine to be given at birth are BCG, OPV, Hepatitis B.

As per the National Immunization Schedule, newborns are given one dose each of the three vaccines, OPV, BCG, and Hepatitis B, irrespective of the place of delivery.

Hence, the correct option is (B).

58. Adequacy of breast feeding can be assessed by all of the following signs except crosses birth weight by 3 days.

Signs of breastfeeding adequacy:

- A newborn is breastfed at least every 2 to 3 hours or 8 to 12 times every day and at a time this is an assessment of breastfeeding adequacy
- After the fifth day of life, the baby passes urine at least 6 to 8 times per day and wet diapers should be changed.
- Can hear the baby swallowing during breastfeeding, and can see breast milk in her mouth.
- Breasts feel softer after feeding and not as full as they were before feeding.
- The baby appears satisfied and satisfied after feeding, and he sleeps for 2-3 hours after the feeding.

Hence, the correct option is (D).

59. Normal body temperature of newborn is 36.5 - 37.4 degree celsius.

In general, the body temperature keeps on increasing and decreasing, so a rise in temperature up to 99 ° F cannot be considered a fever. But when the temperature is 100.4°F (i.e. 38°C), the condition of fever arises. In this state, a person starts feeling weak in the body and needs bed rest.

Hence, the correct option is (B).

60. While preparing for neonatal resuscitation, the bag and mask should be checked for all of the following except suction catheter.

Equipment available for PPV in newborns:

Self-inflating bag- The self-inflate bag is designed to automatically inflate as soon as you release your grip on the bag. It does not require a compressed gas source to be filled. You should be able to identify the different parts of the self-inflating bag.

Resuscitation mask- Masks come in various shapes, sizes and materials. The resuscitation mask should have a cushioned rim to prevent injury to the face.

Hence, the correct option is (D).

61. Preterm newborn is a baby born at < 37 completed weeks of gestation.

Most pregnancies last for 40 weeks. But if the baby is born before the 37th week, then it is called a premature or pre-term baby. When the baby is born prematurely. These children are kept in the ICU in the hospital and during this time they are given special care.

Hence, the correct option is (A).

62. Failure of descent of one or both testes at birth in newborns is called Cryptorchidism.

Cryptorchidism basically refers to the condition where a testicle does not fall into the scrotum bag before the baby is born. This condition is mostly rare when it comes to babies serving the full term of pregnancy and often occurs mainly in babies born preterm.

Hence, the correct option is (C).

63. The available strength of epinephrine is 1:1000.

Epinephrine is a clear, colorless, sterile solution containing 1 mg/mL (1:1000) of epinephrine, packaged as a 1 mL solution in a single-use clear glass vial or multi-dose amber glass.

The vial is packaged in 30 mL of solution. In a 1 mL vial, each 1 mL of Adrenaline solution contains 1 mg epinephrine, 9.0 mg sodium chloride, 1.0 mg sodium metabisulfite, hydrochloric acid to adjust pH, and water for injection.

Hence, the correct option is (C).

64. A newborn is assessed for APGAR at five minutes after birth. The score is 8. This indicate no depression.

- APGAR score test is taken from one minute to five minutes after the birth of the child.
- The purpose of this test is to check the heartbeat of the child to check his movement.
- If all the actions inside the child are going well, then the doctor discontinues the APGAR score test. APGAR score test may be done multiple times if the child is not responding well.

Hence, the correct option is (A).

65. In the first day of life of a newborn, the possible causes of seizures are all except Tetanus.

A newborn usually refers to a baby from birth to about 2 months of age. Seizure is a condition in which there is a sudden imbalance in the normal function of the brain. Due to this, the wrong message goes from the brain to the nerves of the body, due to which the body behaves abnormally.

Hence, the correct option is (B).

66. While providing first aid, do not provide anything to eat or drink to all the following persons except diarrhea and fever leading to dehydration.

Nothing should be given to eat or drink while giving first aid to a seriously injured person and a person who has fainted.

Whereas a person suffering from diarrhea and fever whose energy is much less than normal, and to normalize dehydration, eat and drink very light things.

Hence, the correct option is (D).

67. When the victim is 8 years old boy the appropriate method to provide CPR is thumb technique.

CPR(Cardiopulmonary resuscitation) is a method of first aid, when a person has difficulty breathing or a person gets a heart attack or a person becomes unconscious due to an accident, then can save his life by giving CPR at that time.

CPR for children:

- Step 1: First of all, get down on your knees near the child.
- Step 2: If the newborn is in a hurry to perform CPR, use the Thumb technique instead of the palms of the hands.
- Step 3: While applying pressure on the chest, apply only 1/2 to 2 inches of pressure.
- Now repeat this step and take the child to the hospital as soon as possible and inform the doctor that you have given CPR to the child.

Hence, the correct option is (A).

68. The compression ventilation ratio for providing CPR for an adult victim is 30:2.

While giving artificial respiration, press the chest 30 times, then give artificial respiration 2(30:2).

If the newborn is in a hurry to perform CPR, use the fingers instead of the palms of the hands.

Hence, the correct option is (D).

69. Contraction helps the heart to pump blood to all parts of the body.

Contraction of the muscle in the center of your circulatory system pumps blood around the body as the heart beats. This blood sends oxygen and nutrients to all parts of the body and carries away unwanted carbon dioxide and waste products.

Hence, the correct option is (B).

70. The renal arteries carry large amounts of blood from the heart to the kidneys. The kidneys filter waste and excess fluid from the blood.

Humans have two renal arteries. The right renal artery supplies blood to the right kidney, while the left artery sends blood to the left kidney.

Hence, the correct option is (C).

71. The system that is responsible for all the sensations of the body is called Nervous system.

The nervous system is the body's command centre. Originating from the brain, it controls movements, thoughts, and automatic responses. The nervous system includes the brain, spinal cord, and a complex network of nerves.

Hence, the correct option is (C).

72. Bones gives shape and support to the human body.

Bone is a stiff organ that is a component of the skeleton system. Bones protect the body's other organs, create red and white blood cells, store minerals, provide the body structure and support, and allow for motion.

Hence, the correct option is (B).

73. The skin is the largest organ in the human body as it covers the maximum area of the body.

- The skin helps in maintaining body temperature and protecting the other organs from bacteria.
- Skin of an average adult has a surface area of over 21 square feet.
- It performs a plethora of functions important for the basic functioning of the body.
- The skin helps us to feel things by touching, that is hot or cold, smooth or rough, dry or wet, hard or soft.

Hence, the correct option is (C).

74. An hygienic measure to prevent spread of COVID 19 infection is Hand washing.

Handwashing has always been one of the most effective ways to prevent the spread of infection.

Washing hands can prevent many gastrointestinal diseases and respiratory infections, including the novel coronavirus infection.

Hand washing either with soap and water or using hand sanitizers kills the germs that may transmit infections from one person to another.

Hence, the correct option is (B).

75. International Day of the Midwife was first celebrated on May 5, 1991, and since then International Midwives Day is celebrated on May 5 every year.

Midwife providing care to the women during pregnancy and birth, some midwives may also provide primary care related to reproductive health, including gynecological exams and family planning.

The celebrations ensure the quality of care provided by midwives to newborns, women, and their families.

Hence, the correct option is (A).

76. For an unconscious patient the method to remove excess secretions from mouth is Suction.

Suctioning is 'the mechanical aspiration of pulmonary secretions from a patient with an artificial airway in place (endotracheal tube).

It is performed on unconscious patients or when the patient is unable to effectively move secretions from the respiratory tract.

Hence, the correct option is (A).

77. A person with anxiety disorder will have all the following symptoms except Increased sleep.

Anxiety disorder is a mental health diagnosis that leads to excessive nervousness, fear, apprehension, and worry.

Exact causes of anxiety is unknown but there are some factors that can cause anxiety that as environment, stress, genetic factors, etc.

Hence, the correct option is (C).

78. A state in which a person has strong emotions and behaves in an uncontrolled way is called Hysteria.

Hysteria is a state in which a person or a group of people cannot control their emotions, e.g. they cannot stop laughing, crying, shouting, etc. Hysteria is most commonly present in women.

Symptoms of Hysteria:

- Blindness
- Emotional outbursts
- Hallucinations
- Histrionic behavior (being overly dramatic or excitable)
- Increased suggestibility
- Loss of sensation

Hence, the correct option is (B).

79. Fear of closed spaces is called Claustrophobia.

Claustrophobia is defined as a fear of enclosed spaces. The severity of claustrophobia can vary from person to person. There is no specific cause related to claustrophobia but it is considered a defense mechanism technique.

Hence, the correct option is (B).

80. The signs and symptoms of hysteria includes all the following except appropriate thinking and decision making.

Hysteria is described as emotionally charged behavior that seems excessive and out of control. Hysteria is a dissociative disorder that occurs because of any trauma or incidence in past.

Common symptoms of hysteria are:

- Anxiety
- Fainting
- Having epileptic-like seizures
- Increased pain sensations
- Rigid or spasming muscles (Seizure like Movements)

Hence, the correct option is (D).

81. The essentials of primary health care are all of the following except providing higher education for all.

Primary Health Care (PHC) evolved during the 1970s and is the "front door" of the health system. It provides all the essential services and is the first contact between health care for individuals, families, and the community.

There are eight essential components of PHC:

- Education about common health problems
- Maternal and child health care, including family planning
- Promotion of proper nutrition
- Immunization against major infectious diseases
- An adequate supply of safe water
- Basic sanitation
- Prevention and control of locally endemic diseases
- Appropriate treatment for common diseases and injuries

Hence, the correct option is (D).

82. Involvement of individuals and community in the promotion of their own health and welfare in primary health care is called Community participation.

Community participation is one of the most important principles in delivering primary health services. There should be involvement of the community in the planning, implementation, and maintenance of health services.

Hence, the correct option is (B).

83. The antenatal visit should begin soon after conception and continue throughout pregnancy. The first visit should take place in the first trimester, before or at the 12th week of pregnancy.

Hence, the correct option is (B).

84. Antenatal care in a primary health centre includes all of the following except conducting high risk delivery.

- In primary Health Care, all maternal and child health services are given to the individual of society.
- In PHC antenatal registration includes the screening of high-risk pregnancy, lab investigation, Vaccination, nutrition counseling, IFA, and Calcium supplementation provided.
- Referral and follow up care in instances of Gestational Diabetes, and Syphilis during pregnancy.
- Providing a referral system for high-risk delivery.

Hence, the correct option is (D).

85. The term initiation of early breast feeding means Initiating breast feeding within one hour of delivery.

Exclusive breastfeeding means feeding the infant breast milk soon after delivery to 6 months of age.

Breast feeding should be initiated soon after the delivery within one hour as the mother's colostrum, a nutrient-filled fluid produced before milk is released. It helps to protect the newborn from getting an infection and reduces newborn mortality.

Hence, the correct option is (B).

86. For emergency care of sick children at PHC the strategy to be followed is IMNCI guidelines.

The Integrated Management of Neonatal and Childhood Illness (IMNCI) is a key child health strategy within the National Reproductive Child Health Programme II and the National Rural Health Mission.

IMNCI aims to reduce death, illness, and disability and to improve growth and development among children under 5 years of age. IMNCI caters to two groups of children 0-2 months Young infants & 2 months to 5 years Children.

Hence, the correct option is (C).

87. To maintain sanitation at community level the following measures have to be taken except Improper housing.

Sanitation related to clean drinking water and treatment and disposal of human excreta and sewage. Having access to facilities for the safe disposal of human waste

To maintain good sanitation community has to maintain proper waste disposal and proper utilization of water resources. Proper sanitation promotes health, and improves the quality of the environment and thus, the quality of life in a community.

Hence, the correct option is (D).

88. The diseases that are spread through unsafe water are all of the following except Small pox.

Smallpox was a serious, life-threatening illness caused by the variola virus. It was a respiratory disease condition and can spread from one person to another through droplets(cough and sneeze).

It caused pus-filled blisters (pustules) to develop on the skin. Incubation Period is 7 to 14 days after exposure to the variola virus. Symptoms include high fever, muscle aches, backaches, headaches, and vomiting.

Hence, the correct option is (D).

89. Vaccine that is administered in children to prevent diarrhoea is Rota virus.

Rota virus vaccine can prevent rotavirus disease. Rota virus commonly causes severe, watery diarrhea, mostly in babies and young children. Vomiting and fever are also common in babies with rota virus.

The first dose of either vaccine should be given before a child is 15 weeks of age. Children should receive all doses of the rotavirus vaccine before they turn 8 months old.

Hence, the correct option is (C).

90. The route of administration of BCG vaccine is Intradermal.

The BCG vaccine (which stands for Bacillus Calmette-Guerin vaccine). The BCG vaccine protects against tuberculosis, which is also known as TB, and the most severe forms of TB, such as TB meningitis in children. BCG vaccine should only be given once in a lifetime.

Hence, the correct option is (B).

91. Vitamin A deficiency causes Night blindness.

Vitamin A plays an important role in vision to see the full spectrum of lights, the eye needs to produce certain pigment for the retina. Vitamin A deficiency stops the production of pigments, leading to night blindness. Without Vitamin A eyes can't produce enough moisture for lubrication.

Hence, the correct option is (C).

92. Oral polio vaccine (OPV) is an antiviral vaccine because it prevents the polio virus which causes poliomyelitis.

OPV produces antibodies in the blood ('humoral' or serum immunity) to all three types of poliovirus. This protects the individual against polio paralysis by preventing the spread of poliovirus to the nervous system.

Hence, the correct option is (C).

93. Scurvy is a condition characterized by general weakness, anemia, gingivitis (gum disease), and skin hemorrhages caused by a prolonged deficiency of vitamin C (ascorbic acid) in the diet.

The human body needs vitamin C to produce collagen, heal wounds, and support the immune system. The first symptoms of scurvy will typically develop after at least three months of extremely low vitamin C levels.

Hence, the correct option is (C).

94. The programme that has permitted to use drugs by ANM's in case of specific emergency situations to reduce maternal mortality is RCH Phase II.

- RCH II stands for Reproductive and Child Health. RCH first launched in India in April 2005.
- The main six key components of the RCH program are Maternal Health, Child Health, Nutrition, Family Planning, Adolescent Health (AH), and PC- PNDT.
- Under RCH II ANM are empowered to give a pre-referral dose (Dexamethasone) to pregnant women in preterm labour.

Hence, the correct option is (D).

95. The three critical determinants for declaring a facility as first referral unit include 24 hours availability all of the following facilities except Immunization facility.

First Referral Unit comes under the National Rural Health Mission. First Referral Unit or "FRU" means a clinical facility equipped to provide round-the-clock services for emergency obstetric and newborn care.

Hence, the correct option is (D).

96. While providing feed to a bed ridden patient the ideal position the patient has to be kept is Fowler's position.

- For Feeding the patient Should be sitting up at 30 to 45 degrees (Fowler's Position) with a pillow under the head and shoulders.
- Semi-Fowler's or full-Fowler's position prevents aspiration pneumonia and possible death due to pulmonary complications.
- Fowler's position allows for better chest expansion, improving breathing by facilitating oxygenation.

Hence, the correct option is (C).

97. An infant attains head control by 3-4 months.

Baby's head needs a lot of support during their first few months until their neck muscles get stronger. By age 3 months, the baby can control his or her head movements. At age of 6 months, infants have neck muscles that are strong enough to hold their head up and turn it from side to side.

Hence, the correct option is (B).

98. The mode of transmission of Hepatitis C is Contaminated Blood.

Hepatitis C is a liver infection caused by the hepatitis C virus (HCV). Hepatitis C is spread when blood from an infected person enters the body of someone who is not infected.

HCV is a leading cause of liver transplants and liver cancer. The two most common modes of transmission of HCV are blood transfusion and injection drug use.

Hence, the correct option is (C).

99. Pig is amplifier of Japanese encephalitis.

Japanese encephalitis (JEV) is a viral brain infection that's spread by caused by a flavivirus, through mosquito bites. JEV is cannot transmit from one person to another. Incubation Period is 5 to 15 days after being infected.

Hence, the correct option is (C).

100. World Breastfeeding Week is celebrated every year across the world from August 1 to August 7.

It was first started in 1992 to promote the benefits of breastfeeding for both mother and the baby. This global campaign aims to raise awareness about breastfeeding and its advantages.

Hence, the correct option is (B).

// Notes //

// Notes //

www.ingramcontent.com/pod-product-compliance
Ingram Content Group UK Ltd.
Pitfield, Milton Keynes, MK11 3LW, UK
UKHW061704190726
13853UKWH00008B/2387